Ancient
WISDOM

A Contemporary Application of the
Proverbs of Solomon

Jon Tal Murphree

CreateSpace
Charleston, South Carolina

Ancient Wisdom: A Contemporary Application of the Proverbs of Solomon

ISBN-13: 978-1492840978

Printed in the United States of America
CreateSpace, Charleston, South Carolina

Cover Design by Brenda Ritchey
Author photo by Kevin Klucas

Author's Preface

These are the proverbs of ancient wisdom. They were forged and fashioned in a venerable Mideast culture that distinguished itself from neighboring people-groups and all distant cultures by one immutable conviction—monotheism. Century after century the people preserved their cultural identity by reciting together their unique creed, called the *Shema*: "Hear, O Israel, the Lord our God is *one* Lord . . ." While other cultures worshipped multiple gods, this exceptional enclave broke out of the mold and pledged allegiance to a singular, monotheistic God. Judaism, Christianity, and Islam all built on that basic presupposition.

When ancient King David bequeathed his throne to Solomon, he said to his son, "The Lord give thee wisdom and understanding" (1 Chron 22:12 KJV). When Solomon accepted the throne, one of his first acts of royalty was to bow the knee to his God and make one special request. He did not ask for victory in battle, or for a strong arm to rule an intractable people, or for economic success. His one petition was for a wise and discerning heart. For forty years Solomon reigned over a people that became in many ways the most advanced in the Mideast. News of his sagacity spread and his name became prominent throughout the area. King Solomon was known as the wisest person in the world.

Solomon's wisdom penetrated political, economic, and social conditions. But he followed the founders of his culture in accenting ethical, religious, and practical values. He composed and/or hammered out and honed three thousand proverbs, five hundred of which were included (along with a few proverbs from others) in the biblical book of The Proverbs.

Solomon lived four centuries before Confucius, four centuries before Guatama the Buddha, four centuries before Zoroaster. He lived five centuries before Socrates and Plato, six centuries before Aristotle, ten centuries before Jesus. He lived fifteen centuries before the beginning of Zen. The ethical wisdom of his proverbs predates any body of comparable wisdom in recorded history. Here we find ancient wisdom, by an ancient sage!

What makes Solomon's proverbs so astonishing is their surprising contemporaneity for the twenty-first century. They reflect a penetrating analysis of human nature and social situations that flow throughout all generations. They appeal to permanent human interests that are not eroded by time.

The word "proverb" means *pro verb*. That is to say, it is "for talking or writing about." A proverb is a short, crisp, axiomatic saying that stands for more than is said. It contains more than immediately meets the eye. Being concise and tersely cogent, it implies more than is immediately inferred. It is to be opened up and discussed. It is to be talked about and written about. Most of Solomon's proverbs make their point either by synthesis or antithesis—that is, either by comparison or contrast.

A cursory reading of Solomon's proverbs may not impress one as being particularly profound, witty, or insightful. Some of them may seem trite. But we must remember that we are standing on Solomon's shoulders. Some of the support material from classical literature that I have used here says the same thing that Solomon said. But Solomon said it first. Most of classical literature came later.

When I began to study these proverbs closely, I was surprised that they are so rich and weighty, full of thought, copious with ideas that deserve further explication. Especially was I startled by two discoveries. The first is the many and varied subjects that Solomon addresses. The second is the multiple practical ways that he approaches the same subjects. He keeps coming at some of them from many angles, cracking them open for practical application to various areas of life. Many of the subjects are interwoven, showing how virtues interrelate and vices contribute to each other.

Some religionists may think that many of the proverbs are not religious. But they are given to show that theistic religion has implications for the secular. To the ancient Hebrews, God covers all of life!

Because a proverb is concise, it cannot elucidate all its exceptions and disclaimers. All variables cannot be factored in. Most of the proverbs are general factual statements of the way moral and practical principles ordinarily work. By appropriate application, the general needs to be applied to specifics.

4

Since most proverbs lace together more than one subject, the original compilers did not arrange them in thematic order. Many may seem disjointed and disconnected, not needing a literary context for their interpretation. Consequently, I have followed the order in which they were originally compiled, without trying to categorize them into sectional subjects.

Attempting to open up the proverbs with application for the contemporary mindset, I have been consistently frustrated by wanting to say more than my one-page limit for each proverb allows. Hence I have compacted this entire volume, sacrificing a rapid-reading flow for punchy, proverb-like lines that encapsulate ideas, staccato style. For the most part, I have screened out anecdotes and personal experiences, and drawn most of my support material from classical literature.

In these 367 essays—one for each day of the year with two extra—I have covered (or touched on) each of Solomon's five hundred proverbs, doubling up on some that address the same subject. Only the last essay (# 367) is on a proverb generally thought to be from a non-Solomon source, though in the biblical book of The Proverbs.

For those concerned about mechanical linguistics, I have avoided using plural pronouns (they, their, theirs, them) to stand for singular in the common gender (i.e., neither masculine, feminine, nor neuter). In doing so, I have avoided the clumsy "he or she" or "him or her" by allowing both masculine and feminine to be used for common gender, sometimes using one and sometimes the other. That allows pronouns referring to the singular to stay in the singular while still avoiding the sexism of using the generic masculine exclusively for either gender.

Suggestions for Reading This Book

Most of you will *not* want to read through this volume rapidly. Some may wish to read only one essay a day, or a few each day. The essays will mean more if you will first take time to read the proverb at the top of the page, and have it in mind as you read the application essay. Then when you have finished the page, rereading the proverb will help lace the thoughts together.

Codes for Biblical Versions Used

In this volume, proverbs are used from various versions or translations of the Bible, which are identified by code after each quotation. Scriptures used in the text itself are also identified by code UNLESS the scripture is from the same version as the proverb at the top of the page. If the version used in the text is not identified, it is the same version as the proverb being discussed. The following code will identify the various versions/translations used:

AAT — The Bible: An American Translation (J. M. Powis Smith and Edgar J. Goodspeed)

ABPS — The Holy Bible Containing the Old and New Testaments: An Improved Edition (American Baptist Publication Society)

ASV — The American Standard Version

Bas — The Bible in Basic English

Ber — The Modern Language Bible: The New Berkeley Version in Modern English

CEV — Contemporary English Version

Jerus — The Jerusalem Bible

KJV — King James Version

Lam — The Holy Bible From Ancient Eastern Manuscripts (George M. Lamsa)

Mof — A New Translation of the Bible (James Moffatt)

NAB — The New American Bible

NASB — New American Standard Bible

NEB — The New English Bible

NIV — New International Version

NKJV — The New King James Version

Rhm — The Emphasized Bible: A New Translation (J. B. Rotherham)

RSV — Revised Standard Version

Sprl — A Translation of the Old Testament Scriptures From the Original Hebrew (Helen Spurrell)

Tay — The Living Bible: Paraphrased (Kenneth Taylor)

To Bruise or to Bless 1

A wise son makes a glad father, but a foolish son is the grief of his mother (10:1 NKJV).

Warm fatherly feelings toward children are not products of 21st century family counseling. From the several proverbs urging fathers to discipline their children and children to honor their parents, we can infer that fathers 3,000 years ago were generally indulgent rather than harsh toward their sons and daughters. An earlier Hebrew poet spoke of the "pity" fathers had for their children (Ps. 103:13). Those male progenitors may have been more humanized than the later fathers whom Paul warned not to "provoke their children to anger" (Eph. 6:4; Col. 3:21).

Youth often push the limit to test their parents' blood pressure, but a healthy family usually survives those fractious periods. The love of good parents outweighs their egotism, and they know how to make necessary concessions. Robert Louis Stevenson's character said, "It is a small love that shies at a little pride."[1] Children from a happy childhood often look back on those delightful days and feel with Elizabeth Akers Allen, "Backward, turn backward, O time, in your flight, / Make me a child again just for tonight!"[2]

Adult children are in a position either to make their parents' hearts heavy with hurt or light with laughter. Loving always makes the lover vulnerable to the one that is loved. What people *are* and what they *do* affect those who love them most. Daring to love their children makes parents vulnerable to what a child does. That is included in the nature of love. Sons and daughters are in a position to place highest happiness or inflict heaviest sorrow on the parents. They can bruise their spirits or bless their souls. Folly or wisdom makes the difference between disappointment and delight, between grief and gladness, between parental pain and pleasure.

---

[1] Robert Louis Stevenson, "The Sire de Malétroit's Door," *The Great Short Stories of Robert Louis Stevenson* (New York: Pocket Books, Inc., 1951) p. 219.
[2] Elizabeth Akers Allen, "Rock Me to Sleep," Richard C. MacKenzie, ed., *The New Home Book of Best Loved Poems* (Garden City, NY: Doubleday & Co. Inc., 1946) p. 58.

2 Loss and Profit

Treasures of wickedness profit nothing, but righteousness delivers from death (10:2 NKJV).

Very evil people are gratified by evil itself, apart from its "treasures." The majority of evil people have not yet sunk to that devil-like level. They commit fraud not for the joys of committing fraud, but for the profit they gain from it. They rob a person's dignity and self-respect for the gratification of putting another down and the "profit" of feeling superior.

Sinning for profit, however, is a losing business deal. It has diminishing returns. Pursuing evil treasure becomes a relentless scavenger hunt, sucking all the possible profit out of the smallest situations. C. S. Lewis said that evil can "sate itself with the tiniest cruelties, as love does not disdain the smallest kindness."[1] Eventually it costs much more than is gained.

In many ways today, righteousness gets bad press, and evil "treasures" are overcooked in the public imagination. What follows is worse than disappointment. Evildoers, to prevent their overcast skies from dripping with heavy guilt, adjust their values and deaden their consciences with moral anesthesia. Those who fall into that syndrome lose their moral sensitivities and become moral corpses. Eventually the profit from ill-gained goods becomes like ashes in one's mouth. Life turns dead on your hands. Life loses its freshness. Zest and zing evaporate.

When the treasures of selfish living are finally lost, a person is left with only a deficit balance. The gains add up to a loss. The entire payoff slips away. That person ends up dying in a thousand ways. "The wages of sin is death . . ." (Rom. 6:23).

Right living prevents the death of conscience, the death of moral value, and the fatality of a life that is lost. Deficits become dividends. Losses become profits. Righteousness turns the debit to a surplus. What otherwise would have been eternal loss is replaced with eternal gain!

---

[1] C. S. Lewis, *Perelandra* (New York: Macmillan Pub. Co., 1944) p. 123.

Disciplined with Diligence 3

He who deals with a slack hand becomes poor, but the hand of the diligent makes one rich. / He who gathers in summer is a wise son, but he who sleeps in harvest is a son who causes shame" (10:4,5 NKJV). Also 10:3.[1]

Laziness is sometimes triggered by low blood sugar or slow metabolism. The body affects the mind, sometimes shifting it into neutral gear. That is called psychosomatics.

Fortunately for us hypoglycemiacs, the principle works both ways. By exercising determination our minds can control our bodies. Sharp minds with intentional purposes activate languid bodies. If allowed, sluggish bodies will make us lazy, but prudence can trigger the mind to make us diligent. Developing special interest in our professions or vocations, getting into special projects, concentrating on our responsibilities, prizing the fruits of our labors, prioritizing worthy goals—these mental disciplines can activate our bodies and drive our lives. To settle for slothfulness is to engage in selfishness. Diligence is a matter of discipline.

Work schedules must be seasonally adjusted, otherwise the effort is wasted. Cultivating crops must be done in spring, and harvesting in autumn, otherwise there is no yield to be harvested. Prudent diligence means meeting responsibilities *on time*. Leisure living during the cultivation season is selfish. Sleeping at harvest time is shameful. Slack hands allow opportunities to slip by unused, but active hands are quick to seize the moment. Shakespeare had his character Othello to say, "We must obey the time."[2] Idle hands contribute to poverty, but active hands lead to abundance.

---

[1] This proverb (10:3), stating that God will not allow the righteous to famish, enunciates a general principle rather than making a biblical promise. It is the ordinary outcome of the principle of diligence stated in 10:4 and 10:5. Those who are disciplined with diligence as a rule can sustain their lives with adequate nutrition. Being a righteous person includes a diligent work ethic. In that way the righteous are not expected to famish. Beyond the general principle, God adds an additional ingredient. He does provide special assistance to righteous people who are eager to work.

[2] Shakespeare, *Othello*, Act I, Scene 3, line 301.

4 Transparency and Deception

Blessings are on the head of the righteous, but the mouth of the wicked conceals violence (10:6 NASB).

Evil people cannot be trusted because of the "political" spin they put on their deeds. Devious actions are shielded by excuses. Their wickedness is concealed by well-thought-through explanations that are made to seem plausible. Evil is dressed up, toned down, doctored up, shaded, processed and refined, made civil. The sinfulness of sin is masked by clever speech. Badness hides behind the words of those who are bad. "The mouth of the wicked conceals evil."

Shakespeare's character Duke Frederick, unconvinced of Rosalind's innocence after her strong defense of herself, cynically but correctly said, "Thus do all traitors. If their purgation did consist in words, they are as innocent as grace itself."[1]

Sooner or later, however, excuses wear thin and deception is exposed. Deceivers overplay their hand. The odds catch up with them. Their public image collapses. They are seen for what they are. They lose the honor and blessing of others.

Those who live righteous lives, however, are transparent. They have nothing to hide. They have no need to play games. They stand as tall in the public eye as in their own. Respect is earned. Approbation is deserved. They are honored with noble acclaim. Righteous people stand in for the blessing that evil people have sought in the wrong way and lost.

To live righteously is to live without ulterior purposes, simply for the sake of rightness itself, because rightness is right. Then the inner cacophony of dissonance subsides, and inner chaos is resolved because motivation is simplified.

And as a bonus, you gain the blessing of self-respect and public esteem that those who attempt short-cuts never find. You gain honor that you did not seek. Your head is crowned with blessing.

---

[1]Shakespeare, *As You Like It*, Act I, Scene 2, lines 54-56.

Sowing and Reaping 5

Blessings crown the head of the righteous, but violence overwhelms the mouth of the wicked (10:6 NIV).[1]

Just as an entombed corpse had a cloth covering its face, the mouth of wicked people is soon covered with insult and untimely grief. They are "choked by their own violence" (NEB). The bad person's "face shall be darkened with disaster" (Mof). The wicked are "overwhelmed" (NIV) with their own wickedness. Given an inch, evil will take a mile.

Interpreting liberty to mean license, evildoers push their luck too far. Going for thrill-kicks, they get kickbacks. Sowing wild oats, they reap a crop of thorns and thistles. Sowing to the flesh, they reap corruption (Gal. 6:8 KJV)). Spin-thrills of violence spin out of control.

Committing sin pulls down on one's head its own consequences. One cannot outfox the law of sowing-and-reaping, the principle of cause-and-effect, the maxim of sin-and-its-consequences. One can smoke cigarettes until he dies with lung cancer. One can carry hostility until her soul burns with acid. One can do illicit drugs until his emotions are baked and his brain is fried. One can develop patterns of self-centeredness that bind her like chains.

Causes and effects have a way of equalizing themselves. Effects are proportionate to their causes. "Be sure that your sin will find you out" (Num. 32:23). Eventually, the life that people live catches up with them. The evil are "overwhelmed" with bitter regret, haunting memories, burning remorse, tormenting guilt. Evil people are victimized of their own evil.

That condition is punctuated by its contrast to the blessedness of righteous living. The effects of both good and evil are accented against the backdrop of the other. Without having to be smug, righteous people are crowned with a blessedness that is intrinsic to rightness.

---

[1] Scholars are divided over whether this line should be translated and interpreted as it is in the previous essay, or as it is here. Whichever the original intention, however, both are true. Hence I have done these two consecutive essays on the two translations, both of which express important messages.

11

Adored or Abhorred 6

The memory of the righteous will be a blessing, but the name of the wicked will rot (10:7 NIV).

In spite of post-modernism theory, words refer to something beyond themselves. A name designates the person that it represents. It is shorthand for the person it stands for. As such, a name is a badge of character, either good or bad. A person's reputation is wrapped up in her name. Simply hearing the name brings to mind the kind of person she is.

And the kind of person so designated elicits a response, usually either positive or negative. Remembering some names warms our spirits, and others chill our hearts. Good people are remembered with praise, and evil people are cursed.

Simply thinking of a virtuous person inspires people toward virtue and nobility. Names of the noble continue to bless after they are dead. Light from their lives shines in their wake, lighting the paths of others who follow. Memorialized, their names beckon like a beacon. Horace said, "Good repute, sweeter than song, charms the human ear."[1]

Conversely, we recoil from the discomfort of even thinking about those who have disappointed or betrayed us. Talebearers, publicity seekers, two-faced dealers in misinformation, and self-centered snobs are irritating and obnoxious. Names of bloody tyrants are repugnant. They are loathsomely disgusting with the sickening odor of putrefying rot. Future generations make special effort to avoid their memory, in order to escape the moral stench!

Throughout life, we humans are in the daily process of making a name to succeed us that will be either adored or abhorred. That name will be chiseled in some mind to be treasured for perpetual blessing, or detested with disdain for years to come. Once the name is made and we are gone, it will likely not be altered.

---

[1] Horace (Quintus Horatius Flaccus), *Satires, Epistles, Ars Poetica,* H. Rushton Fairclough, tr. (Cambridge, MA: Harvard University Press, 1991) Satire II, Book II, p. 145.

The wise in heart accept commandments, but a chattering fool comes to ruin (10:8 NIV).

The choice is between heart and lip, between brain and tongue, between being a deep thinker and a shallow talker. One is to accept your inferiority and welcome instruction and advice. The other is to feel too self-sufficient to listen to others. The options are between humility and arrogance. Between wisdom and folly. Between listening and talking. Wisdom requires humility, and that is a matter of the heart, the attitude, the disposition, as much as the mind. Wisdom is wise enough to be humble. Foolishness reflects limited humility more than limited intelligence. It exposes an intellect that has lost its anchor in humility. Inquisitiveness is replaced with intellectual snobbery. Such a mind loses its ground for intelligence.

Fluency of speech is a worthy talent if it is disciplined with wisdom. Without it, fluency becomes foolishness. A "chattering fool" betrays his own folly. An idle babbler who endlessly prattles with prosaic rambling exposes a mind that is exhausted of creative subjects to discuss. That person needs the humility to listen, to read, to meditate, and to allow the mind to become fertile.

Saying something that is not worth saying—is not worth saying. Empty heads make poor speakers. Being a communicator requires having something worth communicating.

We can either defer to instruction or become shallow and silly with garrulous palaver. The first will stabilize our lives, and give us the humble confidence and gravity that attracts others. The second will cause us to trip and stumble. We fall flat on our faces. With no outside directives to structure our lives, we collapse. We will "come to ruin."

Those lost spirits that Dante encountered in the "Inferno" had come to ruin. One of them said to him, "Our intellects are void. . . . Our knowledge shall be dead . . . when the portal of the future shall close."[1]

---

[1] Dante, *The Divine Comedy*, Carlyle-Wicksteed, trs. (New York: Random House, 1932) "Inferno," Canto X, pp. 56-57.

8 Straight or Crooked

He that walketh uprightly walketh surely, but he that perverteth his ways shall be known (10:9 KJV).

To walk uprightly is to walk "right-up-ly." It is to live with integrity, transparency, and sincerity. The upright person walks forward in life with confidence and security.

To pervert one's own way is to deviate from a straight path, to walk in a crooked way, attempting to accommodate devious interests, without singleness of purpose. When interests are split and splintered rather than integrated, they shoot in all directions and drive a person down a crooked path. No single controlling purpose consolidates his motives. They pull and tug and bump in every direction. His way is "perverted."

Walking straight toward our priority goal, we cover the shortest distance to arrive. But when we are diverted on detours, crooks and curves, we cover miles and miles and years and years before arriving. Going a curvy road is a longer distance than going straight. Lacking integrity, some are so diverted that they end up going in circles and never arriving.

With conflicting motives, hypocrites recoil from straight walk also for fear their ways will be detected. To them, straight is dangerous. Like a fox darting along a crooked line to keep from being tracked out, they attempt to conceal their secret wickedness. However studiously they disguise their ways, they do not escape the radar screen. They cannot avoid the scrutinizing eye of God. Always they are spotted by the divine laser beam.

Upright people have nothing to hide. They do not have more than one character role to support. They have only one image to protect. Their forces are not divided and their energies are not depleted. They are not living as aliens, obscuring their real identity. Nothing needs to be concealed from exposure. Their eye is fixed on the target goal. They stay on a direct route. They "walk surely" because they walk straight.

Body Language or Verbal Language 9

He who winks the eye causes trouble, and a babbling fool will be thrown down (10:10 NASB).

Which is preferable, the winker or the babbler? Winkers are scarce with words, concentrating on their actions. They use body language. Babblers are sparse with actions, issuing a steady stream of unwanted verbosity.

Winking implies intended mischief, whether or not it is malicious. Secrecy is involved. It carries an esoteric connotation that is understood by both winker and winkee. Winkers feign good, often with evil intent. They are deceptive. They pretend benevolence, but it is for ulterior purposes. They propose get-rich-quick schemes designed to pad their own pockets with the exploited expectations of the gullible. Their commercials are flashy, but the products are faulty. Kindness is feigned for the sake of the sales pitch.

Babblers specialize in blabbing. With profuse expression, they betray their own intent. They divulge more about themselves and their motives than others want to know. They reserve no personal secrecy to attract people and inerest them. Babblers exhaust their own mystery by unknowingly blabbing on themselves. The rest of us are buried by an avalanche of wordiness.

Here we have two extremes—the winker and the babbler. The manipulator and the bore. The cunning and the common. The artificial and the artless. Yet the two are juxtaposed as equally dangerous. Persons of both extremes create serious problems. Winkers damage other people with faulty schemes and promises. Babblers hurt themselves by alienating other people. In the end, both will be "thrown down." Neither will be appreciated. Our mandate is to constrain the eyelid and curtail the tongue, to control both the eyelid and the lip, both the actions and the words, both the walk and the talk. That puts us in a position to help others instead of "causing trouble"—and to stand tall and not be "thrown down."

10 Helping Talk or Hurting Talk 10

The mouth of the righteous is a fountain of life, but violence overwhelms the mouth of the wicked (10:11 NIV), or, *The talk of good men is a life-giving fountain; the talk of bad men overflows with harm* (Mof).

Both goodness and badness express themselves most clearly within the context of community. Both are visible in relation to other persons. Each comes into clear focus by the way people talk as much as the way they live. What people say betrays their character as much as what they do. Words express both ideas and attitudes, hitting both mind and heart of other people with powerful impact. Good talk is "a life-giving fountain."

Genuinely good people are driven by the one most positive ingredient in human relationships. "Love" is the most relational word in the language. Motivated by love, their language is positive and encouraging, calculated to be helpful to others. Like a fountain of life, like the aorta artery that distributes life to every cell, the mouth of the righteous overflows with comforting, motivating, healing thoughts and attitudes.

Dante prayed, "Give my tongue such power [to] leave a single sparkle of Thy glory unto the folk."[1]

Conversely, the evil mouth runs over with an invective stream of damaging denunciations, derogatory accusations, or depressing ideas and moods that hurt and harm those who hear. Shakespeare's character Brabanto was wrong when he said: "But words are words; I never yet did hear / That the bruised heart was pierced through the ear."[2] Verbal bullying can be more degrading than many kinds of physical abuse.

Words are powerful, delivering incalculable relief and support, or producing unthinkable damage. "Good" people with damaging mouths need to give their goodness a love check. The shortage needs to be replenished with the strength of genuine love.

---

[1] Dante, *The Divine Comedy* (New York: Randon House, 1932) "Paradiso," Canto XXXIII, p. 604.
[2] Shakespeare, *Othello*, Act I, Scene 3, lines 218-219.

Hating and Loving 11

Hatred stirs up strife, but love covers all sins (10:12 NKJV).

The antithesis of love is indifference, not hate, but love and hate do produce opposite effects. While love *covers* the sins of others, hate *uncovers* those sins, exposes them, keeps them in mind. They are too good of an excuse for enmity to let go. Hatred feeds on contentions and strife. It delights in provocations and altercations. It lifts the spear that has lain unused, and stirs up strife that has been dormant.

Hating is painful. It hurts the hater more than the hated. Yet bitter persons continue to torture themselves, while the pain of their animosity fires their insatiable cravings to torture the other person. In ancient Greek tragedy, Sophocles' Creon says to Oedipus, "Natures like yours are hardest to bear by their owners."[1]

The effects of love are quite the opposite. Love reduces the tension and relieves the strife that hate stirs up. It overlooks insult, removes aggravation, seeks to conciliate, puts the best face on offenses, makes excuses for the offender. Love throws a cover over the neighbor's sin. It puts water, not fuel, on the fires of rage.

To "cover" is to conceal. Though we may not be able to forget with the mind, the love-controlled person conceals the offense from her heart. To pardon is to clear a person from punishment, but to forgive adds the personal touch. It restores the relationship; it is willing to be a friend."

Haters hold on to their enemies, not allowing them to go. Those who are disciplined by love remove as many enemies as possible by making them their friends. Kipling's Dick Heldar said, "I can't help purring when I'm rubbed the right way."[2] Lon Woodrum's character said, "Forgiveness . . . helps two hearts at once—the sinner, and the one sinned against."[3]

---

[1] Sophocles, *Oedipus the King* (New York: Washington Square Press, Inc., 1959) pp. 47-48.
[2] Rudyard Kipling, *The Light that Failed* (New York: Books, Inc., n.d.) p. 99.
[3] Lon Woodrum, *Eternity in Their Heart* (Grand Rapids: Zondervan, 1955) p. 246.

12 Punishment and Consequence

Wisdom is found in the lips of him who has understanding, but a rod is for the back of him who is devoid of understanding (10:13).

The "rod for the back" is understood in two valid ways—the first in terms of *punishment*. If wisdom is not learned from the words of the wise, the foolish must be taught by "the rod." This is not necessarily a statement on *physical* punishment at all. "The rod" is used as a metonym for punishment, whatever the form. Appropriate punishment can be used both as a motivation tool for learning and as a valid teacher.

Capable people who refuse to learn should be made to learn. If the teaching of the schoolmaster fails, other motivation may be used. The student who does not respond to Plan-A may be referred to Plan-B. Rather than being punitive, "the rod" is intended to be corrective and educative, as behavior modification. Those who reject positive incentives may be motivated by negative. Those who refuse the one could receive help from the other.

Second, foolishness has repercussions. "Punishment" is built into life in the form of *consequence*. It is automatic rather than arbitrary, but it is just as certain. Discretion prevents the consequences that come from imprudence, but folly makes a person vulnerable. Wise people are adorned with the beauty of wisdom, but the foolish are disgraced with the ugliness of folly. The first is worn on the lips. The second is borne on the back.

Not only that. Discreet people are admired and sought as counselors. Those who are devoid of wisdom are disdained and beaten as slaves. Of course, slaveholding should be condemned as evil, but the warning here is about the consequences of indiscretion. Whether the result comes as punishment or consequence, the negative experience is the same. Those who are "devoid of understanding" are exhorted to learn from the wise and avoid what otherwise would come as an inevitable result.

Vocal or Silent   13

Wise people store up knowledge, but the mouth of the foolish is near destruction (10:14 NKJV).

We all know that speaking what is good has positive value, both to those who hear and those who speak. Negative impact comes from telling the bad, and also from telling the good at the wrong time. *What* we say and *when* we say it are heavy-duty matters. Some things should be kept to ourselves, and others should be reserved for the right time. "He that thinketh by the inch and speaketh by the yard should be kicketh by the foot."

Wisdom is not only marked be saying the right thing. It is distinguished from folly by not saying the wrong thing. In some situations, silence is eloquent and talk is dangerous, precipitating "destruction." The disciplined life includes disciplined talk.

Generally there is more virtue in learning and knowing than in telling. Good conversationalists are better at listening than talking. They specialize in getting others to talk. Knowledge should be "stored up," it should be treasured, and retained. Each day we should take in more than we let out. That way knowledge is cumulative.

The healthy brain has an abundant supply, but only allows a little to trickle out at a time. If you tell me all you know, then I know all you know plus all I already you knew. That puts me far ahead of you in the game.

Good speaking and writing come from the overflow. Poor expression attempts to think of enough to say. Good expression has to filter out what should not be said. When we know more than we say, we can be selective. Refusing to tell all we know about a subject, we have something leftover to say next time. We have a reservoir of knowledge to draw from. With few thoughts of their own, foolish people often parrot only what they have heard. Ovid referred to them as echoes, "who must speak if any other speak and cannot speak unless another speak."[1]

---

[1] Ovid (Publius Ovidius Naso), *Metamorphoses*, David Damrosch and David L. Pike, eds., *The Longman Anthology of World Literature* (New York: Pearson Longman, 2008) p. 780.

14 Material Values and Moral Values

The rich man's wealth is his strong city [or fortress]; *the destruction of the poor is their poverty. / The labor of the righteous leads to life, the wages of the wicked to sin* (10:15, 16 NKJV).

Security sits in wealth, and peril crouches in poverty (vs. 15). It is more than a statement of fact. It is an unfortunate attitude often embraced by both the wealthy and the poor. It can make affluent people vulnerable to economic collapse and paralyze the poor with fear. Both the excess elation of the rich and the emotional prostration of the needy often result from placing an unhealthy premium on material wealth.

Facing subsistence as a lone person on an isolated island, Robinson Crusoe said, "Abused prosperity is often . . . the means of our greatest adversity."[1] And some who are moderately poor sacrifice their happiness to an attitude that prioritizes wealth.

Contrary to popular opinion, the original "American dream" was for liberty more than economic security, for freedom to pursue security rather than entitled security. Much of the dream was for freedom from political and religious oppression rather than for the security of wealth. Unfortunately, the contemporary American dream is primarily economic.

In contrast to those material values (vs. 15), we observe the moral values of the righteous and the immoral values of the wicked (vs. 16). For the righteous, whether wealthy or poor, the "wages" of their labor support life rather than luxury—their own lives and the lives of those less fortunate. Gain from their enterprises "tendeth to life" (KJV) in helping others who are plagued with poverty.

For self-centered, evil-driven persons, the fruit of their labor is wasted in indulgence, easy living, and cholesterol! They work hard and have little to show for it.

In the end, the righteous discover LIFE in capital letters, with God through Christ, while the labors of the wicked add up to a big fat zero!

---

[1] Daniel Defoe, *Robinson Crusoe* (Garden City, NY: Doubleday, 1945) p. 45.

Great Opportunity and Grave Obligation 15

He who heeds discipline [i.e., instruction] *shows the way of life, but whoever ignores correction leads others astray* (10:17 NIV).

The influence of humans on humans is greater than our wildest calculations. Human personalities emit "force fields" around them like force fields in outer space. When others come into those fields of influence, they surrender themselves, sometimes unknowingly, at times willingly. They become eager slaves. In *Uncle Tom's Cabin*, Harriet Beecher Stowe's character said, "We might as well allow small-pox to run among our children" as to allow bad influence.[1] Even with the demise of behavioristic psychology, social stimuli are still influential.

The power of influence is both a great opportunity and a grave responsibility. Unknown persons observe us from a distance, sometimes not even knowing who we are. Facial nuances, body language, vocal overtones point others in various directions. Moods, dispositions, reactions to situations shout with silent eloquence. We are investing influence, good or bad, in other lives.

Desperately we need an instruction manual. It is so difficult "to see ourselves as others see us."[2] We need frequent midcouse corrections. We need regular counsel. If some people oppose us, their criticism comes free of charge. We can profit without having to pay a counselor's fee! The Bible itself is a roadmap, filled with directions for "the way of life."

If we are willing to be disciplined, to make corrections, to accept advice, we are in a position to point others up the road of life. If we are too arrogant or stubborn to seek and follow directions, we become roadblocks, turning others away. We must not duck out of responsibility. Out influence is influential, one way or the other. Attempting to be neutral is to be negative. If we take our responsibility as a serious opportunity, our lives will make an eternity of difference!

---

[1] Harriet Beecher Stowe, *Uncle Tom's Cabin* (New York: Alfred A. Knoph, Inc., 1994) p 260.

[2] Robert Burns, "To a Louse," in Richard Aldington, ed. *The Viking Book of Poetry*, vol. I (New York:: The Viking Press, 1958) p 631.

16 To Hide and to Harm

*He who conceals his hatred has lying lips, and whoever spreads slander
is a fool* (10:18 NIV).

Long ago the human race discovered two evil ways to
handle hatred—to lie about one's own attitude and to slander the
one who is hated.

Filled with hate and fantasizing revenge, too many people
have pretended magnanimity by lying about their animosity, playacting nobility. All the while they were devising malicious ways
to settle the score in secret without damaging their public image.
Hiding behind lying lips, they fabricated gentility. As Lady
Macbeth advised her perfidious husband, "Look like the innocent
flower, but be the serpent under it."[1]

In *The Shack*, Papa says to Mackenzie, "Lies are one of the
easiest places to hide. It gives you a sense of safety. But it's a
dark place."[2]

The other evil option is to malign the other person with
slander. It is always done behind the person's back, not having to
confront him face to face. Punishing the person without having to
defend oneself is the ideal role for a coward. He cherishes the play
part.

The two options employ a subtle touch of irony. The first
makes one a knave. The second makes him a fool. Both reveal
evil intent—one to hide, the other to harm. Both tell lies, one to
defend oneself, the other to defame someone else. Both sins are
committed with the same tool, one with lying lips, the other with
slandering lips. The human tool that can best bring help and
healing is perverted to bring hurt. As an instrument for good, the
tool is useless.

Part of the irony is that in the end the two are connected.
Hatred is concealed in order that it may erupt in slander that
appears to be credible precisely because the hatred is concealed.
That is vicious malevolence!

---

[1] Shakespeare, *Macbeth*, Act I, Scene 5, lines 66-67.
[2] William P. Young, *The Shack*, (Newbury Park, CA: Windblown Media, 2007)
p. 187.

Silent or Sorry 17

When there are many words, transgression is unavoidable, but he who restrains his lips is wise (10:19 NASB).

To speak or not to speak; that is the question.[1] At times we fail to speak up when we should. More often we speak when we should not. The choice between talking and not talking is frequently the choice between transgression and wisdom.

The delicate structure of this proverb, by implication, packages three items in each of two separate bundles. One composite includes excess talk, folly, and transgression. The other is composed of limited talk, wisdom, and avoiding sin. Folly in the first and avoiding sin in the second are implied by their counterparts. The items come in triplicates. Excess talk reflects folly and leads to sin. Controlled talk reflects wisdom and avoids sinning.

Someone is apt to think that what one does is more important than what one says. Deeds are weightier than words. Talking, however, *is* a deed. "Speak" is a verb in the active voice. As an action, it has more consequences than most other acts.

Discretion filters out foolish talk, issuing words of wisdom. Folly regurgitates a reflux of undigested ideas that have turned sour. Both good sense and bad sense are disclosed when one talks. With the one, evil speech is avoided, and with the other, evil is virtually unavoidable.

A wise person thinks through what she says. A foolish person says what she thinks. The first has greater income of ideas than expenditure in speech. The other's outflow is faster than her inflow.

Many people need to take advantage of every opportunity to keep their mouths closed. Ancient Greek philosopher Xenocrates of Chalcedon has been widely quoted as saying, "I have often regretted that I spoke; I have never been sorry that I was silent.[2]

---

[1] Paraphrase of Shakespeare in *Hamlet*, Act III, Scene 1, line 56.
[2] Probably first quoted by Valerius Maximus.

18 Futility or Utility

The tongue of the righteous is choice silver; the heart of the wicked is worth little. / The lips of the righteous feed many, but fools die for lack of wisdom (10:20, 21 NKJV)

When the three ingredients in the last essay's first bundle interact and crossbreed, a fourth ingredient is born. Wisdom, good talk and moral value produce utilitarian value. The instruction, guidance, and encouraging talk nourish other people. "The lips of the righteous *feed* many." Their talk has the value of pure refined silver because they deliver helpfulness and healing. Their words are pregnant with life-changing wisdom.

The three ingredients in the other bundle are barren. Bad talk, folly, and moral evil produce no positive offspring. Spinning their wheels, they get nowhere. They are "worth little." In terms of utility, "the heart of the wicked is trash" (NEB).

The heart is the fountainhead of the tongue's talk. Attitudes, dispositions, and feelings determine what is said. Jesus said, "Out of the overflow of the heart the mouth speaks" (Matt. 12:34 NIV). So, the "tongue of the just" is like rare silver, but the "heart of the wicked" is void of value. The "lips of the righteous" run over with wisdom, but fools cannot draw from their "lack of wisdom." With the wise there is abundance, but with the foolish there is famine. The words of the righteous have much to offer, but the talk of evil fools is empty. With plenty, the wise can share; with poverty, the foolish are bare.

Moreover, while the righteous nourish others from their abundance, the unrighteous themselves perish from their stark desolation. One shares, the other starves. One feeds, the other dies. While the righteous are helping others from their wisdom, the foolish are dying from their folly.

The wicked are malnourished while the righteous are morally nutritious. They are decimated with futility while the other live for utility. Evil people are worthless; righteous people are priceless! To shift from futility to utility, we must travel the path of righteousness and wisdom.

Bane or Blessing 19

The blessing of the Lord makes one rich, and He adds no sorrow with it
(10:22 NKJV).

Unfortunately, some people always interpret "blessing" to mean material or monetary wealth, as if streets of gold and gates of pearl would mean more to us than heavenly relationships. Others wish to spiritualize everything in the Bible, emasculating its ability to address practical issues. Certainly the Lord enriches our lives with spiritual assets, but here we get a sneak peek at God's support in our economic efforts to make a living.

The original *source* of everything good is God Himself. Professional expertise, vocational skill, entrepreneurial enterprise are merely the *means.* No matter how ingenious and industrious one may be, he always begins with something rather than nothing, and that something came from God.

Ordinarily, wealth is not acquired by a manipulative prayer for personal benefit. God is not a lazy person's substitute for preparation and hard work. He expects us to go after it. In addition to being the original source, the "blessing of the Lord" is an additive to one's own industrial effort. God honors those who are diligent and "helps those who help themselves."

He promised the early Hebrew people, "If you walk in my statutes and keep my commandments, . . . the land shall yield its produce" (Lev. 26:3-4).

If "the increase" comes from exploitation, deceit, or unethical alliances, a person is liable to troubles, sorrows, and eventual regret. The profit is a bane rather than a blessing. When the increase is from the Lord's blessing, "no sorrow" is included in the additive. Adam Clarke said, "God's blessing gives simple enjoyment, and levies no tax upon the comfort."[1]

The ancient preacher of Ecclesiastes said, "There is nothing better for a man than that . . . his soul should enjoy good in his labor" (Ecc. 2:24).

---

[1]Adam Clarke's *Commentary* (New York: Eaton and Mains, 1883) Vol III, p 731.

20 Good Sport or Bad Sport

It is like sport to a fool to do wrong, but wise conduct is pleasure to a man of understanding (10:23 RSV).

Philosopher John Locke described pleasure as the process of going from pain to less pain.[1] He uses pain as a category broad enough to include desire. Pleasure flows from the process of moving from desire to less desire; it is derived from the process of gratification.

Very evil people crave evil for its own sake. Foolishly feeding their desires, they develop a hankering to do wrong and then get pleasure from satisfying the crave. They frame themselves for a fall into a state of diminished humanity. Hanging out with folly, they sport with evil.

Conversely, the closer people move toward Christian sanctity, the greater desire they have for goodness, purity, and holiness. They love the principle of goodness itself. Feeding on wisdom, they sport with goodness. The consequent pleasure is unsullied, liberating, and exalting.

In a sense you actually become whatever it is that you like. You internalize it. It becomes you. Basketball players enjoy playing basketball because they *are* ball players. Foolish sinners delight in sin because they *are* sinners. Wise people glory in wisdom because they *are* wise. Loving people long for love because they *are* loving. Good people relish goodness because they *are* good. That is what they are.

Over and again the ancient sage identified folly with evil because it leads to evil. And wisdom is connected with goodness because it leads to goodness. Deferring to folly, people collapse into sin. Functioning from wisdom, they align with goodness. Then they develop yens and yearnings appropriate to what they have become. Evil sport is repugnant to the righteous, and good pleasure seems tame to the sinful. Both end up getting the sport they want.

---

[1] John Locke, *An Essay Concerning Human Understanding* (London: Dent & Sons, LTD, 1961) Vol I, Bk I, pp. 189-192; Bk II, pp 229-230.

Fear of Future or Hope of Heaven 21

The fear of the wicked will come upon him, and the desire of the righteous will be granted (10:24 NKJV).

Both righteousness and wickedness are grounded in a person's deepest desires. Virtue and vice are more than culturally conditioned lifestyles. They are matters of the heart. Any disconnect is only temporal. As a rule, moral value centers more in what one *is* than in what one *does*. In the final analysis, what separates the righteous from the wicked is not found in their moral strength or weakness, but in their motives. Righteous people with God's help have fine-tuned their desires for goodness, moral cleanness, and an eternal life of service to God. What they desire is aligned with the reality of the universe because goodness is the universal norm.

Evil people cling to an abnormal aberration from universal goodness. Serving God has little appeal to those who have solidified their self-centered desires for sensual pleasure or ego fulfillment. A holy heaven would torment them with holiness, and a heavenly community of service to God would burden them with intolerable responsibilities. Milton quotes Satan as saying to Beelzebub, "Better to reign in hell than serve in heaven."[1]

For the average person, a recurring feeling keeps surfacing that somewhere down the long road, either in this life or the next, moral justice will be equalized and people will get what they deserve. Wise is the sinner who takes time to "fear," to ponder the future, and to shift his central desire to a better estate! As Paton's priest said, "Where there is life, there is hope for amendment to life."[2]

Humans are all moving either toward what they dread or what they desire. Evil persons are walking into their most dreaded fear, while righteous people are marching with hope into a future that is filled with what they want most. Solomon says it will be granted.

---

[1] John Milton, *Paradise Lost* (Indianapolis: ITT Bobbs-Merrill Educational Pub. Co., 1962) Book I, p. 13.

[2] Alan Paton, *Cry, the Beloved Country* (New York: MacMillan Pub. Co. 1948) p. 106.

22 The Fickle and the Stable

As the whirlwind passeth, so is the wicked no more, but the righteous is
an everlasting foundation (10:25 KJV).

By elucidating opposite extremes, many proverbs are piquant and intentionally provocative. Solomon often did this by putting the wicked and the righteous in antithetical relationships. Many humans today, however, do not fit comfortably in either category. They sit somewhere on the spectrum between the two extremes. Even the most evil person carries the potential for becoming more evil, and the most righteous has room to grow in righteousness.

Each person, however, is *more or less* in one category or the other. To the precise extent that a person belongs in either category, what its predicate states is true of that person.

By grammatical mechanics, we learn here that a wicked person like a fast-moving storm is soon gone. A whirlwind is stronger and briefer than any other wind. Tornadoes are devastating but short-lived. The more violently evil a person is, the sooner he is gone.

Linguistically, however, we pick up another implication—from the simile that is used and from its opposite in the antithetical clause. A tornado sweeps clean, demolishing everything in its path. Evil persons are not only short-lived *like* a storm, but they are swept away *by* the storm as soon as it strikes.[1] Their foundation is faulty and their anchor is weak.

Those who are righteous overcome the first liability by being stable and steadfast rather than fickle, not swirling and twirling with the tempest. And they overcome the second by being anchored on a sure foundation, grounded in God Himself. Even their happiness is well-founded and secure. Then they themselves become a foundation for society,[2] a mooring for culture, serving the human race with moral continuity in the turbulent typhoons of life.

---

[1] Some versions translate the line by its grammatical structure, and others by its linguistic implications.

[2] Similarly, some versions translate the second clause "*has* an everlasting foundation" and some "*is* an everlasting foundation."

Indolence or Industry 23

As vinegar to the teeth and smoke to the eyes, so is the sluggard to those who send him (10:26 NKJV).

Failure to achieve is not always a matter of indolence, and accomplishment is not exclusively reserved for the industrious. Many energetic people have to labor long hours simply to eke out a meager subsistence. Others are born into privilege, either with inherited wealth or native talent, and success is almost placed in their hands. Achievement itself is not a Judeo-Christian priority, but a commitment to hard work is emphasized from the first chapter of scripture where God is pictured as a diligent and creative worker. Of course, work includes both manual and mental, both of which can be difficult and demanding.

Men do not want slothful wives, and women do not want couch-potato husbands. Management wants motivated labor. Employers refuse to tolerate lazy employees. Indolence is not a self-enclosed package. It not only affects others, bit it draws reaction from others.

This proverb is a comparison rather than contrast, comparing vinegar and smoke with sluggards, and teeth and eyes with employers. The acid of vinegar puts teeth on edge, interfering with their function. Smoke irritates the delicate vessels of the eyes, causing discomfort and distorting the vision. Similarly, sluggards hamper the program, demoralize colleagues, frustrate the manager, and retard progress. Contrast *is*, however, *implied* in the proverb. Diligent workers are like fluoride that toughens the teeth and eyedrops that soothe the eyes. They facilitate the program, expedite the process, raise the morale of colleagues, and please the manager.

God smiles on all worthy work, because it is a part of His program for people. In Ronald Reagan's first year as president, after an assassination attempt almost took his life, he confided in a friend, "I have decided that whatever time I may have left is left for *Him*."[1]

---

[1] Nancy Gibbs and Michael Duffy, *The Preacher and the Presidents* (New York: Center Street, Hatchet Book Group USA, 2007) p. 268.

24 Lifestyle and Life Length

The fear of the Lord prolongs days, but the years of the wicked will be shortened (10:27 NKJV).

Contrary to what this proverb seems to say, we do not always see more years for those who respect the Lord and fewer for those who do not.

Of course, no accurate study can be made of the precise proportionate life-terms of good people to bad people, because there are too many variables. If exact allowance could be made for all extenuating factors, however, those who consistently practice righteousness in both act and attitude certainly average longer lives than they themselves would if they were evil.

Here, however, instead of stating specific numerical calculations, the sage uses "the fear of the Lord" to address the conditions that promote health and happiness, and those that do the opposite. Gluttony, intemperance, indulgence, promiscuity, and violence work against life, while sobriety, self-discipline, and neighborly harmony support life.

The scripture is God's lifestyle manual, and it delineates those practices that prolong life and those that are detrimental. Hostility causes ulcers. Violence precipitates violent reaction. Worry causes headaches. Sexual immorality contributes to disease, fractured relationships, mutilated trust, heartbreak, unwanted pregnancies, and single-parent homes.

Christian love is therapeutic. Righteousness builds self-esteem. Fidelity fosters meaningful relationships. Those things that are *commanded* by God are precisely those things that are *demanded* by our lives. John said, "His commandments are not burdensome" (1 John 5:3 NASB). Jesus said, "My yoke is easy, and My load is light" (Matt. 11:28 NASB).

In his prologue to the proverbs, Solomon stated as a matter of fact, "The fear of the Lord is the beginning of wisdom." In the very next verse he added, "Through [wisdom] your days will be many, and years will be added to your life" (Prov. 9:10-11 NIV).

The hope of the righteous is gladness, but the expectation of the wicked perishes (10:28 NASB).

Evil, self-centered people presumptuously expect a soft lenient God to bail them out in the end. But the entire body of scripture forcefully asserts that those expectations will be disappointed. Presumptuous persons become pathetic when they stand at dead end.

Shakespeare's Player King said for Hamlet to hear, "Our wills and fates do so contrary run / That our desires still are overthrown. / Our thoughts are ours, their ends none of our own."[1]

Christian hope is much stronger than a wistful dream. Throughout scripture, hope includes a focused expectation. The hope of heaven is often disparaged for being otherworldly and having no relation to life on earth. But the *expectation* of heaven is in *this* world in the present, and that expectation can color every temporal situation with light and every personal motive with a positive attitude. That hope has given millions of people a deep and abiding "gladness" in the most difficult and trying circumstances of life.

Then death itself will become an open door to the realization of even more than we have expected for a lifetime. In *Othello*, Roderigo said to Ancient Iago, "We have a prescription to die when death is our physician."[2]

When Uncle Tom finally died, the author of *Uncle Tom's Cabin* wrote, "An eternal lapse of moments is ever hurrying the day of evil to an eternal night, and the night of the just to an eternal day."[3]

When that day occurs, the vain hope of the presumptuous will perish, and the genuine expectation of the righteous will break open with a light that is brighter than their highest hopes. It will be the difference between eternal midnight and everlasting noonday!

---

[1] Shakespeare, *Hamlet,* Act III, Scene 2, lines 203-205.
[2] Shakespeare, *Othello*, Act I, Scene 3, lines 310-311.
[3] Harriet Beecher Stowe, *Uncle Tom's Cabin* (New York: Everyman's Library, Alfred A. Knoph, Inc., 1994) p. 451.

26 Defense or Defeat

The way of the Lord is a stronghold to the upright, but ruin to the
workers of iniquity (10:29 NIV).

The "way of the Lord" is attractive to those who see it as a toll-free ride to heaven, especially if it is popular in a cultural context. But continuing the journey without serious mishap requires a commitment to moral uprightness.

Too many wish to travel comfortably in the way without that commitment. They attempt to continue their evil works while expecting to stay on the road. Playing both sides, as Odysseus' wife Penelope said, is to "weave a web of wiles."[1] England's Lord Shaftesbury said, "What is morally wrong can never be politically right."[2] Being different publicly from what they are privately creates a confrontation of values. They stumble and are subdued. The goodness of God is too much for them to handle. The way of the Lord itself becomes their downfall.

Conversely, the Lord's way is "a stronghold," a fortress, for those who are upright. A hefty pace is like aerobics for the spirit. Running the path is a means of renewable energy. The more carefully they traverse that road, the stronger they become. "They will run and not grow weary. They will walk and not be faint" (Isa. 40:31).

It is an enigma. The same road that leads to the eternal salvation of the godly is the means of destruction for the ungodly. The same sun that melts the ice hardens the clay. The Lord's road defends some and defeats others. It affects the good and the bad in opposite ways. Like an obstacle course, "the way of the Lord" builds the moral muscle of the upright, but allows the muscles of those who drift leisurely to atrophy.

"The ways of the Lord are right, and the righteous will walk in them, but transgressors will stumble in them" (Hos. 14:9 NASB). Their fall will be to their own "ruin."

---

[1] Homer, *The Odyssey* (New York: The MacMillan Co., 1911) Bk. XIX, p. 225.
[2] Kevin Belmonte, "Greatness Upon Greatness," *Christian History* magazine, Carol Stream, IL, Issue 53, n.d., p. 31.

Righteous or Removed 27

The righteous will never be uprooted, but the wicked will not remain in the land (10:30 NIV).

The Christian faith is optimistic, not pessimistic, about the future of the world. Though evil may yet be unleashed on a scale unprecedented, the forces of evil will not write the last chapter of world history. God will write that chapter. The whole point of biblical eschatology is that Christ's Kingdom is coming, and it will entail a worldwide community of righteousness.

Those who live in God's world without being in God's Kingdom are moral misfits because they are moral intruders. They are living life against the inevitable. When the Kingdom of Righteousness captures the entire world, they will face expulsion.

Under this proverb, however, lies a deeper reality. Until the Kingdom comes, God's people hold a continuing estate in God's higher Kingdom that entails larger venues than the earth. Constantly we are bombarded with the advice to "keep up with the times" to keep step with the world. But the temporal movement of our culture is erratic, always shifting directions, frequently mutating. Fads and fashions fade. Styles change. Moving from one craze to the next means living a nomadic life. Without roots, one's direction and destiny are out of focus. Planted in the volatile world system, the wanderer becomes a fugitive. His foliage is sparse because the roots are few. Woodrow Wilson said, "A man's rootage is more important than his leafage."[1]

Our position in the Kingdom is based on God's saving grace, but our commitment to enter and remain in the Kingdom is grounded in moral righteousness. Repentance stabilizes us in righteousness rather than in whim, feeling, or caprice. Those who are so grounded will "stand firm" (CEV), "remain unshaken" (Rhm), "never be disturbed" (NAB). When the Kingdom comes, those not righteous will be removed. But "the righteous will never be uprooted" (NIV).

---

[1] Quoted by Senator Bob Dole in his *Great Political Wit* (New York: Doubleday, 1998) p. 3.

28 Nutritious Talk and Noxious Talk

The mouth of the righteous brings forth wisdom, but a perverse tongue will be cut off. /The lips of the righteous know what is fitting, but the mouth of the wicked only what is perverse (10:31-32 NIV).

In English translations, we often miss the original metaphor in this proverb. The figure is that of a fruit tree that buds, blooms, and bears fruit, either good or bad. What comes from one's mouth is pictured as fruit, either wise and nutritious or perverse and noxious. What one says affects other people, either by helping or hurting.

Warped, twisted, and diseased trees produce deformed, stunted, and tasteless fruit. Jesus said, "Every tree that does not bear good fruit is cut down" (Matt. 7:19). Twisted, perverse tongues with bad and bitter words will be silenced. As worthless trees, they will be cut down.

Body language communicates moods and attitudes, and what a person does makes a character statement about that person. But intricate ideas require verbal communication. God showed us something about Himself through the world—that He is knowledgeable and powerful and skilled—which we call natural revelation. But more complex concepts about God require propositional revelation in the Bible. Shakespeare said, "Words . . . breathe truth."[1]

The words that we speak (or write) communicate ideas and concepts that cannot be otherwise related. The tongue is a conveyor belt to deliver intricate and important truth. Job said, "How forceful are honest words!" (Job 6:25 RSV). Unfortunately, the mouth that can relate helpful truth can also deliver hurtful truth. And the same tongue that can tell truth can convey falsehoods. The difference is whether the tongue belongs to the righteous or the wicked.

The warning is strong, though it is stated factually without a threat. Producing bad fruit will not be tolerated. The perverse tongue will be "cut off." Jesus said, "By your words you will be condemned" (Matt. 12:37 NASB).

---

[1] Shakespeare, *King Richard II*, Act II, Scene 1, lines 7-8.

Detestable or Delightful 29

A false balance is an abomination to the Lord, but a just weight is His delight" (11:1 NKJV).

Our symbol for justice is the blindfolded lady holding a set of balances with equal weights. The blindfold means that justice is impartial, without prejudice or favoritism, with no consideration for payoffs, political connections, or nepotism. The set of balances means that moral value is equalized. Recompense and retribution are equitably distributed. In the economy of goodness, there is no moral deficit. The ledger must balance. Justice means perfect fairness.

Actual weights and balances are still used today in selling commodities that are priced by weight. Balances can be deceitfully constructed and a lighter weight can be marked as heavier, giving the seller a dishonest advantage.

The practice is even more evil because it is disguised under the pretense of justice. Gross injustice hides behind the façade of justice. Pretended goodness is used to disguise evil.

Deceitful dealings are detestable to God, not only because the practice puts people at an unfair disadvantage, but also because it is unjust and therefore morally wrong. And God is perfectly just because justice is a part of goodness and God is morally good. He abhors unfair tricks for profit. He delights in honest scales and accurate weights.

When unjust dealings are institutionalized, they become powerful social systems for political oppression, ethnic cruelty, or economic exploitation. Reinhold Niebuhr emphasized the brutal character of human collectives[1] to inflict large blocks of society with untold torture. Millions of people today are incarcerated under oppressive systems, suffering, starving, and dying. The injustice is reprehensible to good people and abominable to God!

(Continued in the next essay)

---

[1] Reinhold Niebuhr, *Moral Man and Immoral Society* (New York: Charles Scribner's Sons, 1960).

30 Weights and Balances

CONTINUED FROM PREVIOUS ESSAY

Perfect justice means that rewards and punishment are precisely proportionate to the value of the virtue and the weightiness of the crime. When we pledge "justice for all," we mean that the innocent will be acquitted and the guilty will not be over-punished. But we know that all criminals will not be caught, and that all penalties cannot be exact. Sometimes the judicial system is even swayed by public sentiment. King Claudius complained about the excess public sympathy for the criminal, when "the offender's scourge is weighed, but never the offense."[1]

We also recognize that in the congested turbulence of life fairness is not equitably distributed. Chesterton lamented that misfortune here "seems to fall on the wrong person," and he said, "Somewhere else retribution will come on the real offender."[2]

Divine forgiveness for redeemed people seems to throw eternal justice out of balance. Sinners get off scot-free.

God can forgive penitents, however, without violating justice, through a brilliant sacrificial atonement in the death of Christ. At Calvary's cross, mercy complied with all the principles of justice, and a *just* God *justified unjust* people *justly*, without violating *justice*. Now mercy is *justified by justice* itself. God's forgiveness is not cheap.

When people complain about God over any matter, they are actually sitting in judgment of God Himself. C. S. Lewis said that to the modern person, "Man is on the Bench and God in the Dock."[3] Our problem is that we humans do not have accurate weights for judging Almighty God. Our balances are out of kilter. All human judgment of the divine is skewed. In our universe, we are the defendants. God is the judge. And His weights are accurate.

---

[1] Shakespeare, *Hamlet*, Act IV, Scene 3, lines 5-6.
[2] G. K. Chesterton, "The Sins of Prince Saradine," *Favorite Father Brown . . .* (New York: Dover Pub., 1993) p. 24.
[3] C. S. Lewis, *God in the Dock* (Grand Rapids: William B. Eerdmans Pub. Co., 1970) p. 244.

When pride comes, then comes shame; but with the humble is wisdom
(11:2 NKJV).

Many Hebrew proverbs employ a mechanical tool that is puzzling to us contemporary readers. Contrasts seem cloudy. Antithetical categories are not clean. The contrasting notions are not parallel, and the symmetry is lost. Consequently, the proverb seems unwieldy.

The literary trick is subtle and actually quite clever. The missing term in each clause is implied by its opposite in the other clause. What is missing in each is supplied by the other. In this proverb, only one set of contrasts is stated—pride and humility. Both shame and wisdom are left hanging without a counterpart. But shame in the first implies honor in the second, and wisdom in the second implies folly in the first. When the proverb is unpacked, we have: (*Folly produces) pride which brings shame, but wisdom produces humility (that brings honor).* The riddle is solved, and each term is parallel with its counterpart term in the other clause.

We teach our children to have pride in their work and in their personal grooming. Then we tell them to develop humility rather than pride. What they think is double-talk becomes confusing. The contradiction is solved when this proverb is unpacked. We have two kinds of pride. The bad kind is opposite humility, which we call arrogance or conceit. The good is opposite shame, which we call honor or self-respect. Arrogance comes from folly and produces shame. Humility comes from wisdom and produces honor. With humility rather than arrogance, we have honor rather than shame. Wisdom eclipses folly, humility cancels pride, and honor is always preferable to shame. King Hrothgar said to Beowulf: "Your fame . . . is a triumph song that ocean thunders to her farthest shore; it is a whisper in the frailest seashell."[1] Honor is not only personally fulfilling. Your honorable name will inspire all who know or hear of you.

---

[1] *Beowulf the Warrior*, Ian Serraillier, tr. (New York: Henry Z. Walck, Inc., 1961) p. 8.

32 Integrity and Duplicity

The integrity of the upright will guide them, but the perversity of the unfaithful will destroy them (11:3 NKJV).

The word "integrity" comes form the same root as "integrate." To have integrity is to be whole, to be complete, to be integrated, not fragmented with shards and scraps.

First, with integrity one's *public* self is not different from the *private* self. I am the person I really am when nobody is looking, when I think no one will ever know. If the public *I* is different from the private *me*, I am a phony. Chaucer wrote of phony preachers who ". . . spit out their venom under hue / Of holiness, to seem both good and true."[1] When the public and private are integrated as the same person, we do not need to wear masks. No cover-up is necessary. We do not stonewall the evidence. We are comfortable being the persons we are.

Second, integrity means your *desires* are integrated with your *conscience*. In spite of surface motives that are easily triggered, what you *want* on a deep level is not substantially different from what you *ought*. Deeply, you can *want* to do what you *ought* to do more than you *want* to do what you otherwise *want* to do. Desires are aligned with conscience, so you are upright because you want to be that kind of person. You are truthful, not for what others may *think* of you, but for what you *know* about you.

Third, with integrity, *secular* life is integrated with *religious* life. All life becomes sacred. We are the same at work in the world as we are at worship. We are adjective Christian as well as noun Christian, embracing the ethical injunctions as well as the salvation benefits.

Those who have integrity rather than duplicity are "guided" rather than "destroyed." The "integrity of the upright" gives them health and wholeness, but the treachery of the "unfaithful" will eventually disintegrate them, break them to pieces, and "destroy them."

---

[1] Chaucer, "The Pardoner's Tale," *Canterbury Tales* (Garden City, NY: Garden City Pub. Co., 1934) p. 295.

Riches and Righteousness 33

Riches do not profit in the day of wrath, but righteousness delivers from death (11:4 NKJV).

Righteousness and riches are not mutually exclusive, because they are not opposites. Their opposites are wickedness and poverty, which likewise are not exclusive. If we on occasion should have to choose between the two, poverty is not as bad as wickedness, and riches are not as good as righteousness. Righteousness with poverty trumps riches with wickedness.

When we approach the final day of reckoning, however, the "profit" of riches has no redeeming value, but the rewards of righteousness deliver from final destruction.[1] To embrace righteousness, even if it means poverty, is to secure one's future. To abandon righteousness for riches is to sacrifice the eternal for the temporal. It is to sacrifice billions of future wealthy years for one moment of present wealth. Anyone can see the advantage of sacrificing the limited present for the infinite future. But it takes a moral person to make that sacrifice.

On an isolated island, alone and without hope of rescue, Robinson Crusoe exclaimed to himself, "If I had all the world, and should lose the favor and blessing of God, there would be no comparison in the loss."[2] Material riches are not in the same class with spiritual riches.

To invest one's life in the pursuit of wealth only to face eternal bankruptcy is not only insane. It is eternally tragic. To give one's life for moral/spiritual "wealth" is to deposit a principal that accrues eternal dividends. It pays ultimate prosperity. If material wealth has to be sacrificed for spiritual, it is the best bargain in life! To paraphrase a line from Jim Elliot, it is no loss to give what you cannot keep to gain what you cannot lose.[3]

---

[1] This does not violate the Christian doctrine of salvation by grace. The Christian faith prioritizes righteousness, while insisting that eternal righteousness only comes through God's saving grace.
[2] Daniel Defoe, *Robinson Crusoe* (Garden City, NY: Doubleday, 1945) p. 132.
[3] Jim Elliot's precise phrase was, "He is no fool who gives what he cannot keep to gain what he cannot lose." Elizabeth Elliot, *Shadow of the Almighty: The Life and Testament of Jim Elliot* (New York: Harper & Brothers, 1958) p. 108.

34 Moral Evil and Utilitarian Evil

The righteousness of the blameless keeps his way straight, but the wicked falls by his own wickedness (11:5 RSV). Also 11:6.

When I refer to someone as a good person, you understand that I mean she is morally, ethically good. But if I refer to a good government program, I am probably referring to a helpful program for its citizens. Moral goodness is measured by character, conscience, and integrity. Utilitarian goodness is judged by its usefulness, its helpfulness, its ability to produce happiness. Similarly, moral and utilitarian evil are judged by the same criteria. Moral good and evil refer to virtue and vice, but utilitarian good and evil refer to pleasure and pain.

This proverb draws a connection between moral evil and utilitarian evil—"the wicked falls by his own wickedness." Moral evil causes a downfall. The line is variously translated, "By his own lawlessness shall the lawless fall" (Rhm), "The wicked are brought down by their own wickedness" (NIV), "The wicked shall fall beneath their load of sins" (Tay).

Wickedness brings disaster. An immoral act contains its own utilitarian consequences. Moral choices determine practical destinies. Immoral causes have detrimental effects. Creating a morally evil cause releases a chain of painfully evil consequences. Moral evil is a self-destructive kit! It carries its own TNT. Inevitably the explosion comes. Sin is suicidal!

Novelist Lon Woodrum spoke of those "who allowed dark thoughts to beachhead their brains . . . After awhile the government of their minds crashed, and the tyrants took over . . ."[1]

Other proverbs state it: "The wicked are choked by their own violence" (10:6 NEB), "The unfaithful are destroyed by their duplicity" (11:3 NIV), "He who pursues evil pursues it to his own death" (11:19 NKJV), and "Wickedness overthrows the sinner" (13:6 NIV).

(Continued in the next essay)

---

[1] Lon Woodrum, *Stumble Upon the Dark Mountains* (Waco, TX: Word Books, 1956) p. 85.

Moral Goodness and Utilitarian Goodness 35

CONTINUED FROM PREVIOUS ESSAY

We have all been delivered many times from perilous predicaments, either by God or His angelic emissaries. But the point here is that righteous people are delivered also *by righteousness itself.* "The good man's goodness delivers him" (Tay).

Morality is designed to produce utility. Love is therapeutic. Being considerate prevents altercations. Sacrifice is appreciated and rewarded. Selflessness preempts retaliation. Marital fidelity results in long-term happiness. Hard work facilitates success. Moral goodness is programmed for utilitarian goodness. Highest happiness comes from holiness.

This is the flip side of the last essay which showed that evil is prone to disappointment, detriment, and destruction. The reason it is so prone is that moral evil is an aberration from moral goodness. Perversion presupposes goodness to pervert. Corruption presupposes goodness to corrupt. Rebellion requires authority to rebel against. Disobedience implies rules and regulations to disobey. Evil does not exist on its own. It requires goodness as a point of departure. Evil is an abnormal deviation from normality. Goodness is the universal norm.

Eventually evil destroys itself in conflict with goodness. An old Scottish hymn is a translation from Psalm 52: "Why dost thou boast, O mighty man / Of mischief or of ill? / The goodness of Almighty God / Endureth ever still."[1]

When evil people clash with universal goodness, they are in combat with unchangeable reality. The warp is set against the woof. In the end they lose. Goodness is too good to be overcome. Evil is too weak to survive. An evil person does not stand a chance in a universe that is ordered with goodness. Against goodness, the evil person cannot win. With goodness, the righteous cannot lose.

---

[1] *The Book of Psalms in Metre: The Scottish Hymnal* (Edinburgh: Thomas Nelson and Sons, 1882) p. 55.

36 An Endless Hope or a Hopeless End

When a wicked man dies, his hope perishes; all he expected from his power comes to nothing (11:7 NIV).

The hope of heaven makes life worth living even with its most ludicrous absurdities. Hope gives strength, purpose, and a measure of happiness to sustain souls in their darkest hours.

The unique genius of hope is that it borrows happiness from the future for instant delivery. For those whose hope is appropriately based, the joy is drawn from their own future account and therefore requires no repay. It is an advance on their future joy. It comes from anticipating the future while living in the present. Joy is attained from expecting joy.

Too many people, however, focus their hope on a diminutive future based on their own resources and power. Or they hope for heaven based on their own abilities, their public status, and their misunderstanding of God as a pushover. The problem is that they have confiscated a hope that is not rightfully theirs. The hope is drawn on an empty account. It is phantom hope. It has no resources to legitimize it, no future to justify it. The expected future is an illusion. When those people with false hope die, their hope dies with them, and their unjustified expectations add up to zero! They "come to nothing."

In the proverb, the first clause states *whose* hope perishes—that of the evil person. The second says *what* hope perishes—the falsely based hope. In a capsule the proverb says: Evil people with false hope are hopeless. By implication, the proverb suggests the opposite for the righteous on both counts. They have a genuinely based hope that will not perish. They carry their immortality with them. By hope, their future comes to them in the present. As Lon Woodrum wrote, "They outwit time by living in eternity."[1]

For the sinner, life is a hopeless end. For the "saint" life is an endless hope!

---

[1] Lon Woodrum, *Eternity in Their Heart* (Grand Rapids: Zondervan Publishing House, 1955) p. 108.

The righteous is delivered out of trouble, and the wicked cometh in his stead (11:8 KJV). Also 21:18.

Our first reaction is that life does not work that way. The proverbial solution to life's difficulties is too simplistic, and does not account for variables and contingencies. Certainly it does not explain why bad things happen to good people and good things to bad people. In frustration, Prince Hamlet erupted to the ghost of his murdered father, "The time is out of joint. O cursed spite, / That ever I was born to set it right!"[1]

A deeper look, however, will see that the line does not necessarily state a universal, but rather the general inclination of life's episodes, allowing for noteworthy exceptions. It is more of an observation than a promise. Most righteous people, both pagan and Christian, have lived situations in which they could not doubt divine help. Ancient Odysseus, in his heroic journey, confessed to the king, "Some god was our guide . . . Some god took pity."[2]

In this world, we cannot avoid the complex system of causes and effects. From thoughtlessness and folly, people walk directly into trouble. From overt or covert sin, they chance the repercussions for the benefit of the odds. Some become innocent victims of random occurrence, for which no one is responsible. Righteous people are not always sinless, but not sinning does preempt the effects of sin. To the extent that people are wise and cautious and good, they avoid the fallout from personal folly, recklessness, and sin. Further, the proverb is verified in real life that God often undertakes directly to spare specifically His devoted children.

The line, however, does not say that the righteous will *escape* misfortune, but that they will be delivered *out of it*. They have extra resources to handle it. God attends their dilemma. Often they hear in their own spirits an inaudible whisper, saying, "You are not alone!"

---

[1] Shakespeare, *Hamlet*, Act I, Scene 5, lines 188-189.
[2] Homer, *The Odyssey*, S.H. Butcher and A. Lang, tr. (New York: The MacMillan Co., 1911) Bk. X, pp. 115-116.

38 Destroyed or Delivered

The hypocrite with his mouth destroys his neighbor, but through knowledge the righteous will be delivered (11:9 NKJV).

Without any help from tongue-wagging neighbors, most of us too often misrepresent ourselves. Our own loose tongues leave the wrong impression about our motives or attitudes. Our mouths are put on automatic pilot, and we get our big flat foot stuck between our dentures.

The last thing we need is an unfriendly commentator to put the worst possible spin on our words and actions. A sudden strike of innuendo can do irreparable damage.

Some would destroy us by confrontation and rebuke, or by corrupting our values with verbal manipulation. More of them would damage our reputation behind our backs where we are helpless to defend ourselves. That way, they keep a safe distance. Simply by lifting an eyebrow and dropping their voice, they can abuse a good name.

All falsehoods are pretended truth. Yet because they are false, they collapse in the light of genuine truth. Daniel Webster said, "Falsehoods not only disagree with truths, but usually they quarrel among themselves."[1] Truth stands firm, because it never disagrees with itself.

When Othello was lied about and urged to leave, he said, "Not I. I must be found. My parts, my title, and my perfect soul shall manifest me rightly."[2]

Scholars are not sure whether the last clause of the proverb should be interpreted that righteous people escape when the truth is known or that righteous people will set the record straight for neighbors who have been falsely accused. But this we know, that when a person stays with truth, he is safe on the long haul. Sometime, somewhere, he will be exonerated. Knowledge of truth ultimately delivers the falsely accused.

---

[1] Quoted in *Encyclopedia of 7,700 Illustrations*, Paul Lee Tan, ed. (Rockville, MD: Assurance Pub., 1979) p. 563.
[2] Shakespeare, *Othello*, Act I, Scene 2, lines 30-32.

When the righteous prosper, the city rejoices; when the wicked perish, there are shouts of joy. / Through the blessing of the upright a city is exalted, but by the mouth of the wicked it is destroyed (11:10-11 NIV).

Frequently we hear that the personal and the political are separate categories and should not overlap. We are told that moral values are private and should carry no weight in the political process. Usually, however, such claims are intended to apply only to the other person's values rather than one's own. Those with weak values are comfortable with valueless politicians.

The two proverbs above highlight an unavoidable connection between piety and politics. A righteous leader inclines the entire state toward righteousness. An evil leader corrupts the state with vexations, oppressions, and scandal.

The first proverb declares that the citizens rejoice on two occasions—when the righteous are in leadership and when the state is freed from those political pests that plunder the process. People rejoice more when some people are replaced than when they are elected.

The second proverb says the nation is raised up, "exalted," by the blessing of righteous people and "torn down" (ABPS) by the curse of the wicked.

Here we are talking morality, not necessarily religion. In Alan Paton's classic fiction during the apartheid period of South Africa, just before Arthur Jarvis was murdered by an African, Jarvis had written, "The old tribal system was, for all its . . . superstition and witchcraft, [still] a moral system. . . . Today. . . their simple system of order and tradition and convention has been destroyed."[1] His own death underscored his point.

Even the morality of a righteous pagan nation disposes its people toward success. Moral rightness has its own positive effects. Another proverb says, "Righteousness exalts a nation, but sin is a disgrace to any people" (14:34).

---

[1] Alan Paton, *Cry, the Beloved Country* (New York: MacMillan Publishing Company, 1948) p. 146.

40 To Deride or to Defer

He that is devoid of wisdom despises his neighbor, but a man of understanding holds his peace (11:12 NKJV).

Few people can despise a neighbor without expressing it. That is implied by its antithesis in the other clause—"holding one's peace." To despise a person is to belittle her (RSV), to deride her (NIV), to pour contempt on her (AAT). To hold one's peace is to keep silent (NASB), to hold one's tongue (NIV). Foolishness does the first, and wisdom does the second.

Those without wisdom effuse their animosity in a stream of contempt, either to the person's face or behind her back. The problem is complicated when the defects are seen in one so close as a neighbor. Being a part of one's own community or social circle magnifies the shortcomings and aggravates the disapproval. What casual friends easily overlook stick out like thorns to close acquaintances. Neighbors scrutinize neighbors with mental binoculars.

Expressing ill will or resentment is foolish because it hurts the other person or her reputation, and it makes an enemy out of a potential friend. Hearing yourself condemn a person intensifies rather than mitigates your own feelings and convinces you that she is deplorable. Also, it breaks down your own inhibitions, making it more difficult to refrain the next time.

When his brother wanted to rail against those who had caused him so much misery, Shakespeare's Orlando said, "I will chide no breather in the world but myself, against whom I know most faults."[1]

When I was a youth, I heard the voice of wisdom from my own father who said to me, "Son, always be harder on yourself than on others."[2]

Rather than exposing faults, the prudent person is preoccupied with helping, protecting, and deferring to others, concealing their faults where feasible, otherwise putting on them the most charitable face possible.

---

[1] Shakespeare, *As You Like It*, Act III, Scene 2, lines 297-298.
[2] Hobart Murphree, Wedowee, Alabama.

A talebearer reveals secrets, but he who is of a faithful spirit conceals a matter (11:13 NKJV).

Once I heard the late Christian novelist Lon Woodrum satirically say, "Don't tell anyone I said that, but when you do, tell them not to tell anybody, and tell them when they do to tell them not to tell anybody."[1] In some minds, classified information is too active to be kept.

Grapevines are never idle. Buzzing with information, they transfer private matters into public domain. Once a secret is expressed, it spreads. And as it spreads, it inflates. As a rule, to tell one person is to tell a greedy public with itching ears. A top secret can only be kept in the bottle by keeping the cork in the bottleneck.

The gossip network rarely picks up good stories to broadcast. It traffics in scandal, or in private items that are innocuous only as long as they are kept private. The grapevine is a transportation system exporting smuggled contraband. Because it is a person-to-person network, false baggage accumulates, dispensing cargoes of misinformation.

But even if a personal item does not snowball, it properly remains personal unless the public is a stakeholder in the matter. A talebearer does not necessarily traffic in false information. He is a self-appointed news-hawk, peddling truth that others have no right to know. Telling the truth is morally wrong when it is only right to say nothing at all.

"A faithful spirit" that "conceals a matter" is an entrusted confidant who is impeccably trustworthy. With integrity and sobriety, he is a solemn and worthy trustee of the secret that has been shared. It is protected behind the walls of moral principle. In his head, the secret is safe.

Laertes said to his daughter, "Farewell, Ophelia; and remember well what I have said to you." Ophelia replied, "'Tis in my memory locked, and you yourself shall keep the key of it."[2]

---

[1] At Brasher Springs Camp, Gallant, Alabama.
[2] Shakespeare, *Hamlet*, Act I, Scene 3, lines 84-86.

42 Closed Minds or Open Ears

Where no counsel is, the people fall; but in the multitude of counselors there is safety (11:14 NKJV).

Implications and overtones of this proverb apply to leadership of a political entity. A people-group will be either victim or victor, determined by the counsel the leader is willing to hear and to heed. Every leader needs a staff of reliable advisors.

Between the lines, we also read that the counselors must be capable persons, otherwise they would do more harm than good. Multiple opinions of unseasoned advisors bring confusion. A leader needs wise guidance from experienced statesmen, people with no ulterior agenda, not voting for their own political pork. When he got word that he had a new granddaughter, President Herbert Hoover, dismayed with fragmented congressional opinion, remarked, "Thank God she doesn't have to be confirmed by the Senate."[1]

A problem for strong leaders is that the advisors may be too intimidated to express honest opinion, and they tell the leaders only what they want to hear. Another problem is that strong leaders tend to disregard their counsel in making decisions. Old Testament King Rehoboam lost five-sixths of his kingdom by refusing to listen to wise counsel (I Kgs. 12). Conversely, weak leaders are paralyzed by conflicting advice and disabled from making pivotal decisions.

While this proverb applies first to city-state or national leaders, the capsule is packed with potent advice for other institutional leaders as well: As far as possible, listen to everybody and govern by consensus with the team approach. Make decisions in the context of community rather than in isolation. Pick the minds of capable counselors. Expose yourself to differing views, and analyze the reasons for opposing opinions. Making a crucial decision takes courage, but making the right decision takes the humility to listen.

---

[1] Bob Dole, *Great Political Wit* (New York: Doubleday, 1998) p. 79.

*He who is surety for a stranger will surely suffer for it, but he who hates
going surety is safe* (11:15 NASB).

Now learn a new word. This proverb was written as a
"paronomasia," which means a word trick or pun. To capture the
original mechanics, it has been variously translated, ". . . shall be
broken with breakage," ". . . shall be evilly entreated with evil," or
"shall find evil upon evil."

The proverb assumes that moral responsibility includes
economy. Righteousness applies to more than religious ritual or
lifestyle values. It entails economic frugality and stewardship of
financial matters. Earlier Solomon had written: "If thou be surety .
. ., thou art snared. . . . Deliver thyself as a bird from the hand of
the fowler" (Prov. 6:1-5 KJV).

Charitable giving to needy people is not banned at all.
Standing surety for a responsible acquaintance is not strictly
prohibited. The warning is against incurring obligations that could
jeopardize our ability. The caveat could be expanded to include
credit cards and excessive home mortgages. In times of national
prosperity, we develop the cultural feeling that we can have
whatever we want, and money is no problem so long as credit is
available.

The warning is against making bail for a "stranger" or co-
signing a loan for someone you simply assume is safe. In this
situation, knowing the person includes knowing his economic
status, his dossier, his financial respectability. Many unsafe people
have sincere intentions, and standing surety does them a serious
disservice. Refusing their request helps save them from
themselves.

And it saves you from liability. Your signature takes the
legal burden off the other person and places it on yourself. The
borrower is free because you shoulder his responsibility. When he
defaults, he avoids you. The one you thought was a friend
becomes a stranger. Complying with the request runs a greater risk
of losing the friendship than you have by refusing the request.
You end up losing a friend and incurring a debt.

44 Grace or Grit

A gracious woman retaineth honor, and strong men retain riches (11:16 KJV).

This little nutshell holds a lot of goody, though it begins with a *faux pas* in political correctness. By favoring the woman, some might smell the sexism of a patronizing chivalry.

Her gain comes from what she *is* and his from what he *does*, implying that *being* has more value than *doing.*

She obtains by *grace*, by charm, by loveliness. Othello's ancient Iago described in verse a gracious woman: "She was ever fair and never proud, / Had tongue at will and yet was never loud. . . . / She could think and ne'er disclose her mind, / See suitors following and [never] look behind."[1]

But the man gains by activity, by energetic *force,* by grind and grit. The original word even had the nuance of ruthless violence often used in acquiring riches.

And too, the woman gains *honor* and *respect* while the man gains only *riches.* Important as capital assets are, some intangibles are much more valuable. It is futile to waste one's life for nothing more than wealth. Someone said, "He spent his health to gain his wealth, / And then turned round again / And spent his wealth to gain his health / Which never came back again."[2]

We can become so attached to what we have that we end up *belonging* to what we have. Instead of owning our wealth, our wealth owns us! David Neff wrote, "Bullion in bulk cannot be made to serve us. We can only serve it."[3] Money is useful as a servant, but deadly as a master.

Three millennia ago the world did not understand stereotyping as we do today. The proverb, however, does not say that men do not have grace and women do not work hard. It does point out differences that were generally associated with each. If we men fit the category, we should take lessons from the other gender.

---

[1] Shakespeare, *Othello*, Act II, Scene 1, lines 149-150, 158-159.
[2] Author unknown.
[3] David Neff, "Drunk on Money," *Christianity Today*, April 8, 1988, p. 15.

The merciful man does good for his own soul, but he who is cruel troubles his own flesh (11:17 NKJV).

Judicial mercy refers to clemency toward the guilty, but the scriptures use mercy many times in nonjudicial ways, referring to benevolence toward needy persons. Mercy entails little gestures of generosity, and cruelty includes subtle maneuvers from heartlessness.

The mathematical formula is this: Doing good to others ends up doing good to oneself. Giving results in getting. Helping others elicits help from others. Both cruelty and mercy are reciprocated, one with retaliation and the other with response. The first is to one's own detriment, the second to one's profit.

Not only is mercy reflexive, but acts of mercy are *intrinsically* valuable to the one who gives. They enrich, deepen, and bless one's own spirit. They expand a person's soul. Focusing on the needs of others detaches a person from her own needs, and unfetters her from self-centered entanglements. It is liberating! Shakespeare's Portia said, "Mercy . . . is twice blest; it blesseth him that gives it and him that takes."[1]

The formula, however, is elusive. Attempting to use it, we cannot grasp it. It has no handle to hold. Feeding the formula for personal benefit clogs its mechanisms. Giving for the purpose of getting is not mercy at all. It is pretended mercy. Investing in others for personal profit under the guise of mercy is self-centered rather than other-centered.

Genuine mercy is preoccupied with the other person, and it is its own reward. The purest of benefits come in the joy of knowing the needy person has been helped. That is a joy that only the merciful know.

Jesus lifted the first clause of this proverb, refined and polished it, and made it a beatitude: "Blessed are the merciful, for they shall obtain mercy" (Matt. 5:7).

---

[1] Shakespeare, *The Merchant of Venice*, Act IV, Scene 1, lines 184-187.

46 The Work and the Reward

The wicked man does deceptive work, but to him who sows righteousness will be a sure reward (11:18 NKJV).

The work of the wicked is deceitful in that its result is not durable. In another place Solomon complained that most human work "is vanity"—that is, it is empty and ephemeral, like a bubble that bursts (Ecc. 1:14). The work is deceitful also in that it does not produce what was expected. So the wicked earns "deceptive wages" (NIV), "wages of falsehoods" (Rhm), "empty profits" (NAB). When they work for themselves, they attempt shortcuts and are shortchanged.

The metaphor in the second clause is assumed in the first. A wicked worker is like a sower that spreads weed seed expecting to produce a bountiful harvest of grain. What he gets is crabgrass and ragweeds. Even hard work that is done the wrong way with wrong materials and wrong tools does not produce what is desired. Houses are not built with forest foliage. Crops are not cultivated by sitting at the keyboard of a word processor. Taking shortcuts with quick-fixes does not build an empire! And sowing evil seed does not yield a harvest of righteousness.

This is a figure of life's ultimate values and its final destiny. Careless, self-centered persons may work hard to have what they want, and discover in the end they never got what they really wanted. Temporarily they were pleased, but their harvest was temporal rather than eternal. For the one who spreads the seeds of righteousness, the yield is quite the reverse. Instead of being transient and temporal, the harvest is durable and eternal.

"Sow for yourselves righteousness, reap the fruit of unfailing love" (Hos. 10:12 NIV). "He who sows wickedness reaps trouble" (Prov. 22:8 NIV). "Whatsoever a man soweth, that shall he also reap. For he that soweth to the flesh shall . . . reap corruption, but he that soweth to the Spirit shall . . . reap life everlasting" (Gal. 6:7-8 KJV). The law of sowing and reaping is operative. The final harvest corresponds to the seed that is sown. The reward correlates with the work.

The Way of Life and the Pursuit of Death 47

As righteousness leads to life, so he who pursues evil pursues it to his own death (11:19 NKJV).

The pursuit of evil was not begun as a pursuit of evil itself. It was a diversion from the search for love, beauty, goodness and truth for which the human mechanism is specially adapted. We looked within ourselves for our own fulfillment and found only an empty void. Then we discovered that our personal fancies are more easily fulfilled than our deeper longings, so we refocused our quest on self-centered yens and urges. Living on self-centered motives led to a self-centered lifestyle that became an entrenched pattern of embedded evil.

Selfish satisfactions, however, are only flimsy substitutes for the righteousness that we deeply crave. George Eliot referred to "those foolish habits that were no pleasures, but only a feverish way of annulling vacancy."[1] The longing for better living is eclipsed by a fragmented series of momentary satisfactions, and the urge for higher fulfillment is frustrated. Seeking life at its best, we have taken a detour that leads to "death."

Self-centeredness by its nature is habit-forming. Finding temporary props for living without higher-level commitment, a person becomes addicted. We can become enslaved *by* ourselves *to* ourselves. We can be hooked *on* ourselves! Evil leads its suitor "to his own death."

The ancient proverb depicted the problem, but the solution awaited the New Testament gospel. The strength of sinfulness and the vulnerability of human personality require a radical disturbance of the self-centered pattern, and higher-level fulfillment requires a solid replacement for the disappointing substitutes. Paul said, "I have been crucified with Christ and I no longer live, but Christ lives in me" (Gal. 2:20 NIV). Again Paul said, "Therefore, if anyone is in Christ, he is a new creation; the old has gone, the new has come" (2 Cor. 5:17 NIV)!

---

[1] George Eliot, *Silas Marner*, in *Adventures of Appreciation*, Walter Loban and Rosalind Olmsted, eds. (New York: Harcourt, Brace & World, Inc., 1963) p. 645.

48 The Abomination of Transgression

They that are of a froward[1] heart are abomination to the Lord, but such as are upright in their way are his delight (11:20 KJV).

Sir Winston Churchill is quoted as saying that Sir Cripps had "all the virtues I dislike and none of the vices I admire."[2] Of course, he was using satire to disparage straitlaced piety. God, however, never saw a virtue that He did not like nor a vice He did not hate. In an astounding gesture of divine humility, the God of all eternity stoops to allow us humans to affect His feelings with displeasure or delight.[3] He is not emotionally distant or detached. He is alert, not apathetic. He is responsive, not impassive.

Goodness does not mean softness toward evil. An infinitely good God detests the abominable badness of those with rebellious hearts. Hawthorne spoke of "the taint of deepest sin in the most sacred quality of human life."[4] While God loves all sinners, He deplores all sin. It is not something that is nicely naughty, giving zing, zest, and gusto to life. Sin is a moral malignancy that results in eternal fatality! A holy God cannot wink at "the sinfulness of sin" *(Rom. 7:13)* without violating His holiness.

Little white lies are big and black in His eyes. Profanity, obscenity, and racial slurs strike like a thunderstorm in His Ears. Irreverence and indecent attitudes toward other people confront His righteous nature with repugnance, and fire the fierceness of His goodness with holy indignation—precisely because He is good.

An old Puritan proverb states: "What righteousness doth God require of thee but that righteousness which His righteousness requireth Him to require of thee?" (Continued in the next essay)

---

[1] In the phrase "to and fro," *to* means toward and *fro* means backward, away from, or *froward*

[2] Quoted by Senator Bob Dole in his book, *Great Political Wit* (New York: Doubleday, 1998) p. 35.

[3] Today most of the church has moved beyond Augustine's, Anselm's, and Aquinas' view of divine impassibility—that an immutable God cannot be emotionally affected by anything His creatures do.

[4] Nahaniel Hawthorne, *The Scarlet Letter* (New York: Books, Inc., n.d.) p. 45.

CONTINUED FROM PREVIOUS ESSAY

In the fantasyland of Narnia, all the creatures wept when Prince Caspian died. And the majestic lion Aslan who personified Christ wept too, "great Lion-tears, each tear more precious than the Earth would be if it was a single solid diamond."[1]

That God has voluntarily allowed Himself to feel deeply about humankind, human sin and human righteousness cannot be missed when one takes a long look at Calvary. The cross of Christ shows that God left His feelings unguarded. He made Himself vulnerable to human sin. He placed Himself in a position to allow us to crucify His feelings. He did not play it safe. The eternal God has stooped to allow you and me to affect His feelings with pain or pleasure.

To allow unworthy persons like us to please Him, to contribute to His pleasure, to become the subjects of His delight—that is at once both humbling and honoring. Unworthy as we are, we are yet worthful to Him. We need no longer feel like a "nobody" because to Him each of us is "somebody." Our value is not intrinsic. It is bestowed. It is not earned. It is derived from the premium He places on us. We are important because we are important to Him!

To think that God can delight in our uprightness is surely presumptuous beyond words. Perhaps the Psalmist's term would be more modest—"be *acceptable* in Thy sight" (Ps. 19:14). Yet the Psalmist was so bold as to announce, "He delighted in me" (Ps. 18:19 NIV). He "delights" in His people (Ps. 37:23). God even uses us as object lessons to the world. He takes great pleasure in presenting us in His program of "show and tell."

It is incomprehensible that we have been placed in a position either to pain Him or please Him! God is not detached and aloof. The eternal God of all reality is not embarrassed to *delight* in His people!

---

[1] C. S. Lewis, *The Silver Chair*, Book 4 of the Chronicles (New York: Collier Books, Macmillan, 1953) p. 211.

50 Acted or Acted Upon

Though hand join in hand, the wicked shall not be unpunished, but the seed of the righteous shall be delivered (11:21 KJV).

Since the advent of psychology, the world has wondered just how much and in what way people can point to their heritage to account for their behavior. The old philosophy of behaviorism attributed every human action to external stimuli, which included parental conditioning. Instead of acting, we were acted upon. That left no place for personal accountability, and made all judicial punishment misplaced and unfair.

More recent schools of counseling emphasize individual responsibility. Nobody ever had perfect parents. The parents themselves were reared by imperfect parents, and so were their parents. We cannot help where we came from, but we are responsible for where we are going. Personal choice, freedom, and responsibility figure largely in human behavior. Shakespeare's Cassius said to Brutus, "The fault, dear Brutus, is not in our stars, but in ourselves."[1]

God said to Jeremiah, "People will no longer say, The fathers have eaten sour grapes, and the children's teeth are set on edge. Instead, everyone will die for his own sin" (Jer. 31:29-30 NIV). The proverb here says no one will be excused by claiming the sin was handed down, "hand to hand," from parents. Robinson Crusoe, blaming no one but himself, said, "I was still . . . the willful agent of my own miseries. . . . I, born to be my own destroyer, could not resist the offer."[2]

This is not to deny strong parental influence, either environmental or genetic, but we are judged for refusing to veto the bad influences. Those who respond to the righteous rearing they inherited will be spared the punishment. Those who reject their righteous rearing or refuse to reject their unrighteous rearing will be judged proportionately.

---

[1] Shakespeare, *Julius Ceasar*, Act I, Scene 2, lines 140-141.
[2] Daniel Defoe, *Robinson Crusoe* (Garden City, NY: Doubleday, 1945) p. 46, 48.

As a ring of gold in a swine's snout, so is a beautiful woman who lacks discretion (11:22 NASB).

Gender egalitarianism was never intended to eliminate differences between male and female. It is foolish to pretend that men are as beautiful as women, or that men are no more attracted to the form and figure of a woman than a woman is to that of a man.

The simile in this proverb compares a woman's beauty with a precious, valuable jewel, and the indiscretion of some women with the filth and stench of a swine. We have no problem with either gems or swine, but the force of the word picture comes in connecting the two. Attempting to cover indecency with outward beauty is just as incongruous as an ornament in a pig's snout. A hog uses its grotesque nose to root in the mire for swill, which makes the adornment seem most out of place.

The ghost of Hamlet's murdered father tells him that "lewdness takes the shape of heaven" in its attempt to seduce virtue. The ghost adds, "So lust . . . will sate itself in a celestial bed, and prey on garbage."[1] Just as a man of love desires to feast at the festival of feminine beauty, so a man of lust craves a banquet of beauty to devour. The proverb by implication condemns the voracious appetite of some men as much as the cheap beauty of some women.

A jewel is an admirable gem, not to be discredited. But its location in a swine's snout calls attention to its ugly venue. It is perfectly appropriate for a woman to want her appearance to reflect her inward beauty. And it is understandable that persons who are inwardly ugly should want to cover with outward beauty. Yet when the inward is markedly different from the outward, the contrast is distasteful, sickening, and revolting—not because of the outward beauty, but because the beauty makes its opposite so unsightly.

---

[1] Shakespeare, *Hamlet*, Act I, Scene 5, lines 53-57.

52 Good Desires or Bad Desires

The desire of the righteous is only good, but the expectation of the wicked is wrath (11:23 NKJV).

The good desires of the righteous in the first clause imply the evil desires of the wicked in the second. And the bad end of the wicked in the second implies the good end of the righteous in the first. Each is implied by its counterpoint. Then the proverb reads: *The good desires of the righteous end in God's good favor, and the bad desires of the wicked end in God's wrath.*

It is a heavy message. Final favor or disfavor turns on our present desires, because they determine our direction. Here we are not speaking of surface desires that are easily triggered by temptation or situations. We are talking the deep controlling motive that directs our lives. That righteous motive can be strong enough to flip the circuit breaker on conflicting surface desires.

Self-centered desires are addictive. By gratifying ourselves, the chains strengthen and we become more helpless. Incarcerated by our own *will* and *will not*, we require the Spirit of God to remotivate our will toward repentance and righteousness. In that moment of motivation, inspiration or conviction, we are genuinely free to choose between God and self.

After the righteous motive is firmly in place, it can be strengthened by daily use until the unworthy motives are reined in. That is the process of moral growth and sanctification. We can reach the point that we can do whatever we want to do, because on that deep level we *want* to do what God *wants* us to do more than we *want* to do what we *want* to do. We are more *pleased* when we *please* Him than when we *please* ourselves. We *will* His *will* more than we *will* our own *will*, so our *will* becomes one with His *will*. Whittier said, "Doing God's will as if it were my own,/ Yet trusting not in mine, but in His strength alone!"[1] That radical level of sanctification makes life easier, and it is available for every Christian. (Continued in the next essay)

---

[1] John G. Whittier, "First-Day Thoughts," Donald McQuade, ed., *The Harper American Literature* (No city: Addison-Wesley Educational Publishers, 1994) Vol. I, p. 2132.

CONTINUED FROM PREVIOUS ESSAY

The idea of an angry God is repulsive to those of us who resonate with a loving God. But the wrath of God comes through clearly from the Old Testament prophets, the New Testament writers, and from Jesus Himself. The proverbs do not say much about God's wrath, but when they do, the subject is stated strongly.

Our confusion comes from the model of wrath that we are accustomed to seeing. We have witnessed humans that are driven by uncontrollable bursts of rage, and we do not wish to ascribe to God that kind of madness. It smacks of emotional volatility.

What we overlook is that there are two kinds of wrath, a bad and a good. Both are emotional, but one is immoral and the other is moral. The first controls the person, and the second is controlled by the person. One is unholy anger and the other is righteous wrath. The first is a reaction to an offended self, and the second is a reaction to an offended principle or to an abused person.

Because emotion is integral to personality, to ask us not to respond to situations emotionally is to ask us to be fragmented rather than integrated persons. Anger is morally appropriate to some situations.

Standing passively on the sidelines while innocent people are abused with cruelty is no exhibition of moral character. Recent reports of ethnic cleansing should fire our blood with burning indignation! To say God is incapable of holy anger is to say He is ethically neutral. Of course, any divine punishment is morally rather than emotionally determined. Because His wrath is righteous, it is always under ethical control.

God's good wrath is bad news for the wicked. Their *appropriate* "expectation" is wrath. In the end, their false hope for escape will be disappointed. The righteous will be surprised with favors greater than they could have anticipated.

54 The Seed and the Grain

There is one who scatters, yet increases more; and there is one who withholds more than is rght, but it leads to poverty (11:24 NKJV).

The metaphor is that of sowing seeds. The farmer needs to calculate closely just how much grain he needs to withhold for stockfeed and how much he can use to seed the next production. Withholding too much will guarantee fat stock for the first year, but not enough seed is left for next year's crop. Using more grain for seed to assure a future harvest requires some sacrifice in the present. The more that is used for sowing, the greater the harvest next time.

The principle is important in a monetary economy. Laying aside enough for retirement is worth the present sacrifice. The long view should eclipse our nearsightedness. Sacrificing the future on the altar of the present is not worth the present comfort it gives. Because unforeseen contingencies rule out meticulous calculations, any capital cushion should favor the future. Recognizing uncontrollable variables, however, the sage of the proverb is careful not to state a precise mathematical formula. He deals in generalities rather than universal absolutes.

The larger metaphorical application highlights the importance of contributing to God's work and distributing charity to persons in need. Investing that way for monetary profit is self-defeating, for God honors generosity for its own sake rather than for a return on the investment. Making a contribution as "seed faith" for a future yield is a pure business move and accrues no merit to your account with God. The right motive should accompany the good deed.

A wealthy businessman benefactor lost all his assets and neared the end of life in poverty. He said, "All I have left is what I gave to God and to hurting, hungry people. I am so happy I gave it. Everything else is lost."[1] The psalmist said, "He has scattered abroad his gifts to the poor; his righteousness endures forever" (Ps. 112:9 NIV).

---

[1] Told of one of his friends by Dr. John R. Church, Winston-Salem, NC.

The generous man will be prosperous, and he who waters will himself be watered. / He who withholds grain, the people will curse him, but blessing will be on the head of him who sells it (11:25-26 NASB).

Social responsibility was accented as far back as ancient times. Selfish speculators who connived to profit on unfortunate people by withholding needed commodities to inflate prices were accursed. Though generosity was urged for the sake of those who benefited, the good that came to the giver from giving was not overlooked. Those who refresh others—like a soft "watering" rain on dry land—will themselves receive corresponding refreshment. They are refreshed by refreshing others.

The idea of getting from giving is foreign to an IBM machine. It would give an electronic brain a nervous breakdown. But it is an operative principle in the social and spiritual mechanics of life. By a willingness to follow, one learns how to be a good leader. By being a good student you pick up how to be a good teacher. By being a good listener, you learn what it takes to be a good speaker. By giving, you receive. The way up is down.

Jesus said if you save your life you will lose it, but if you lose your life—in the right way for the right cause—you will find it (Matt. 16:25). We lose to Him our self-centered lives, and we discover in Him our new liberated lives.

When all that we own belongs to Him, we gain riches in a dimension of life that was otherwise impoverished by our miserliness.

Like the lad with the loaves and fish, we give our meager baskets and He returns a banquet of plenty. A cup of water given in His name returns to us a Mediterranean of mercy! The poorest person on earth may be the wealthy miser who hoards his possessions. The richest ones may be the poor "Mother Teresa's" who expend themselves in the needs of others for the sake of Christ. You cannot outgive God!

56 Seeking and Finding

He who diligently seeks good finds favor, but trouble will come to him who seeks evil (11:27 NKJV).

Life experiences are not mathematically predictable. Outside input beyond our ability to calculate often alters the sum or product of the equation. This proverb contains a paradox that can neither be explained nor denied.

Those persons who seek to do good, and to find goodness to feed on, are not aware of the secondary effects of the search. Favor comes back as a by-product of the good they sought. Unknown to them at the time, while seeking ways to help others they were befriending others. Good favor seeks those who seek what is good. Jesus said, "Seek and you will find" (Matt. 7:7), but He left us to be surprised that the find would be more than we sought!

What is predictable is that whatever comes back eventually will be in the same moral area of what was sought—either good or bad.

What you fantasized will be actualized, with unexpected consequences. Mischief will come back on the one who sought to do mischief to others. "If a man pursues evil it turns upon him" (11:27 NEB). Haman was hanged on the gallows he prepared for Mordecai (Es. 7:10). A man fell into the pit he dug for another (Ps. 7:15). The wicked are snared in their own net (Ps. 9:15). Isaiah speaks of those who kindle their own fire, encircle themselves with their own firebrands, and walk among the brands they themselves have set ablaze, and then lie down in their own torment (Isa. 50:11). Kipling has his character Dick Heldar say: "I have my own matches and sulfur, and I'll make my own hell, thanks."[1]

Each new day of life, earthlings are on a quest, some on scavenger hunts, others on noble pursuits. Sooner or later they discover the corollary of what they have sought—either sorrow or surprise, either suffering or serendipity!

---

[1] Rudyard Kipling, *The Light that Failed* (New York: Books, Inc., n.d.) p. 131.

World Wealth or Other-World Wealth 57

Whoever trusts in his riches will fall, but the righteous will thrive like a green leaf (11:28 NIV).

Musing about his future, Linus says, "I'd like to make a lot of money, but I'd hate to be a snob. I've given this a lot of thought." Charlie Brown asks, "So what did you decide?" Linus replies, "I've decided to be a very rich and famous person who doesn't really care about money, and who is . . . very humble and rich and famous." Charlie Brown says, "Good luck!"[1]

The scripture never condemns material possessions, but it does say "the love of money is the root of all kinds of evil" (1 Tim. 6:10). The prosperous and the pauper alike can over-prioritize the value of wealth. Money cannot even secure itself against the inflation and recession that reduce its value and diminish its ability to perform.

This proverb enunciates the problem of relying on affluence for what it is not strong enough to support—personal worth, genuine love, happiness, eternal life. These are treasures no money can buy. Synthetic status, momentary pleasures, superficial love, elusive happiness are only the empty ghosts of the real. Expecting money to perform beyond its ability places it under too heavy a strain. As a foundation for life, it collapses under the weight it is not able to support. In the larger economies of life, wealth is a perilous priority.

Peter said, We "are not redeemed with corruptible things, as silver and gold" (1 Pet. 1:18 KJV).

The proverb implies that some unrighteous people place undue trust in riches, and the righteous do not. The metaphor is that of a verdant leaf. Those who trust in riches wither and fall like a leaf that loses its connection with its source of life. Those who anchor their trust in something richer than money are like flourishing foliage, healthy and wealthy with riches that are more valuable. The greater wealth comes from a higher economy.

---

[1] Charles M. Schulz, *The Complete Peanuts, 1963-1964* (Seattle: Fantagraphics Books, 2007) p. 23.

58 Home and Family

He who troubles his own house will inherit the wind, and the fool will be servant to the wise of heart (11:29 NKJV).

A mother stuck her head in the playroom where she heard a furious fuss. The little girl exclaimed, "We're having fun! We're playing husband and wife!" Most people handle conflict very much as their parents did. Some are yellers. Some pouters. Some divorcers. Some are peacemakers and forgivers. The effects of family relationships, either helpful or hurtful, are disproportionately large. Small acorns grow into huge oaks. Facial frowns and accusatorial tones feed negative attitudes. A climate where love is expressed reproduces itself.

For those who neglect their families for strangers in the chat rooms, family friendship becomes empty air. Those who upset their families with tension produce tempestuous wind. Little whirlwinds become cyclones and typhoons, and the home becomes a storm center.

Adolescents, craving approval and self-esteem while being locked into a social environment that puts them down, are incarcerated in an emotional syndrome, complicated by hormone-driven bodies. The stress of disappointments and inadequacies can immobilize them. Some become impulsive and impetuous. Anger erupts against those who represent repression. Ronald Reagan spoke tongue-in-cheek when the president wrote, "Insanity is hereditary. You catch it from your kids."[1]

Youth desperately need a home that is a haven. They need an orderly atmosphere of relaxed relationships to which they can resort. They need an environment of acceptance and understanding, without critical barbs, where they are treated with adult respect. Robert Frost wrote: "Home is the place where . . . they have to take you in."[2] Youth need to live in a house that is a home! The apostle Paul wrote, "Do not provoke your children to anger" (Eph. 6:4 NASB).

---

[1] Associated Press article in *The Atlanta Journal-Constitution,* Atlanta, GA, May 3, 2007, p. A12.
[2] Robert Frost, "The Death of the Hired Man," Louis Untermeyer, ed., *Modern American Poetry* (New York: Harcourt, Brace and Co., 1950) p. 189.

The fruit of the righteous is a tree of life, and he who wins souls is wise
(11:30 NKJV).

Whether righteousness produces wisdom or wisdom produces righteousness—that we would like to know. Then we could know where to begin with one to gain the other. The proverbialist keeps implying they go together, though with different definitions. Certainly each motivates and complements the other, and each feeds the other and feeds *on* the other, causing them to grow holistically and exponentially. Each needs the other, not only for itself, but also for its influence on people. Wise rascals and righteous fools alike have little appeal.

The sage keeps saying that both wisdom and righteousness have something to do with God. Earlier he said, "The fear of the Lord is the beginning of wisdom" (Pro. 9:10). When God is brought in on the act, wisdom and righteousness soar. And shine. And sway others.

What first appears here to be two separate proverbs are really two parts of the same. The righteous in the first implies the same in the second, and the wise in the second implies the same in the first. The two go together. The proverb says those who are both wise and righteous both produce healthy fruit and attract sincere souls. By their words and actions, the wise-righteous *impart* an influence that stands as a living tree with nutritious fruit. And they *impact* people by making virtue so attractive that it "wins their souls." Profoundly influenced, people partake and benefit from the fruit's salutary value, and they respond with their hearts to righteous living. A broader application can serve Christian evangelism.

Florence Nightingale's biographer wrote that her "mere presence brought with it a strange influence" and imparted "something of the forgotten charm of life."[1] She had both wisdom and righteousness, both of which are prerequisites for nourishing and impacting people.

---

[1] Lytton Strachey, *Eminent Victorians* (London: Bloomsbury Publishing Ltd., 1988. First published in 1918) p. 84.

60 Rewards and Retribution

If the righteous receive their due on earth, how much more the ungodly and the sinner (11:31 NIV)!

When scholars disagree, we are left confused. Some interpret this proverb to mean the righteous will be rewarded on earth and the wicked will be punished. But we do not see that regularly occurring. The befuddled ecclesiastic of the Old Testament observed common problems for both "the righteous and the wicked, the good and the bad" (Ecc. 9:2), though we do note frequently granted requests of the righteous.

Probably a better interpretation comes from the ancient Greek translation[1]: "And if the righteous scarcely be saved, where shall the ungodly and sinner appear?" Peter quotes that line verbatim in the context of suffering (1 Pet. 4:18), stating positively that the righteous are not spared suffering on earth. How much more is it true that the sinner will not be spared.

We must be cautious about attempting to trace God's activity with meticulous precision, but as a general rule He seems to postpone rewards and retribution until a later life. Yet the system on earth is set up so that both goodness and evil have their respective consequences. At least, the righteous have better equipment to handle their adversities. If God does not save them *from* affliction, He certainly helps them *in* affliction. When adversity is complicated with guilt, it is much harder to handle. When guilt switches to anger, then to self-pity, the problem is further complicated. Righteous people can avoid those complications.

My personal friend[2] had been misdiagnosed with a heart attack. When I visited him in the hospital, Bob said, "If I had been a smoker, I don't think I could handle the guilt of a heart attack." Then a broad grin lifted his slumping face, and he exclaimed, "You can't imagine how good it feels to have a heart attack and not feel guilty!"

---

[1] The early translation of the Hebrew Old Testament into Greek is called *The Septuagint*.
[2] Robert A. Perry, Wedowee, Alabama.

Whoever loves instruction loves knowledge, but he who hates reproof is stupid (12:1 NKJV).

Billy Graham ended a preaching tour in Russia and said to a Russian Orthodox leader, "You have listened to many of my sermons. Do you have any suggestions?" The reply was, "Yes. Emphasize the Resurrection more." Graham later remarked, "God took me all the way to Russia to be reminded in a fresh way" of the importance of Christ's Resurrection.[1] In the prologue to Proverbs, Solomon said, "Let the wise listen and add to their learning, and let the discerning get guidance" (Prov. 1:5 NIV).

The word for "instruction" includes a connotation of being corrected. It implies that one important source of knowledge is the correction we get when we have been wrong. Brutus said, "The eye sees not itself but by reflection." And Cassius replied, "I, your glass, will modestly discover to yourself that of yourself which you know not."[2]

A Hebrew writer said, "No discipline seems pleasant at the time, but painful. Later on, however, it produces . . . righteousness" (Heb. 12:11 NIV). For continuing education, we all need peer reviews and evaluation.

One function of wisdom is to increase itself, because the wise are wise enough to wish for more wisdom. Since wisdom requires knowledge to work with, how better to get the knowledge than from others? Wise people are humble enough to learn from those who know.

Today we are swimming in a pool of polling statistics. We are weighted down with information overload. The reading public consumes myriad volumes of "how to" books. Instead of using our minds as a repository for temporary trivia that can always be found on-line, we need to go after basic, eternal truth about reality, God, and righteousness. That knowledge will anchor us in life and sustain us in death.

---

[1] In a printed letter by Billy Graham sent to the Billy Graham Evangelistic Association supporters April 2009.
[2] Shakespeare, *Julius Caesar*, Act I, Scene 2, lines 52-53, 67-70.

62 Favor or Disfavor

A good man obtains favor from the Lord, but a man of wicked devices He will condemn (12:2 NKJV).

Some people sin without being tempted to sin. They need no outside influence to trigger an evil impulse. Their minds grind out evil plots and plans with carefully calculated procedures. They are not lazy. They are highly motivated, crafty, creating their own temptations with devious designs and cleverly crafted schemes and strategies.

Here we have more than wicked works or deeds. We have a person of evil thoughts. In the drama, Julius Caesar said to Mark Antony, "Yon Cassius has a lean and hungry look; he thinks too much. Such men are dangerous."[1]

Rudyard Kipling spoke of one whose "revolving thoughts ground against each other as millstones grind when there is no corn between . . ."[2] When there is no grist to grind, the mental millstones grind out the grit of one's own evil mind. Thoughts activate motives that incite intentions to live out the thoughts. A morally weak, struggling sinner is not as dangerous as a conniving, deceptive, intentional rogue.

God's love for us comes from what He is rather than from what we are. And our salvation is never earned. But God's "favor" is His response to our devotion and goodness. And God's "condemnation" is His response to our badness.

C. S. Lewis said, "When we merely say that we are bad, the 'wrath' of God seems a barbarous doctrine; as soon as we *perceive* our badness, [God's wrath] appears inevitable."[3]

A sweeping dialectical difference stands between God's favor and His disfavor. His frown is worth everything in life to avoid. His smile is worth everything to gain.

---

[1] Shakespeare, *Julius Caesar*, Act I, Scene 2, lines 194-195.
[2] Rudyard Kipling, *The Light that Failed* (New York: Books, Inc., n.d.) p. 203.
[3] C. S. Lewis, *The Problem of Pain* (New York: Macmillan Publishing Co., Inc., 21st printing, 1978) p. 58.

Precarious or Secure 63

A man shall not be established by wickedness, but the root of the righteous shall not be moved (12:3 KJV).

Ancient Greek philosopher Heraclitus said, "One cannot step twice into the same river,"[1] meaning that the water is different each time you step in.

Like the changing world, evil is variable, constantly changing. Its only fixed principle is that its root is in the human heart, and that takes different forms from place to place and from time to time. Evil rides with the flow of fads and contemporary situations. But fads change, and time is rapidly slipping into history. Time is in fast forward. There is no pause button, and no rewind.

C. S. Lewis said, "We know where times move. They move *away*. But in religion we find something that does not move away."[2]

By fraud or by force, evil may establish prosperity for a period, but it is precarious. Evil people stand on tenuous ground, subject to seismic convulsions. Without moral roots, they have no security because they have no anchor. They live outside God's safety zone.

Though we humans cannot be established *by* wickedness, we can certainly be established *in* wickedness, because evil will clutch our wills and capture our characters. Unable to shake loose, sinners are enslaved to a changing temporality, with no permanency.

The taproot of the righteous goes deep into the moral subsoil of life. Amid tornadic and tectonic turbulence, they stand tall like titans, still smiling when the disturbance subsides. Righteousness centers in God, and the righteous are anchored in the unchangeableness of God. The ancient psalmist sang, "The heavens . . . shall perish, but Thou shalt endure. . . . Thou art the same, and Thy years shall have no end" (Ps. 102: 25-7).

---

[1] Douglas J. Soccio, *Archetypes of Wisdom* (Belmont, CA: Wadsworth Pub. Co., 1998) p. 47.
[2] C. S. Lewis, *God in the Dock* (Grand Rapids: Eerdmans, 1970) p. 65.

64 A Crown or a Curse

A virtuous woman is a crown to her husband, but she that maketh ashamed is as rottenness in his bones (12:4 KJV).

The virtuous wife is contrasted with the woman who shames her husband, and crowning her husband is contrasted with rotting his bones. The original word is broader than what we know as virtue, including excellence, nobility, character, worthiness, dignity, strength of soul. That woman is different from the shameful wife who shamelessly disgraces her husband.

A virtuous wife is the husband's chief ornament, his crown, who brightens his life with a splendor that authenticates his value. As a crown, she sits on his brow, vindicating him as her prince. But the shameful wife with questionable social values and irregular manners is like an incurable disease, a curse that plagues the privacy of the home and the family name in public.

Some 200 years before this proverb, the Hebrew prophetess Deborah was respected as the judge and followed as a successful leader. Rather than reflecting a cultural sexism, this proverb reveals the monumental place of a wife. She is in a position to make or break her husband.

What is left unsaid is that honor or disgrace moves both ways between spouses. A noble, virtuous man can adorn his wife with luster like a tiara on her brow, announcing to the world that she is a princess. Or, he can disgrace her with disrespect like a disease.

Christian marriage is not a mutual agreement to eat and sleep together while living otherwise separate lives. Marital unity is forged by mutual affection, enhanced by common values, lifestyle, and Christian experience. We-ness and us-ness replaces I-ness and me-ness. Each ego-center shifts to the other. It is identity rather than diversity, each happy when the other is happy and hurting when the other hurts, each protecting the feelings of the other. Self-interests are secondary to spouse-interests. Each boosts and blesses the other as a cherished crown, fulfilling Paul's ideal that they "two shall become one" (Eph. 5:31 RSV).

Morally Righteous and Factually Right 65

The thoughts of the righteous are right, but the counsels of the wicked are deceitful (12:5 NKJV).

"The righteous are right" seems to be a tautology, for if the righteous were not right they would not be righteous. But there are two meanings to the term "right"—moral goodness and factual correctness. Being morally good has nothing to do with knowing the right answer on an algebra test. But it does have something to do with character, integrity, and ethical principles.

The original term translated "thoughts" is a judicial term referring to correct judgments, which is why several versions translate the word "right" as "just." Correct judgment is just, which implies both moral goodness and correct analysis of the facts. If a person's thoughts (that is, plans and purposes) are judicially right, they are both morally right and factually accurate.

The "counsels" (that is, the designs) of the wicked are intentionally deceptive. They violate what is *true* in order to get what is *best* for themselves. Shakespeare's Iago, deceptively maneuvering for personal advantage, boasts: "I follow [the Moor] to serve my turn upon him. . . . [Like those] who . . . keep their heads attending on themselves. . . . And such a one do I profess myself; . . . not for love of duty, but seeming so, for my peculiar end. . . . I am not what I am."[1]

How dreadful to be someone different from what you pretend to be! The attempt to get what is best for oneself can never be morally right when pursued outside the context of what is factually right. Rather than adjusting truth to accommodate our wishes, our lives must adjust to the truth. Righteous plans and purposes entail honest attempts to know the truth and a willingness to comply. Then truth is liberating from the shackles of deception. Duplicity is a frequent pattern of the unrighteous. Without honest integrity, those who think they are righteous are not.

---

[1] Shakespeare, *Othello*, Act I, Scene 1, lines 42-65. In the end, Iago's duplicity was exposed by his own wife, and he was imprisoned to suffer regular torture till his death.

66 Entrapped or Enlightened

The words of the wicked are to lie in wait for blood, but the mouth of the upright shall deliver them (12:6 KJV).

An expanded translation could read something like this: With deceptive talk, low-down people entrap those who are vulnerable for disaster, but with wise and truthful talk, upright people enlighten them to steer clear.

It may take the form of temptation, to lure them to sin. Sometimes it is a persuasive sales pitch, to bait them and exploit their needs for a commodity they really cannot afford. At times it is the "appeal-to-pity fallacy," preying on their sympathy to bilk them out of funds for personal profit. On occasion it may entice them into positions to be ambushed for destruction.

The trusting disposition is a worthy attitude that we do not want to lose. Some have been burned once and refuse to trust anyone again. When Mr. Dimmesdale became suspicious of everyone, Hawthorne wrote, "Trusting no man as his friend, he could not recognize his enemy when the latter actually appeared."[1] The positive attitude enables us to put the best face on other persons' motives. That is a boon to them and a benefit to us.

On the other hand, being gullible is dangerous. Suckers not only lose their shirts. They can lose their self-respect, their morals, and even their lives. Wise persons refuse to be manipulated by sensational or bizarre appeals. They stand their ground.

The object is to walk the fine line between paranoia and gullibility. It is not always easy. The attempt to manipulate by personal influence is often an indicator. That is a red flag. Genuine friends do not use their friendships for manipulation. Friendship protects the freedom of friends. Advance help comes from hearing the advice of the upright. It comes from rubbing shoulders with those who have integrity, picking their minds, and receiving their counsel.

---

[1] Nathaniel Hawthorne, *The Scarlet Letter* (New York: Books, Inc., n.d.) p. 106.

The wicked are overthrown and are no more, but the house of the righteous will stand (12:7 NKJV).

Astute debaters have a keen ear for what is called "the excluded middle," which is the fallacy of contrasting dipolar opposites while overlooking items in the middle. It is not a fallacy, however, to contrast opposites *with the understanding* that some items stand between the poles.

That is the form taken by many of Solomon's proverbs. Without attempting to sweep everyone into opposite extremes, this proverb contrasts the righteous and the wicked poles without pretending that both camps together include everyone. Most people are more righteous or less righteous or more evil or less evil, with a mixture of goodness and badness.

Most people, however, are more in one category or the other, and they may continue to drift in the direction to which they are inclined. Straddling the fence is not a permanent position. Eventually the middle will be emptied, both extremes will be full, and the sheep will be separated from the goats (Matt. 25:32-33). Ultimately, goodness and badness cannot cohabit.

Though we theists deny the materialist philosophy of prebiological macroevolution, we recognize a broad view of natural selection and the survival of the fittest. The view also applies to moral selectivity. Evil itself diminishes or destroys evildoers, increasing the proportion of goodness in the world. Culture survives by the perpetuity of goodness. On a slippery slope with no anchor, evil people will collapse. With solid support, the righteous will continue to stand.

Sooner or later, either in this life or at its end, spiritual selectivity occurs. Spiritual laws transcend natural laws, and the human spirit that is cursed with moral evil will be culled from the community of the righteous. God steps in on the scene and calls an end to the narrative that He himself began. He allows humans to write the body of their own autobiography, but the Author who wrote the introduction will write the last chapter.

68 Commended or Despised

A man will be commended according to his wisdom, but he who is of a perverse heart will be despised (12:8 NKJV).

We do not have as good an angle on ourselves as others have on us. We want to be recognized for our merits, but those merits are shaded by our desire to be so recognized. Our conceit is more obvious than our credits. And conceit is a deficit that cancels the credits.

Colonel Roosevelt said that his father, President Theodore Roosevelt, so wanted to be the star of every show that he "never went to a wedding without wanting to be the bride, and he never went to a funeral without wanting to be the corpse."[1]

The person with a "perverse heart" is turned away from reality into fantasy. The warped mind has a distorted understanding of oneself. In her world of make-believe, she pretends the very popularity that is prevented by her pretensions. Instead of honor, she gets hatred—because she is haughty. Self-respect destroys itself by self-conceit.

Wisdom and humility are so interlocked that each helps produce the other, supports the other, and protects the other. Being humble does not mean to grovel on the ground. It means to recognize and accept yourself as you are. Then you can acknowledge your inferiority without deprecating yourself, and you can accept public praise without bloating your mind with vainglory. Humility is a relief from the relentless crusade to convince others of your merit!

Commendations will come in proportion to your wisdom, and hostility in proportion to your warped, self-centered mind. The pride of the perverted heart cannot handle *praise without pretentiousness*, which brings on disapproval. The humility of the wise can accept *compliments without conceit*, which evokes commendation. The bigger you become in your own eyes, the smaller you are in the eyes of others. The smaller you are willing to be, the bigger you become!

---

[1] George C. Wise, *Rev. Bud Robinson*, a biography (Louisville, KY: The Pentecostal Pub. Co., 1946) p. 65.

Better is he who is lightly esteemed and has a servant, than he who honors himself and lacks bread (12:9 NASB).

Self-honor is dishonoring to oneself. The effort is wasted because the attempt is futile. A big brag loses respect by seeking it, and only cheapens himself. Eliciting acclaim gets disdain. The proverb says it is better to settle for public modesty and have a means of livelihood than to have an expensive automobile on your drive for your neighbors to see, and not be able to support your family. Humble egos and full stomachs are better than bloated egos and starved stomachs.

When he lost his good reputation, Lieutenant Cassio complained, "I have lost the immortal part of myself." Iago replied, "Reputation is an idle and most false imposition, oft got without merit and lost without deserving. You have lost no reputation at all, unless you repute yourself a loser."[1] What others think of you is less important than what you know about yourself. The proverb urges a self-esteem that is not under the mandate of public esteem.

Too many impoverished egos crave approval and applause. They want to be thought of as bright personalities, brilliant intellects, shrewd entrepreneurs, skilled artisans, or accomplished professionals. If they cannot achieve by labor and talent, they boost their image by boasting. Confusing success with superiority and failure with inferiority, they pretend a superiority that automatically assigns others to a position of inferiority. Ostentatious people spend freightloads of energy jockeying for position in a game of one-upmanship!

Attempting to jump-start public praise for an ego trip is a self-defeating game. It is not only evil; it does not work. Trying to gain your self-image by improving your public image is an endless crusade of frustration. Pomposity loses public-esteem. People tire of the drumbeat. Happy is the person who is comfortably at home with himself!

---

[1] Shakespeare, *Othello*, Act II, Scene 3, lines 263 ff.

70 Brute Cruelty and Human Kindness

A righteous man has regard for the life of his beast, but the compassion of the wicked is cruel (12:10 NASB).

When I was young, I heard that persons who love kittens rarely become murderers, and violent criminals rarely exemplify a pattern of kindness to animals.

While pain itself may not be intrinsically evil, *causing pain* is a grave moral evil—unless it is necessary for a higher good, like the pain endured in a dentist's chair. Hamlet applied a principle to a wrong situation with the wrong word, but he did have the idea right when he said, "I must be cruel, only to be kind."[1] If causing pain, however, is required by a good that one is morally responsible to bring about, it is not cruelty. It is a kindness that is tough and severe.

Many otherwise civil people, however, who would not dare abuse other humans, consider it an incidental gesture to inflict pain on an animal.[2] I am appalled at those who inflict innocent suffering on helpless animals purely for sport. This we see in the sponsors and viewers of dogfights and cockfights, and no less in those who justify hunting with equipment that is painful. Their rationale is that the prey is not a member of our species.

The point is that pain *is pain*, wherever it occurs! And pain is painful! Causing pain is extreme cruelty! Those who have a heart should be engaged in reducing pain wherever it is. God required the Hebrews to rescue even their enemy's donkey that had fallen under a load (Ex. 23:5). He mandated a weekly day of rest for their work animals (Ex. 20:8).

In the proverb, even what passes as the "compassion" of the wicked is but cruelty. Once begun, cruelty hardens one's heart. Animal cruelty is cold-blooded barbarity committed by heartless human monsters! It is a great evil against God and His creation.

---

[1] Shakespeare, *Hamlet*, Act III, Scene 4, line 178.
[2] Here I do not condemn killing animals for justified purposes, provided the death is done in a painless way.

He who tills his land will be satisfied with bread, but he who follows frivolity is devoid of understanding. / He who tills his land will have plenty of bread, but he who follows frivolity will have poverty enough (12:11; 28:19 NKJV)!

My father was a clergyman, a high school teacher, and a farmer, so he had perspective from experience on all three professions. Once he told me that working the soil with my own hands would keep me close to the basics of life, give emotional stability, confirm solid values, and enable me to view other areas of life in appropriate relationships. Unfortunately, most youth today do not have the opportunity that ancient Hebrew youth had in their rural culture.

Both these proverbs contrast diligent workers with those who "follow vain persons" (KJV), "pursue vain things" (NASB), "follow worthless pursuits" (RSV), "chase fantasies" (NIV and Jerus), are "daydreamers" (CEV), and have "useless interests" (Mof). Void of understanding, they will be void of bread. Wise people choose their interests carefully, are diligent and disciplined in work, and stand a much better chance of professional and economic success than do indolent sloths.

Broader applications are so apropos they are hard to miss. Diligent students get a better education. Those who work hard at a successful marriage are more apt to succeed. Those who are disciplined in personal prayer develop a depth of devotion that enriches their lives a thousand times over! Readers who lay aside the shallow trade books and force themselves to read the classics become broader and deeper in their sympathies. Those who log off line and turn off the television to read, or to fellowship with family, or to participate in nature's environment, build for themselves a meaningful life that does not ride piggyback on the entertainment industry.

Wasted time arrests human development and impedes personal progress, stunting your growth and leaving you as only the shell of the person God intended you to be. Wisely investing your time keeps you growing and expanding with no limit to the person you can become.

72 Outer Props or Inner Roots

The wicked desireth the net of evil men, but the root of the
righteous yieldeth fruit (12:12 KJV).

Does "the net" refer to entrapment or to a fortress for defense? The Hebrew word can mean either, which leaves us uncertain.

Assuming the first, evil people have a penchant to use the evil snare for its loot—for its plunder (NIV), its booty (NASB), its prey (Sprl). The loot may consist of pleasure, false emotional goods that give ego trips, or even the bounty of material gain. They refine their trickery and deception to ensnare their victims. On the contrary, righteous people have a fertile root that proliferates whatever they need to prosper. Evil people get their goods deceptively, from without. The righteous get theirs honestly, from within.

Entrapment is always a chance game, sometimes yielding much, sometimes nothing. But the good root of the righteous is consistent, never failing to yield. And it is satisfying, while the evil net is always yawning for more. Chesterton said, the deceiver develops "a delicate intellectual art in which he may achieve masterpieces which he must keep secret . . . A really accomplished imposter is the most wretched of geniuses: he is a Napoleon on a desert island."[1]

Assuming the second meaning, "the net" refers to a stronghold of protection that evil people pursue, looking for support in a network of like-minded people. To them, there is safety in numbers. They can hide behind the network of mutual imposters. Deceiving oneself because "others do it" is a dangerous exercise. But "the root of the righteous yields" the support that the wicked miss. Their pleasure is honest and their self-esteem needs no ego trip. Their defense is not found in numbers, but in themselves. They carry their safety net with them, wherever they go, perpetually refortified with righteousness. The inner root is safer than the outer prop.

---

[1] G. K. Chesterton, *Robert Browning* (Teddington, Middlesex, UK: Echo Library, n.d.) p. 102.

The wicked is snared by the transgression of his lips, but the just shall come out of trouble (12:13 KJV).

The "transgression of the lips" does not refer to lip-syncing, whistling a secular tune, or kissing your fiancé. Our appliance for articulating words is appreciated most by those who are mute, but it is an arsenal of injury for victims of slander and verbal abuse.

Most sins are either wrong by their nature or by their consequence,[1] but the lips are uniquely equipped for both evils. Even if telling a falsehood does no harm on the occasion, it is wrong by nature because it does the opposite of what it purports to do. It reports nonfacts while claiming to report actual facts. There is no way to tell a falsehood without claiming to be telling the truth. To achieve its end, lying exploits the listener's trust by betraying that trust.

Other kinds of articulation are wrong because they are malignant and malicious. Curt remarks with accusatorial overtones stab and slash like switchblades. Behind-the-back slander ambushes a person with verbal artillery. Some people lumber through life leaving a trail of damage when they could leave blossoms and fragrance. Hurting rather than helping, their lives are worse than useless—they are injurious! Job spoke of those who "torment me with words" (Job 19:2). That is the sin of using the good gift of communication for purposes that are grossly evil.

The principle of retribution, however, reflects one's damage back on oneself. People are "snared by [their own] lips," either by life itself or by supernatural order. By injuring others they injure themselves. Jesus said, "By your words you shall be condemned" (Matt. 12:37).

With sobriety and word discretion, righteous people who avoid damaging talk can vocalize blessing and inspiration, encouragement and enlightenment, to others along the way. As a bonus, they circumvent the potential trouble to themselves.

---

[1] Philosophers use the terms "deontological" and "consequential" ethics.

74 Input and Output

From the fruit of his words a man is satisfied with good, and the work of a man's hand comes back to him (12:14 RSV).

The sage of the proverbs keeps returning to a law that is elucidated throughout the Bible and exhibited in life. It is the law of sowing and reaping, the law of cause and effects, the law of sin and its consequences, righteousness and its rewards, input and output, the law of what you do and what you are, the law of the past and the future.

Ben C. Johnson writes: "The past does not disappear just because you refuse to acknowledge it. The past invades every moment, coloring feelings, motivating decisions, and controlling behavior. We cannot run away from our history; it is us!"[1]

This proverb accents the positive rather than the negative, both from what we say and from what we do. Good decisions determine good destinies. Good deeds entail good consequences. Upright living sets the stage for a pleasant future. What you do forms within you what you are.

Aristotle said, "States of character arise out of like activities."[2] I have learned more from my own teaching than my students have learned. I have been shaped by my own preaching more than those who sat in the pews.

Of course, if we do good simply for the good we expect to get out of it, what we do ceases to be good. It is selfish, and it can disrupt the formula and preempt the good that otherwise would come. That is because this is more than a natural or behavioral law. It is a divinely arranged principle, and God Himself makes His own input.

Hamlet said, "There's a divinity that shapes our ends, rough-hew them how we will."[3] Jesus said, The one who does good "will certainly not lose his reward" (Matt. 10:42 NIV).

---

[1] Ben Campbell Johnson, *To Will God's Will* (Philadelphia: The Westminster Press, 1987) pp. 30-31.
[2] Aristotle, *Nicomachean Ethics*, Book II, Chapter 1, p. 332 in McKeon.
[3] Shakespeare, *Hamlet*, Act V, Scene 2, lines 10-11.

The way of a fool is right in his own eyes, but a wise man listens to counsel (12:15 RSV).

A popular public mood is that moral and religious opinions are impertinent so long as a person is sincere. Postmodernism holds there is no correct view about such things because it is all a matter of personal opinion. It is all subjective and relative.

One afternoon a neighbor girl said to Charlie Brown, "You sure were dumb in school today. . . . You got all the answers wrong." Charlie Brown replied, "I didn't think being right mattered as long as I was sincere!"[1] Correct opinion matters on an academic test, and it makes a world of difference in the way one lives. I felt sure I was on the road that led to our home and needed no suggestions from my wife, but finally I had to defer to her advice. I was sincerely wrong. Even bigoted tyrants are unfeigned. Adolf Hitler was sincere in causing the holocaust.

Someone says, "To me, God does not exist." But God either does or does not exist, quite apart from anyone's opinion. Reality does not bend to opinion; opinion has to adjust to reality. Thinking the road is clear does not prevent you from getting killed by an oncoming car. Aloof attitudes about truth can be fatal! Being "right in the eyes of a fool" does not make it right. A fool is a fool because he is too foolish to listen to advice, but a wise person is wise enough to listen. Wisdom wishes to be directed by wisdom rather than folly.

Aristotle said, "Wisdom . . . [includes] intuitive reason combined with scientific [i.e., factual] knowledge."[2] Wisdom begins with an analysis of factual situations, and it is therefore based on factual knowledge. Wisdom goes far beyond knowledge, but it starts with knowledge. First you must find the facts. Foolish people begin with a hunch. Wise people begin with knowledge. One begins with a feeling; the other begins with the facts.

---

[1] Charles Schulz' *Peanuts* comic strip, 14 September 1955.
[2] Aristotle, *Nicomachean Ethics*, Book VI, Chapter 7, p. 430 in McKeon.

76 Response and Reaction

A fool's wrath is presently known, but a prudent man covereth shame (12:16 KJV).

Every club, community, and church has quick-tempered people that others are acutely aware of. They bristle like porcupines. Their firearms are stacked and soon fired. In their hearts they carry firecrackers with short fuses. Brutus said that Cassius "carries anger as the flint bears fire . . . [and] shows a hasty spark."[1]

Radioactive people rarely respond positively—they react negatively. They cut no slack for others. Temper is easily triggered. Like a rumbling volcano, they are constantly ready to erupt. Every little annoyance is immediately expressed. Their vexation is sprayed in the faces of all who are close by. Some were conditioned with inner anger early in life, and for years they have practiced the art of expressing it without restraint. Foolish they are, for not reining it in!

Sir Winston Churchill said, "Anger is a waste of energy. Steam which is allowed to blow off a safety valve would be better used to drive the engine."[2] Anger requires energy and soul, and those resources should not be spent on situations that are not serious enough to deserve our anger. Most insults are not big enough to be honored by a big person. Most indignities are not worthy of our emotional attention.

Wise persons are like a veteran bulldog walking down the drive unperturbed by the feisty yapping of puppies on the sideline. Prudent people ride above the dishonor of little insults, exuding poise and confidence. They allow little irritations to go by. They have bigger goals and nobler interests. They respond positively to what is wholesome and good. They reserve their reaction for something serious. Paul said, "Let . . . wrath and anger . . . be put away from you" (Eph. 4:31). James said, "Be . . . slow to anger" (Ja. 1:19).

---

[1] Shakespeare, *Julius Caesar*, Act IV, Scene 3, lines 111-113.
[2] Jon Meacham, *Franklin and Winston* (New York: Random House, 2003) p. 30.

Truth and

He that speaketh truth showeth forth righteousness, but ι witness deceit (12:17 KJV).

These original Hebrew words carry special nuances that are difficult to wrap into a concise English proverb. The term for "speaks truth" means something like "breathes out truth," implying that telling truth can be consistent and habitual. The honest person does not have to strive to tell truth because it is a part of her nature. It comes as automatically as breathing.

"Shows righteousness" means "gives evidence for a just case." Rather then being a simplistic truism, the proverb gives a glimpse of a court scene that is followed through in the second clause with the "false witness." With the metaphor in place, we see that truthness and justice are inseparable. False witnesses subvert the justice of a judicial system. Honest witnesses shape a court of justice rather than a counterfeit court of injustice. Genuine justice cannot be established with dishonesty. Truthfulness is basic to the very notion of justice.

Telling the truth does not mean a person is honest, for liars generally tell truth when it is to their advantage. So you cannot assume something is wrong simply because a perjurer said it. That would be the *ad hominem* fallacy—an argument "against the person." But telling an intentional falsehood even one time does make a person a liar. Dishonest persons often tell truth, but truthful persons do not tell lies. Telling truth does not identify one as honest, but telling one lie does identify one as dishonest. That is the reason, in ancient Greek mythology, Creon said to Oedipus, "Time alone reveals just men—the unjust you can recognize in one short day."[1]

Truth telling is a lifelong occupation. Perpetual effort is required to become the person who by nature "breathes out truth." Patterns are established by practice, and they become habitual by diligence and constant caution.

---

[1] Sophocles, *Oedipus the King* (New York: Washington Square Press, Inc. 1959) p. 41.

78 Hateful Hurts and Healing Help

There is that speaketh like the piercings of a sword, but the tongue of the wise is health (12:18 KJV).

Words are dangerous! Using the dictionary in the wrong way for the wrong purposes can be lethal. When tongue and lips consort to spew out words, they extrude more than vowel and consonantal tones. Each word is freighted with meaning beyond syllabic sounds, and those meanings are delivered to the minds and moods of people via vocalized words.

Some of those words can be used for torture. Tongue and lips can be dangerous, spraying verbal bullets like a shotgun, or rifling shots like a semiautomatic with a precision sight. The tongue is a deadly weapon! An old Hebrew dirge deplored those whose "teeth are spears and arrows, whose tongues are sharp swords" (Ps. 57:4 NIV). Sometimes the assault is packaged in culturally acceptable ways, modified a bit by civility—sharp remarks that pierce and puncture like daggers, and cut and slice one's personal worth, sometimes with pretended goodwill.

The dictionary is just as heavy with helpful words of healing. The very instrument one uses for stabbing can be used by another for salving the wound. One sword brings blood and another brings balm. With words, one person hinders and hurts; another helps and heals.

Sometimes important words of healing and health give temporary discomfort, like a hypodermic needle. A prominent Presbyterian author was converted to Christ as a youth when a friend said to him simply, "If Christ returned, would you be on His side?" The words stung, but captivated his mind, and that night the young man who later founded the Lay Witness Movement across America whispered to the Lord, "Yes, God." Thirty-five years later, Ben Johnson said, "The experience continues to give both rootage and direction to my life today."[1] The simple words gave the motivation for a move that motivated words of help and health to many others.

---

[1] Ben Campbell Johnson, *To Will God's Will* (Philadelphia: The Westminster Press, 1987) p. 28-29.

The truthful lip shall be established forever, but a lying tongue is but for a moment (12:19 NKJV).

Now note the difference between *truth* and *reality*, which many confuse. A shining sun is reality but it is not truth. But if a shining sun is reality, the statement "The sun is shining" is true, and then what the statement reports is called truth. Truth and falsehood refer to the propositions that statements make. Statements make truth-claims about reality, and if those claims accurately report the reality they refer to, the propositions are true.

The truth of some propositions is temporal and that of others is eternal. "The sky is overcast" may be true today and false tomorrow, yet the statement is always true *if* it always refers to the day in which it was made. In that sense, divinely authenticated propositions are always true. Statements about God's character, His nature, His purposes, however, are true every day, for every period of history, under every situation, because they do not change.

Falsehoods are always corrected by the reality to which they refer. That is why falsehoods are covert, couched in deceit, with efforts to prevent exposure to reality. Sooner or later, however, the efforts fail, false veneers fall off, because reality stands on its own, untarnished. "Lying tongues" are ephemeral, temporal, "but for a moment." Those who expose false truth-claims to reality are not long deceived. Sophocles said, "No lie reaches old age."[1]

A true truth-claim stands alongside reality, consonant with reality, supported by reality, "established" by the reality to which it refers. It makes no attempt to alter reality, to tweak it or tarnish it, to redress it with different garb. Reality stands undisputed, vindicating those reports that are accurate. After the lying tongue falls victim to reality, the truthful lip remains unchallenged and unchanged.

---

[1] Quoted in Jamieson, Fausset, and Brown, *Commentary* (Grand Rapids: Eerdmans., 1945) Vol. III, p. 454.

80 Plotting Evil or Promoting Good

There is deceit in the hearts of those who plot evil, but joy for those who promote peace (12:20 NIV).

The world's program of evil includes a vast network of those who have signed on for personal advantage, unaware that the program is coordinated by what Paul called "principalities and powers, spiritual wickedness in high places" (Eph. 6:12 KJV). Unwittingly they have become stakeholders in the network, promoting the program even when they are least aware they are doing so. Every adherent is a contributor, helping to implement the program.

It is open to question whether the proverb means they use deceit in promoting evil or that they themselves are deceived in what they are doing. One version translates the line: "Disappointment comes to those who plot evil" (AAT), implying they themselves are deceived in expecting more than they get. Disappointment comes from deception.

Whichever the proverb originally intended, both propositions are true because each feeds on the other. Disillusion comes to the stakeholders. In using deceit they are deceived, because deceit is deceitful! It turns on the one who uses it. It is a trap that traps the trapper.

Similarly, those who promote goodness will gain good in return. Peace and joy come to those who promote peace and joy in others. We reap the harvest of the kind of crop we cultivate. Aristotle said, "Happiness is activity in accordance with . . . the highest virtue . . . [which is] the most divine element in us."[1] When God deposits peace in our hearts, we develop an affinity with peace. When we are noble we love nobility. When we love goodness, we are overjoyed with goodness. As Aristotle said again, "Lovers of what is noble find pleasant the things that are by nature pleasant."[2] In the New Testament, Peter says those who have been given a "new birth into a living hope . . . are filled with an inexpressible and glorious joy!" (I Pet. 1:3, 8).

---

[1] Aristotle, *Nicomachean Ethics*, Book X, Chapter 7, p. 532 in McKeon.
[2] *Op. cit.*, Book I, Chapter 8, p. 312 in McKeon.

Useful or Futile 81

No harm befalls the righteous, but the wicked are filled with trouble (12:21 NASB).

Our initial reaction is disbelief. "No harm to the righteous" does not square with human experience. In this upside-down world, values are turned on their head and retribution is reversed. The innocent suffer while the guilty are exempt. Other proverbs specifically say that all have adversity (cf. 17:17, 24:10), yet this one seems specific and definite in stating the opposite.

Here are two possible solutions. First, the word "harm" literally meant iniquity, and "trouble" is sometimes translated "mischief" (KJV). Then the proverb reads: "No fallout from iniquity falls on the righteous, but the mischief of the wicked comes back on them."

Second, God turns adversity to advantage for those who love Him (Rom. 8:28). He had no purpose *behind* it, but He finds a purpose *for* it. He did not *cause* it, but He *uses* it, so that our suffering need not be futile. Rather than sanctioning it, He sanctifies it. Instead of becoming bitter, His people can become better, utilizing it instead of criticizing it. What would otherwise be futility becomes utility. In the end, no permanent harm will have been done. Banished to the forest of Arden, the Duke said to his lords, "Sweet are the uses of adversity, which . . . finds tongues in trees, books in the running brooks, sermons in stones, and good in everything."[1]

Moreover, God's people have access to a storm shelter. Their relationship with Him becomes their refuge. In God's heart they find a sanctuary in adversity.

Evil people have no such retreat. They have no safe haven for resort. They suffer trouble without the support of a supernatural Companion. And, too often they find no use for their adversity, no higher purpose to plug in to. They make the investment and get no return. They pay the price and have nothing to show for it. Their suffering is in vain.

---

[1] Shakespeare, *As You Like It*, Act II, Scene 1, lines 12 ff.

82 Lying Lips and Delightful Dealings

Lying lips are abomination to the Lord, but those who deal truthfully are His delight (12:22 NKJV).

In Shakespeare's comedy, Petruchio wooed the shrew for marriage and then tormented her incessantly while constantly declaring his affection. Katharina complained, "That which spites me more than all [is that] he does it under the name of love."[1]

Whether in marriage, business bargaining, or any other human transaction, God is concerned with both our speaking and our dealing. He expects the deeds to confirm the talk. When we speak one way and do another way, our lips have lied and the deal is dishonest.

If the two are not the same, both are abominations to the Lord. In any human relationship that entails both speak and deed, our dealing can be either despicable or delectable to God.

The burden of this proverb is that all human transactions include a divine transaction. All horizontal relationships entail a vertical relationship. The person who looks every direction to see if anyone is watching must not forget to look up. God is the constant in every moral equation, and He cannot be left out.

Sin is not just sin against our neighbors or ourselves. All sin is against God. After King David committed adultery and murder, in repentance he prayed, "Against You . . . have I sinned, and done this evil in Your sight" (Ps. 51:4). Paul warned his friends, "When you sin against your brothers . . . you sin against Christ" (I Cor. 8:12 NIV).

In choosing our value system, we cannot afford to drift on the current of contemporary opinion. We are looking into the face of a God who "cannot tolerate wrong!" (Hab. 1:13 NIV). Because God is absolute righteousness, deceitful dealings are detestable and deplorable.

For the same reason, acts of integrity are deliciously delightful!

---

[1] Shakespeare, *The Taming of the Shrew*, Act IV, Scene 3, lines 9-12.

*A prudent man conceals knowledge, but the heart of fools
proclaims folly* (12:23 NASB).

Lucy was out of hearing distance when Charlie Brown
yelled, "You're not as smart as you think you are. . . . If you were
as smart as you think you are, you wouldn't think you were so
smart!"[1] Most who have their knowledge on display do not *know*
enough to *know* how little they do *know*, so they broadcast what
knowledge they do have. To cope with their inferiority, they
project an attitude of superiority. Proclaiming their knowledge,
they unwittingly proclaim their folly. Foolishness rides piggyback
on whatever they say.

While folly spends what it has, the nature of wisdom is to
be economical with its knowledge. Only the knowledgeable know
enough to know how much they do *not* know. Understanding the
limits on their knowledge forces on them the wisdom of
intellectual humility.

African American scientist George Washington Carver
discovered almost 200 new products he could get from the peanut.
Earlier one October morning, he had gone into the woods before
day, and looking up he cried out, "Oh, Mr. Creator, why did You
make the universe?" He said the Creator whispered, "You want to
know too much for your little mind. Ask something more your
size." So he said, "Dear Mr. Creator, tell me why You made man."
Again God whispered, "Little man, you are still asking for more
than you can handle." Finally he asked, "Mr. Creator, why did
You make the peanut?" The Lord said, "That's better!" And he
went to his lab and was shown multiple reasons God made the
peanut.[2]

"The heart of fools proclaims folly." A fool's folly is in his
prideful heart, and a wise person's wisdom is in his humble heart.
Each attitude controls what the person says.

---

[1] Charles M. Schulz, *The Complete Peanuts 1957-1958* (Seattle: Fantagraphics
Books. 2005) p. 41.
[2] Lawrence Elliott, *George Washington Carver: The Man Who Overcame*
(Englewood Cliffs, NJ: Prentice Hall, Inc., 1966) pp. 155-156.

84 Laboring Hands or Lazy Hands

Diligent hands will rule, but laziness ends in forced labor (12:24 NIV).

Pity the creatures that have no hands. Longhorns use their heads to gore. Burros use their hind feet to kick and snakes their fangs to bite. Humans have hands that can grip and turn, pass and catch, dribble and shoot, steer the wheel and shift the gears. Hands can wield swords and trigger handguns to kill, or they can lift and caress and embrace. Strong tough hands do manual labor, and skilled hands do pen strokes or clatter at the keyboard. Delicate, dexterous hands do artistic sketches or perform surgical procedures.

We need to develop the habit of hard work with our hands. Charles Dickens' insolvent pauper Mr. Micawber admonished young David Copperfield, "Never do tomorrow what you can do today. Procrastination is the thief of time. Collar him!"[1] Talent and personality can never substitute for industry. Diligence earns promotion while indolence does well to hold its own. Easy careers, like get-rich-quick schemes, are virtually nonexistent.

One way or the other, most people have to work, either by self-motivation or from economic necessity. Their perseverance is either inwardly initiated or outwardly enforced. Self-industry promotes independence, and "forced labor" fosters dependence.

When all other motivation languishes in lazy lethargy, self-motivation kicks in to drive a person with nothing more than a dogged sense of responsibility. Character in labor stands out best against the backdrop of weariness and discouragement. Diligent, laboring hands mitigate the drag of discouraging work. Dawdling, leisure hands make work more laborious. In another place (Eccl. 9:10), translated into Scottish verse, Solomon exhorts: "Then what thy thoughts design to do, / Still let thy hands with might pursue."[2] Today, the sage's work ethic still works!

---

[1] Charles Dickens, *David Copperfield*, in *Best Loved Books* (Pleasantville, NY: Reader's Digest Ass'n., 1966) p.229.
[2] *The Book of Psalms in Metre: The Scottish Hymnal* (Edinburgh: Thoman Nelson & Sons, 1882) p. 166.

Heavy Hearts and Helpful Words 85

Anxiety in the heart of a man weighs it down, but a good word makes it glad (12:25 NASB).

Hamlet spoke of "the dread of something after death, / The undiscovered country from whose bourn / No traveler returns . . . / And thus the native hue of resolution / Is sicklied o'er with the pale cast of thought."[1]

In *The Shack*, William Young clarifies the difference between rational fears and imagined fears. In our ungrounded anxieties, we imagine the danger but rarely imagine The Christ standing with us in it. In our fantasies, God is rarely present.[2] Legitimate concerns about life after death are perfectly appropriate for those who have not found peace with God. But most of us are saddled with other unfounded worries that reflect a lack of faith.

It is true, as Shakespeare said, "There are many events in the womb of time [yet to] be delivered."[3] But when we worry about what we cannot prevent, we are borrowing pain from the future to make our present painful. Living through it in advance is often worse than going through it when it occurs. At that time, the worry will change to sorrow. What the old African minister Kumalo had feared so long did finally come to him. Then the Anglican priest consoled him by sayng, "Sorrow is better than fear. . . . Fear is a journey, but sorrow is at least an arriving. . . . When a storm threatens, a man is afraid for his house. . . . But when the house is destroyed, there is something to do. About a storm he can do nothing, but he can rebuild a house."[4]

It is amazing how weighted hearts are lifted and saddened hearts are gladdened by the appropriate word from the right person. Words are heavy with help, but even more so when expressed with warmth by a respected person. We gain courage, and life turns good again.

---

[1] Shakespeare, *Hamlet*, Act III, Scene 1, lines 78-85.
[2] William P. Young, *The Shack* (Newbury Park, CA: Windblown Midia, 2007) pp. 141-142.
[3] Shakespeare, *Othello*, Act I, Scene 3, lnes 377-379.
[4] Alan Paton, *Cry, the Beloved Country* (New York: MacMillan Publishing Company, 1948) p. 108.

86 Fight or Flight

*A righteous man is cautious in friendship, but the way of the
wicked leads them astray* (12:26 NIV).

Hebrew scholars wish they could get inside Solomon's
mind on this proverb. It may mean that righteous people are more
richly abundant with excellence than the unrighteous, yet the
unrighteous are led astray by the temporal advantages of evil.
Others think it means that the righteous point out or demonstrate a
better way, but unrighteous people refuse to follow the better lead.
The moral lessons from both, however, are entailed in the NIV
translation above.

Both good and evil people are attracted to abundance and
excellence, but one has a long-range eye for the spiritual and
eternal, while the other has nearsighted focus on the material and
temporal. Both good and bad people are influenced by those
around them, and both gravitate toward those of their own like
interests. Cassius said, "Therefore it is meet that noble minds keep
ever with their likes, for who so firm that cannot be seduced?"[1]

Of course, we should build relational bridges with secular
or evil people to influence them for God and goodness—and for
friendship's own sake—but we need to have around us a support
group of like-minded people to protect ourselves from counter
influences.

In Homer's *Odyssey*, the fair goddess Circe warns
Odysseus to sail on by the coast of Charybdis where the demon
goddess in the cave would prey upon his men with irresistible
temptation. "She . . . is an immortal plague," Circe said, "dread,
grievous, and fierce, and not to be fought with; against her there is
no defense. Flight is the bravest way. . . . So drive past with all thy
force."[2] Overestimating one's own moral strength can be fatal.
The righteous must be cautious. In vulnerable encounters, flight is
braver than fight. It is smarter because it is safer. Enticing
situations should be avoided.

---

[1] Shakespeare, *Julius Caesar*, Act I, Scene 2, lines 315-316.
[2] Homer, *The Odyssey of Homer*, Butcher & Lang, trs. (New York: The
MacMillan Co., 1911) Bk. XII, p. 137.

The lazy man does not roast his game, but the diligent man prizes his possessions (12:27 NIV).[1]

Smoked ham was not originally smoked to accommodate the appetites of those who like the charbroiled flavor. Before freezing food was an option, ham was salted and smoked for preservation to be used many months later. Simply cooking meat preserves it for several days after raw meat has spoiled.

Without refrigeration in ancient Judea, game had to be roasted quickly to prevent spoiling. Hungry men pumped up their motivation to hunt down their prey for lunch. When their stomachs were satisfied, the lazy lounged on their mats and the sluggards slept in their huts, leaving the leftover to spoil. They quit the job and left the task half done.

In every culture and every period of history, the slothful follow the same pattern. Indolent farmers plant crops which they neglect to harvest. Unmotivated students succumb to discouragement, leaving the term paper half-finished by the deadline date. Some who initially make Christian commitments become disheartened and fail to follow through to preserve their commitments. Lon Woodrum said, "Nothing really good is easy. Gold must be gouged from quartz. Oil must be pumped from the bowels of the earth. Pearls must be plucked from water."[2]

Diligent persons prize what they have worked to acquire. They sacrifice comfort and ease to complete and preserve their projects. Then their *diligence* becomes their precious possession (cf. 12:27 RV & NASB). Losing that, they lose all else. Retaining it, they retain much more. Here is the lesson: prize your diligence, protect it, preserve it! It is your most valuable possession. Without it, you are a poor person. With it, you are rich! Preserving diligence preserves for you much more than diligence. It preserves your other valuable possessions.

---

[1] Obscurity in the original text and the difficulty in decoding its meaning account for the various translations.

[2] Lon Woodrum, *Stumble Upon the Dark Mountains* (Waco, TX: Word Books, 1956) p. 105.

88 A Shrinking Life or an Expanding Life

In the way of righteousness is life, and in its pathway there is no death (12:28 NASB).

Here we have the law of double negation, which ends up as a positive. "No nonlife" equals "life." The first clause states the positive value of righteousness and the second gives the flip side. Righteousness works on two fronts, giving life and preventing nonlife.

The proverb highlights the integral relationship between moral ethics and life. Several Hebrew authors spoke of life beyond death. Unfortunately, some religionists today have pushed the important doctrine of "salvation by grace" into antinomianism— that they can live unrighteous lives and still be saved. Even though the ticket to heaven is by grace apart from merit, moral ethics and eternal life are both found in the same package.

Included in these lines, however, is the notion of fuller, deeper, richer living *in the present*. It implies that some persons live shallow, superficial, barren lives on earth. Miss Ophelia spoke of those who "in the midst of life are in death."[1] But "its pathway" connotes a narrow footpath, different from a cart-road. Here it also implies the existence of its opposite, a devious, crooked way that unrighteous people turn into.

Dickens' protagonist Sydney Carton lived a purposeless life that turned back and forth on a crooked path. One afternoon he "lingered [beside a stream], watching an eddy that turned and turned purposeless, until the stream absorbed it, and carried it on to the sea." Carton blurted out, "Like me!"[2] Later he did get back on the straight footpath and life became meaningful.

On that path, life can be lived at its fullest and its best. Unrighteousness shrinks life, draining its beauty and its value. Righteousness expands life, pumping it fuller and fuller with more and more life! And when the footpath of life finally reaches death, there is no death!

---

[1] Harriet Beecher Stowe, *Uncle Tom's Cabin* (New York: Everyman's Library, Alfred A. Knoph, Inc., 1994) p. 344.
[2] Charles Dickens, *A Tale of Two Cities* (New York: Books, Inc., n.d.) p. 312.

*A wise son hears his father's instruction, but a scoffer does not
listen to rebuke* (13:1 RSV).

In an earlier day when school administrators were allowed
to paddle students for misbehavior, the paddle was sometimes
referred to as "the board of education." Discipline more than
instruction is often more educational, especially in driving a lesson
home. Among ancient Hebrews, instructing an underling in
correct reasoning often included a rebuke for faulty reasoning.

Parents are sometimes more trustworthy than some teachers
because they genuinely want what is best for their sons and
daughters. And all parents are older and therefore more
experienced than their progeny.

Young people are often more abreast of local current
moods and mindsets than their parents, but their cultural roots are
more shallow. Consequently cynicism comes easily, and
instruction is rejected. At times they are correct in thinking their
parents are locked into a narrow antiquated temperament, which
reduces respect for the parents' opinions.

Wise is the son or daughter, however, who rejects scoff and
scorn, listens to a parent's instruction, and accepts whatever rebuke
may be included.

The words "cunning," "crafty," "sly," "tricky," and "wily"
all entail cleverness, but they usually refer to attaining one's ends
by devious methods. Wisdom may use cleverness and ingenuity,
but it includes a willingness to evaluate one's own ends
themselves.

Aristotle said, "Not all ends are final ends, but the chief
good is evidently something final."[1] Wisdom focuses on long-
range goals and includes higher values in decision-making.

Prefacing the proverbs, Solomon said, "Your father's
instruction and . . . your mother's teaching . . . will be a garland to
grace your head and a chain to adorn your neck" (Pro. 1:7-9 NIV).

---

[1] Aristotle, *Nicomachean Ethics*, Book I, Chapter 7, p. 316 in McKeon.

90 Giving Out and Getting Back

A man shall eat good by . . . his mouth, but the soul of transgressors shall eat violence (13:2 KJV).

This proverb has to be unpacked. It is structured as an antithesis, yet not all the elements are uniform. Eating good and eating violence are clear contrasts, and transgressors in the second clause implies good persons in the first. But mouth and soul are hardly parallel, until we assume that each stands for something that is hinted at by the other. The word for "soul" included appetite, and is sometimes translated "desire," somewhat corresponding to the appetite of the mouth. The word "mouth" is an outward expression of the soul, and therefore represents "living out" the soul's desires. By including their subtle insinuations, mouth and soul are parallel.

The point of the proverb is that what people "live out" returns to them "in kind." They get back what they give out. Good people want to give good and to feast on the good return, but evil people crave to give evil while desiring to feast on the good. They have conflicting desires between their giving and their getting, creating clashing discords in their souls. While good people are feasting on their good returns, the bad are forced to swallow the bitter effects of their actions. Brutus warned Cassius, "You shall digest the venom of your spleen!"[1]

The obvious solution is to suppress the inner evil yens and live righteously. Shakespeare spoke of "the expense of spirit in a waste of shame." He added, "All this the world knows well; yet none knows well / To shun the 'heaven' [that is, pleasure] that leads men to this hell."[2] Evil people do not have within them the ability to adjust their basic likes and dislikes, to rein in their unbridled cravings, and to develop an appetite for what is good. Both Solomon and Shakespeare could analyze the problem and its consequences, but the ability to shift the soul's desire awaited a "power that works within us" (Eph. 3:20). It is the enabling of the indwelling Christ (Eph. 3:17).

---

[1] Shakespeare, *Julius Caesar*, Act IV, Scene 3, line 47.
[2] Shakespeare's *Sonnets*, # 129.

He who guards his mouth preserves his life; he who opens wide his lips comes into ruin (13:3 RSV).

The chatter of talk-show chitchat is burying our nation under an avalanche of verbosity! Facial expressions punctuate an endless stream of meaningless verbiage, intended to showcase the brightness of a personality under the disguise of communicating ideas. Without the visual props, radio is often worse, attempting to rely on vocal expression alone to sustain interest.

Some people have the ability never to say anything in fewer words if it can possibly be said in more. As an orator, Senator Hubert Humphrey was well-known for his fluency. Senator Barry Goldwater, referring to his political opponent, joked, "Hubert has been clocked at 275 words a minute with gusts up to 340!"[1] In our culture, words are losing their ability to relate substance. Pieces of heavy earth-moving equipment are becoming spades and garden hoes. Pulpits are losing power, posturing as fireside chats rather than proclaiming scriptural truth. Give Solomon credit in these proverbs—in urging economy of speech, he modeled his advice. Shakespeare said, "Where words are scarce, they are seldom spent in vain."[2]

My friend Ted Yannayon became a victim of Lou Gehrig's Disease that developed until he could barely speak with great effort. He said, "The Lord is using it in my life. I have learned to say only what I need to say, and skip everything else!"

Solomon warned of the peril. Every time we spread our lips we become vulnerable. Misunderstandings occur. People are hurt. Our intentions become suspect. Talking on automatic pilot can take us places we do not wish to go. Here is a good rule: If you do not have a thought, do not express it! Solomon said to guard your life by guarding your lips. Jesus said, "By your words you will be condemned!" (Matt. 12:36-37). And those are sobering words!

---

[1] Quoted by Senator Bob Dole in his book, *Great Political Wit* (New York: Doubleday, 1998) p. 16.
[2] Shakespeare, *King Richard II*, Act II, Scene 1, line 7.

92 Hungry Spirits or Healthy Souls

The soul of the sluggard desireth and hath nothing, but the soul of the diligent shall be made fat (13:4 KJV).

A fast-food menu of carbs and cholesterol is clogging our arteries and cursing us with obesity. Couch potatoes inflame their appetite with constant snacks, soft drinks, and beer, and the more they eat, the more they crave. Foodoholics are never satisfied. But in lands of scarcity where people are blighted with malnutrition, bodily weight is a sign of robust health. In this proverb, it is used metaphorically for fiscal and economic health.

The twice-used term "soul" (so translated also by the RSV and the NASB) may justify a spiritual application as well. Our souls need a healthy menu of biblical truth and spiritual food. Our minds hunger for transcendent truth, and our impoverished spirits crave to feast on the personality of Christ and drink from His spirit. We need nutritional meals. Without regular intake, our souls become anemic, they shrink and shrivel, turn pallid and pale, and become feeble and frail. For daily devotional experiences, diligence and discipline are required.

Dangerously, some religionists substitute sensational experiences for spiritual. They swell and bloat on gaseous imaginations, but do not expand and grow with solid substance. True worship is not unfocused meditation. It is a restricted focus on God Himself.

Ancient Hebrews never promoted the ecstatic trances that were prevalent in neighboring pagan communities. Christian "experience" is *a certain kind* of religious experience—it is a subjective experience *within objective guidelines* that are delineated in scripture. Our souls need more than tapioca pudding. We need beefsteak, baked beans, and brown bread.

More than two hundred years after Solomon, God through the prophet Isaiah invited His people to a sumptuous spiritual feast: "Hearken diligently unto me, and eat ye that which is good, and let your soul delight itself in fatness" (Isa. 55:2).

A righteous man hates lying, but a wicked man is loathsome and comes to shame (13:5 NKJV).

Because goodness is the universal norm, evil operates best under deception, in the dark, behind a mask. Falsehood is often a cover for a more consequential evil.

While plotting to take the king's throne, Macbeth looked up into the night skies and pleaded, "Stars, hide your fires; / Let not light see my black and deep desires."[1] When his plans were set to murder the king, he instructed his accomplice Lady Macbeth, "Mock the time with fairest show. / False face must hide what false heart doth know."[2]

We often hear that a person should be herself, without attempts to deceive. But because a deceptive person is by nature deceptive, when she deceives she is actually being herself. Between the lines, the proverb hints that most persons generally do act in character, in harmony with what they love and opposite what they hate.

Righteous people live righteously because they love righteousness. They do not hate liars, but they do hate lying. The more one grows in Christian sanctity, the more she identifies with the principle of goodness, not just its good consequences. And the more she loves goodness, the more she hates evil itself, not just its evil effects. The psalmist declared that God "loves righteousness and hates wickedness" (Ps. 45:7). He hates deception because He loves truth.

The righteous not only abstain from lying; they hate lying. They not only hate being duped by deception; they hate deception itself. They not only detest the falsehood they see in others. They abhor any falsehood they may note in themselves. The hate is simply a corollary to their love for goodness that drives their lives. The second clause is strong: An evil person emits a repugnant odor—and the odor is repulsive to those who have refined their taste for the good.

---

[1] Shakespeare, *Macbeth*, Act I, Scene 4, lines 50-51.
[2] *Op. cit.*, Act I, Scene 7, lines 81-82.

94 Safe Tread or Slick Soles

Righteousness keepeth him that is upright in the way, but
wickedness overthroweth the sinner (13:6 KJV).

"The way" refers to a *manner* of living, but it does so by alluding to the road of life. Literally translated, "overthrows" means *causes to slip*, implying a roadway. To capture the imagery, the proverb could be loosely translated: In the road we travel, righteousness gives the upright safe tread and the sinner slippery footing. Written alliteratively, it could be: Goodness gives good persons good ground, but sin sets sinners on slippery slopes.

The point of the proverb is that righteousness affects the righteous and evil affects the evildoer. Both are destiny prone. The roadway itself is slippery for all who travel, but God's children wear boot treads and orphans have sleek-soled slippers. The righteous ride on snow-grip radials and sinners roll on well-worn tires that are slick.

The lesson applies to the end of the road as much as to the journey itself. Both heaven and hell are automatic consequences for those who befriend the Lord as their eternal companion and those who reject His friendship. Forcing an unwilling person into an eternal companionship with God would be "hell" to an incorrigible recalcitrant. Those who have embraced the divine Companion as their Father will be kept safe all the way across to the next life.

When Bunyan got his two pilgrims to the end of the road of life, Hopeful stepped first into the river of death. Then Christian stepped in and screamed, "I sink in deep waters, the billows go over my soul!" Then Hopeful, in the swift of the current, looked back to his friend and exclaimed, "Be of good cheer, my brother. I can feel the bottom, and it is good!"[1] Many other Christian pilgrims ahead of us can verify the proverb by saying to us, "Be of good cheer, my fellow pilgrims, for I have felt the bottom, and it was good!"

---

[1] John Bunyan, *The Pilgrim's Progress* (Philadelphia: Universal Book and Bible House, 1933) p. 161.

The Poor Rich and the Rich Poor 95

One man pretends to be rich, yet has nothing; another pretends to be poor, yet has great wealth (13:7 NIV, RSV).

Five of the world's most highly reputed financiers met at Chicago's Edgewater Beach Hotel to pool their financial brilliance—presidents of a large steel company, the largest utility company, the largest gas company, the New York Stock Market, and the Bank of International Settlements. The year was 1923. Within the next 25 years, victimized by the great depression, one had committed suicide, one became psychotic, one was released from Sing Sing, one died insolvent as a fugitive from justice, and the other died bankrupt, living on borrowed money.[1]

Yet millions of sharecroppers and one-dollar-a-day laborers had reared their families well in difficult times, and now in their old age had the satisfaction of a well-lived life. All the while, though unknown at the time, the rich were really poor and the poor were rich.

Jesus denounced "the man who . . . is not rich toward God" (Lu. 12:21 NASB). He condemned those who say they are "rich and . . . and do not know [they are] wretched . . . and poor" (Rev. 3:17 NASB). But He commended the Smyrnans: "I know your . . . poverty, yet you are rich!" (Rev. 2:9 NIV).

James spoke of those who are "the poor of this world, rich in faith and heirs of the kingdom" (Ja. 2:5 KJV). Paul spoke of himself as "having nothing yet possessing all things (2 Cor. 6:10 NASB).

Spiritual wealth often lies beneath material poverty, and spiritual poverty below worldly wealth. James Wells wrote: "You can't buy the green of the meadowland fair, / You can't buy a little one's love; / You can't buy the smile of a friend that's worthwhile, / And you cannot buy heaven above."[2]

Peter said, You "were not redeemed with perishable things like silver and gold . . . but with the precious blood of Christ" (1 Pet. 1:18-19 KJV).

---

[1] Bill Bright, ed., *Teacher's Manual* (Campus Crusade Publishers, n.d.) p. 328.
[2] James Wells' gospel hymn "Treasures" in *Gospel Harmony* (Dalton, GA: The A. J. Showalter Co., 1936) p. 6.

96 Prosperity and Poverty

A man's riches may ransom his life, but a poor man hears no threat (13:8 NIV).

Some spiritualize this to mean those with spiritual riches are redeemed from sin, but others are spiritually empty because they refuse to hear warnings or heed directions.

Probably it rather means that a wealthy person is vulnerable to extortion, fraud, threats and blackmail, while those without property or wealth are never threatened. Family members of notable tycoons are kidnapped and held for ransom. Extortioners get hush money from affluent people as payment for keeping quiet. False accusations are made and innocent persons are blackmailed with threats for regular payoffs. Some wealthy people have more trouble keeping their money than they had getting it. Wealth brings its own problems that poverty never knows.

The old shepherd in the forest of Arden was asked by Shakespeare's clever clown for his philosophy of life. He replied, "Sir, I am a good laborer. I earn what I eat, get what I wear, owe no man hate, envy no man's happiness, glad of other men's goods, content with my own harm, and the greatest of my pride is to see my ewes graze and my lambs suck."[1] Certainly such a simplistic lifestyle has its rewards. The person who owns nothing can relax in the presence of a robber. While prosperity has its advantages and poverty its disadvantages, wealth has its bane and privation its blessings.

The proverb can be further applied without violating its principle. Those Christians who, on a deep level, have "forsaken all to follow Christ" (Matt. 19:27, 29 KJV) are not threatened with loss, for what they own is not their own. Having given everything up, they have nothing left to lose. What they have belongs to Christ, so any loss is His to suffer, not theirs. Those who live lives of reckless abandonment can even be killed, and they will not die! And that is the way to live!

---

[1] Shakespeare, *As You Like It*, Act III, Scene 2, lines 76-81.

The light of the righteous rejoices, but the lamp of the wicked will be put out (13:9 RSV, NKJV).

Since photons have no ability to rejoice, the phrase "the light rejoices" is obviously a metaphor. Light and darkness are richly symbolic, here in the areas of (1) good and evil and (2) joy and sorrow.[1] In this proverb the two areas are provided in the same package, because righteousness contributes to joy and wickedness brings on sorrow.

Here the term for "rejoices" is frequently translated "shines brightly," for it seems to cover both ideas. The sage is saying that righteousness "shines joyously," and evil will suppress the joy of the wicked until it is finally snuffed out like a darkened lamp.

What gives the righteous the joyous light is thought by some scholars to include material success and posterity. While those may often be the case, the symbolism is broad enough to include any worthy source of joy, all of which comes from God. An old Scottish hymnal translates a line from Psalm 18 into rhythmic verse: "The Lord will light my candle so / That it shall shine full bright. / The Lord my God will also make / My darkness to be light."[2]

If God's joyous light shines in our lives, it should shine joyfully to "joyfullize" others in times of sorrow. Tolkien refers to humans as "the refracted Light, through whom is splintered from a single White to many hues . . ."[3] The white light of God through our human prisms may shed different shades and tints through different persons. Together God's good light of joy and truth is adjusted and adapted to flush out like liquid light the various pockets of darkness in the world. Paul said, "In the midst of a crooked and perverse generation . . . you shine as lights in the world" (Phil. 2:15 RSV).

---

[1] A third primary area of this symbolism, though not used in this proverb, is knowledge and ignorance.

[2] *The Book of Psalms in Metre: The Scottish Hymnal* (Edinburgh: Thomas Nelson and Sons, 1882) p. 16.

[3] J. R. R. Tolkien, "On Faerie Stories," in *The Tolkien Reader* (New York: Ballantine, 1966) p. 67.

98 Natural Pride and Human Pride

By pride only comes contention, but with the well-advised is wisdom (13:10 KJV).[1]

The nature of pride is to crave superiority, but I cannot be superior to you without making you inferior to me. The problem comes when your pride refuses to accept the inferiority that I have assigned. In order to become superior, you must reverse the order and make me inferior. Then combat begins. But pride is unwilling to settle for a deadlock, so we go into overtime to break the tie. For some, the extra innings continue throughout life!

Here we see a distinction between natural pride and human pride. In the wild kingdom, animals have a built-in adjustment to reality that we call the law of the jungle. The "peck order" is easily recognized by the animal and soon accepted. Each animal by nature falls in line at its true position, superior to some and inferior to others.

Human haughtiness, however, precludes appropriate adjustment to the real situation. We keep attempting to change the peck order. We keep pretending we are superior and demanding others to accept their inferiority. When they refuse, contention erupts. Carried to its extreme, we have racism, sexism, homicide, exorbitant nationalism, ethnic cleansing, and wars of aggression.

Thus the human species seems to have fallen morally lower than the lower species. Truth claims are more vulnerable to falsehood than nontruth expressions. Beauty is more subject to being marred than nonbeauty. Moral subjects are capable of immorality that amoral things are not. Similarly, beings with greater potential for goodness, when exploited and perverted, have greater potential for evil. Shakespeare said, "Sweetest things turn sourest by their deeds; / Lilies that fester smell far worse than weeds."[2]

---

[1] In these antithetical clauses, contention in the first implies peace in the second, and wisdom in the second implies folly in the first. So the first says the foolish are proud and contentious, and the second says the wise are humble (well advised) and peaceful. The lesson is that pride refuses advice and humility accepts advice, resulting in peace.

[2] Shakespeare's *Sonnets*, # 94.

Sudden Wealth or Incremental Gains 99

Wealth gotten by vanity shall be diminished, but he that gathereth by labor shall increase (13:11 KJV).

Good composition makes good use of metaphorical imagery, at which the ancient Hebrews were specialists. But figures of speech when translated lose much of their pristine symbolism. Here the imagery is so rich with varied implications that translations come in a variety of shapes and sizes.

What is translated "by vanity" is literally "by a slack hand," and is variously translated "without effort," "from nothing," "hastily," "dishonestly," "by scheming," "by a sudden fortune," "from gambling." What is translated "by labor" says literally "with a hand," and is diversely translated "by single handfuls," "little by little," "gradually," "by diligence," "from hard work," "by toilsome labor." Together it says gains from honest labor come incrementally.

The proverb seems to make two points. First, those who have get-rich-quick illusions are only propping up false hope. Shuffling cards, rolling the dice, or playing the odds will be disappointed. Whatever casino success one person scores comes at the expense of multiple others who have lost. Gains from a bank heist are soon gone, to support a drug habit. Second, rather than simply giving the natural effects of "going for a fast buck," the proverb states the policy of Providence in stretching and blessing what is earned from honest work. It stands in contrast to the dwindling nature of what comes easily. Another proverb says, "An inheritance may be gotten hastily at the beginning, but the end thereof shall not be blessed" (Prov. 20:21).

Another advantage, that may or may not be implied in the proverb, is the personal satisfaction enjoyed from the fruit of one's labor. When David Copperfield lost his inheritance, Dickens says he told his fiancée that "a crust well-earned was sweeter than a feast inherited."[1]

---

[1] Charles Dickens, *David Copperfield* in *Best Loved Books* (Pleasantville, NY: Reader's Digest Asso., 1966) p. 348.

100 Failed Hope or Fulfilled Hope

Hope deferred makes the heart sick, but when the desire comes, it is a tree of life (13:12 NKJV).

After 18 years in prison on a false charge, his constant hope for release periodically denied, Dr. Manette's faint voice "was like the last feeble echo of a sound made long ago . . . like a once beautiful color faded away into a poor weak stain," said Charles Dickens.[1]

Delayed expectations make the heart sick. Ultimate disappointment of one's highest hope can devastate the heart with death. Shakespeare's Ophelia referred to the "form and feature of blown youth, blasted with ecstasy."[2]

That is in stark contrast to fulfilled hopes, which are like a tree of life-giving fruit. The actualized dream may not be as fanciful as the dream itself, but the reality is usually more solid and satisfying. The tree-of-life metaphor is used by Jesus as the final fulfillment of the soul's highest hope of heaven, a tree that is planted "in the Paradise of God" (Rev. 2:7).

The lesson is easily drawn: Be cautious what you fix your hopes on. Do not set yourself up for a fall. Make sure your hopes are limited to feasible expectations, not capricious fantasies with little chance of fulfillment. Indulging unjustified fancies can doom us with disappointment.

The proverb contrasts lost hope with fulfilled hope. But there is another option, understood but not stated. That is a firmly grounded hope. When expectations are set on something sure, soul energy is replenished. Hope invigorates. Expectations motivate. The future is integrated into the present, giving life a forward look. The scripture says, A "hope [that is] both sure and steadfast" is "an anchor of the soul" (Heb. 6:19).

Incorporating the future into your present is not borrowing an experience, like a *loan* to be repaid. It is an *advance* on the future that awaits you! That life-giving fruit from "the tree of life" comes to you while you live.

---

[1] Charles Dickens, *A Tale of Two Cities* (New York: Books, Inc., n.d.) p. 37.
[2] Shakespeare, *Hamlet*, Act III, Scene 1, lines 163-164.

He who despises the word will be destroyed, but he who fears the commandment will be rewarded (13:13 NKJV).

Gullible people often believe whatever is proclaimed by the most engaging personality or the most emphatic speaker. The proverb does not ask us to accept everything we hear. We are expected to love and obey the word of *truth*. Whether it is the word of God or the word of wisdom is irrelevant, for in the end they are the same. God's commandments are simply the eternal ethical law that is codified for our clarity.

Something is not wrong because God prohibits it. Rather God prohibits it because it is wrong. But because He forbids it, all transgression is sin against Him. Lawlessness is godlessness. It is treason against the Creator. God's rules are unalterable. Lon Woodrum says, "The changes we make are illegal. . . . All our revisions are unconstitutional!"[1]

Our option is either to *despise* the word or to *respect* and obey it.

Too many people choose arbitrarily to believe or disbelieve based on their likes or dislikes rather than on its truthness or falsity. Emotionally driven rather than truth-driven, they use their disbelief as a cover for a disobedient lifestyle. Rather than honest doubt, it is an accommodation to their preferences. They disbelieve the word because they hate what it says. But disbelief does not change truth. It only deceives those who choose to disbelieve.

Some "despise the word," trudging the trail of deception for a lifetime, on a collision course with final ruin. Others "respect the word," trekking the trail of truth through life, on a pilgrimage that leads to final reward. The scripture declares, "Forever, O Lord, Your word is settled in heaven" (Ps. 119:89). A Hebrew psalmist confided, "Your word is a lamp to my feet, and a light to my path" (Ps. 119:105).

---

[1] Lon Woodrum, *The Rebellious Planet* (Grand Rapids: Zondervan, 1965) p. 31.

102 Life Fountains or Death Traps

The teaching of the wise is a fountain of life, turning a man from the snares of death (13:14 NIV).

What immediately leaps out to the sophisticated student is the problem of mixed metaphors. A fountain and a snare hardly belong together in the same sentence. Closer study, however, may show they are justified because they contrast opposites. One is a fountain of *life*, the other a snare of *death*. A fountain cannot illustrate death and a snare does not describe life.

The force of the proverb is felt in the way the positive preempts the negative. Instead of a warning to avoid the snares, something more attractive is offered to divert the person from the snares. Behavior modification should first come from positive reenforcement, leaving negative threats as secondary inducements.

We should never measure our righteousness by the bad we do *not* do, while neglecting to do the good. One child hears her father say that hers is a church-going family. A neighbor hears his father boast that he has never been taken to jail. A girl cries because she did not make all A's—she got one B. Her brother rejoiced that he did not fail even one subject—he got all D's. If the positive is made more attractive than the negative, more people will gravitate to the good. Jesus strongly warned of judgment (Matt. 23:33, 24:46), but He first promised positive rewards to those who follow Him (Matt. 19:29). The average person prefers life fountains to death traps.

To heed the wise is to enjoy the fountain, but to shun the teaching is to be trapped in the snares. One adds up to life. The other spells out death. The first is a promise, the second a warning. The positive does not negate the negative, but it does make the negative superfluous for those who respond to the positive. Our option is between fountains and snares, rewards and punishment, promises and warnings, between life and death.

Earlier Moses had declared God's word to the people: "I have set before you life and death . . . therefore choose life" (Deut. 30:19 NKJV).

Good understanding giveth favor, but the way of transgressors is hard (13:15 KJV).

When they begin the devious odyssey, turning back seems so easy to do. The farther they go, the more difficult it becomes to get out of the rut, yet the harder it is to continue.

Hebrew scholars have trouble with the word "hard." It connotes a rugged, desolate trek on soil unfit for vegetation, void of health and vigor. Transgressors never imagined their journey would be so difficult. I see them often, some of my childhood friends, now locked into habits they cannot break, entangled with hostilities and guilt, the fresh vibrant spirit of youth that I once knew now crushed and dead within them. Most sinners pay a greater price to destroy their own souls than most righteous people pay, even with their cross-bearing, to have their souls redeemed. The way of the transgressor is a harsh, dilapidated track.

Nathaniel Hawthorne wrote of Hester Prynne's attempt to "hide her character and identity under a new exterior," but "her sin, her ignominy, were the roots she had struck into the soil."[1]

Charles Dickens' character Sydney Carton said to Lucie, "The life I lead is not good for one's health. God knows it is a shame." She said, "Then why not change it?" Lucie saw tears in his eyes and heard tears in his voice as he replied, "It is too late for that. I shall never be better than I am. I shall sink lower and lower."[2]

But—"good understanding," kindly wisdom, can place a person on a different road, in another direction, with the favor of God. The good news is that both Hester Prynne and Sydney Carton did an about-face. They turned 180 degrees! The message of the Gospel is that God is available to help a person turn, and then pick him up and give a new life. Solomon knew the importance of wisdom, but Jesus added the power of transformation!

---

[1] Nathaniel Hawthorne, *The Scarlet Letter* (New York: Books, Inc., n.d.) p. 64.
[2] Charles Dickens, *A Tale of Two Cities* (New York: J. J. Little & Ives Co., Inc., 1941) p. 69.

104 Prudence and Folly

Every prudent man acts with knowledge, but a fool lays open his folly (13:16 NKJV).

President Calvin Coolidge, known as "Silent Cal," sat at dinner beside a guest who said to him, "I have made a bet that I can get more than two words out of you." He replied, "You lose."[1] Whatever folly he may have had, he was wise enough to conceal it.

Foolish people empty their limited knowledge at the wrong place, at the wrong time, in the wrong situations, to anyone who will listen. In doing so, they lay their folly bare. They have little sense of what is appropriate to say. Playacting their imagined roles as venerable gurus, they actually think they know what they need to know. Fools act like fools because they *are* fools, flaunting their folly. Thinking they understand, they are hopelessly confused. Always, rationality bows out when folly takes the stage. Shakespeare's Banquo wondered, "Have we eaten on the insane root that takes the reason prisoner?"[2]

To act with knowledge, the discreet person must have knowledge to act with. And once she has the knowledge, she must know how to deal with it. It is not only important for conversational situations. It applies to politicians, preachers, and motivation speakers. And it applies to our actions as much as our speaking.

No one becomes an authority simply by reading a magazine article on the subject. Prudent persons are wise enough to research their subjects, and to familiarize themselves with both sides of the issues. They try on various opinions for size and fit. By trial and error, they learn from experience. Nothing should be proclaimed that does not wear well in life. Knowledge itself should never be used without the wisdom to use it well. Knowledge without wisdom is inadequate. Wisdom without knowledge is less than wisdom.

---

[1] John McCollister, *God and the Oval Office* (Nashville: W Publishing Group, Thomas Nelson, 2005) p. 149.
[2] Shakespeare, *Macbeth*, Act I, Scene 3, lines 84-85.

A wicked messenger falls into trouble, but a trustworthy envoy brings healing (13:17 NIV).

Here is a picture of an ambassador representing his government to a foreign country. He is negligent, carelessly wicked, even tampering with the message he is charged to deliver, leaving misunderstandings between the countries. Then a trustworthy emissary is assigned to deliver a message to repair the damage. As a responsible diplomat, he brings healing to the broken relationship, and restores the honor of his own country.

A one-person representative of a sovereign state carries a heavy-duty responsibility. The president or premier places the reputation of the entire country in his hands. As the voice of his government, he holds a position of power. Abraham Lincoln said, "Nearly all men can stand adversity. But if you want to test a man's character, give him power."[1]

The message is more important than the messenger. If he fails, the message does not get through. When the people wanted to know who John the Baptist was, he did not give his résumé. He said simply, I am a "voice" (Matt. 3:3). We clergy are not called to establish our reputation or climb the professional ladder. We are envoys representing another Kingdom. We have been given a message to deliver to a hurting world, to repair its damaged relationship with God. Using that assignment to boost our own prominence is so dishonoring! And so damaging to the world! We are citizens of another country. We have directions from a different source. The message must not be tampered with or altered to please those who hear.

The unfaithful envoy not only brought trouble *to* his country, but he himself fell into trouble *with* his country. That is a liability we cannot allow to happen to us! Paul said we have been "entrusted with the Gospel" (I Thes. 2:4). Whatever the cost, we must protect that trust!

---

[1] Helen Buss Mitchell, *Roots of Wisdom*, (Belmont, CA: Wadsworth Publishing Co., 1996) p. 462.

106 Disgraced or Praised

All who refuse correction will be poor and disgraced; all who accept correction will be praised (13:18 CEV).

Today our western culture is like that of the ancient Hebrews, but in opposite ways. They retained a strong ethnic community consciousness, but were economically independent. We prioritize our personal independence, but require a collectivism for economic survival.

Our autonomous individualism is fast becoming pathological. We do not wish to take directions. We resist instruction. As self-made persons, we pride ourselves in the knowledge we think we have acquired. When learning requires being corrected or disciplined, we rationalize our ignorance and refuse to change.

The word "correction" is variously translated instruction, discipline, and training. Perhaps "disciplining instruction" comes nearest covering its nuances. Knowledge is best retained when it is learned by being corrected after we have erred. Disciplining a student is probably the best educational tool a schoolmaster can use.

Many athletic contests simulate the pressurized experiences of life in a concentrated way. Playing requires close attention to the teaching of the coach. When infraction occurs, players are penalized. The other team gets free shots or free yards. The coach spares no words in rebuking the offenders. At times they are benched, or even ejected from the game. Players learn their lessons the hard way. Playing well requires subjugating one's ego and accepting the correction.

You and I keep committing fouls, fumbling the ball, and missing tackles. We need frequent instruction and correction. We are people under orders. We have a divine mandate. We are playing for the Coach, not for the fans. When correction comes, we can either refuse it or use it. We can be either the goat or the hero, either shamed or honored, either disgraced or praised. Our best option is to listen, to learn, and to love it.

A desire fulfilled is sweet to the soul, but to turn away from evil is an abomination to fools (13:19 RSV).

We humans are built with a desire and capacity for God, without whom our souls will never be satisfied. Feeding our surface desires with pleasure and pride nourishes those incentives, while neglecting our desires for God starves and deadens our deepest motives. Then we drift along, losing the higher joys of goodness, as one loses the joys of real life by sleeping.

A desire that at first seems inconsequential can filter down in the psyche to become a deep sentiment. Consistently placated, it becomes an entrenched pattern of embedded evil, enslaving one's motives and overwhelming one's desire for God. Indulging that sentiment is the sin-oholics' fix for pleasure. For them, to give it up would be like "an abomination."

They are hooked! Shakespeare's Rosalind complained about a deep love that held her in its clutches, "Oh, how full of briars . . . ! I could shake them from my coat, but these burs are in my heart!"[1]

Foolish sinners are like ill persons who want the joys of good health, but are unwilling to turn from fried foods, concentrated sugars, and nicotine. They want the pleasures of indulgence more than they want the sweet joys of health.

We humans become willing slaves to what we want most. We *could* give it up if we *would*, but we cannot because we will not. Enslaved to our *will* and our *will-not*, we lack the willpower—which is simply intensified want-power. We will do what we want to do if we want to do it strongly enough.

The secret of success comes in readjusting our desires. With God's help, those unworthy desires can be preempted by a stronger motive for God. The fulfillment of that desire is "sweet to the soul." We can have the pure pleasure that those who are hung-up on themselves can never have. Christ can free us from our bondage to ourselves.

---

[1] Shakespeare, *As You Like It*, Act I, Scene 3, lines 12ff.

108 Walk with the Wise

*He who walks with the wise grows wise, but a companion of fools
suffers harm* (13:20 NIV).

Saadi, an ancient moralist in Persia, said he held in his hand
a piece of pottery scented with a pleasing aroma. He asked the
object what it was, and got the reply, "I was a despicable piece of
clay, but I was in the company of a rose . . . and the sweet quality
of my companion was communicated to me."[1]

An old Persian proverb said, "To know a plant, you must
know the spot where it grows."[2]

Solomon made the application to life. We humans are like
sponges absorbing our social environment. We pick up accents,
feelings, knowledge and values, often without realizing we are
doing so. By nature we are chameleons, changing colors to
conform to new environments. We are assiduous imitators,
inadvertent copycats, emulating and duplicating those with whom
we associate. Their values, good or bad, rub off on us.

Patterned after the social nature of God in the dynamo of
the Trinity, we are inveterate social creatures with the herd instinct.
That can be either good or bad, determined by the company we
keep. Two angles on this are important. First, we need to use our
good influence on as many people as possible, and be cautious not
to have any bad influence.

Second, we need the good influence of others. Spiritual
isolation can leave us vulnerable. We need Christian community
with Christian companions for reciprocal influence. Their wisdom
will become our wisdom, their knowledge our knowledge, their
values our values—and ours theirs. And we must guard ourselves
when in company with foolish or evil people. Polluted air can
erode the best health, and a bad community of companions can
debilitate the best mind, deactivate the most virtuous values, and
damage the saintliest soul.

---

[1] Daniel D. Whedon, ed., *Whedon's Commentary* (New York: Phillips and Hunt,
1885) Vol. VI, p. 385.
[2] Isaiah Reed, *Boyhood Memories*, Jim Kerwin, ed. (Chesapeake, VA: Parbar
Westward Publications, 2007) p. 51.

Misfortune pursues the sinner, but prosperity is the reward of the righteous (13:21 NIV).

In simplistic ancient cultures, economic misfortune or prosperity may have been more precisely related to sin and righteousness than in our complex interdependent culture. But still today, consequences automatically follow the principles of good and evil—hard work, discipline, and thriftiness, or indolence, extravagance, and wastefulness.

Misfortune and prosperity, however, are not limited to economy. Recklessness is accident-prone, and caution tends toward safety. Indulgence causes illness, while self-discipline fosters health. Love unites families, and hostility disintegrates them. Misfortune stalks the steps and dogs the heels of evil people. We can assume this proverb refers also to spiritual misfortune and prosperity, for the Hebrews were a religious people to whom all life was sacred.

The system is set up, however, so that evil pursues the evildoer and goodness tracks the trail of the righteous, automatically rather than arbitrarily. Nathaniel Hawthorne said, "Heaven promotes its purposes without aiming at the stage-effect of what is called miraculous."[1] Like thornbush seeds contain thorns, dahlia seeds contain blossoms, and acorns contain oaks, causes are programmed with effects. Actions are pregnant with their aftermath. Deeds determine destinies. As C. S. Lewis said, "This moment contains all moments."[2]

In addition to this, the scripture is clear that God is directly involved in the lives of His people. When Woodrum's protagonist suffered a great loss, he drove into the sunset thinking to himself that the "future was an unmarked sheet of paper. But the pen was in God's hands. Whatever should be written on the sheet of paper would be right."[3]

---

[1] N. Hawthorne, *The Scarlet Letter* (New York: Books, Inc., n.d.) p. 98-99.
[2] C. S. Lewis, *The Great Divorce* (New York: Macmillan Publishing Co., Inc., 1978) p. 100.
[3] Lon Woodrum, *Stumble Upon the Dark Mountain* (Waco, TX: Word Books, 1980) p. 145.

110 Heritage Received, Heritage Given

A good man leaves an inheritance for his children's children, but a sinner's wealth is stored up for the righteous (13:22 NIV).

We do not ordinarily note a disproportionate transfer of wealth to the posterity of good people. Hebrew proverbs were forged in a moral/religious context, and this one is predicated on good and evil people, so we may assume that it was intended to include religious application.

One lesson is that evil persons' badness so eclipses their goodness that only their evil influence is passed on to descendants. Mark Antony said, "The evil that men do lives after them; the good is oft interred with the bones."[1]

Another lesson is that good people leave a supply of moral capital that filters through succeeding generations. When young Orlando learned that he was spurned by Duke Frederick because of his father, he declared: "I am more proud to be Sir Rowland's son . . . and would not change that calling to be adopted heir to Frederick."[2]

At this point, I am one of those fortunate persons. Proudly and humbly, I acknowledge generations of God-fearing forbears. They have left for me a moral reservoir that I have d rawn from through life. I would not exchange my heritage for the world! I believe the Lord is still answering prayers that my grandparents prayed for me when I was a child. In heaven, God has prayer files marked "pending," awaiting the appropriate time to be opened. We are often unaware that God is still granting requests our foreparents filed on our behalf.

The big lesson here is that we can leave for our children and grandchildren, or nieces and nephews, a heritage of values, piety, and prayer. Those moral treasures will be priceless to enrich their lives. Our influence will become a part of them, though they are not aware of it, and we will continue to live in their lives long after we are gone.

---

[1] Shakespeare, *JuliusCaesar*, Act III, Scene 2, lines 80-81.
[2] Shakespeare, *As You Like It*, Act I, Scene 2, lines 245-247.

A poor man's field may produce abundant food, but injustice sweeps it away (13:23 NIV).[1]

Two economic philosophies dominated the 20th century, often called *redistribution* and *developmentalism*. The first spawned extreme socialism and Marxism, and generally undermined industrial motivation, resulting in personal irresponsibility and slothfulness. The second accommodated capitalism, motivating diligent effort for personal gain, but resulting in economic competition that left helpless those who were not in a position to compete. Consequently both theories functioned in ways that marginalized people with injustice.

Now in the 21st century, multiple millions of people are victimized with economic exploitation, political oppression, and institutionalized injustice. With highly mechanized farmlands producing more food than ever, we live in an age of stark malnutrition. Anger, futility, and tears are the language of the hurting.

Wealth is probably the most common idol of the western world. Centuries ago the word of the Lord came to Ezekiel saying, "The people of the land practice extortion and commit robbery; they oppress the poor and needy, . . . denying them justice" (Ezek. 22:29). God declared to Jeremiah, "Woe to him who builds his house without righteousness, and . . . without justice, who uses his neighbor's services without pay, and does not give him his wages" (Jer. 22:13 NASB).

Ronald Sider said, "If a few million Christians in affluent nations dare to join hands with the poor around the world, we will decisively influence the course of world history. . . . We must pray for the courage to bear any cross, suffer any loss, and joyfully embrace any sacrifice that biblical faith requires in an Age of Hunger."[2]

---

[1] The wording of this original proverb is confusing and can suggest various meanings. Most prominent contemporary versions interpret it as it is translated here by the NIV.

[2] Ronald J. Sider, *Rich Christians in an Age of Hunger* (Downers Grove, IL: InterVarsity Press, 1977) pp. 225-226.

112 Diligent to Discipline

He who spares the rod hates his son, but he who loves him is diligent to discipline him (13:24 RSV).

Here the word "hate" is used loosely, perhaps as a hyperbole to emphasize the point. To be more accurate it should probably be read, ". . . is *as if he hates*" his son. The term is used as a contrast to parental love in the other clause that prioritizes the child's long-term well-being.

Discipline, of course, does not have to take the form of spanking or paddling with "the rod." Physical punishment should be the last resort, but it does have the advantage of having the matter quickly resolved, preempting a prolonged period of drawn-out punishment in which the child's anger or guilt continues to build up. The danger of corporal punishment is that it can easily become child abuse when the parent is angry or without discretion.

Paul said, "Do not provoke your children to anger" (Eph. 6:4 NASB).

To reconcile this proverb with Paul's injunction, I make the following suggestions. (1) Never punish when you are angry. (2) You may tell the child what he/she did was bad, but never say, "*You* are bad." Instead say, "You are too good a person to be doing that."

(3) Make prohibitions clear, but not oppressive. Give the child leverage to be a child. Never punish for using poor judgment. As a general rule, punishment should be limited to intentional disobedience and sassy insolence. (4) Minimize threats, so that you are not caricatured as a constant threat.

(5) Know each child's "pinch point." Children are different. Some respond to being grounded, some to losing an allowance; some may require a spank.

(6) Create a relational dynamic with the child. Make frequent eye contact when you are in a good mood, rather than primarily when in a stern or angry mood. Let the child absorb the feeling that you are primarily a relating parent rather than a disciplinarian. Long before the child reaches adolescence, you need to have an adequate store of relational capital to draw from during those difficult years.

To Pamper or To Temper 113

The righteous has enough to satisfy his appetite, but the stomach of the wicked is in want (13:25 NASB)

Righteousness and wickedness are generic terms that need to be broken down to specifics. Some people are righteous in other ways but evil in ways that contribute to poverty. Others are evil in more important ways but quite righteous in ways that support adequate food.

Here we are talking good and evil in specific ways that relate to plenty and poverty. The proverb assumes a tenuous economy in which people walk the tightrope between having and not having what is needed. Whether it applies to those in robust or barren economies is not clear.

The principle relating righteousness with satisfaction and evil with hunger operates two ways—one by the *arbitrary* assistance of God and the other by the *automatic* consequences of lifestyle. Some of us believe God is operative in economic ways to help responsible persons, and we can point to specifics in our own lives. The following application, however, depicts the principle in terms of automatic consequences.

First, *evil people often have less.* They bring themselves to poverty by an extravagant lifestyle, while economically righteous people budget their income, avoid unnecessary luxuries, and save for the future.

Second, *evil people desire more.* They pamper and inflate their sensual desires and develop insatiable appetites. Instead of eating to live, they live to eat. But indulgence is always "in want." It is never satisfied. Economically righteous people temper their desires, content themselves with prevailing situations, and cultivate higher-level appetites.

This evil problem and righteous remedy may carry over to the next life where insatiable selfish desires with no means of gratification can become unbearably frustrating. For others, being gratified by the presence of Christ will be perpetually fulfilling. Some will be eternally hungry and others eternally satisfied.

114 Held Together or Torn Apart

The wise woman builds her house, but the foolish tears it down
with her own hands (14:1 NASB).

When Goethe brought Faust's tragic life to an end, the earthly and heavenly realms were bridged by the spirit of wisdom and love in the figure of a woman. The mystical chorus sang: "Here it is done. The Woman-soul leadeth us upward and on!"[1] Throughout human history, tenderest human love and inspiration are figured and felt in the image of motherhood.[2]

When Uncle Tom was sold away from his family, he said to the slave-seller's son, "The Lord gives a good many things twice over, but he don't give you a mother but once."[3] Political correctness notwithstanding, our judicial system recognizes the preeminent place of the mother in the home, and unless it is unfeasible, custody rights of children are granted to their mothers.

That the home and family are the mother's nest and brood is illustrated in nature by wing-feathered vertebrates. The notion here is descriptive rather than prescriptive. But those who argue that the role is only a cultural practice have the problem of explaining why it has always been embraced even by remote and isolated cultures. Because the mother carries the child during gestation, births the child even when the father is absent, and alone is equipped to breastfeed the child, many fathers feel out of the loop. Many times I have been surprised by the unique wisdom of my own wife in domestic situations when I am sadly lacking.

It is precisely because a mother has such privilege and power that she can destroy the home simply by default. When the foundation cracks, the entire home collapses. One version translates the proverb, "A woman's family is held together by her wisdom, but it can be destroyed by her foolishness" (CEV).

---

[1] Johann von Goethe, *Faust*, Bayard Taylor, tr. (New York: Macmillan, 1937) Part II, Act 5, Scene 7, p. 506.
[2] Unfortunately, this led to the radical theological feminism of Naomi Goldenberg who followed feminine witchcraft to the "divine-feminine principle" for harmony with the "Mother Goddess."
[3] Harriet Beecher Stowe, *Uncle Tom's Cabin* (New York: Everyman's Library, Alfred A. Knoph, Inc., 1994) p. 117.

Upright Walk or Underhanded Ways 115

He whose walk is upright fears the Lord, but he whose ways are devious despises him (14:2 NIV).

An academic word study of the proverbs would be an interesting project. In these essays I am avoiding most of that for fear of being too pedantic, but some of it is necessary for grasping the message. Most translations of this proverb use the word "despise." But the term has two definitions, one stronger and one weaker. The stronger means to *detest*. The weaker means to *disregard* as negligible or trivial. As used here, the meaning can run the range, from the stronger to the weaker. An evil person may not consciously detest the Lord; he may simply disregard the Lord and sink further into evil.

The point of the proverb is that piety and principle are not disconnected. Fearing the Lord results in uprightness, and devious living amounts to despising the Lord. The religious includes the moral. Faith without fruit is false faith. The walk of the upright and the way of the devious have to do with God, because He requires uprightness. Every moral choice is a choice either to obey or disobey God.

When religion is isolated, cozy religious feelings of worship can act as a dangerously deceitful cover for ethical irresponsibility. What is morally right is not determined by subjective experience. Warm religious fuzzies can anesthetize a person to ethical responsibility and produce moral anesthesia that enables one to live a lie.

In the land of Narnia where Aslan the lion personified the Lord, Tirian said to Griffle: "I serve the real Aslan. . . . I [do not] keep him in my wallet. . . . He's not a tame lion."[1] The God of eternal reality is not our domesticated pet! He is a righteous God who by nature cannot settle for sin in His people. The Lord declared, "Those who honor me I will honor, but those who despise me will be disdained" (1 Sam. 2:30).

---

[1] C. S. Lewis, *The Last Battle: Book 7 in the Chronicles* (New York: Collier Books, Macmillan, 1978) p. 72.

116 Foolish Tongue and Wise Lips

In the mouth of the foolish is a rod for his back, but the lips of the wise will preserve them (14:3 NASB).

Foolish persons are foolish because they understand neither folly nor wisdom. They are like party bores who think they are entertaining the guests, or people with halitosis who never know their breath is foul.

As those who are asleep do not understand sleep, or those making mistakes do not understand their mistakes as they make them, foolish people cannot perceive their foolishness as long as they are foolish.[1]

Foolish talk brings repercussions that the foolish cannot anticipate. Deception brings loss of credibility, harsh talk gets harsh reaction, unsolicited advice loses appreciation, threats precipitate violence, faultfinders are faulted, blamers are blamed. Jesus said, "In the way you judge, you will be judged; by your standard of measure, it will be measured to you" (Matt. 7:2).

The tongue of the foolish is "a rod" that ricochets off whatever it hits and strikes back at the person using it. He may think he is being persecuted, but he is really punishing himself. Every stroke on the back is a rebound of his own stroke, usually in kind. The rod for the fool's back is in the fool's own mouth. It is a dangerous weapon for a person to use.

Fortunately, the rod is locked inside a gate, and the latch is on the inside. Others cannot reach the latch. Those who are wise are cautious about opening their lips. They keep the gate closed on the punishing rod, and open it only to use the rod as a staff for support and comfort. The Shepherd Psalm says, "Thy rod and Thy staff they comfort me" (Ps. 23:4).

Polonius warned his daughter Ophelia, "Give thy thoughts no tongue. . . . Give every man thy ear, but few thy voice."[2]

---

[1] cf. C. S. Lewis, *Mere Christianity* (New York: Macmillan, 1960) p. 73.
[2] Shakespeare, *Hamlet*, Act I, Scene 3, lines 59, 68.

Where no oxen are, the crib is clean, but much increase is by the strength of the ox (14:4 KJV).

A fascinating analogy—to something! But what is it analogous to? The first view: Without oxen, the ox stall is clean from a buildup of muck and scraps of hay. Keeping the stall clean requires keeping the oxen out, which is too high a price to pay for sanitation. Too much preoccupation with hygiene produces sterility.

You do not eliminate the oxen to keep a clean stall. You do not kill the dog to eliminate the fleas, or burn down a house to get rid of a mouse. Without an ox the farmer has no grain, and without a willingness to tolerate messiness, and work through stench and disorder, nothing worthwhile can be gained. The lesson applies to everything from changing baby diapers to working through a million technological details to get to the moon. The road to achievement is an obstacle course. Prep time is not orderly. It is messy.

The other view: Without oxen the crib is bare of stock feed. In those days, farmers required oxen to raise their crops to feed the rest of the livestock. Without an ox they had no produce. *No oxen, no corn . . .* (Mof). Dirt farmers discovered that oxen were much better utility for crop yield than horses. They are steadier, less fractious, not as accident-prone, they consume less feed, their hides are more valuable, and their horns have considerable utility.

The second clause avers that an ox can produce much more than its maintenance cost. Its yield is disproportionately high to the energy it expends. It can produce enough to feed itself plus many more. Without the ox, the stall may be clean but the crib is empty. Better to have a full corncrib than a clean ox stall. But the strength of the ox is useless if it is not used. A grass-grazing, cud-chewing ox that is workless is high maintenance. Unactualized potential is wasted.

Too much good and gain are lost by under-using our assets. Our potential far exceeds our competence. If we are usable, our usefulness can be stretched many times over our abilities.

118 Faithful Witness or False Witness

A faithful witness does not lie, but a false witness breathes out lies
(14:5 RSV).

To be truthful does not mean you have to tell everything you know. Things that do not merit public exposure should be kept silent. You are not a falsifier for refusing to address those items. Much of the news media needs to know that.

Being truthful means you are a faithful witness to the facts in not telling what is false, *and* it means you are not so selective in what you say that it shades the truth with false impression. To lie is to commit intentional deception whether spoken or implied. If you ate a dozen cookies and said, "I ate two cookies," it is a true statement—you did eat *two* (and more)—with a false implication. It is a "fallacy of accent," and it is intentional deception.

One of the many problems with lying is that it affects the one who lies. It not only makes you a liar in practice, but the lying is internalized and makes you a liar by nature. Actions affect and alter your affections. One-time falsifiers soon become habitual liars, "breathing out lies." The line between truth and falsehood gets fuzzy and fades. The mind gets muddled and muddy.

Inevitably, consistent falsifiers contradict themselves, because their standard for truth-claims is expediency rather than actuality, and expediency changes. Then they lose all credibility. When asked what a liar gains from telling falsehoods, Aristotle said, "Not to be credited when he shall tell the truth."[1]

Without factuality as the standard, the falsifier's deceptive nature is brought out under oath by a skilled attorney, and he perjures himself with legal problems. Hearing contradictory witnesses, Shakespeare's Helena erupted to Lysander: "When truth kills truth, O devilish-holy fray! . . . / Weigh oath with oath, and you will nothing weigh."[2]

False witnessing is dangerous all the way around the circle of many reasons. Faithful witnessing is safe.

---

[1] Paul Lee Tan, *Encyclopedia of 7,700 Illustrations* (Rockville, MD: Assurance Publishers, 1979) p. 563.
[2] Shakespeare, *A Midsummer Night's Dream*, Act III, Scene 2, lines 129-131.

Haughty Scoffing or Humble Seeking 119

A scoffer seeks wisdom in vain, but knowledge is easy for a man of understanding (14:6 RSV).

Goethe's Dr. Faust exclaimed, I "see that nothing can be known! / *That* knowledge cuts me to the bone!"[1] Of course, the idea that you *"can know* that you *cannot know"* undermines its own proposition by its own assertion.

Most of us have encountered the kind of insolent attitudes and haughty arrogance depicted in this proverb toward differing opinions. Ruling out a large body of evidence by nothing but a sneer is not a proper academic move. Questioning has value, but when it becomes cynical it is dangerously debilitating to the intellect. Scorning and scoffing is the shortcut to a scholarly self-image taken by some would-be intellectuals. C. S. Lewis distinguished between a proper and improper educational process by what he described as *propagation* and *propaganda.*[2]

In the proverb, wisdom and knowledge stand in the contrasting clauses as two labels for the same package, lost by the scoffer but gained by the person of discernment. The two belong together because each requires and complements the other. The best knowledge goes beyond itself and addresses basic issues of life. A recent educational emphasis on technological science at the expense of liberal arts is unfair to students who want answers to the existential questions of identity and meaning—"Who and I? Where am I? Why am I? Am I? What is this crazy mixed-up business of living all about?" Paul wrote to Timothy of those who are "ever learning and never able to come to the knowledge of the truth" (2 Tim. 3:7 KJV).

When knowledge embraces the overwhelming evidence for theism and when wisdom understands it as the most coherent system to explain human life, human nature, and human destiny, then the wise person zeroes in on transcendent reality.

---

[1] Johann Wolfgang von Goethe, *Faust* (New York: The Macmillan Company, 1937) Part I, Scene 1, p. 19.
[2] C. S. Lewis, *The Abolition of Man* (New York: Macmillan Publishing Co., Inc., 1947) pp. 32-33.

120 Wise Wisdom and Foolish Folly

Go from the presence of a foolish man, when you do not perceive in him the lips of knowledge. / The wisdom of the prudent is to understand his way, but the folly of fools is deceit (14:7-8 NKJV).

To the foolish, Faust declared: ". . . Thou hollow skull . . . like a cloudy mirror / . . . In twilight dull . . . Went wretchedly to error!"[1]

Of course, wise people should fellowship with the unwise, realizing that every person has something to offer that can contribute to their lives. But consistently fraternizing with the foolish can create an identity that will curtail your influence. Dolly Parton sang, "You're known by the company you keep."

The primary reason to limit your time with the foolish is found in the second proverb above. "To understand" is stated in contrast to "deceit." By deceiving themselves, foolish persons deceive their friends. Both wisdom and folly are contagious. You catch them from your associates. From the wise you will *learn* your way, and from the foolish you will *lose* your way. Wisdom is *directive* and foolishness is *deceptive*.

First you become fascinated with the foolish. Then, as Macbeth said, you "dress in borrowed robes."[2] When those robes adjust to your body, the fit becomes comfortable. Then you confiscate them, and they become your own. The folly of the foolish should never even be test-worn for size.

A dog in a pack becomes fiercer with each additional dog. Wise persons become wiser from wise discourse. Social influence multiplies. In varying degrees, we are all products of our social environment. An anonymous person wrote: "Friends that don't help you climb will want you to crawl. Friends will stretch your vision or choke your dream. If you run with the wolves you will learn to howl. If you associate with eagles you will learn to soar."[3]

---

[1] Johann Wolfgang von Goethe, *Faust* (New York: The Macmillan Company, 1937) Part I, Scene 1, p. 29.
[2] Shakespeare, *Macbeth*, Act I, Scene 3, lines 8-9.
[3] Internet, Google site for "The Company You Keep," listed as anonymous.

Fools make a mock at sin, but among the righteous there is favor
(14:9 KJV).

Opposites are left to be supplied. "Fools" and "a mock at sin" in the first clause imply "wise persons" and "taking sin seriously" in the second. "The righteous" and the "favor" in the second suggest "the evil" and the "disfavor" in the first. When all are supplied, the proverb reads: "Evil fools mock sin and incur God's disfavor, but the righteous wise take sin seriously and enjoy God's favor." When the skeleton is fleshed out, it makes a body of profound truth.

When American clergy largely quit preaching against sin, the public began supplying a plethora of euphemisms to mitigate its seriousness—unsocial behavior, a complex, sociological maladjustment, failure to cope with one's environment, the eruption of an inhibition.

If evil people only knew the gravity of sin and its consequences, they could not mock! But sinning by nature blinds the sinner to its severity. In C. S. Lewis' space fiction, the earthling Ransom said, "In my world, [sin] would pass for folly. We have been evil so long." The King replied, "We have learned better than that . . . for it is waking that understands sleep and not sleep that understands waking. There is an ignorance of evil . . . that comes from doing it, as men sleeping lose the knowledge of sleep."[1]

It is open to question whether the subject and object in the first clause should be reversed, as some scholars translate it. Both propositions, however, are true. Fools make a mock at sin, and sin makes a mock of fools. Those who make sport of sinning will not find the punishment to be sport. Those who make life a moral chess game may know that God made the first move. Then He allows them to make any moves they wish. They may not realize, however, that God always makes the final move. In the end, they will be put in checkmate!

---

[1] C. S. Lewis, *Perelandra* (New York: Macmillan Publishing Co., Inc., 1944) p. 209.

122 Isolated or Inhabited

The heart knows its own bitterness, and a stranger does not share its joy (14:10 NASB, NKJV).

Charles Dickens wrote, "Every human creature is constituted to be that profound secret and mystery to every other. . . . Every beating heart . . . is a secret to the heart nearest it!"[1]

In grammatical construction, reflexive pronouns show a special relationship with their antecedents that other pronouns do not have. You relate with yourself in a way that you cannot relate with others. I can hurt you or help you, but I cannot hurt or help yourself. Others may know you, but only you can know yourself. You have an intimate consciousness of yourself that others can never have. I may sympathize with your sorrows and share in your joys, but never in as personal a way as you feel your own. To some extent, I am a stranger to my best friend.

Maxwell Anderson's drama measures the distance between separate souls as thousands and thousands of miles. Only love can span the distance to unite them. Then the chorus swells in a surging refrain: "Each lives alone in a world of dark / Crossing the skies in a lonely arc, / Save when love leaps out like a leaping spark / Over thousands, thousands of miles!"[2]

What the proverb says is true. What it does not say is also true. In our innermost spirits, we can be conscious of a divine Presence that is closer and more intimate than even our spouses can be. Once a stranger, He becomes our closest Companion. The One who embodies and unites both perfect knowledge and perfect love can cross millennia of miles to bond with our spirits. He homesteads our hearts and inhabits our lives. We become His residences.

When we reciprocate His love, it moves in both directions with mutual interrelationship. Inhabited rather than isolated, we know that He feels our most bitter hurts and shares our most exalted joys!

---

[1] Charles Dickens, *A Tale of Two Cities* (New York: Books, Inc., n.d.) pp. 9-10.
[2] Maxwell Anderson, *Lost in the Stars*, in Henry Hewes, ed., *Famous American Plays of the 1940s* (New York: Dell Pub. Co., 1960) p. 369.

The house of the wicked will be destroyed, but the tent of the upright will flourish (14:11 RSV, NASB, NIV).

Here the terms "house" and "tent" seem to be used two ways—literally, referring to the residence, and as a metonymy, referring to the family. They are used for both *house* and *home*.

The home is a social entity initiated by God to provide a haven from a hostile world. Ideally the family is a matrix of supportive relationships. It is a retreat center from a raucous, ravaging world. Being "upright" includes positive response to both love and law. Young people do not want "to live in a cage," but for both emotional and moral support, they "want to live on a leash," says Jay Kesler. "They keep running until they feel the tug of love and concern."[1] On average, parents who feed the children wholesome menus of loving, positive attitudes succeed in being an "upright" home. Nourishing parents have flourishing children. "Those who are planted in the house of the Lord shall flourish in the courts of our God" (Ps. 92:13 NKJV).

When relationships break down, the home is said here to be "wicked," in the sense that self-centered, inconsiderate relationships preempt other-centered relationships. Conversations are accented with accusations. Family members live together in a house without a home.

Using the terms "house" and "tent," the proverb suggests a distinction between a larger abode and a humbler dwelling. The upright or the wicked home can be paired with either, but the upright *home* will flourish even when it occupies a humble *house*, and the wicked *home* will disintegrate even in a better *abode*. The quality of the home is not determined by the house. External prosperity does not make a flourishing home, and economic privation does not prevent it.

A humble hovel that houses an upright home is a thousand times preferable to a palace with a broken, dysfunctional family!

---

[1] Jay Kesler, *Too Big to Spank* (Glendale, CA: Regal Books, G/L Publications, 1978) p. 70.

124 The Wrong Road and the Right Road

There is a way which seems right to a man, but its end is the way of death (14:12 NKJV). Same as 16:25.

A man told me he was sure he would go to heaven because he paid off his home mortgage and charge cards accounts without default. He had "figured out" for himself the way of eternal salvation, and his ears were plugged. Refusing to listen, he protected his false security by pretending the truth of a falsehood. Haughty attitudes on some subjects can be fatal!

Our thoughtless propensities need to be checked. Regarding theistic faith, Pascal said if there is no God, you lose nothing by believing there is. But if there is, you lose everything by believing there is not. "Pascal's Wager" is rational wisdom.[1]

"Reason is always reasonable," said the priest in Chesterton's story. "People charge the Church with lowering reason, but it is just the other way. . . . Alone on earth, the Church affirms that God Himself is bound by reason."[2] Isaiah Reed said: "The Holy Spirit is not a substitute for lack of brains; rather, He works with the best brains He can find. God does not make brains and then set them aside. They are too expensive a product."[3]

What initially seems to be right can be wrong. The road can lead in the wrong direction to the wrong destiny. Substituting feelings or wishes for truth is a precarious game of Russian roulette. Arriving at your moral code by the way you feel without objective guidelines is to play Ostrich. Resting on a hunch is like stepping into quicksand. Without solid support, it will swallow you up. C. S. Lewis has the pilgrim's guide singing: "Therefore, oh man, have fear / Lest oldest fears be true, / Lest thou too far pursue / The road that seems so clear."[4]

---

[1] Blaise Pascal, *Pensées*, A. J. Krailsheimer, tr. (London: Penguin Books, 1995) pp. 121-127.
[2] G. K. Chesterton, "The Blue Cross," in *Favorite Father Brown Stories* (New York: Dover Pub., 1993) pp. 12-13.
[3] Isaiah Reed, *Boyhood Memories and Lessons* (Chesapeake, VA: Parbar Westward Publications, 2007) p. 64.
[4] C. S. Lewis, *The Pilgrim's Regress* (Grand Rapids: Wm. B. Eerdmans Publishing Co., reprint 1979) p. 182.

Even in laughter the heart may ache, and joy may end in grief (14:13
NIV).

Though they are opposites, joy and sorrow exist in life so close together that it is hard to speak of one without thinking of the other. Macbeth spoke of "so fair and foul a day."[1] Happiest times are often sabotaged by tragedy. As night follows day and winter follows summer, sorrow follows joy and sadness follows gladness. Shakespeare's queen of the fairies rued, "Hoary-headed frosts fall in the fresh lap of the crimson rose."[2]

Yet always we can observe others who hurt more than we. When the banished duke met hungry homeless men in the forest, he said, "This wide and universal theatre presents more woeful pageants than the scene wherein we play."[3] And we can always know that our own lives could be worse. After Robinson Crusoe had been isolated for years on the island, he hand-made a little boat and tried to escape, but a storm at sea took him so far out that he thought he faced certain death. He said, "Now I looked back on my desolate solitary island as the most pleasant place in the world, and . . . all the happiness my heart could wish for was to be there again."[4]

The old broken African minister in his far-out village, while his own son sat on death row in Johannesburg awaiting the scaffold, confided in a friend that he could not understand suffering. "I have learned that . . . pain and suffering, they are a secret. Kindness and love, they are a secret. But I have learned that kindness and love can pay for pain and suffering."[5]

Goodness in the world is greater than evil, and joy can overcome sorrow. Daybreak follows darkness, and spring follows winter. For God's people, in the end gladness follows sadness!

[1] Shakespeare, *Macbeth,* Act I, Scene 3, line 38.
[2] Shakespeare, *A Midsummer Night's Dream,* Act II, Scene 1, lines 107-108.
[3] Shakespeare, *As You Like It,* Act II, Scene 7, lines 137-139.
[4] Daniel Defoe, *Robinson Crusoe* (Garden City, NY: Doubleday, 1945) p. 159.
[5] Alan Paton, *Cry, the Beloved Country* (New York: Macmillan Publishing Co., 1948) p. 226.

126 Self-Hate or Self-Love

The backslider in heart shall be filled with his own ways, and a good man shall be satisfied with himself (14:14 KJV).

Eminent 19th century Presbyterian evangelist Charles G. Finney ordinarily began his campaigns by preaching several consecutive sermons from the first phrase of this proverb. It was used by God's Spirit to precipitate revival that still benefits the church today.

Many faithful churchpersons retain the outward form of religion who are "backslidden in heart." Their souls have sprung a leak that flows out faster than they are refilled. Outgo exceeds income. They are empty and barren. The void is filled with self-centeredness resulting in folly and sin until they are nauseated with themselves. Civil war rages in their chests. Loving themselves while paradoxically hating themselves, their forces are depleted. Jesus spoke of those who "have left their first love" (Rev. 2:4). No longer satisfied with God, they are dissatisfied with themselves. Making miserable company for themselves to live with, they get sick of self.

The proverb labels the backslider's counterpart "a good man." One is "filled with his own ways." The other is "satisfied with himself." One hates himself for what he *does*; the other loves himself for what he *is*. Self-love is better than self-hate. It is not incompatible with loving God if one loves God more. Exorbitant self-love is sick, but appropriate self-love is healthy. With the self-respect of wholesome self-love, the good person's happiness is self-contained, independent of external sources. It does not even come from religious creeds or faith, but from his relationship with God. He "has the witness in himself" (1 Jno. 5:10).

Those who through difficulties have kept intact their heart devotion can happily sing the psalm of the ancient Hebrews, "All this is come upon us, yet have we not forgotten Thee . . . Our heart is not turned back, neither have our steps declined from Thy way" (Ps. 44:17-18). They are satisfied with themselves because they still find their chief satisfaction in God.

The simple believes every word, but the prudent man considers well his steps (14:15 NKJV).

Whether to believe or doubt can be a paralyzing problem. Earlier proverbs urged us to seek counsel, but this one warns us to beware of the advice we get. Tennyson said, "There lives more faith in honest doubt, believe me, than in half the creeds."[1]

Thoughtless, simple minds can believe everything they hear or read, without running it through a test grid. They are quick to believe flattery, or to be sucked in by shysters with false promises of personal profit. Others are naïve enough to favor both sides of an issue, without having their own worldview as a reference point. Suspended in perpetual doubt, they unwisely adopt doubt itself as their worldview. They become skeptics. Victimized by the paralysis of analysis, they become comfortable with a closed mind. C. S. Lewis said, "The trouble about trying to make yourself stupider than you are is that you often succeed."[2]

Prudent persons check out a claim before committing themselves. Hamlet said, "He that made us . . . gave us not . . . god-like reason to [grow moldy] in us unused."[3] At the point of theistic faith, George Washington said, "It is impossible to reason without arriving at a Supreme Being."[4] If the search by logical reasoning fails, wise persons look to its practical effects to determine its value—they "consider well [their] steps." Practical wisdom should lead a person to commit on the basis of theism's coherent explanation of the world. If logical reasoning falters from inadequate premises, practical wisdom is the safest resort. Too much is riding on this commitment to remain neutral!

[1] Alfred Lord Tennyson, *In Memoriam*, poem 96, M.H. Abrams, ed., *The Norton Anthology of English Literature*, Vol. 2 (New York: W.W. Norton & Co., 1962) p. 764.
[2] C. S. Lewis, *The Magician's Nephew*, Bk. 6 in The Chronicles (New York: Macmillan, Collier Bks., 1978) p. 126.
[3] Shakespeare, *Hamlet*, Act IV, Scene 4, lines 36-39. Shakespeare used the word "fust"which means "grow moldy."
[4] John C. McCollister, *God and the Oval Office* (Nashville: W Publishing Group of Thomas Nelson, 2005) p. 1.

128 Cautious or Careless

A wise man is cautious and turns away from evil, but a fool throws off restraint and is careless (14:16 RSV).

The difference between being cautious and careless is often the difference between life and death. Wisdom and folly have direr consequences in moral matters than in any other. At that point, an eternity of difference stands between "turning away" and rushing in.

Courage is usually lauded as a virtue, but the courage to pursue evil belongs to the stupidity of a fool. Throwing off moral restraint is the kind of thing done by foolish cowards who have neither the wisdom nor the courage to opt for goodness.

Dickens' character Martha Endell came to London as a rural girl and was caught up in the nightlife of street women. David Copperfield found her one night at the edge of the city where the polluted river with its scum and filth connected with the sea. Ruefully she confided, "Oh, the dreadful river! It's like me! It comes from country places where there was no harm in it—and it creeps through the dismal street, defiled and miserable—and it goes away, like my life, to a great sea that is always troubled. It's the only thing in all the world that I am fit for."[1]

Choices that start a person down an evil road are not only sinful—they are asinine, made by thickheaded natives of idiocy! Turning back to an earlier way is many times more difficult than "turning away" at the start.

Kipling's character Dick Helden said the tempter "holds the bank. Fly from him. Pack your things and go!"[2] Get off the beaten paths! Wear the yoke of restraint!

Solomon said, "My son, let not them depart from thine eyes; keep sound wisdom and discretion. So shall they be life unto thy soul, and grace to thy neck. Then shalt thou walk in thy way safely, and thy foot shall not stumble" (Prov. 3:21-23 KJV).

---

[1] Charles Dickens, *David Copperfield* in *Best Loved Books* (Pleasantville, NY: Reader's Digest Ass'n., 1966) p. 379.
[2] Rudyard Kipling, *The Light that Failed* (New York: Books, Inc., n.d.) p. 149.

Hot Heads and Heartless Hearts 129

He that is soon angry dealeth foolishly, and a man of evil devices is hated (14:17 KJV).

Solomon's metaphor deserves a chuckle. For "soon angry," he used the phrase "short of nostrils." Quick-tempered people have a short fuse. Hotheads with short nostrils vent quickly and speak foolishly. But they are soon over it. Damage is done, but more people are likely to chalk it up to folly rather than evil intent.

These impulsive, impetuous people are contrasted with those who hold their anger inside and continue to feed it. All the while they are deliberately devising malicious revenge. As they wait for the opportunity, their veins expand with rage and their evil intentions go into overdrive. When the eruption occurs, others around them are shredded with shrapnel! Rather than tolerated, those with long nostrils are hated. Devising despite, they are despised.

In Greece, Aristotle distinguished between hot-tempered and bad-tempered people when he said: "Hot-tempered people get angry quickly . . . but their anger ceases quickly. . . . Bad-tempered [people] . . . cannot be appeased until they inflict vengeance."[1] Solomon had made much the same distinction six centuries earlier. Righteous people are expected not to be either hot-tempered or bad-tempered. A psalm says, "Cease from anger, and forsake wrath" (Ps. 37:8).

We should also have wisdom to handle the anger of the hot heads and the malice of the heartless hearts. Hot heads need to be *defused*. Heartless hearts can often be *diffused*, over a period of time. The big thing is to keep yourself functioning from cerebral wisdom rather than emotional reaction. The psalmist said, "Fret not yourself over him . . . who carries out evil devices" (Ps. 37:7 RSV).

With apologies to three successive generations of American youth, I interpret the psalm to be saying: "Don't get all shook up," "don't get bent out of shape," and "keep your cool, dude!"

---

[1] Aristotle, *Nicomachean Ethics*, Book IV, Chapter 5, p. 390 in McKeon.

130 The Simple and the Prudent

The simple inherit folly, but the prudent are crowned with knowledge (14:18 KJV, NKJV, NIV).

Wisdom is not expected from the limited knowledge of infants. Regretfully, as they grow older many do not acquire the knowledge to make them wise. They settle for the simplicity and folly they had as infants. But the prudent go for knowledge that increases their prudence.

In church history, erudite church leaders have always countered the anti-intellectualism of some religious zealots. When asked, "How does scholarship enhance your faith?" Erasmus has been widely quoted as saying, "How does ignorance improve yours?" Tertullian's question, "What does Athens have to do with Jerusalem?" was resoundingly answered in the positive. Most people who are inspired by Isaac Watts' 600 hymns do not know that he wrote 52 books—on grammar, astronomy, geography, philosophy, and one on logic that was widely used in universities.[1] Rather than demolishing faith, knowledge should strengthen it.

Many have been inspired to minister by stories of John Wesley crisscrossing England on horseback to preach four-to-five times a day for fifty years. It all sounded adventurous and romantic! They were not told, however, that Wesley always read a book while riding horseback to preach, usually a cultural classic in literature or philosophy. He read Homer's *Iliad* and *Odyssey*, Virgil's *Aeneid* and Cicero's *Letters*. He read Plato, Demosthenes, Horace, Voltaire, Rousseau, Shakespeare, Milton, Lock, Pope. The list goes on and on. Wesley read easily in several languages. He himself authored more than 30 volumes.[2]

Not only does knowledge contribute to wisdom, but wisdom also contributes to knowledge. Simple people preserve their folly as a crown of disgrace, while prudent people acquire knowledge that adorns their head with a crown of eminent honor.

---

[1] See Robert J. Morgan, *Then Sings My Soul: . . . Hymn Stories* (Nashville: Thomas Nelson, 2006) p. 63.
[2] C. T. Winchester, *The Life of John Wesley* (New York: The Macmillan Company, 1906) pp. 273-274.

The evil will bow before the good, and the wicked at the gates of the righteous (14:19 NKJV).

During the unrelenting days of southern reconstruction, my maternal grandfather at age 13 was left by his father's death to support his mother and sisters on a small dirt farm. Without work shoes for plowing, he asked the neighborhood storekeeper for shoes on a credit, promising to pay when the crops were harvested. Instead of simply refusing, the neighbor mocked and sneered. More than 50 years later the youth had become a successful merchant in town, and the earlier storekeeper's daughter came to him asking to purchase foodstuffs on a credit to feed her family. Immediately the earlier incident popped into his mind, but he said, "Sure Suzanne, get whatever you need and pay whenever you can."

In the Old Testament, Joseph's brothers who had sold him into slavery came to his home needing food and "bowed to the ground before him" (Gen. 43:26 NASB).

The proverb says evil people will "bow" before the good (NKJV), "have to bend the knee" (Sprl), "prostrate themselves . . . and beg" (Lam), "go down to the dust" (Bas), "come crawling" (CEV).

In a morally ordered universe, evil by its nature loses and goodness by nature wins. In a frightening scene, two women got into acute combat, one of them hating Lucie and wanting to kill her, the other loving Lucie and fighting to protect her. Dickens wrote, "It was in vain [for the one who hated] to struggle and to strike" because "love [is] always so much stronger than hate."[1] Fighting for love's sake, Miss Pross won the brawling battle, and Lucie was spared.

On occasions when badness seems not to bow by nature to goodness, we can be sure that the God behind the moral order will eventually effect retribution. Providence has not abdicated "the throne of His holiness" (Ps. 47:8 KJV), and every situation will come under His moral dominion!

---

[1] Charles Dickens, *A Tale of Two Cities* (New York: J.J. Little & Ives Co., Inc., 1941) p. 179.

132 Friend or Fake

The poor are shunned even by their neighbors, but the rich have many friends (14:20 NIV).

Fair-weather friends are falsifying fakers. The proverb is using the term loosely, referring only to staged friendships. The nature of friendship is so deeply grounded in interrelational love that it has no reference to economic conditions. Those who shun the poor and embrace the affluent profane the term "friendship' by using it.

True friendship is for its own sake. It does not ride on wealth. It is not a commodity to be used. Pretended friendships are not friendships. Shallow friends are not friends. They plagiarize the word for personal advantage, claiming what is not theirs. Genuine friendships take time to develop. Meaningful relationships require a reservoir of relational equity that builds up over a period. Instant friends are rare commodities. Most instant marriages face instant collapse. We recoil from fundraisers who feign instant, intimate friendship. We do not want new friends who attempt to pick our pockets with the left hand while shaking hands with their right.

Being friendly is quite a different thing from claiming friendship. Friendliness to a casual acquaintance is a valuable virtue, and being willing to become a friend is a commendable attitude. But the word "friend" encapsulates such deep camaraderie and commitment that it is dishonored and debased when used for personal profit.

Because friendship is so interrelational, the relationship becomes a part of you. To bury a friend is to bury a part of yourself. But losing a friend by rejection over something as trivial as economic status is much more painful than losing a friend by death. And shunning a former friend because of his/her misfortune is to reject a big part of yourself. Thus Creon said to Oedipus, "To reject a good friend is the equivalent of throwing away one's own life."[1]

---

[1] Sophocles, *Oedipus the King* (New York: Washington Square Press, Inc., 1959) p. 41.

He that despises his neighbor sins, but he who has mercy on the poor, happy is he (14:21 NKJV).

The previous proverb says that the poor are despised by neighbors. This sequel states the moral character of that attitude— it is a brazen sin! The impudence is toward the victims of misfortune, even if the misfortune did not come from their fault or folly. Whatever the condition, poverty, illness, ignorance, or moral weakness, and for whatever reason, unfortunate people are easy prey to all sorts of predators. They need the compassion of others. Joaquin Miller wrote: "That man who lives for himself alone / Lives for the meanest mortal known."[1]

Yes, many with misfortune need handouts, but they also need emotional support. Harriet B. Stowe said, "Everything your money can buy, given with a cold, averted face, is not worth one honest tear shed in real sympathy."[2] It is a moral thing—we *ought* to do it. It is also a *love* thing—we *want* to do it. Law *and* love converge in the law *of* love that Jesus said was the second greatest commandment: "Love your neighbor" (Matt. 22:39).

When other-centeredness replaces self-centeredness, selfish concern shifts to compassion. German philosopher von Leibniz said, "To love is to place our happiness in the happiness of another."[3] The enigma is like a riddle—you find happiness where it is least looked for. When you seek it for yourself, it is elusive. When you get interested in making others happy, you strike gold! You become happy by making them happy. And if making them happy makes you happy, then—you are happy! The way to be happy is to give up your happiness for others to be happy. Then happiness comes to you as a big-time bonus!

---

[1] Quoted in William C. Ringenberg, *Letters to Young Scholars* (Upland, IN: Taylor University Press, 2003) p. 125.
[2] Harriet Beecher Stowe, *Uncle Tom's Cabin* (New York: Everyman's Library, Alfred A. Knoph, Inc., 1994) p. 113.
[3] This line has been attributed to Leibniz in several places, but not documented with specific references. I have read considerably in Leibniz' works, but I have not found it, though he did write much about happiness. An internet Google site attributes the line to Leibniz without further documentation.

134 Plotting Evil or Planning Good

Do they not err that devise evil? But mercy and truth shall be to them that devise good (14:22 KJV).

Those who devise evil are not good-intentioned people who stumble in a trap of moral weakness. They are not nice guys with a few problems. They are schemers who plan and plot with evil intentions from an evil mind. Lady Macbeth, urging her husband to murder the king so that he could become king, lauded his ambition but complained that he was "without the illness" necessary to kill the king. Then she implored evil spirits to "fill me . . . full of . . . cruelty! Make my blood thick!"[1] Devising evil is more than mental illness; it is outrageous moral debauchery!

In contemporary usage, to "err" covers mild, incidental infractions, but the word here is stronger. Devising evil sends one diametrically astray (NKJV, NIV), to fare miserably (Mof), and to perish. The point is that evil takes a person where she does not want to go, to a futility described by Robert Frost (though in a different setting) as "nothing to look backward to with pride and nothing to look forward to with hope."[2] Lady Macbeth ended up wringing her hands, attempting to wash away the guilt blood, and bewailing that "these hands [will] never be clean." She lamented, "All the perfumes of Arabia will not sweeten this hand!"[3] It is dangerous to be hijacked by evil!

For those who devise what is good and purpose what is right, "goodness and mercy follows them" (Ps. 23:6) with "good measure, pressed down, shaken together, and running over . . . poured into [their] lap" (Lu. 6:38 NIV). Jesus said, "With the measure you use, it will be measured to you" (vs. 39 NIV). And the rewards continue into the next life with surprises beyond our ability to imagine! Paul said, "Eye hath not seen, nor ear heard, neither have entered into the heart of man, the things which God hath prepared for them that love Him" (1 Cor. 2:9).

---

[1] Shakespeare, *Macbeth*, Act I, Scene 5, lines 20-21, 43-44.
[2] Robert Frost, "The Death of the Hired Man," in Louis Untermeyer, ed., *Modern American Poetry* (New York: Harcourt, Brace and Co., 1950) p. 189.
[3] Shakespeare, *Macbeth*, Act V, Scene 1, lines 48-49, 57-58.

Toil or Talk 135

In all labor there is profit, but mere talk leads only to poverty (14:23 NASB).

This was written in an agrarian culture consisting primarily of manual workers. In that context, loud lips belonged to lazy laborers. Less talk meant more work. The principle of work, however, has its source in God Himself, said Jesus (John 5:17), and a good work ethic is always an indispensable code of conduct for people in any area. Every field of activity exacts relentless effort. Longfellow wrote: "Each morning sees some task begun; / Each evening sees it close. / Something attempted, something done, / Has earned a night's repose."[1]

Good public speaking that looks easy requires diligent work to make it look easy. Unprepared speakers are verbose and disorganized, which undermines their impact. The homiletical rule of thumb for preachers is one hour of prep time for every one minute of the message. A big part of the preparation is reducing the palaver to a lean style for impact. "Mere talk" misses the mark. Whatever the field, a strong work ethic is imperative.

When I was a child, I was puzzled when my father, not referring to income, often thanked the Lord for work to do. My style was to work hard to complete the job so that I would *not* have work to do. My industry was motivated by laziness. Now I know my father was correct in promoting the intrinsic value of work. Part of the "profit" comes from the work itself rather than from what it accomplishes. It prevents boredom, it builds character, and it is signally satisfying. Work provides its own joy. Speculating about our expected work in the next life, Kipling writes: "And only the Master will praise us, and only the Master will blame; / And no one shall work for money, and no one shall work for fame, / But each for the joy of working . . ."[2]

---

[1] Henry Wadsworth Longfellow, "The Village Blacksmith," in *Best Loved Poems of Longfellow* (Chicago: The Spencer Press, 1949) p. 12.
[2] Rudyard Kipling, "When Earth's Last Picture Is Painted," in Miles and Pooley, eds., *Literature and Life in England* (New York: Scott, Foresman and Co., 1943) p. 603.

136 Bountiful Wisdom and Barren Folly

The crown of the wise is their riches, but the foolishness of fools is folly (14:24 KJV, NKJV).

"The *foolishness* of *fools* is *folly!*" It is a fascinating phrase that sounds like a tautology. You can turn the line several ways and always come out at the same point. Initially it looks like a riddle. By repeating the word three times, the writer makes the answer seem obvious: Foolishness is nothingness, emptiness, poverty. After folly has done its best work with its best efforts, you still have nothing but folly.

It is contrasted with all the riches that wisdom produces. Here we have an antithesis between the riches of wisdom and the poverty of folly. One is a crown of honor to the wise, the other a mark of shame to the foolish. While material wealth is sometimes a product of shrewd sagacity, the rich result of wisdom goes far beyond the material. It includes riches in relationships, morality, lifestyle, increased knowledge, greater freedom, less stress, fewer complications, the liberty of living a structured life. Wisdom is wealthy with life's higher values, while folly is barren. In another place, Solomon said, "Wisdom excelleth folly as far as light excelleth darkness" (Ecc. 2:13 KJV). Job said, "The price of wisdom is above rubies" (Job 28:18).

Being human, all our minds have been clouded with the fog of foolishness. Shakespeare's Robin Goodfellow said, "What fools we mortals be!"[1] Some of us may learn our lessons only by painful experience. Coleridge said his Wedding-Guest was "a sadder and wiser man."[2]

As a general rule, being sadder is not a bad price to pay in order to be wiser. The price may be only temporary, but the product will last into the future—to enrich our lives with the wealth of wisdom!

---

[1] Shakespeare, *A Midsummer Night's Dream*, Act III, Scene 2, line 115. The line, generally attributed to Shakespeare, actually originated with the ancient Roman writer Seneca.
[2] Samuel Taylor Coleridge, "The Rhyme of the Ancient Mariner," Part VII, in Richard Aldington, ed., *The Viking Book of Poetry* (New York: The Viking Press, 1958) Vol. II, p. 698.

A truthful witness saves lives, but he who speaks lies is treacherous
(14:25 NASB).

John Davidson's character said, "I never lie outright,"[1] but covert deception is no less deceptive than overt. Intentional falsehood is morally wrong because it reports fiction as fact. Dressing and refining it does not change its intention. Honest people do not alter truth.

Falsifiers damage themselves by tarnishing their image and losing their credibility. Once the genie is out of the bottle, it grows too big to put back in. Spurgeon is quoted as saying, "A lie travels around the world while truth is putting on her boots."[2]

This proverb, however, identifies the severest practical consequence of dishonesty in the damage it does to other people. In jurisprudence, telling the truth and refusing to tell a lie are not the same. Silence gives consent to a false accusation simply by being mum. To neutralize a falsehood, the truth must be known. We should never underestimate the positive power of truth-telling to expose falsehood and defend the innocent.

The same is true outside the courtroom, in everyday informal situations. Reputations of innocent people are constantly at stake. Exaggerations and insinuations put their character on trial. The accused are placed at a disadvantage because the "court scene" is behind their backs. In their absence they cannot defend themselves. Desperately they need a truthful witness to defend their integrity and protect their name.

Future lives are jeopardized by treacherous people who betray them with innuendoes, and their only defense is the courage of others to speak the truth. In doing so, the "truthful witness" salvages a life that is threatened, and preserves a person's future influence for good in the world.

---

[1] John Davidson, "A Ballad of Hell," in Louis Untermeyer, ed., *Modern British Poetry* (New York: Harcourt, Brace and Co., 1950) p. 73.
[2] Charles Spurgeon, quoted in Paul Lee Tan, *Encyclopedia of 7,700 Illustrations* (Rockville, MD: Assurance Publishers, 1979) p. 563.

138 Fearing but Fearless

He who fears the Lord has a secure fortress, and for his children it will be a refuge (14:26 NIV).

Public clamor against the notion of "fearing" the Lord is justified if fearing implies that God is a tyrant. For that reason, some have translated "fear" as "respect" or "reverence."

Respect means a willingness to defer to the one respected, whether it is from honor or fear. Public school teachers get respect from students either by their position, or by their personal warmth and likableness, or from the fear of corrective punishment. A strong hand of discipline gets respect when other attempts fail. To fear the Lord does not necessarily mean to be paralyzed from committing evil by the threat of reprisal. Preferably it should mean to be activated for righteousness by the honor He deserves.

But if we think God is a pushover to be taken advantage of, He has methods of capturing our respect that we would prefer to avoid. Our security is not in *our* respect for the Lord. Our confidence is in His care and concern rather than in ourselves. He is our fortress, available for those who respect Him. He provides Himself as a refuge for those who obediently acknowledge Him as Lord of their lives.

Trusting our own cunning to exploit His generosity will not permanently succeed. He is not duped by pretended respect. Attempts to appropriate His benevolence for personal advantage deserves the strongest divine reaction. To place your confidence in an indulgent, permissive god is to wrap yourself in the arms of a fantasy. Your supposed security is in a daydream. When reality dawns, the god that does not exist will let you down.

In the precarious instability of our lives on earth, we need a divine fortress. In the fragile position that our children feel in their social group, they need a refuge! In God we have found a security pocket in the universe. Our fortress is a refuge. "Fearing" Him, we can be fearless!

Fountain of Life and Snares of Death 139

The fear of the Lord is a fountain of life, that one may avoid the snares of death (14:27 RSV, NASB).

Long before Ponce de León's quest for the fountain of youth ended in futility, Solomon had already discovered the fountain of life. This fountain has a double function in human life, a positive and a negative. It nourishes the spirits of those who drink, and it draws them away from the pitfalls of evil. Life is sustained and death is averted.

Steering clear of land mines and death traps is an arduous undertaking, because we all are vulnerable. Spurgeon warned his students, "The strong are not always vigorous, the wise not always ready, the brave not always courageous, and the joyous not always happy."[1] In our low or weak moments, when we bite on the bait and trigger the trap, we are ensnared. Goethe's personification of the fallen Lucifer tells his attending spirits to seize Faust while he is asleep: "With fairest images of dreams infold him. / Plunge him in seas of sweet untruth." Later, when Faust felt illicit lust, he said, "Within my breast [Mephistopheles] fans a lawless flame."[2] Paul said, "We wrestle . . . against principalities, against powers, against the rulers of the darkness of this world, against spiritual wickedness in high places" (Eph. 6:12 KJV).

We need more than negative moral laws. We need resources to avoid the snares. We need higher ideals to sustain us in weakness and foresight to alert us to lurking danger. We need constant inflow to nourish our souls and refortify our character. The stream of life flows from the fountainhead of God when we have a positive relationship with Him. When we respond to His relational overtures, that relationship is established.

Jesus said, "Whoever drinks the water I give him, . . . [it] will become in him a spring of water welling up to eternal life" (John 4:14 NIV).

---

[1] C. H. Spurgeon, "The Minister's Fainting Fits" (Lecture XI), *Lectures to My Students* (Lynchburg, VA: The Old Time Gospel Hour, n.d., reprint from edition in England, 1875) p. 167.
[2] Goethe, *Faust* (New York: The Macmillan Co., 1937) Part I, Scene 3, p. 60, and Scene 14, p. 142.

140 Profuse Populace or Sparse Society

In a multitude of people is the glory of a king, but without people a prince is ruined (14:28 RSV).

King Solomon did not write much in his own area of professional expertise. He was a specialist in political leadership, but his proverbs reflect his concern to guide his people in moral, pedagogic, religious, and practical matters.

This proverb, however, is a statement of political fact. Being a leader requires followers, and being a ruler requires subjects. A diminishing population reduces the chances for a prince to become a king. Also, the statue and prominence of a president or premier stands in proportion to the number of people that he/she leads. Leading for self-glory requires a glorying people. More people provide more glory. Population is a popularity prop.

My first reaction is that people do not exist to promote a leader. Rather a leader is in place to lead the people. In priority, a people is above its leadership. The leader exists to serve, not to gain glory from the people. After President Lyndon Johnson lost his popularity rating, in a sobering remark he confided, "I'd have been better off looking for immortality through my wife and children . . . instead of seeking all that love and affection from the American people. They're just too fickle."[1] Promoting oneself is self-defeating.

For more than half a century, we have heard dire predictions about the world's exploding population. More congestion creates more problems in human relationships and in food distribution. More people, however, do bolster a robust economy and supply more specialists for the collective benefit of the individual. The principle of interdependency operates more efficiently when a nation is well-occupied with people. Each person serves others and is served by the others. Creating an opportunity for a leader to lead is only a secondary effect.

---

[1] Gibbs and Duffy, *The Precher and the Presidents* (New York: Center Street, Hatchette, 2007) p. 156. The president's popularity was lost because of the Viet Nam War. The quote was made to Doris Kearns Goodwin.

He who is slow to anger has great understanding, but he who is quick-tempered exalts folly (14:29 NASB).

Some complacent people are too placid, and have to be prodded to worthy anger. When Macduff got word the king had slaughtered his wife and children, Malcolm said, "Be this the whetstone of your sword. Let grief convert to anger. Blunt not the heart. Enrage it."[1]

This proverb does not condemn righteous anger, but hasty anger. Moral anger should shake us out of cowardice and make us courageous, but even then it must be under control. Quick-tempered rage "exalts folly." It hangs the banner of foolishness on a pole to wave in the wind for the world to see. Goethe spoke of the person who is "incompetent to rule his own internal self."[2]

Remarks and real-life situations trigger what is already embedded in one's nature. Good moral natures are incensed by evil, and selfish people become indignant from personal offense. C. S. Lewis said, "Provocation does not make me an ill-tempered man. It only shows me what an ill-tempered man I am."[3]

In tranquil environments beside pacific seas, retaining serenity is not a problem. But in turbulence, stress, and tensions, personal control has high value and exhibits wisdom and "great understanding."

Our dispassionate composure in stormy tumults exposes a self-control to the world that needs to see it modeled. Orlando said, "Let gentleness my strong enforcement be, in hope [of which] I . . . hide my sword."[4]

Negative mindsets and internal hostilities can be dissolved in God's love that can fill the human heart. Paul said, "Love is patient, love is kind. . . . It is not rude, it is not self-seeking, it is not easily angered" (1 Cor. 13:4-5 NIV).

---

[1] Shakespeare, *Macbeth*, Act IV, Scene 3, lines 228-229.
[2] Goethe, *Faust* (New York: The Macmillan Co., 1937) Part II, Act II, Scene 3, p. 305.
[3] C. S. Lewis, *Mere Christianity* (New York: The Macmillan Co., 1960) p. 150.
[4] Shakespeare, *As You Like It*, Act II, Scene 7, line 119.

142 Living Flesh or Rotting Bones

A sound heart is life to the body, but envy is rottenness to the bones
(14:30 NKJV).

When the scripture speaks of the heart, ordinarily it does not refer to the organ that churns in the chest. Because the physical heart is the circulatory center that distributes nourishment to the entire body, it is used as a figure for one's spiritual heart. That heart is so deep inside that no surgeon has discovered it with a knife. It is the personality center, where intellect, sentiment, and volition converge into personhood. Since the personality is the driving dynamo for interpersonal relationships, the biblical heart is the seat of affection.

For many years, medical science has recognized an undeniable relationship between the spiritual heart and the body. Stress drains physical energy, guilt causes insomnia, hostility produces ulcers. Love is physically therapeutic. Positive attitudes invigorate the body. A chemical imbalance causes depression. Despair shortens life and hope lengthens life.

In the mystery of sleep, body and mind join hands to bow out of activity together. If either refuses, the other cannot go it alone. Macbeth said sleep is "labor's bath, balm of hurt minds, nature's second course, . . . nourisher of life's feast." He said it ruefully and pensively because his mind burned with so much guilt that he could not sleep.[1]

The word "sound" is a general term with various translations. "Rotting bones" is a graphic metaphor of declining health. The wholesome heart contributes to physical life, and the diseased heart can eventually deteriorate the skeleton.

God's x-ray vision diagnoses the moral problems of the heart. His visual beam can perform laser surgery. He can give a new personality center. He is a specialist in thoracic surgery, to do a heart transplant! He said through Ezekiel, "A new heart will I give you. . . . I will put my spirit within you" (Ez. 36:26 KJV).

---

[1] Shakespeare, *Macbeth*, Act II, Scene 2, lines 38-40, 43.

148

He who oppresses the poor reproaches his Maker, but he who is gracious to the needy honors Him (14:31 NASB).

In the Protestant church, the fundamentalist-modernist polemic of the early 20th century drove a wedge between evangelism and what was called the Social Gospel. To engage in one was understood to oppose the other. While the disputation raged, responsible elements of the church, without capturing headlines, were actively engaged in both. The Christ of God was on a mission to provide eternal salvation, yet He had time to heal the sick, feed the hungry, and give sight to the blind. Unsaved souls in healthy bodies need salvation. Healthy souls in hungry bodies need food. Neither can be avoided when the church is motivated by compassion.

Poverty is a downward spiraling syndrome that robs the poor of ambition, silences their music, buries their dreams, deprives them of higher education, and divests them of health, happiness, and hope. Of the hard-working poor man, Edwin Markham wrote, "The emptiness of the ages [is] in his face, and on his back the burden of the world."[1]

To be a part of an economic enterprise that oppresses the poor is to insult the Maker of all people. But *not* exploiting the poor is not enough to honor Him. Only those who are gracious and giving to help the hapless respect and honor Him.

The One who gave His life for the eternal salvation of humankind nevertheless wept with those who were bereaved (John 11:35). He so identified with needy people that He stood in their shoes. When we feed the hungry, clothe the naked, and visit the sick, we are feeding, clothing, and visiting Him. When we refuse to do so, we are refusing Him (Matt. 25: 35-45).

Here is what drops like a bombshell: Jesus intimated that Christians will be judged by their social service (vs. 46). And that should shock us! And sober us!

---

[1] Edwin Markham, "The Man with the Hoe," in Louis Untermeyer, ed., *Modern American Poetry* (New York: Harcourt, Brace and Co., 1950) p. 107.

144 Victim or Victor

When calamity comes the wicked are brought down, but even in death the righteous have a refuge (14:32 NIV).

As long as life runs smoothly, evil people fare rather well with temporal support. But when they are snagged on stubs and stumps, they have no retreat center. Life's greatest calamity is to have no resort in times of calamity. Righteous people can download a divine dimension as a refuge. "Under His wings" (Ps. 91:4) they have an emotional nest.

For many, death comes as a major disaster. It levels the playing field leaving no one standing. Against death, all are losers. Longfellow wrote, ". . . our hearts, though stout and brave, / Still, like muffled drums are beating / Funeral marches to the grave."[1] Humans are biodegradable. One time through is their only run. They cannot be recycled. Victimized by death, the unrighteous collapse in utter ruin!

What is life's greatest calamity for some is for others the fulfillment of life's highest hope. The bane becomes a bountiful benefit. Condemnation for one is commendation for another. At death, the unrighteous are losers and the righteous are eternal winners! Some are victims. Others are victors!

For righteous people who are prepared for death, Harriet Beecher Stowe said, "There is no . . . darkness nor shadow of death; only a bright fading as when the morning star fades in the golden dawn."[2]

C. S. Lewis further elaborated, "The dream has ended; this is the morning." Life in the Shadow-Land "was only the beginning of the real story . . . [It was] only the cover and the title page. [This] is Chapter One of the Great Story . . . which goes on forever, in which every chapter is better than the one before."[3]

---

[1] Henry W. Longfellow, "A Psalm of Life," Longfellow, *Best Loved Poems* (Chicago: Spencer Press, 1949) p. 316.
[2] Harriet Beecher Stowe, *Uncle Tom's Cabin* (New York: Everyman's Library, Alfred A. Knoph, Inc., 1994) p. 330.
[3] C. S. Lewis, *The Last Battle: Book 7 in the Chronicles* (New York: Collier Books, Macmillan, 1978) pp. 183-184.

Resting Wisdom and Growing Wisdom 145

Wisdom rests quietly in the heart of him who has understanding, but what is in the heart of fools is made known (14:33 NKJV).[1]

Superficial wisdom is spluttered and squirted from the lips of those who are only wistfully wise. Never allowed to "rest in the heart," it is kept on exhibition for instant expression. Unsolicited advice sputters out like undulating ripples from an inexhaustible spring of pretended wisdom. What others hear may resemble wisdom, but is soon recognized as folly. It is only dressed up as wisdom. Foolish people cannot for long disguise their folly. It betrays itself. The fool's foolishness is soon "made known."

Those who "have understanding" keep their wisdom in reserve, not requiring constant display. The supply is stored in the inner recesses of the mind and "heart" rather than camping out on the lips. It does not need public recognition, but it is available when needed, not used randomly, never soliciting attention. It is allowed to "rest," to repose in its resting-place, to lie tranquil in the modest attitude of the wise. Wisdom by nature is quiet.

While resting from use, wisdom by nature is also expanding. It grows when fed and diminishes when deprived. It does not simply hold its own. Like fire, wisdom cannot exist in a static state. Philosopher Douglas Soccio said, "The lessons of wisdom are . . . hard to take . . . and easy to forget."[2] Retaining wisdom requires growing in wisdom. That requires an open mind. Ideas must be bounced off other ideas in a network of notions. The process keeps the wise person alert, which keeps her humble. And that humility accelerates the wisdom.

---

[1] Translating ancient idioms and word usage into contemporary English is hard enough, but it is doubly confusing when different ancient manuscripts have various wording. That is the case with this proverb. One interpretation is that a measure of wisdom is discovered even in foolish people. Another is that foolish persons recognize wisdom when they see it in the wise. One manuscript suggests that wisdom is *not* known to fools. Here I am opting for the interpretation that seems to be most plausible—that the folly of the foolish is not concealed from public view. There is no confusion, however, about the meaning of the first clause.

[2] Douglas J. Soccio, *Archetypes of Wisdom* (Belmont, CA: Wadsworth/Thomas Learning, 2001) p. 545.

146 Noble Nation or Crumbling Culture

Righteousness exalts a nation, but sin is a reproach to any people
(14:34 NKJV).

During the Civil War, when someone wondered whether the Lord was "on our side," President Lincoln said that he was more concerned whether we were "on the Lord's side." He added, "I know the Lord is always on the side of the right."[1] Contrary to the opinion of some, the Christian religion holds no monopoly on moral righteousness. Social mores among all people groups are surprisingly similar. Comparable cross-cultural moral codes are noteworthy. Ethical universals are startling! Chesterton said, "On plains of opal, under cliffs cut out of pearl, you would still find a notice-board, 'Thou shalt not steal.'"[2] A nation's moral DNA is in the center of every cell of public life as a blueprint either for health or a crumbling culture.

Cultural evil is a curse and a scandal. The Bolshevik revolution with its millions of atrocities is off the stage. Nazism with its holocaust was wiped out. Slave-holding states were soundly defeated and suffered the devastation of reconstruction. In the Old Testament, God precipitated the destruction of those groups that ceremonially burned their children in fire. Both institutionalized evil and cumulative personal immorality are repugnant to a righteous God. Hating homosexuals and condoning their sin are both loathsome evils to God. Marketing entertainment to the worst human instincts is morally nauseating.

Some of our American ideals and sacrificial acts of goodness make my chest swell with patriotic pride. Some of our publicly approved corruption drives me to pray with Rudyard Kipling, "Judge of all nations, spare us yet, / Lest we forget—lest we forget!"[3]

---

[1] John C. McCollister, *God and the Oval Office* (Nashville: W Publishing Group of Thomas Nelson, 2005) p. 81.
[2] G. K. Chesterton, "The Blue Cross," *Favorite Father Brown Stories* (New York: Dover Pub., Inc., 1993) p. 13.
[3] Rudyard Kipling, "Recessional," Louis Untermeyer, ed., *Modern British Poetry* (New York: Harcourt, Brace, & Co., 1950) p. 136. This poem-prayer was about the United Kingdom.

The king's favor is toward a servant who acts wisely, but his anger is toward him who acts shamefully (14:35 NASB).

This is a picture of the king's minister who serves as what we Americans call Secretary of State, or Secretary of Defense, on the president's cabinet. Those are positions of service, and those who fill them are public servants.

Discreet servants know well their areas of service, and they have relational skills in representing their nation. Their wisdom wins respect, and they dignify their nation by their own distinction. The president reciprocates with favor. Those who shame their nation by foolish maneuvers or tactless relationships jeopardize their nation and incur the president's anger. In this proverb, we see basic principles of servanthood.

A slight change in the proverb's translation will point out basic principles of leadership. Kings who favor their subjects produce servants who reciprocate the favor by representing their king wisely. And stern, angry leaders create morale problems and produce subjects who dishonor their leader and shame their nation. The treatment works both ways.

King Duncan thanked his army general for conquering the opposition by saying, "More is thy due than more than all can pay." The general responded, "The service and loyalty I owe, in doing it, pays itself."[1] That is the kind of mutual respect, appreciation, and honor that builds empires. And successful businesses. And close-knit families!

More is accomplished by relationships than by the strong hand of power or the timid response of fear. Good leaders have the attitude of servants. Successful leaders know how to follow. When their humility kicks in, they get what they want from other people the easy way.

---

[1] Shakespeare, *Macbeth*, Act I, Scene 4, lines 21, 22-23. These lines illustrate my point, but the story is skewed because the general was not sincere and was plotting against the king.

148 Harsh Reaction or Gentle Response

A soft answer turns away wrath, but a harsh word stirs up anger
(15:1 NKJV).

Pain inflicted by the tongue goes deeper and lasts longer than pain produced by the fist. Confrontational people expend their lives making people around them unhappy, accumulating to their own record untold volumes of hurt in unknown numbers of people.

Those who are not mature enough to absorb the pain attempt to throw it back on the one who caused it. But that person is often out of reach, so their pop-off valve bursts on whoever is in the way.

George Eliot said, "It is seldom that the miserable can help regarding their misery as wrongfully inflicted by those who are less miserable."[1]

Usually those who speak sharply are communicating a message that is not included in the definition of their words. They are saying, "I am hurting," and they are attempting to shift some of the hurt on you to lighten the load. If you do not pick up the subliminal message, you are apt to react by throwing your hurt back on them to get relief for yourself. Now their hurt is further compounded, and they return it to you. The conflict becomes a fistfight with the tongue, each attempting to land the last punch. At this point, whoever started the spat is beside the point. Each is simply reacting to the latest provocation. You have allowed yourself to be pulled into a duel using tongues as swords.

How much easier it would be to have "turned away" the initial insult with a softer response! By "losing your cool" you lose control of the situation. By "keeping your cool" you stay in control.

When Orlando threatened to use force, the Duke said, "Your gentleness shall force more than your force [will] move us to gentleness."[2] Soft answers work!

---

[1] George Eliot, *Silas Marner*, in Loban and Olmsted, eds., *Adventures in Appreciation* (New York: Harcourt, Brace & World, Inc., 1963) pp. 689-690.
[2] Shakespeare, *As You Like It*, Act II, Scene 7, lines 102-103.

Using Wisdom or Gushing Foolishness 149

The tongue of the wise uses knowledge rightly, but the mouth of fools pours forth foolishness (15:2 NKJV).

Humans are inveterate talkers. Gag orders rarely work. From foolish mouths, folly *gushes* out (NIV), *spouts* out (NASB), *pours* out (RSV), *spews* out (Jerus). Those who are quick-speaks cut out those who are slow of speech, and strong, penetrating voices overwhelm those with weaker voice. Tongues that are placed on automatic pilot are unbearably boring. Those speakers delude themselves to believe they are entertaining performers! With foolishness, as Kipling said, we are "shouting across seas of misunderstanding."[1]

Wise tongues *utter useful* knowledge (ABPS), *adorn* it (Rhm), *distill* it (Jerus), *commend* it (NIV), *dispense* it (RSV), *use* it *aright* (KJV). Wisdom knows when to speak, how to speak, and what to say for the circumstance.

Distributing information appropriately is both an art and a science. Here are suggestions to improve both conversational talk and public speaking.

Have something worth saying. Talking about nothing conditions people to tune you out. Curtail your speak. Verbosity detracts. Silence can be eloquent. Some big-boulder ideas cannot be delivered with words. They deserve speechlessness. On some subjects, "the greatest eloquence seems to stutter," said the Chinese mystic Lao-tzu.[2] Keep it interesting. Make every word count. Lazy lines lull people. Speak with staccato. Too much flow is sleepy. Vary the speed. Run nonsubstantive lines rapidly. Vary the emphasis, inflection, and modulation. Generally, curtail hand motions, and limit body language to "suggestive" facial expressions. Give creative vocal interpretation. Do not allow your personality to overshadow the content of what you say. Allow words to do their work, and trust them to do what only words can do.

---

[1] Rudyard Kipling, *The Light that Failed* (New York: Books, Inc., n.d.) p. 169.
[2] Douglas J. Soccio, *Archetypes of Wisdom* (Belmont, CA: Wadsworth/Thomas Learning, 2001) p. 31.

150 Everything Seen, Nothing Concealed

*The eyes of the Lord are in every place, keeping watch on the evil
and the good* (15:3 NKJV).

The biblical notion of God's omnipresence is not that He is
so vast that He fills all of space. That would limit our access to
that small portion of God nearest us. Rather the picture is that God
occupies every mathematical point in space as a whole, complete
Person at every moment of time. He is indivisible and undiluted.
C. S. Lewis said, "He dwells within the seed of the smallest flower
and is not cramped."[1]   Those who have difficulty discovering
where God *is* find it even harder to say where He *is not*.

That means not only that we have access to Him, but He
has unlimited access to us. We have no place to hide from His
ubiquity. God's vision is not limited to light rays and photons. He
sees in the dark. He eyeballs us when we are crouched behind
blind corners or concealed in dark pockets. He reads between
every line of our lives. God said, "My eyes are on all their ways;
they are not hidden from me, nor is their sin concealed from my
eyes" (Jer. 16:17 NIV).

Browning's Paracelsus said, "I want to be forgotten by
God,"[2] but Solomon warned, "God will bring every deed into
judgment, including every hidden thing, . . . good or evil" (Ecc. 12:14
NIV).

Whatever God has that are analogous to eyes, they are
intensely focused on His devout children. He sees in detail the
pain and the problems. Civilla Martin wrote the gospel song, "His
eye is on the sparrow, and I know He watches me." No good deed,
no honorable thought, no noble motive escapes His scrutiny.
Alone, isolated on a lonely island with little hope of rescue,
Robinson Crusoe said, "The eyes of an infinite power search into
the remotest corner of the world and send help to the miserable."[3]

---

[1] C. S. Lewis, *Perelandra* (New York: Macmillan Publishing Co., Inc., 1944)
pp. 214-215.
[2] Robert Browning, *Paracelsus*, Horace E. Scudder, ed., *The Complete Poetic
and Dramatic Works of Robert Browning* (Cambridge, MA: Houghton Mifflin
Co., 1895) p. 44.
[3] Daniel Defoe, *Robinson Crusoe* (Garden City, NY: Doubleday, 1945) p. 295.

A wholesome tongue is a tree of life, but perverseness in it breaks the spirit (15:4 NKJV).

In a funny little scene in *Don Quixote*, a curate, a parson, and a barber enter and purge the knight's library to cure him of his "knightly disease." Some books are sentenced to death and are thrown out the window to be burned. One volume is sentenced to prison never to be read.[1]

In our morally fallen world, all humans have been wounded and their spirits crushed. Petulant tongues have stabbed their egos. The problem is too dire to be corrected by burning their books. They need friends with wholesome tongues through whom God's Spirit can apply medicinal balm, like the life-giving fruit of a living tree. Band-aids are not adequate. Too many torturing tongues keep re-opening old wounds. The life of God is best appropriated through the warm expressions of Christian friends.

The difference between the two tongues is seen in the works of two American authors. Edgar Allan Poe was a mechanically perfect poet and brilliant storywriter, whose talent I love, but whose dark themes are discouraging and depressing. Henry Wadsworth Longfellow did not avoid life's pathos, but his works are encouraging and optimistic. He wrote: "The unattained / In life at last, / When life is past, / Shall all be gained."[2] When he heard church bells on Christmas morning, he disdainfully wrote: "Hate is strong, and mocks the song / Of peace on earth, goodwill to men." Then on better thought, he wrote: "Then pealed the bells more loud and deep: / 'God is not dead, nor doth He sleep; / The wrong shall fail, the right prevail, / With peace on earth, goodwill to men.'"[3] Bad tongues give wounding words; good tongues give healing hope.

---

[1] Miguel de Cervantes, *Don Quixote of the Mancha* (New York: P. F. Collier & Son, 1909, 1937) pp. 48-54.

[2] Henry Wadsworth Longfellow, "Some Day, Some Day," Richard Aldington, ed., *The Viking Book of Poetry* (New York: The Viking Press, 1958) Vol. II, p. 828.

[3] Longfellow, "I Heard the Bells on Christmas Day," *The Broadman Hymnal* (Nashville: Broadman, 1940) # 148.

152 To Reject or to Regard

A fool despises his father's instruction, but he who receives reproof is prudent (15:5 NKJV).

Prudent persons are separated from the foolish by many huge chasms, one of which is their willingness to hear advice. Good counsel is often screened out by sleepy, insolent ears. Priceless advice is deemed worthless by the cynic who dismisses it with a sneer. Oscar Wilde said, "A cynic is a man who knows the price of everything and the value of nothing."[1] Because parental advice sometimes includes reproof, it is rejected before it is heard.

Many who refuse advice from their parents take advice too quickly from others. Suggestion-prone persons have no cognitive or moral mesh for evaluating and screening unsolicited suggestions. Lacking self-confidence, they are easy prey for misdirection.

Wise people attempt to learn something about the advisor's worldview, values, biases, integrity, and experience, and they measure the advice against their own values and experience. They are cautious about personality appeal and bandwagon psychology ("everybody's doing it"). They analyze *why* one says *what*. They ask for reasons, and weigh them. Being clever, they are quick to perceive and avoid clever tricks and traps.

Getting wise professional counsel can be expensive, but people with parents can have free counsel from persons who are rich in experience and who care deeply about their children. Parental advice is a short-cut to knowledge. It is the easy way to get direction. Some are wise enough to regard it, and gain from it. Others are foolish enough to reject it, and lose by it. Those who refuse to listen usually have to learn the lessons they have rejected by painful or humiliating experience. Others never learn.

Here is the best advice on this page: Invite advice from your parents. Do not wait until it is offered. They will be complimented, and you will be wiser.

---

[1] Manuel Velasquez, *Philosophy: A Text with Readings* (Belmont, CA: Wadsworth Publishing Co., 1999) p. 496.

The house of the righteous contains great treasure, but the income of the wicked brings them trouble (15:6 NIV).

This conversation is not about either wealth or poverty. It is about what we do with what we have and what we allow it to do for us. Righteousness or unrighteousness in financial matters determines our wealth or poverty in values that are deeper and higher. Material income is the tool for something better or something worse. For the righteous, prosperity is a blessing. For the wicked, it is a bane. We can use it either to help us or to harm us.

The righteous keep prosperity in perspective, yielding deeper treasures of gratitude, humility, faith, generosity, family bonding, appreciation for the intangibles of art, spiritual realities, and moral character. Our lives are enriched with greater treasures. The unrighteous lose perspective on prosperity, leading to pride, selfishness, excess emphasis on luxuries and pleasure, distorted relationships, irresponsibility in other areas, loss of appreciation for the intangibles of life.

Righteousness makes what one has mean more, with ever increasing benefits. Unrighteousness makes what one has mean less, with diminishing returns. For one, it is the means to a greater end. For the other, it is the end in itself. A dead-end!

Because righteousness keeps prosperity in perspective with greater values, poverty is likewise kept in perspective. The treasures of righteousness are retained when prosperity is gone, and even poverty can be used for greater values. After runaway slaves George Harris and his wife were reunited in a Quaker home, he said, "Eliza, people that have houses, and lands, and money . . . can't love as we do, who have nothing but each other."[1]

When our lives are seasoned with righteous attitudes and motives, losses can become gains, misfortune can produce treasures, and deficits can become dividends.

---

[1] Harriet Beecher Stowe, *Uncle Tom's Cabin* (New York: Everyman's Library, Alfred A. Knoph, Inc., 1994) p. 215.

154 Wise Lips and Foolish Hearts

The lips of the wise disperse knowledge, but the heart of the fool does not do so (15:7 NKJV).

"He who *knows* and *knows* that he *knows* is wise—follow him. He who *knows not* and *knows not* that he *knows not* is a fool—shun him."[1] The two lines of this abridged paraphrase from Lady Burton depict the two categories of the proverb. Archbishop Fulton Sheen distinguished between *the intellectuals* and *the intelligentsia.* "The intelligentsia," he said, "are those who are educated beyond their intelligence."[2] The fools in the second category may have knowledge, but they do not have wise hearts for dispersing it appropriately.

The Hebrew word translated "disperse" means also to "winnow," as in separating the chaff from the wheat. The idea is that wise lips act as a winnowing machine, filtering good ideas and important knowledge. Wisdom culls the useless from the useful and scatters only the seeds of knowledge that are valuable and helpful. The rest is not expressed.

The foolish have no mechanism for screening out the bad, so the lips spit it all out. Instead of sifting their knowledge and distributing what is needful, they dump it all on whoever will listen. Freight loads of folly are unloaded without discrimination. Eager for others to think they are knowledgeable, they lack the lips of wisdom to spread pristine knowledge and virgin truth. In a culture that accents sensationalism, truth and value are too much accepted or rejected by the mood of the moment. Wise ears are scarce. Many are left without an intelligent guide. Disseminating religious, moral, or practical truth is a hefty responsibility. James cautioned against "presuming to be teachers," warning that teachers "will be judged more strictly" (Ja. 3:1 NIV). The challenge is to podium professors, pulpit preachers, Sunday School teachers, and group leaders—yes, and to writers. A word to the wise . . . !

---

[1] Quoted by Manuel Velasquez, *Philosophy: A Text with Readings* (Belmont: CA: Wadsworth, 1999) p. 466.
[2] Fulton J. Sheen, "Bottom-Line Theology," *Christianity Today*, June 3, 1977, p. 11.

Evil Sacrifices or Upright Prayers 155

The sacrifice of the wicked is an abomination to the Lord, but the prayer of the upright is His delight (15:8 KJV, NKJV, NASB, RSV).

In many pagan religions, sacrifices were made to win the favor of the gods, hoping against hope for forgiveness and life after death. Hebrew sacrifices testified to the people's strong faith in God's provision for forgiveness, not fully realizing it entailed the future sacrifice of Christ. But another important difference grabs our attention. Hebrew sacrifices were acts of obedience to God's specific requirement, symbolizing their willingness to live morally righteous lives. Observing the ceremonial law was never a substitute for complying with moral law.

In the Christian faith, prayers for forgiveness replace ceremonial sacrifices, but living by the moral law has not been displaced. Petitions without obedience are just as fruitless as empty sacrifices. Religious observance without a reformed lifestyle "is an abomination to the Lord." Playing religious playhouse stands a person in no better stead for salvation than ritual routines. God is not an angry deity waiting to be pacified by pagan sacrifices! He cannot be bought off by the religious gestures of evil persons hoping to strike a bargain!

After King Claudius killed his own brother to take his wife, he bewailed his dastardly deed and cried: "My offence is rank. It smells to heaven!" Then he complained, "I cannot pray. . . . I cannot be forgiven because I still possess the effects for which I did the murder. May one be pardoned and retain what he won from his offense?"[1]

The answer is a resounding no! God scolded the Hebrews: "To what purpose is the multitude of your sacrifices? When you make many prayers, I will not hear. Put away the evil doings from before mine eyes. Cease to do evil." Then, "though your sins be as scarlet, they shall be as white as snow!" (Is. 1:11-18 abridged, KJV).

---

[1] Shakespeare, *Hamlet*, Act III, Scene 3, lines 35-57. These lines, while using the original words, are here paraphrased for clarity.

156 Devine Displeasure and Delight

The way of the wicked is an abomination to the Lord, but he loves him who pursues righteousness (15:9 RSV, NASB).

God's emotional feelings are not loosely attached and left to flutter in unpredictable ways. His displeasure with the sinner and delight with the righteous are feelings that arise from a sentiment that is deeper and more enduring than either.

That sentiment is something like a disposition or a basic motive. It is like patriotism, which is a sentiment that can cause gaiety or festivity or pride, or even shame. It remains in place through the ebb and flow of feelings that are attached. Sentiment is that part of love or friendship that is deeper than momentary feelings. Marital love is constant while the feelings connected to the love fluctuate with various situations. I can even feel anger if my spouse is insulted, and that anger is specifically an expression of my love for her. Love is a sentiment that can throw up all sorts of emotions.

God's immutable moral sentiment is for goodness and righteousness. It is permanent and unalterable, and precipitates feelings in agreement with itself. Those feelings are automatic to an integrated personality with a holy disposition. God is repulsed by "the way of the wicked" and pleased with the pursuit of righteousness. The way we live gives Him displeasure or delight!

In Hebrew, the verb for "pursue" is intensive, implying an intensified intention that stretches every effort for righteousness. That kind of resolve requires the regenerating work of God's Spirit in the human heart. Even Aristotle who knew nothing of the Hebrew God said, A virtuous life is "too high for man; for it is not insofar as he is man that he will live so, but insofar as something divine is present in him."[1]

Paul said we can have "regeneration and renewal in the Holy Spirit" (Tit. 3:5 RSV), and Christ can "dwell in our hearts" (Eph. 3:17). That presence can continually regenerate our intentional purposiveness to pursue the righteous life.

---

[1] Aristotle, *Nichomachean Ethics*, Book X, Chapter 7, p. 533 in McKeon.

Correction and Reproof 157

Correction is grievous unto him that forsaketh the way, and he that hateth reproof shall die (15:10 KJV).

Whether "the correction that comes is grievous" or "grievous correction will come," as the alternate translation says, they broadly shake out to the same thing. Correction is something that the best people do not need and the worst people will not take. It can be avoided by staying on the right path.

For those who attempt a detour, grievous times await. First off, they are grieved by correction. If they continue to stray, grievousness is hardened into "hating reproof." To run free from "the way" is to run out of control. It is living life against itself. As one continues to resist reproof, repercussions become increasingly severe until one abruptly reaches dead end. Derek Kidner says, "To be wayward is asking for a lesson; to be unteachable is asking for death."[1]

In this proverb, "shall die" may refer to premature death as a bad end. Solomon did not generally appeal to life after death, but some think "death" in this proverb implies the future state. In his drama, Goethe says emphatically, "What's done's already done, alas! / What follows it must come to pass." Then the sinner falls into the prison of evil spirits who torment her. When Faust attempts a rescue, she refuses, saying, "There's no hope any more. . . . Tis all in vain."[2] In life, detours are divergent routes that do not reconnect! Destinations are altered!

Correction though grievous is better than death, whatever death means. We can accept reproof and get back on path. And heed Browning's advice: ". . . welcome each rebuff / That turns earth's smoothness rough. / . . . Be our joys three parts pain, / . . . Hold cheap the strain."[3] Paul said, "Now is the time of God's favor, now is the day of salvation" (2 Cor. 6:2 NIV).

---

[1] Derek Kidner, *Proverbs*, D. J. Wiseman, ed., *Tyndale O. T. Commentaries* (Downers Grove, IL: IVP, 1964) p. 114.
[2] Goethe, *Faust* (New York: The Macmillan Co., 1937) First Part, Scenes 19, 25, pp. 165-169, 204-205.
[3] Robert Browning, "Rabbi Ben Ezra," *Norton Anthology of English Lit* (New York: Norton Co., 1962) p. 864.

158 Hidden but Visible

Sheol and Abaddon lie open before the Lord, how much more the hearts of men (15:11 NASB, RSV)!

Getting inside the minds of ancient writers is not easy. The weird words that open the proverb are cloudy and confusing. Whatever specifics they may connote, they refer in general to the dark netherworld of departed human spirits, a social environment that is opaque and invisible to human eyes. The point of the proverb is that, if the sharp eyes of God can penetrate that subterranean darkness, He certainly can read the thoughts and motives of human hearts.

Lady Macbeth, strategizing criminality, prays to the darkness, "Come, thick night, and [cover my sin] in the smoke of hell, . . . that heaven peep [not] through the blanket of the dark."[1] Evil people may delude themselves in thinking God "covers his face and never sees" (Ps. 10:11 NIV), but the scripture declares, "[God] alone knows the hearts of all men" (1 Kgs. 8:39 NIV).

Heaven's laser light not only penetrates the dark to expose every act of evil, but God's X-ray eyes see every evil intent of the heart that has not yet been actualized. God sees beneath what we do. He sees what we are. All our secret thoughts are naked before Him. He sees the motive that we ourselves are not aware of—that latent motive which in a certain circumstance could be activated for atrocious evil. We need to pray with the psalmist, "Search my, O God, and know my heart. . . . See if there is any offensive way in me, and lead me in the way everlasting" (Ps. 139:23-24 NIV).

Here is the good side of the truth. Those divine eyes that cannot miss the bad see also every good deed, every unselfish motive, every noble impulse, every generous intent! Nothing is concealed. Everything is disclosed. The virtues in you that others have missed are not overlooked by God. His eyes are wide open to every upright act. And He rejoices! Selah!

---

[1] Shakespeare, *Macbeth*, Act I, Scene 5, lines 51-54.

164

A scoffer does not love one who reproves him, nor will he go to the wise (15:12 NKJV).

Whether the original meant "does not like the one who reproves" or "does not like to be reproved" is open to question. But the two ordinarily go together. In time, those who do not like to be reproved come to dislike those who do the reproving. Students who do not want to be taught do not like their teachers. Those who reject behavioral correction shun prophetic preachers and moralists. Freeloaders resent the lessons that come from hardworkers.

Those who do not want to hear truth detest those who refuse to shade the truth. King Ahab said, "There is still one man through whom we can inquire of the Lord, but I hate him, because he never prophesies anything good about me, but always bad" (1 Kgs. 22:8 NIV). A reproof is gentler and kindlier than a rebuke or a reprimand, yet those who reject reproof may become insolent scoffers, disrespectfully scorning those who would admonish them to higher ideals.

Not all advice, of course, is good. The bad should not be taken to heart. We are in as much trouble taking all advice as refusing all advice. Wise persons accept wise advice from wise people. And they are humble enough to solicit it without waiting for it to come unsolicited.

Many today lay out large sums for professional counsel, but divine direction from the Master Sage comes free of charge and is rarely sought. Those who will can digest daily counsel from the written Word of God. Isaiah said Christ is the "Wonderful Counselor" (Is. 9:6). A Hebrew psalmist declared, "O how I love Thy law! It is my meditation all the day. Thy commandments make me wise. . . . I have more insight than all my teachers. . . . I understand more than the aged" (Ps. 119:97-100 NASB). Another psalmist sang: "How blessed is the man who does not walk in the counsel of the wicked . . . nor sit in the seat of the scoffers! But his delight is in the law of the Lord, and in His law he meditates day and night" (Ps. 1:1-2 NASB).

160 Joyful Heart or Broken Spirit

A joyful heart makes a cheerful face, but when the heart is sad, the spirit is broken (15:13 NASB).

A broken spirit is worse than a sad heart. The implication here is that a sad heart can lead to a broken spirit, which gives a glum face. The secret solution is never to allow heart-hurt to break the spirit. Switching a sorrowful heart to a joyful heart can brighten the face with a cheerful smile. Sympathy between mind and body causes each to affect the other.

The hymnist Fanny Crosby was blind from infancy, had a disappointing marriage, and was devastated by the death of her only child. Yet at age 84 she said, "People grow old because they are not cheerful."[1] She lived cheerfully until she died at 95. Shakespeare said, "Receive what cheer you may. / The night is long that never finds a day."[2]

Bypassing the heart when reaching for happiness places happiness on a tenuous foundation. Happiness based on happenings is collapsible. Our limited ability to manipulate circumstances should force us to develop a joyful heart. No happiness is stable when what produces it is out of control. We need something to fall back on. Those who would have joy must go beyond fun-thrills in packaged entertainment and physical pleasures. Goethe said, "Who seeks for good must first be good; / Who seeks for joy must moderate his blood."[3]

When we prioritize God in our lives, we have an unshakable source of joy to sustain us in the darkest hours of circumstance. His fellowship supports our spirits. His assurance of a bright future boosts our hope. C. S. Lewis said, "God . . . is the fuel our spirits were designed to burn, the food our spirits were designed to feed on."[4] A psalmist sang, God is "my exceeding joy" (Ps. 43:4). God Himself said, "I will . . . give them joy for their sorrow" (Jer. 31:13).

---

[1] Robert J. Morgan, *Then Sings My Soul: Hymn Stories* (Nashville: Thomas Nelson, 2006) p. 435.
[2] Shakespeare, *Macbeth*, Act IV, Scene 3, lines 239-240.
[3] Goethe, *Faust*, Second Part, Act I, Scene 2, p. 226.
[4] C. S. Lewis, *Mere Christianity* (New York: The Macmillan Co., 1960) p. 39.

Heart Seeking and Mouth Feeding 161

The discerning heart seeks knowledge, but the mouth of a fool feeds on folly (15:14 NIV).

Note four contrasts in this capsule: the heart and the mouth, the discerning and the foolish, seeking and feeding, knowledge and folly. To seek with the heart means the search is sincere rather than serendipitous. Goethe's Wagner said, "Erudition . . . is my ambition."[1] Longfellow's Evangeline said, "Whither my heart has gone, there follows my hand."[2]

The difference between seeking and feeding is that one is purposeful and the other is perfunctory. One is focused while the other is random. One goes for knowledge; the other settles for folly.

There are short cuts to getting degrees, but no short cuts to an education. In our culture more people are reading trade books and cheap novels while their exposure to the classics is through abridged editions, films, and comic book versions. Biblical knowledge comes through Bible stories, videos, and power-point presentations rather than the text itself.

"Fools feed on folly!" Solomon used strong language. Instead of hungering for knowledge, they salivate for what is stimulating. They relish the clever. Minds that flit and flutter require no discipline.

In our culture, we nibble around the edges of knowledge while Homer, Horace, Virgil, Plato, Aristotle, Augustine, Anselm, Aquinas, Dante, Milton sit on the library shelves waiting to make our acquaintance.

Our inadequate store of knowledge should give us the attitudes of humility and inquisitiveness, which are the two basic ingredients in the recipe for being wise, discerning persons. Instead of foolishly feeding our faces on trifling trivia, as we focus our hearts on the knowledge that belongs to the discerning, we become wiser and weightier persons.

---

[1] Goethe, *Faust*, First Part, Scene 1, p. 27.
[2] Henry W. Longfellow, "Evangeline," *Best Loved Poems of Longfellow* (Chicago: The Spencer Press, 1949) Second Part, Section I, p. 65.

162 Bad Days but Glad Hearts

All the days of the afflicted are bad, but a cheerful heart has a continual feast (15:15 NASB).

King Claudius said, "When sorrows come, they come not is single spies, but in battalions!"[1] So it seems to many people. Suffering is not equitably distributed, but it is thorough. Even the most fortunate have not escaped. Since it is not possible to avoid all afflictions, our recourse is to minimize their effects. Orlando said, "Live a little! Comfort a little! Cheer thyself a little!"

By default we have to resort to inner resources that can dilute and dispel the effects of outward problems. If those resources are lacking, we have little to fall back on. Instead of *sparing* us *from* all trials, God wants to *equip* us *for* the trials, with inner joy and strength.

The final solution to suffering is to be found in the next life. Some disparage that solution for resorting to a future world. But the anticipation of that solution is in this present life, giving hope to the hopeless and cheering the sad. It can motivate hope when there is otherwise no hope. "If in this life only we have hope . . . , we are of all men most miserable" (1 Cor. 15:19 KJV).

When Uncle Tom finally died, after a lifetime of unthinkable suffering, the "last ray of earthly hope went out in night, and . . . in the blackness of earthly darkness, the firmament of the unseen . . . blazed with stars."[3] For those prepared for the next life, the firmament of the unseen will someday blaze with starlight! Oliver Wendell Holmes spoke of the "endless melodies" of life, "as sad as earth, as sweet as heaven."[4] Furnished and fortified with the expectation of future life with Christ, our hearts can "continually feast" on "cheerful" joy while background dinner music rings in our souls—as sweet as heaven! We can have glad hearts even on bad days.

---

[1] Shakespeare, *Hamlet*, Act IV, Scene 5, lines 66-67.
[3] Harriet Beecher Stowe, *Uncle Tom's Cabin* (New York: Everyman's Library, Alfred A. Knoph, Inc., 1994) p. 451.
[4] Oliver W. Holmes, "The Voiceless," *The Viking Book of Poetry* (New York: Viking Press, 1958) Vol. II, p. 831.

Better is a little with the fear of the Lord than great treasure with trouble (15:16 NKJV).

Schumacher said, "Small is beautiful,"[1] and Solomon said, "Little is better." A little with righteousness is better than a lot with trouble. A modest income is not better than riches, but it is better than the problems that often attach to riches. A package of modest and righteous living is better than a package of "treasure with trouble" or "wealth with worry" (Mof).

The anxiety and vexation that frequently accompany wealth can be tormenting. Those with heavy investments fret over the stock market. The wealthy are more vulnerable to robbery, or to kidnapping for ransom. An inflated lifestyle can capture and control one's psyche. It becomes mentally addictive. Heavy consumers are themselves consumed with consumerism. Working for more wealth can become habitual, preempting adequate diversion. A woman wrote to Ann Landers' advice column that she was "trapped by success." She said, "I envy the modest families who have one car and a small house."[2]

Of course, many wealthy people are righteous and many poor are evil. But for some, the loss of affluence can be liberating, like a heavy load rolling off the back. *Rich* treasures become greater than "*great* treasures." When Mr. Micawber was reunited with his wife, he exclaimed, "Welcome poverty! Welcome hunger, rags, and beggary! Mutual confidence is restored. . . . [It] will sustain us to the end!"[3] Over 150 years ago Adelaide Procter prayed: "I thank thee, Lord, that thou hast kept / The best in store; / We have enough, yet not too much, / To long for more; / A yearning for a deeper peace / Not known before."[4]

---

[1] *Small Is Beautiful* is the title of E. F. Schumacher's book (New York: Harper & Row, 1973).
[2] "Ann Landers" newspaper column, P*ittsburgh Post-Gazette,* Pittsburgh, PA, 17 Feb. 1969, p. 24.
[3] Charles Dickens, *David Copperfield,* in *Best Loved Books* (Pleasantville, NY: Reader's Digest As'n., 1966) p. 407.
[4] Adelaide Anne Procter's hymn, "My God, I Thank Thee," *The Methodist Hymnal* (Nashville: The Methodist Publishing House, 1966) p. 50.

164 Vegetable Plate or Stall-fed Steak

Better is a dinner of herbs where love is, than a fatted calf with hatred (15:17 NKJV).

Dining is social rather than solitary. When eating alone, food loses its savory seasoning. It is bland and boring. Flavors become flat and unfriendly. Solo eating is unfair to the chef's recipe. Fellowship dinners are lavishly gratifying. Together, food and fellowship make for fun!

Eating in a context of antisocial relationships is even worse than eating alone. Bitterness and hostility, though served with civility, drain off piquant flavors, leaving the experience dull and disappointing. Even a meager meal with loving relationships is preferable to a sumptuous supper with tension and conflict. Vegetable plates combined with love are exquisitely delicious, but a mixture of stall-fed veal cutlets with hate is nauseous to the delicate taste. The human soul has fastidious taste buds that are not satiated with food alone.

Family table time should be served with delicious dishes of fellowship and positive support. It should include genuine interest in what each is willing to share. It should be free from little barbs and pricks. Parental scolding and correction should be reserved for other times. All parents need frequent attitude checks. Going through the motions of pretended love will soon betray your real disposition. Brutus said, "When love begins to sicken and decay, it uses an enforced ceremony."[1] Genuine love is expressed in transparent attitudes more than in words.

Lon Woodrum's character says, "Make me not a stranger to your mind. . . . I must not be half-resident, half-guest. I must be at home in your heart."[2] Making others feel at home in your heart requires forgetting yourself and focusing on them, not attempting to make an impression but willing to be impressed. It requires a measure of self-deprecation and vulnerability, because that is the nature of love. And that multiplies the merit of a meal!

---

[1] Shakespeare, *Julius Caesar*, Act IV, Scene 2, lines 20-21.
[2] Lon Woodrum, *Eternity in Their Heart* (Grand Rapids: Zondervan Pub. House, 1955) p. 190.

Arousing Strife or Allaying Strife 165

A wrathful man stirs up strife, but he who is slow to anger allays contention (15:18 NKJV).

Altercations come more from emotional discord than from mental disagreements. When anger is out of control, it loses direction and focus. It shoots shotgun style instead of rifle, hitting anyone in a broad range. Shakespeare's character was so inflamed with indignation that he said, "Had I power, I should pour the sweet milk of concord into hell, uproar the universal peace, confound all unity on earth."[1] The primary principle in producing terrorism is to create such anger that terrorists have no problem taking it out on innocent people.

Craving a fracas, angry persons find an easy fight with like-tempered people, which cool-natured persons avoid. Those who are out of control resonate with those who are out of control. Angry persons first attract each other and then repel each other, resulting in a feud. They are pawns to the situation because they are slaves to their uncontrolled temperament. Goethe said, "They fight, we're told, their freedom's right to save; / But, clearlier still, tis slave that fights with slave."[2] Most brawls require two people who are enslaved to their anger.

Those who control themselves can more easily control relationships and situations. Instead of entertaining the monster inside, they find appropriate ways to vent. Grudges dissolve in a sympathetic disposition. Love begins to function, creating an inner climate in which the negative reactionary pattern is modified and eventually broken.

When being loved by God grips them, they "learn to live loved," as William Young said.[3] Living as a loved person, they are equipped to be catalysts for defusing the conflicts of the world. Hot-tempered persons arouse strife while cool-natured people allay strife.

---

[1] Shakespeare, *Macbeth*, Act IV, Scene 3, lines 97-99.
[2] Goethe, *Faust*, Second Part, Act II, Scene 2, p. 303.
[3] William P. Young, *The Shack* (Newbury Park, CA: Windblown Media, 2007) p. 175.

166 Learning to Labor

The way of the sluggard is as a hedge of thorns, but the path of the upright is a highway (15:19 NASB).

In one of Aesop's fables, a hungry jackdaw perched on the limb of a fig tree waiting for the figs to ripen. A clever fox came by and said, "Don't fool yourself, my friend. You can feed on hopes, but they won't make you fat!"[1]

A slothful sluggard, too lazy to work, hopes against hope that his hopes will be handed to him. He is facing an imagined "hedge of thorns" that he is too work-shy to tackle. If he were energetic, he would discover the difficulties are not invincible. Unwilling to expend the effort, his own imagination becomes a thorny hedge that he cannot get through.

Feeding on futile hopes that end only in themselves will not nourish one to health. "They won't make you fat." False hope makes us lethargic, demotivating us from the pursuit of enterprises that genuine hope can motivate us to achieve. The result is fruitless and frivolous futility.

Goethe's chorus sang: "Wouldest thou win desires unbounded, / Yonder see the glory burn! / Lightly is thy life surrounded— / Sleep's a shell, to break and spurn!"[2] It is true that what you *do* is less important than what you *are*, but what you *are* determines what you *do*, and what you *do* reflects what you *are*.

Industrious people focus on the goal and give themselves courageously to accomplish it. "The path of the upright"—the forthright, the straightforward—is an open "highway" to their goals. Thorns are not fabricated into hedges, obstacles are overcome, barriers are banished, blockades are broken!

Longfellow exhorted us to a strong work ethic: "Let us, then, be up and doing, / With a heart for any fate; / Still achieving, still pursuing, / Learn to labor and to wait!"[3]

---

[1] Aesop, *The Fables of Aesop* (New York: Dorset Press, 1975) p. 16.
[2] Goethe, *Faust*, Second Part, Act I, Scene 1, p. 212.
[3] Henry W. Longfellow, "A Psalm of Life," *Best Loved Poems of Longfellow* (Chicago: Spencer Press, 1949) p. 316.

A wise son makes a father glad, but a foolish man despises his mother (15:20 NKJV, NASB).

Parents are pleased both by what a son *is* and by what he *does*. They appreciate his wisdom, and they enjoy the fruits of his wisdom in his efforts to please them. The burden of the proverb is in the second clause. Here the word "despises" is used for more than thoughtlessness. The original term is forceful, meaning to treat the mother with contempt. The mother's hurt is implied by the heartlessness of the son who carelessly imposes the pain.

We cannot wrap our minds around the tenderness and depth of a mother's love. Rudyard Kipling wrote: "If I were hanged on the highest hill, / I know whose love would follow me still. / If I were drowned in the depths of the sea, / I know whose tears would come down to me."[1]

Mental suffering may not be as acute as some physical pain, but it is deeper. The anguish of rejected love cuts as deeply as the love has gone. To love is to make oneself voluntarily vulnerable to the pain of rejection. Most mothers would endure the pain of childbirth many times over the pain of neglect and abuse from a child they love. Loving is dangerous activity! To love is to chance the most devastating liabilities. There is no way to love and play it safe!

The pain inflicted on a parent by an unworthy trustee of love is sickening to the soul! For a vile, corrupted, self-centered son or daughter to crucify a mother's heart is outrageously nauseating! The proverb designates "a foolish *man*" to make sure we understand that a child's responsibility "to honor thy father and mother" (Ex. 20:12, Deut. 5:16) continues throughout adulthood. That command is so strong that it is repeated four times in the New Testament![2] Obedience to the command is a matter of moral character, and that is a matter of moral wisdom.

---

[1] Rudyard Kipling, "Mother O' Mine," Richard C. MacKenzie, ed., *The New Home Book of Best Loved Poems* (Garden City, NY: Garden City Books , Doubleday, 1946) p. 65.
[2] Matt. 15:4, Mk. 7:10, Lu. 18:20, Eph. 6:2.

168 Folly Fun or Wise Walk

Folly is joy to him who is destitute of discernment, but a man of understanding walks uprightly (15:21 NKJV).

"Walks uprightly" here is translated from a phrase that really means "keeps a straight course" (NIV), "follows a straight path" (CEV), or "leads a straightforward life" (Mof).
One of the strongest temptations is to divert from straightness to crooks and curves. Doing the unconventional, the socially unacceptable, gives zing and zest. Folly becomes thrilling precisely because it is unwise. For young single persons, part of the appeal to sex is the appeal of stepping outside one's usual self into an altered ego state. The detour is fun because it has no road marks. Not knowing where you are going gives a sense of freedom from direction. Inhibitions fall off. Being lost is a daring thrill. Pleasant vibrations like electrical currents tease the arteries.

Being destitute of wisdom is a perilous condition, but it is stimulating simply because it is perilous. Wisdom is paralyzed by the fun of folly.

Yet on that foolish alternate route, the human conscience still has a feel for the straight path. In *Faust*, the Lord said to the sinister Mephistopheles, "Stand aside when thou art forced to say, / . . . Man . . . has still an instinct of the one true way."[1] Some people have the good sense to tilt toward wisdom, and when they do, wisdom neutralizes and deactivates folly. C. S. Lewis said, "Virtue—even attempted virtue—brings light; indulgence brings fog."[2]

Wisdom is at once both restricting and liberating. It restricts foolish behavior and thinking, and it liberates from the shallow simplicity and consequences of folly. The constraint and direction of the straightforward course give security and stability that belong only to the wise. Solomon said: "Let your eyes look straight ahead, and your eyelids look right before you. Ponder the path of your feet, and let all your ways be established. . . . Do not turn to the right or the left" (Prov. 4:25-27).

---

[1] Goethe, *Faust*, Prologue in Heaven, p. 14.
[2] C. S, Lewis, *Mere Christianity* (New York: The Macmillan Co., 1960) p. 80.

Without counsel purposes are disappointed, but in the multitude of counselors they are established (15:22 KJV).

A purpose usually begins with a seed idea or a wish dream that must be either discarded or firmed up. Prince Hamlet said, "A dream is but a shadow," and his courtier replied, ". . . it is but a shadow's shadow."[1]

When a dream is given substance it solidifies into a purpose. Then a blueprint is adopted to implement the purpose. The goal is set in concrete, but the plan is placed in sand, subject to change. Blueprints often must be redrawn.

Counselors are most useful in shaping the plan. Everyone may agree on the ultimate goal, but they have different ideas to actualize the goal. The various opinions need to be shaken together to see what rises to the top.

In one of Chaucer's Canterbury Tales, Nicholas said to the carpenter: "If you will work by counsel of the wise, / You must not act on what your wits advise. / For so says Solomon, and it all is true, / Work by advice and thou shalt never rue."[2] What Nicholas said was true, and he appealed to Solomon for support. But what he did not say proved to be the carpenter's downfall. Solomon specified a "multitude" of counselors, and the carpenter settled for one. He did as Nicholas said.

Limited counsel can deceive a dupe, but conflicting counsel can paralyze one who is naïve. Consultation must be filtered through a person's rational grid before it is accepted. The one making the decision is not simply directing the traffic of various opinions. We all need advice from trusted consultants, but in the end we make our own choices. A responsible decision requires us to be humble enough to seek counsel, but courageous enough to be decisive. Here is the formula: C+C=Dr. Consultation and courage equal responsible decisions.

---

[1] Shakespeare, *Hamlet*, Act II, Scene 2, lines 262-264.
[2] Geoffrey Chaucer, "The Miller's Tale," *Canterbury Tales* (Garden City, NY: Garden City Pub. Co., 1934) p. 97.

170 Words that Work

A man finds joy in giving an apt reply—and how good is a timely word (15:23 NIV)!

Most of us have suffered embarrassing moments from speaking amiss. The "unbridled tongue" (Ja. 1:26 KJV) slips out of control, making clumsy, humiliating remarks. Right answers, at the right time, in the right way, require wisdom, caution, and practice. My father said to me as a youth, "Always think before you speak."

The proverb highlights the value of "a timely word," "spoken in due season" (NKJV). In our day of interminable chitchat, this accent on a single word is refreshing. Words lose their force when they are smothered by multiple meaningless syllables. A free-flowing tongue betrays a slaphappy rattlebrain! When the *London Times* asked several eminent authors to submit articles on what is wrong with the world, Chesterton wrote: "Dear Sirs: I am. Sincerely yours, G. K. Chesterton." Catholic chaplain John Kelly advised, "Say nothing often."[1]

Words are powerful forces, delivering cargoes of meaning that can change lives. But each word needs space to do its work. When other words crowd in, its force is diluted and its power is weakened. If you "say nothing often" enough, what you do say will pack a heavy punch. "How good that timely word" will be!

Civilla Martin visited a happy Christian who had been bedridden for 20 years, and asked how she stayed so bright and cheerful. Instead of launching into an explanation, Mrs. Doolittle replied, "His eye is on the sparrow, and I know He watches me." The simple line, unadorned with superlatives, lodged in Martin's mind and refused to leave, until she had written the gospel hymn with that title.[2] Whether the handicapped woman felt joy from her apt reply, no one knows. But it has brought blessing to millions of people for more than a hundred years!

---

[1] Both items are taken from Cal and Rose Samra, *More Holy Humor* (Nashville: Thomas Nelson, 1997) p. 58.
[2] Robert J. Morgan, *Then Sings My Soul: Hymn Stories* (Nashville: Thomas Nelson, 2006) p. 509.

The wise man's path goes upward to life, that he may avoid Sheol beneath (15:24 RSV).

The two roads lead in opposite directions, neither of which is level. The only way to avoid the downward destiny is to travel the upward incline. Here "Sheol" means more than physical death, as some translate it, otherwise the two paths would end at the same place. The Old Testament preacher said, "The wise man dies just like the fool" (Ecc. 2:16)!

Coasting downhill is easier than climbing uphill. But those on the downward road soon lose their higher human propensities. They have no GPS unit to know where they are, or to locate their destination. C. S. Lewis says, "At the bottom of all worlds, that face is waiting whose sight alone is the misery from which none . . . can ever recover."[1]

Paracelsus spoke of those "upward tending" people "like plants in mines which never see the sun, but . . . do their best to climb and get to [it]."[2] Faust spoke of "the wings that lift the mind" to "a glorious dream! . . . Each soul is born with the pleasure of yearning onward, upward, and away."[3] Paul said, "Set your hearts on things above" (Col. 3:1 NIV). Our noblest dreams will be ultimately fulfilled in realities greater than we ever dared to dream! Browning said, "A man's reach must exceed his grasp, or what's a heaven for!"[4]

Lewis describes the continuing journey in the next life: "The further up and in you go, the bigger everything gets. The inside is larger than the outside, . . . world within world, . . . like an onion, except that as you continue to go in and in, each circle is larger than the last."[5]

---

[1] C. S. Lewis, *Perelandra* (New York: Macmillan Pub. Co. Inc., 1944) pp. 111.
[2] Robert Browning, "Paracelsus," *The Complete . . . Works . . .* (Cambridge, MA: Houghton Mifflin, 1895) p. 48.
[3] Goethe, *Faust,* First Part, Scene 2, pp. 44-45.
[4] Robert Browning, "Andrea del Sarto," *The Poems of Robert Browning* (London: Oxford U. Press, 1928) p. 132.
[5] C. S. Lewis, *The Last Battle: Book 7 in the Chronicles* (New York: Collier Books, Macmillan, 1978) p. 180.

172 The Proud and the Poor

The Lord will destroy the house of the proud, but he will establish the boundary of the widow (15:25 NKJV).

The question is whether God gets involved in human affairs to help the unfortunate and defeat the evildoers. First, connotations must be clarified. The "house" refers to the home and family. The "proud" connotes the haughty and high-minded. The "widow" represents the oppressed and exploited.

Ordinarily, the proud are powerful and the exploited are helpless. That sets up the proud as predator and the powerless as prey.

Exploiting the poor for personal advantage is intolerable! Jesus condemned even our refusal to help the poor (Matt. 25:41-46). Complacently protecting social and political inequities while the wealthy prey on the pauper is outrageous! Dante said, "The hottest places in hell are reserved for those who, in . . . great moral crisis, maintain neutrality."[1]

The point of biblical eschatology is that someday all social antitheses will be synthesized. The Kingdom of God will include neither exploitation nor oppression, and "the lamb will lie down with the lion" (Is. 11: 6-9). Until then God is at work, sometimes directly, always indirectly through secondary causes, to neutralize social evils and level the fields of opportunity. We are those secondary causes He wishes to use to work His will in the world.

God's time line may be different from what we prefer, because He values human freedom, and for a period He chooses to protect the freedom of the insolent. But eventually, the house of the haughty will be overthrown, and the property line ("boundary") of the poor will be "established." Jesus said, "Whoever exalts himself shall be humbled, and whoever humbles himself shall be exalted" (Matt. 23:12 NASB). Those who reject voluntary humility will be victims of enforced humiliation. Those who are deprived of equity will be exalted.

---

[1] Quoted without citation by Helen Buss Mitchell, *Roots of Wisdom* (Belmont, CA: Wadsworth, 2002) p. 449.

The Lord detests the thoughts of the wicked, but those of the pure are pleasing to him (15:26 NIV).

Even if "the thoughts" refer specifically to the plans and plots of the wicked, the lesson is broad enough to include all evil thoughts. First, a disclaimer: The proverb refers to evil thoughts rather than thoughts about evil. Thinking evil is quite different from thinking *of* evil. The second is unavoidable in this life. The first is wickedly dangerous!

Moral battles are fought out on the battlefield of the mind. Your constitution cannot handle overtime imagination. Being unselective in movies, DVDs, television channels, and novels can fill your mind with garbage until it reeks with the putrefying stench of a city dump! The mind plays tricks on us. Its center of gravity shifts quickly from your home base to what you begin fantasizing. Too soon you have a new home base. The mind is frighteningly accommodating to the direction of your drift. You can become hooked! Mental obsession can be harder to break than chemical addiction.

Winning the battle of the mind gives you victory in your own life. The scripture says, "Whatsoever things are pure, . . . think on these things" (Phil. 4:8 KJV).

Mark Twain said that "man . . . is the only creature that has a nasty mind."[1] Some men feel more like themselves when out with the guys using obscenities than when out with their wives controlling their tongues. Some feel more at home watching Internet porn in their offices than being with their families in their own homes. They have wallowed in filth and grime until they are obsessed with it. Having to live in a phony shell as an alien in one's own home must be tormenting!

A grievous, somber line comes through the last chapter of the Bible. It says in the end the "filthy [will be] filthy still" (Rev. 22:11 NASB). Our minds are for keeps! Anything "the Lord detests," whose opposite is "pleasing to Him," is a matter of grave concern!

---

[1] Quoted without citation by Manual Velasquez, *Philosophy: A Text with Readings* (Belmont, CA: Wadsworth, 1999) p. 79.

174 Hating Bribes and Loving Bribers

A greedy man brings trouble to his family, but he who hates bribes will live (15:27 NIV).

Some people have courage to resist threats who do not have the character to refuse bribes. So they rearrange their values to accommodate their own desires and rationalize their dishonesty. In our postmodern mindset, personal utility becomes the false standard for moral value. Then we have no inner resources to prevent bribery. Greed like an albatross drives us into trouble.

Bribery is more than offering a justified incentive. It includes corrupting one's conduct for personal advantage. It is done "under the counter," dishonestly and deceptively, to pervert the policy of common good. The previous proverb says God *hates* wicked thoughts. This one says we should not only abstain from evil, but we should *hate* evil. We can hate bribery while still loving both the briber and the bribed. Hating bribery is primarily on moral grounds.

Bribery is wrong because it is deceptive and damaging, but when it is wrong it is a moral issue. We have a greater reason for refusing bribery than its detrimental effects. We refuse it because it is wrong. Our reason is based on the principle of morality that is inherent in the heart of God. There is no greater reason for doing right or not doing wrong than the fact that it is right or wrong.

Conscience has more inhibiting power than utility. We tell our children that honesty is the best policy, but why do we not say that honesty is the *right* policy? Those who live close to God develop a penchant for goodness itself and repulsion to evil itself, apart from their effects.

There is no greater reason to love goodness and hate evil than the fact that goodness is good and evil is evil! Loving the right because it is right and hating the wrong because it is not right, we become like God in that respect.

Then we have a bonus benefit: Doing right comes more easily when we love the right, and resisting evil is easier when we hate evil. And a double bonus: We spare ourselves and our families considerable trouble!

The heart of the righteous weighs its answers, but the mouth of the wicked gushes evil (15:28 NIV).

Frederick the Great is quoted as saying, "Every man has a wild beast within him."[1] We can hardly deny that humans are animalistic in many ways. After all, they eat like a pig, they are sly as a fox, they are proud as a peacock, they are stubborn as a mule! *And*, they talk worse than beasts. No animal ever burped a bad word! Standing beside humans, animals look saintly!

When the mouth gushes out evil, it draws from a store of inner supplies. Some people may not be what they *say* they are, but what they say, they *are*. They *are* what they say. Their speech betrays the beast within. The careless heart bypasses the mind, short-circuiting courtesy and conscience. When one's tongue goes on automatic pilot, it is fed directly by a self-centered heart without a filter system. What is said is a "gully gusher."

The righteous heart is cautiously concerned about the effects of what it says. A new heart may not automatically replace established patterns of speech, but it does deposit a new sensitivity to conscience that can bring the tongue under control. Foul language is utterly incongruous with a righteous heart. Chaucer's character Prudence advised her husband, "Strive to conquer your own heart."[2]

The problem is that one's own heart is unconquerable without divine grace. Its self-centered nature is too solidified, too set in concrete, to conquer itself. Something bigger than oneself is needed. God is required! In the Bible, Peter speaks of those with new hearts and "purified souls" who "have been born again not of seed which is perishable but imperishable" (1 Pet. 1:23 NASB). Paul said, "If anyone is in Christ, he is a new creation; the old has gone, the new has come!" (2 Cor. 5:17 NIV). Slowing the gutter gushing begins with a new heart.

---

[1] Manuel Velasquez, *Philosophy: A Text with Readings* (Belmont, CA: Wadsworth Pub. Co., 1999) p. 76.
[2] Chaucer, "The Tale of Melibeus," *Canterbury Tales* (Garden City, NY: Garden City Pub. Co., 1934) p. 235.

175 Distant Silence or Close Fellowship

The Lord is far from the wicked, but he hears the prayer of the righteous" (15:29 NKJV).

Since God is ubiquitous, we would expect no one to be far from His presence, whatever one's location. Yet the proverb declares God "is far from the wicked." Both notions, however, are true, each on a different definition of "distance." By *spatial* distance, an omnipresent God is close to everyone. *Relational* distance is something different. A child may live in the same home with an abusive parent, while relationally being in a different world. With God, moral proximity refers to *relation* rather than *location*. To allow sin to keep a person removed from a God who is relationally accessible is an unthinkable tragedy!

Prayer is a relational term, and "hearing a prayer" means to interrelate with the one who prays. When a child of God lifts her heart in prayer, she does not get a recorded message from an answering machine. She is not given a mechanical menu to choose from. She is not put on hold while heavenly music is piped into her ears. She does not even get a secretary or sales rep.

Too many Christians fail to realize God's relational closeness. They are like Jacob who said, "Surely the Lord is in this place, and I was not aware of it" (Gen. 28:16 NIV). In the Vietnam War, the first American pilot shot down and rescued in North Vietnam went through weeks of intense "soul-searching emotion." Then Jon Harris "reached a sense of the presence of God so profound it has never left me. If I were killed, I would be with God. If I were captured, He would be with me."[1] In his drama, Shaw has Joan of Arc saying, shortly before she was burned as a martyr, "It is better to be alone with God. His friendship will not fail me!"[2] And that friendship did not fail her! God-consciousness for instant access can only be cultivated by daily fellowship with God in Christ. Our cell phones need to be recharged daily! To seven bars!

---

[1] Jon R. Harris, *Wings of the Morning* (Xulon Press, 2006) p. 33. The above lines have been abridged.
[2] George Bernard Shaw, *Saint Joan* (London: Penguin Group, 1946) p. 112.

The light of the eyes rejoices the heart, and a good report makes the bones healthy (15:30 NKJV).

The proverb may mean that what you see can inspire your spirit and what you hear can invigorate your body. Together, seeing spring flowers and hearing songbirds can rejuvenate your total person, soul and body.

More likely the sage is saying that the spirit-body combo rides heavily on inspiration from other persons and motivation from temporal facts. We live *on* interpersonal relationships and we live *with* factual situations. Our world is teeming with unfortunate millions who feel isolated from meaningful relationships and victimized by unavoidable circumstances. They feel hopeless, like Oscar Wilde who wrote: "We were as men who through a fen / Of filthy darkness grope. . . . / Something was dead in each of us, / And what was dead was hope!"[1]

The world's hopeless people need Christians to make two contributions. First, they need friendship. They need inspiring friends with smiling eyes and cheerful dispositions. Contact with bright eyes and an optimistic face can bathe a dejected person in a heaven of hope, and lift the cloud of despair. More inspiration comes from friends than from situations or other sources.

Second, Christians have heard the greatest good news flash ever to hit the planet! God loves and cares, and is eager to forgive, to save, and to be a friend. He can lace together the tattered edges of life into a rich tapestry. God's people can help others to realign their antennae to pick up the divine signal. Lord Tennyson wrote, "Closer is He than breathing, and nearer than hands and feet."[2] That is the good news of the Gospel! When that "good report" comes from a relational person, it can put joy in "the heart" and a spring in the step ("make the bones healthy"), enlivening the lives of those who otherwise languish without hope.

[1] Oscar Wilde, "The Ballad of Reading Gaol," *The Works of Oscar Wilde* (Leicester, UK: Bookmart, 1990) p. 831.
[2] Alfred Tennyson, "The Higher Pantheism," *The Poetical Works of Tennyson* (New York: Crowell, n.d.) p. 444.

178 Payoff or Penalty

The ear that hears the reproof of life will abide among the wise. /
He who disdains instruction despises his own soul . . . / . . . Before
honor is humility (15:31, 32, 33 NKJV).

Imagine traveling 70-mph on a crowded superhighway without regulations or lane directions. Picture yourself playing basketball with no game rules, where everyone is blocking and tackling. We need training programs for both driving and playing, and we need police officers and referees to enforce the rules. I am a better driver because I have been given traffic citations and a better player because I have been whistled for fouls. "Instruction" and "reproof" go together in teaching-learning experiences, because learning from one's own mistake is one of the best teaching methods.

These three proverbs are in orderly procession, highlighting the *payoff* from *respecting* reproof, the *penalty* for *refusing*, and the *price* for the *rewards.*

The payoff is given first as a positive incentive to heed instruction and accept reproof. Wisdom is its own reward for its own sake, but the payoff is even more than that. Those who become wise "abide among the wise." They are accepted among the sages and recognized as colleagues with the honor of the wise.

The penalty for refusing instruction and rejecting reproof is self-imposed, as if a person "despises his own soul."

In effect, he hates himself by dishonoring, disfavoring and disgracing himself with foolishness. Renowned historical theologian Joseph Butler said, "We may . . . make ourselves as miserable as we please." People "do what they know beforehand will render them so."[1]

The misery of self-torture is a heavy punishment for pandering to pride! Too little comfort is gained for the loss of so much wisdom and public respect! If the positive incentive does not have appeal, this negative warning is a back-up motivation to heed the reproof.

(Continued in the next essay)

---

[1] Joseph Butler, *Analogy of Religion* (New York: Eaton and Mains, 1847) p. 69.

CONTINUED FROM PREVIOUS ESSAY

Dame Prudence exhorted her husband, "Drive from your heart three things that are opposed to good counsel—anger, covetousness, and hastiness."[1] Solomon accented a fourth that the dame overlooked. Pride preempts good counsel probably more than the others do. "Before the honor" of standing among the sages "is humility."

Humility is the price for the honor of wisdom. Certainly humility is preferable to honor, but the proverb says it is not an either/or situation. It is both/and. Humility leads the way, and honor follows in her train. The prudent person honors himself with prudence, even if no one else recognizes his honor. Having the humility to accept reproof to become a wise soul makes one an honorable person.

Woodrum wrote, "A man's first step toward being a Christian is his recognition of his own unworthiness and sinfulness. . . . Thus cast down we may be lifted up. Hopeless, we find hope. Knowing our lostness, we may be found. Aware that we are sinners, we become aware that Christ died for sinners. Confessing our status we come to the gate of the Kingdom."[2]

The same humility is necessary for acquiring wisdom and its honor. Recognizing our need, we listen to instruction. Knowing our faults, we accept reproof. Understanding our shortage of wisdom forces us to honest humility. Genuine honor is seldom reached except by the road of humility. Acknowledging our frequent foolishness brings us to the gate of wisdom.

Jesus said that "the meek will inherit the earth" (Matt. 5:5). Sooner or later, either the humiliation of dishonor will force us to our knees or the humility to acquire wisdom will exalt us to honor. Jesus said, "Whoever exalts himself will be humbled, and whoever humbles himself will be exalted" (Matt. 23:12 NIV).

---

[1] Chaucer, "The Tale of Melibeus," *Canterbury Tales* (Garden City, NY: Garden City Pub. Co., 1934) p. 200.

[2] Lon Woodrum, *The Rebellious Planet* (Grand Rapids: Zondervan Pub. House, 1965) p. 73.

180 God's Purpose and Our Plans

To man belongs the plans of the heart, but from the Lord comes the reply of the tongue (16:1 NIV).

The human heart is equipped to focus on transcendent purposes and direct one's life toward its highest destiny. "Daniel purposed in his heart" (Dan. 1:8 NKJV).

We need a controlling purpose that has the gravity to pull all smaller purposes into its sway. When I adopt God's purpose *behind* my life for my purpose *in* life, I am no longer a cosmic misfit. Neatly and snugly I fit into the purpose for which I was born. Smaller purposes defer to the higher purpose, with which I will never be disappointed.

The human heart also has the propensity to plan lesser projects and draft lower designs that may be innocent but turn out to be unfeasible. On these, our hearts should not be firmly set. Chesterton said, "Flambeau . . . had a sort of half purpose, which he took just so seriously that its success would crown the holiday, but just so lightly that its failure would not spoil it."[1] Small purposes should be held loosely, and not too close to the heart.

"The heart" sometimes refers simply to a wish dream, and "the tongue" means a statement of reply. The proverb affirms the adage: "Man proposes; God disposes." We may present our hearts' plans and purposes to Him for ratification, but He retains veto power. One translation says: "We humans make plans, but God has the final word" (CEV).

Some things He withholds for our own benefit, to protect our future from our present desires. Our vision is so short. He has the long-range view. Oscar Wilde's character Sir Robert Chilton, frightened by extraordinary success, exclaimed, "When the gods wish to punish us they answer our prayers."[2] Many of our petitions need to be edited by God. We only present to Him the rough draft.

---

[1] G. K. Chesterton, "The Sins of Prince Saradine," *Favorite Father Brown Stories* (New York: Dover Publications, 1993) p. 17.
[2] Oscar Wilde, "An Ideal Husband," Act II, *The Works of Oscar Wilde* (Leicester, England: Bookmart Limited, 1990, p. 491.

Conscience and Commandments 181

All the ways of a man are clean in his own sight, but the Lord weighs the motives (16:2 NASB). Also 21:2.

Goodness and badness are based on something deeper than outward actions. It is one thing to be righteous in a culturally customized lifestyle, but quite another to be good in one's motives. When culture loses its hold and our actions expose selfish motives, we exonerate ourselves with excuses. As we become more sinful, we keep redrawing the line between good and evil just below ourselves. We know how to rationalize our behavior to accommodate our desires. Our standards slide to conform to our lifestyle. We are experts in self-delusion.

"Letting your conscience be your guide" is a dangerous standard, on two counts. The first is that conscience does not give a code of ethics. Rather than making laws or defining the law, conscience is designed to enforce what we think is the law. When our opinions become too rigid, conscience produces false guilt. When they are too lax, conscience loses its grist for grinding out guilt.

Because opinions are fluid and self-serving, we need objective commandments. Over and over the scriptures refer to "the law of the Lord." In Psalm 119, God's law (or its synonym) is mentioned in *every* single one of the 176 verses!

Second, the conscience can be inoculated by sin until it becomes immune to guilt. Anesthetized to the principle of morality, it sounds no moral alarm. Paul spoke of those whose "conscience [is] seared with a hot iron" (1 Tim. 4:2 KJV). Eventually the conscience expires. When it is gone, there is no alert to moral danger. The victim becomes a moral corpse in a morally alive universe.

Paul said, "My conscience is clear, but that does not make me innocent. It is the Lord who judges. . . . He will bring to light what is hidden in darkness and will expose the motives of men's hearts" (1 Cor. 4:4-5 NIV).

Absence of guilt feelings means nothing when the conscience is dead. Nor can our opinions make a case for our innocence. The verdict comes from God!

182 Your Plans with God's Help

Commit to the Lord whatever you do, and your plans will succeed
(16:3 NIV).

Two lessons leap up at us. First, this promise is not given to the indolent idler, who lazily waits for a divine jump-start. When a shipwrecked passenger, without attempting to swim, implored the goddess Athena to rescue him, Aesop said, "Look to Athena if you like, but look to your arms as well."[1] The promise is made to industrious persons who plan with ingenuity. Success requires a plan. Ordering and arranging the procedure through analysis and feasibility studies is a prerequisite.

Goethe said, "Your mind will shortly be set aright / When you have learned, all things reducing, / To classify them for your using."[2] God honors diligent planning with the right motives, and He is willing to partner with us in the projects.

Second, the promise is to those who submit their plans and programs to the Lord for input and approval. Pushing our own program is precarious, without His sanction and direction. Too many tenuous details can go awry. Convoluted contingencies turn and twist, congesting the arrangements. Even when our plans go amiss, He can manipulate the particulars for a better outcome, bringing good out of the bad.

An additional bonus is His influence on our own mindset and attitudes. Kipling's artist said to his artist friend, "The instant we begin . . . to play with one eye on the gallery, we lose power and touch. . . . If we make light of our work by using it for our own ends, our work will make light of us."[3]

Carefully made plans, with the right motives, done in the right way, with the right attitude, for the right reasons, approved by God and with His blessing, "will succeed." In successful undertakings, God is more than an additional chance for good luck. He is not the fortunate draw in a raffle. He is the basic ingredient in the enterprise!

---

[1] Aesop, *The Fables of Aesop* (New York: Dorset Press, 1975) p. 20.
[2] Goethe, *Faust*, First Part, Scene 4, pp. 74-75.
[3] Rudyard Kipling, *The Light that Failed* (New York: Books, Inc., n.d.) p. 92.

The Lord works out everything for his own ends—even the wicked for a day of disaster (16:4 NIV).

The intricately entangled wording of this original proverb has put translators gyrating in twisting, twirling tizzies. Some say the Lord made all things "for Himself," "for His ends," or "to answer His designs." Others say He made everything "for its own purpose," or "to answer its own end." Both interpretations, however, strongly oppose a current opinion that was expressed 2,450 years ago by King Oedipus' wife: "Life is governed by the operations of chance.[1] Nothing can be clearly foreseen. The best way to live is by hit and miss, as best you can."[2]

Astute analysis will discover a pattern running throughout all existence. The design includes logical relationships between premises and conclusions, moral relationships between virtue and rewards or vice and punishment, natural and transnatural relationships between causes and effects, volitional relationships between choices and consequences. God's system coordinates a pattern between antecedents and their subsequent counterparts. Outcomes are matched with input. Entities and experiences shape their own ends as a part of God's systematic design. Both translations suggest this, making both true, whichever is accurate.

Nonnatural causes include psychological, emotional, personal, and spiritual causes. God remains in a position to initiate *nonnatural* causes for *natural* effects, thus operating within the causal system for human benefit. Protecting the integrity of the natural system, God is reluctant to produce chaos by interfering arbitrarily with the system itself. When people are innocent victims of a pattern that others have misused, God remains in a position to make it up to them in other ways, either presently or eventually.

(Continued in the next essay)

[1] "Chance" is used by scientific materialists to refer to effects of causes too remote or obscure to discover. The term is used here philosophically to mean *uncaused* occurrences.
[2] Sophocles, *Oedipus the King* (New York: Washington Square Press, Inc., 1959) p. 67.

184 Evil and Its End

CONTINUED FROM PREVIOUS ESSAY

God created the pattern of the natural system, but the logical and moral systems are objective principles inherent in God's nature. What follows is a sketch of how the logical and moral patterns interplay in God's effort to redeem humankind.

The moral pattern of deserts and rewards/punishment is a matter of moral justice that is included in the goodness of God. Justice requires moral equalization, which includes evenhanded rectitude and redress.

Extending unjustified mercy to guilty humans would violate His own goodness, which He logically cannot do and remain a good God.

Moral redemption was a logical problem that was resolved by a brilliant stroke of both genius and sacrifice in Calvary grace, justifying God's mercy without dishonoring His justice. On that basis, God can redeem the entire human race in a way that supports rather than violates His moral goodness.

God's effort to redeem all humans, however, faced another logical problem. Goodness by its nature has to be chosen rather than imposed. Forced goodness is not goodness. In order for human goodness to be genuine, the freedom to reject goodness has to be protected. God cannot force people to be morally good while protecting their freedom to be bad. It would be a logical contradiction. He cannot redeem those who freely refuse to be redeemed.

The relation between "the wicked" and "the day of trouble," stated in the proverb, is depicted by C. S. Lewis as "the frightening abyss which separates ghosthood from manhood." Referring to Weston after his death, Lewis said, "The intoxicated will, which had been poisoning the intelligence and the affections, had now at last poisoned itself, and the whole psychic organism had fallen to pieces. Only a ghost was left—an everlasting unrest, a crumbling, a ruin, an odor of decay."[1]

---

[1] C. S. Lewis, *Perelandra* (New York: Macmillan Pub. Co., Inc., 1944) p. 130.

Pride and Humility 185

*Everyone who is proud in heart is an abomination to the Lord;
assuredly, he will not be unpunished* (16:5 NASB).

Positive self-regard is a proper pride that is not condemned in the Bible. But the "proud *in heart*" have an exaggerated, sickly self-esteem that the scripture strongly denounces.

Pride is the one sin that drives a wedge into human relationships. Committing other sins together can facilitate camaraderie, but committing personal pride together creates antipathy and sets two persons up for hostility.

But the sin cuts even deeper. Pride toward people corrodes one's relationship with God, driving one farther and farther away from congeniality with Him. C. S. Lewis said, "A proud man is always looking down on things and people, and as long as you are looking down, you cannot see something that is above you."[1] Focusing on yourself, you lose sight of God. Pride eclipses His presence, leaving you anchored only in yourself. Little wonder it "is an abomination to the Lord," deserving retribution.

Perhaps the most profane sin that can eat away at the soul of a Christian worker is to take credit for what God has done through you. Accepting praise for what *you* have done is different and is often justified, but to usurp God's glory for your own glory is utterly dishonoring and defiling! Genuine humility will recoil from such presumptuous profanity!

Feeling his own inadequacy to help so many with the plague, Dr. Faust prayed for God's help. When his prayer was answered and they were spared its worst effects, the crowds lavished praise on him and his father. In deep humility Faust said to Wagner: "Now like contempt the crowd's applauses seem. / Could'st thou but read, within mine inmost spirit / How little now I deem / That sire and son should praises merit!"[2]

Undeserved applause seems cheap when the glory belongs to God.

---

[1] C. S. Lewis, *Mere Christianity* (New York: The Macmillan Company, 1960) p. 96.
[2] Goethe, *Faust*, First Part, Scene 2, p. 43.

186 Initial Salvation to Final Salvation

By mercy and truth iniquity is purged, and by the fear of the Lord men depart from evil (16:6 KJV).

Those who love to solve riddles and work puzzles should enjoy tackling and tangling with this proverb. Obscure nuances of the ancient phraseology produce scholarship diversity that precludes consensus. Is iniquity purged by *God's* mercy and truthfulness, or is the purging verified by *our* mercy and faithfulness toward others? Both propositions are true, but which one was intended is not clear.

The second clause is easier. The purging in the first clause is expected to result in the "departure from evil" in the second. The repentance necessary for salvation results in a Christianized lifestyle. Becoming a noun-Christian includes the willingness to be adjective-Christian. That is, being *a* Christian results in being Christian, in attitudes and actions. The regenerated heart of the believer attempts to break the pattern of sin.

Salvation from sin's guilt should be followed by salvation from its power and its practice. God's provision for redemption ultimately includes the entire scope of sin. The redemption process only begins with forgiveness. It moves from "justification" to "sanctification." God's ultimate purpose is not to save us *in* our sins, but *from* our sins.

That is part of the positive side of the Christian gospel. God plans for us a future that is free from all sin, more exciting and fulfilling than we can imagine!

Our final salvation comes at "glorification"—when we are escorted into the heavenly venue that "nothing impure [can] enter" (Rev. 21:27 NIV). The final, full redemption is what God has in mind for the filthiest sinner and the feeblest Christian. When Faust finally ascended immortally to the heavenly regions, the angels sang: "The noblest spirit now is free, / And saved from evil scheming: / Whoe'er aspires unweariedly / Is not beyond redeeming!"[1]

---

[1] Goethe, *Faust*, Second Part, Act V, Scene 7, p. 500.

From Foes to Friends 187

When a man's ways please the Lord, he maketh even his enemies to be at peace with him (16:7 KJV).

The general principle of the proverb was understood at the time not to apply to every particular. Hebrew psalms acknowledged the enemies of innocent people. Jesus blessed the persecuted as well as the peacemaker in consecutive beatitudes (Matt. 5:9-10). He told the disciples they would be hated and persecuted precisely because they followed Him (John 15:18-19).

Notwithstanding enculturated hostility, the principle generally does operate personally, one-on-one. What pleases God usually facilitates human relationships, and what displeases Him distorts relationships. Attitudes and actions that promote peace or enmity are generally the same that please or displease God. Love or hostility, generosity or selfishness, humility or pride, honesty or falsity, pity or apathy, helping people or using people. Pretending friends can ape the positive virtues for personal advantage, but they are soon recognized as counterfeit. Genuine virtues are authenticated in real-life situations, and over time they build up a cumulative inventory of relational capital. Enmities dissolve, hostilities fade out, foes become friends.

When I was a six-year-old lad in the first grade, my mother suggested that I might take two extra apples in my lunch box to give to two bullies who had been harassing me. Reluctantly I agreed, the bullying immediately stopped, and they both became my lifelong friends. I learned an important lesson! The proverb works! Chaucer said, "Let each of us hold up his hand to other / And each of us become the other's brother."[1] Whittier wrote a passionate hymn: "O brother man, fold to thy heart thy brother! / Where pity dwells, the peace of God is there; / To worship rightly is to love each other, / Each smile a hymn, each kindly deed a prayer."[2]

---

[1] Chaucer, "The Pardoner's Tale," *Canterbury Tales* (Garden City, NY: Garden City Pub. Co., 1934) p. 303.
[2] John Greenleaf Whittier, "O Brother Man," in *The Broadman Hymnal* (Nashville: Broadman Press, 1940) p. 403.

188 Earning without Burning

Better is a little with righteousness than great revenues without right (16:8 KJV).

The long-distance phone call was seeking my direction. Joe's long ambition had been to climb the corporate ladder, and now he held an executive position in a prominent company. Recently having been converted to Christ in one of my meetings, he said, "Intentional deception is built into the system as a part of company practice. Now I am a Christian, and I do not know how to handle it." He ended up resigning his position, sold his nice home, unable to make mortgage payments, and traded his gasoline guzzler in on a midsize car. Later he told me that he and his family were happier than ever before, even in their rented house!

The proverb addresses ethical ways to gain income. Proverb 15:16 (Essay 162) advocates religion over trouble, giving a *practical* reason for discretion in making a living. Proverb 15:17 (Essay 163) promotes love over hatred, giving a *relational* reason. This proverb insists on rightness over unrightness, giving an *ethical* reason. Sophocles said, "Wisdom outweighs wealth."[1] Solomon said religion, relationships, and righteousness each outweighs wealth.

In our day, marketing has become a science that can easily slide into something unethical. Disclaimers are buried in fine print, promoting a product's advantages while concealing its disadvantages. Technical correctness can be intentionally misleading. An impersonal corporation can use individuals to do its dirty work, as Faust said to Mephistopheles: "To use me like a cat is thy desire, / To scratch for thee the chestnuts from the fire."[2] Those who are required to participate in the deception hide behind company policy. But participating in institutionalized evil is a serious personal evil. Worse than not giving help to the poor is to profit by making them poorer! Burning guilt is tormenting! God's way, we can do our earning without burning.

---

[1] Quoted by Douglas J. Soccio, *Archetypes of Wisdom* (Belmont, CA: Wadsworth/Thomas Learning, 2001) p. 17.
[2] Goethe, *Faust*, Second Part, Act I, Scene 5, p. 270.

The Heart Devises and God Revises 189

A man's heart deviseth his way, but the Lord directeth his steps (16:9 KJV).

We humans devise divers plans to fulfill our diverse dreams. Many of our plans are fickle, volatile, and shortsighted. We are like George Eliot's character who said, "I think of too many things. . . . I flutter in all ways, and fly in none."[1]

The Lord gives us the freedom to fantasize, and within bounds to choose our direction. Perhaps Oedipus was right when he said that "no man can . . . compel the gods to act against their will,"[2] but God does allow *us* to act against His will. It is a frightful freedom, because a small step in the wrong direction can determine our wrong destiny and ultimate doom. Robert Frost wrote: "Two roads diverged in a wood, and I— / I took the one less traveled by, / And that has made all the difference."[3]

If we choose God's major thoroughfare and allow Him to *revise* whatever we *devise*, the proverb says God will direct, or "make firm and safe," our steps. A Hebrew psalm exhorts us to "commit [our] way to the Lord" (Ps. 37:5). Homer said, "Thou wilt in no sort be a weakling, if . . . the gods follow thee to be thy guide."[4] Solomon said, "In all your ways acknowledge Him, and He will make your paths straight" (Prov. 3:6 NASB). Our footfalls are precarious on the slippery slopes of life, and we need security. If we are committed to His continuing direction, God will steady our footsteps and direct them aright. That is not a pipe dream. It has been verified through life by many of us who are older. In the hectic journey of living, we can affirm with the psalmist: "In Thee do I trust. Cause me to know the way wherein I should walk. . . . Thou art my God. Lead me into the land of uprightness" (Ps. 143:8,10).

---

[1] George Eliot, *The Mill on the Floss* (New York: Dodd, Mead and Co., 1960) pp. 319-320.
[2] Sophocles, *Oedipus the King* (New York: Washington Square Press, Inc., 1959) p. 17.
[3] Robert Frost, "The Road Not Taken," Untermeyer, ed., *Modern Am. Poetry* (New York: Harcourt, 1950), p. 203.
[4] Homer, *The Odyssey of Homer*, Butcher & Lang, trs. (New York: The MacMillan Co., 1911) Bk. III, p. 32.

190 God's Wisdom for Leadership

The lips of the king speak as an oracle, and his mouth should not betray justice (16:10 NIV).

Probably no other proverb is translated into more meanings than this one. (1)Whatever rulers say is from God and is never wrong. (2) Because their decisions are considered to be from God, rulers cannot afford to be wrong. (3) Rulers must have divine wisdom to prevent them from being wrong. (4) Even if divination should influence them toward wrong decisions, righteous rulers will not allow themselves to be wrong. One thing is certain from the various translations: Rather than *being* authority, political leaders are *under* authority. They need divine wisdom for fair, evenhanded decisions, and are accountable to God. Legal justice must not trump moral justice. Some think the proverb implies that supernatural wisdom is always given to *righteous* rulers. Certainly the scripture states that was true with Solomon.

Plato said, "[When] political greatness and wisdom meet in one, . . . then only will our state . . . behold the light. . . . [Only the wise] are able to grasp the eternal and unchangeable."[1]

Righteous leadership includes not only wisdom of the mind but love and pathos of the heart. During apartheid in South Africa, Alan Paton's character feared the opposition would gain power and then be corrupted by its power. He said, "Only one thing has power completely, and that is love. Because when a man loves, he seeks no power, and therefore he has power."[2] Robert Browning spoke of the "proportion love should have with power . . .: love preceding power, and with much power, always much more love."[3]

To be a political leader who seeks God's wisdom requires a heart that will use wisdom in the right way. What is true for political leaders holds also for community leaders, church leaders, small group leaders, family leaders.

---

[1] Plato, *The Republic*, Bk. V, Dagobert Runes, ed., *Treasury of Philosophy* (New York: Philosophical Library, 1955) pp. 935-936.
[2] Alan Paton, *Cry the Beloved Country* (New York: MacMillan Pub. Co., 1948) p. 39.
[3] Robert Browning, "Paracelsus," *The Complete . . . Works . . .* (Cambridge, MA: Houghton Mifflin, 1895) p. 48.

A just balance and scales belong to the Lord; all the weights of the bag are His concern (16:11 NASB).

Human justice means fairness and equitableness in human dealings. Because many commodities are sold by weight, scales with balancing weights have long been used in the commerce of merchandise. Vendors often took with them their own scales with a bag of various weights. If the weights had been altered to cheat the buyer, they were known as "unjust" weights.

The proverb says the notion of justice with accurate weights originated with God and remains one of His major concerns. Sophocles' chorus chanted: "Laws that stand above have been . . . born in the upper air on high . . . In them God is great, and He does not grow old."[1]

In our judicial system, justice concerns the fair treatment of both the criminal and the victim, and that requires punishment. Special attempts should be made to be redemptive, so we use "correctional" rather than "penal" institutions. But all correctional attempts at behavior modification must be inside the context of retributive justice. Those who promote rehabilitation alone do not perceive its liabilities. Without equitable justice, innocent people have no defense against false charges and criminals have no protection against excess penalties. The Soviet system's "re-education camps" used inhumane severity in re-indoctrinating those who did not comply with party line. Someone says, "But that is unfair!" And that is the point! Without justice there is no principle of fairness. Innocent people have no safeguard against a ruthless regime. The attempt to reform an inmate while bypassing justice is to use uneven weights.

As far as possible, justice itself should be used for rehabilitation. Instead of "paying a debt to society," restitution should be made to the victim. That allows criminals to feel that the debt is paid and justice has been done—which helps implement their rehabilitation.

---

[1] Sophocles, *Oedipus the King* (New York: Washington Square Press, Inc., 1959) p. 60.

192 Ruling with Righteousness

It is an abomination for kings to commit wickedness, for a throne is established on righteousness (16:12 NASB).

When the king of Scotland reunited the innocent maiden with her Highlander father, both sire and daughter were ecstatic. Sir Walter Scott wrote: "The monarch drank, that happy hour, / The sweetest, holiest draught of power, / When it can say, with godlike voice, /Arise, sad Virtue, and rejoice!"[1] Righteousness has its own power and its own reward.

Whether the proverb says that kings should be righteous or that they expect the people to be righteous, as some translate it, the proverb points to a chain of command that runs from God through the leader to the people.

It is not a chain of political power but a chain of righteousness that maintains the leader's administration. No chain is stronger than its weakest link. If the moral chain breaks, the leadership position loses both its credibility and the blessing of God. Claiming "the divine rights of kings" is to claim a power chain that does not exist. From top to bottom, the chain is strung by links of righteousness. The strongest draught of power ever drunk is the drink of virtue!

Plato said: "They rule who are truly rich . . . in virtue, . . . who at the same time have other honors and another and better life than that of politics."[2] Standing alone, political life cannot sustain itself. It requires the proper operating context. Unless it functions inside the "better life," one's political life shoots and turns out of control.

Other proverbs point out the important place of wisdom in leadership, but righteousness is included in wisdom, otherwise wisdom is less than wisdom. Righteousness is the home base for the throne, the oval office, the senate chamber, the CEO's chair, the preacher's podium, and the end of the table at family dinner.

---

[1] Sir Walter Scott, *The Lady of the Lake* (New York: The New American Library, 1962) Canto Sixth, Sec. XXVIII, p. 162.
[2] Plato, *The Republic*, D. Runes, ed., *Treasury of Philosophy* (New York: Philosophical Library, 1955) p. 947.

Righteous lips are the delight of kings, and they love him who speaks what is right (16:13 NKJV).

The previous proverb says the king must operate with character, and this one says he must honor truth. The consecutive proverbs insist on integrity in living and integrity in talking. Since both are matters of integrity, the bottom line for both is moral. Personal integrity in private life is the underlying foundation for integrity in public life. Piety shapes policy. One translation of Psalm 47:8 says that God sits on "the throne of His holiness" (KJV). Similarly, premiers, prime ministers, and presidents are expected to occupy seats of righteousness.

As God "loves righteousness and hates wickedness," so righteous political leaders love the right and hate the evil in their subjects. Lady Macbeth lamented, "In this earthly world, . . . to do harm is often laudable [and] to do good is sometimes accounted dangerous folly."[1]

Recalcitrant people refuse to be led, and if they are implacable enough, the leader has to deal with anarchy. All rulers except tyrants know that righteous people are easier to lead. In Scott's epic poem, King James complained about the temperamental volatility of his people: "Vain as a leaf upon the stream, / And fickle as a changeful dream; . . . / Thou many-headed monster-thing, / O who would wish to be thy king!"[2]

Though we applaud much good in American people, our culture has been infected with a plethora of moral viruses. The diseases are contagious. We catch them from watching some Hollywood productions, and listening to some CD hits. Technology has spread our illness throughout the world, infecting other cultures and tarnishing our image abroad. Yet a righteous remnant sits at the core of our culture as a cohesive force in society. God honors a righteous minority in any people group. And righteous rulers are always in their debt.

---

[1] Shakespeare, *Macbeth*, Act IV, Scene 2, lines 75-77.
[2] Sir Walter Scott, *The Lay of the Lake* (New York: New American Library, 1962) Canto Fifth, Sec. XXX, p. 138.

194 Respect the Rage

A king's wrath is a messenger of death, but a wise man will appease it (16:14 NIV).

Our reaction to angry humans is accented here where the lesson is more obvious in dealing with an angry potentate. But people also become victims of homicide by refusing to respect the rage of peers who are taken for granted. Wise people will heed two lessons.

First, give the angry person some leverage. Do not stoke the fires. Allow time for tempers to cool. Those who react too soon should chill out. You can best control others by controlling yourself—by restraining your reaction to the angry actions of others. We should refuse to be needlessly provoked. Coolness reduces heat. A belligerent world needs people who do not snap back at snappers. Facing out-of-control drivers requires drivers who are under control. The pattern of self-control can only be established by practice.

Second, do not be provocative. Do not sport the ability to make others angry. I have known too many Christians who consider themselves pious because they are confrontational. Without being pushovers, we should learn personal warmth by practicing camaraderie. Of course, one must not sacrifice moral principle for friendship, but being friendly is a moral principle itself. Until it conflicts with a higher principle, it should be observed.

The term "gentility" came to refer to social class, because class people were expected to be gentle in style and courteous in conduct, to which the term originally referred. In Chaucer's tale, the old, ugly, outcast woman exclaimed: "Gentility is not . . . / Of ancestors who have some greatness shown, / In which you have no portion of your own. / Your own gentility comes from God alone."[1] True gentility comes to us as a Christian grace. As we thus control ourselves, we make it easier for other people to control themselves around us.

---

[1] Chaucer, "The Tale of the Wife of Bath," *Canterbury Tales* (Garden City, NY: Garden City Pub., 1934) p. 342.

The Face with Favor 195

In the light of the king's face is life, and his favor is like a cloud of the latter rain (16:15 NKJV).

A facial expression can often communicate more than a thousand words. The frown of a furrowed brow is a warning of wrath, and the light of a smile can brighten our lives. This proverb is set against the previous one, contrasting favor with anger and life with death. Both proverbs use the image of a king who is both human and a ruler, standing for the relational attitudes of both human beings and God.

Like the previous proverb, scripture predicts the time when evil humans will cry to the rocks and mountains, "Fall on us and hide us from the face of him who sits on the throne and from the wrath of the Lamb" (Rev. 6:16 NIV). But like this proverb, a psalmist sang about "the light of [God's] countenance" (Ps. 44:3 KJV) and prayed that "the light of your face [would] shine upon us" (Ps. 4:6 NIV). C. S. Lewis spoke of that "one Face above all worlds [which] merely to see is irrevocable joy."[1] It is a happiness, said Lewis, that is "too good to waste on jokes."[2]

One can never know greater joy than comes from God's smile of approval, a happiness that comes from His happiness with us. It is a happiness so focused on His being happy that we are hardly aware of our own happiness. We are lifted out of ourselves into His bliss! At life's end when I stand before Him, if I can but trace on His face a smile of approval, I will be satisfied a million times over! The pleasure of pleasing Christ, at once so supportive and so humbling, will stretch out beyond imagination! Esther Rusthoi wrote: "One glimpse of His dear face / All sorrows will erase."[3] Joy from the favoring faces of human friends will forever pale in light of the eternal joy from That Face that favors us with His approving smile!

---

[1] C. S. Lewis, *Perelandra* (New York: Macmillan Pub. Co., Inc., 1944) p. 111.
[2] C. S. Lewis, *The Last Battle: Book 7 in the Chronicles* (New York: Collier Books, Macmillan, 1978) p. 170.
[3] Esther Kerr Rusthoi, "When We See Christ," in *Great Gospel Songs and Hymns* (Dallas: Stanps-Baxter of Zondervan, 1976) p. 82.

196 Wisdom and Wealth

How much better to get wisdom than gold, to choose understanding rather than silver (16:16 NIV)!

Most people who have neither wisdom nor wealth would probably choose wealth first. Solomon had both, but at the time he made the choice, he was short on both. Fortunately for him, Solomon had enough wisdom to realize he needed more, so he opted for wisdom over wealth. Because he chose wisdom, God honored him with both (I Chron. 1:7-12).

Those foolish persons who opt for gold and silver over wisdom either fail to get what they go for or discover in the end that their wealth has little worth. Either way, it is disappointing. While wealth facilitates comfort, pleasure and prestige, those temporal areas are transient. Scripture says that money only goes "into a bag with holes" (Hag. 1:6 NKJV). But wisdom touches every worthy area of life, both temporal and eternal.

An Aesop fable tells of a miser who buried his gold to preserve it. A wise man told him he would be just as well off to bury a rock and pretend it was gold![1]

Having treasure does you no good as long as you have it. If you invest it for interest, the interest has no practical value until it is spent. Money can only do you good by getting rid of it! It is not for keeps. When you use it, you lose it! On the contrary, you can use wisdom a thousand times a day for practical help on a thousand items, and always gain more by using it! Spending it replenishes it.

The proverb does not condemn acquiring wealth, but it contrasts the value of wealth to that of wisdom. The two are not mutually exclusive, because some people have both and others have neither. Wisdom can even be used in acquiring wealth, and in handling it. Many have moderate wisdom and mediocre wealth. But if a choice between the two is required, to go with wisdom is to go for value. Long before Solomon instructed us to do it, he did it himself.

---

[1] Aesop, *The Fables of Aesop* (New York: Dorset Press, 1975) p. 86.

The highway of the upright is to depart from evil; he who watches his way preserves his life (16:17 NASB).

The Old Testament uses the word "evil" on two definitions, as we do today—moral evil, which is vice or sin, and utilitarian evil which is misfortune or suffering.[1] Since the first often results in the second, we sometimes use "evil" to include both definitions at the same time. In this proverb, the term seems to include the interlocking of both moral evil and its consequences.

Harriet Beecher Stowe said, "The soul awakes, a trembling stranger, between two dim eternities—the eternal past, the eternal future."[2] The road we take between the two is either upright or "downright," leading upward away from evil or winding its way deeper into evil's syndrome of moral indulgence and its consequences. The higher highway departs from moral evil and leads away from its calamities, eventually into an eternity where "there will be no more . . . pain" (Rev. 21:4 NIV). What Franklin D. Roosevelt envisioned for human civilization is certainly true for those who turn away from evil and lift their faces toward the good. He said, "A line drawn through the middle of the peaks and valleys . . . has an upward trend."[3] Those on the upward curve of the graph are moving away from a dark complex of evil and its consequences with faces lifted toward an immaculate city.

Movement from the past to the future is not a quantum leap. It is a journey with constant caution, watching the roadway, guarding one's footsteps to preserve the destiny. Near the end of life, Faust said: "Yes! To this thought I hold with firm persistence; / The last result of wisdom stamps it true: / He only earns his freedom and existence, / Who daily conquers them anew."[4]

---

[1] See, e.g., Jer. 36:3 RSV: God said, "It may be that . . . Judah will hear all the *evil* that I intend to do to them, so that every one may turn from his *evil* way." The first "evil" is utilitarian and the second is moral.
[2] Harriet Beecher Stowe, *Uncle Tom's Cabin* (New York: Everyman's Library, A. Knoph, Inc., 1994) pp. 289-290.
[3] Quoted in Jon Meacham, *Franklin and Winston* (New York: Random House, 2003) p. 17.
[4] Goethe, *Faust*, Second Part, Act V, Scene 6, p. 487.

198 Problems with Pride

Pride goes before destruction, and a haughty spirit before a fall
(16:18 NKJV).

Some think the proverb is personifying pride, picturing pride on a stroll leaving destruction in its wake. The haughty spirit pushes forward leaving disaster behind. Others see the proud person producing her own destruction and the haughty spirit effecting its own fall. But both interpretations agree to a cause-and-effect relationship between pride and its problems.

In the Hebrew text, the words of this proverb stand precisely in the middle of all the words in the Book of Proverbs. Though without intended significance, this observation does *illustrate* that pride is central to most problems depicted in the proverbs.

A self-centered disposition displaces other-centeredness with an attitude so herculean that others cannot miss it. Proud persons are too preoccupied with self to notice that others are not impressed. Party bores think they are entertaining. Playing for applause, they overplay their hand. Turning every relationship into ego fodder, they isolate themselves. Friendships diminish. Relationships crumble. Egotists perch so long on their poles of pride that when they fall they have nothing to fall back on. Haughty attitudes are forced to self-destruct.

When C. S. Lewis' talking horse fell from its inflated self-image, it said, "I've lost everything." The wise hermit replied, "You've lost nothing but your self-conceit. . . . As long as you know you're nobody very special, you'll be a very decent sort of horse."[1]

The best thing that can happen to an inflated ego is to collapse and crash. When our exaggerated position lets us down, we can accept our actual position without having to protect our props. Then we are free from the crusade to convince others that we are more than we really are. A load rolls off our backs. Settling in with ourselves feels good!

---

[1] C. S. Lewis, *The Horse and His Body: Book 5 in the Chronicles* (New York: Collier Books, Macmillan, 1978) p. 146.

Humble or Haughty 199

Better to be of a humble spirit with the lowly, than to divide the spoil with the proud (16:19 NKJV).

When Billy Graham was at the height of public popularity, a woman said to me, "I was sure no one with his fame could be humble—until I heard him in person. He made no attempt to appear humble, but as he preached I got the feeling I was listening to a humble man." Being humble does not mean to pretend to be inferior. It means accepting your position, without pretending inferiority or superiority. Humility neither exalts oneself nor belittles oneself. It does not think in those terms. The humble person is hardly aware of his humility. John L. Brasher said, "The face of humility is so delicate you can't admire it without marring it."[1]

Many people cannot handle with humility the success that Billy Graham has had. When Shakespeare's Orlando scored a big victory with his exceptional strength, his servant warned him, "The abilities of some people serve them as enemies. Virtues become traitors. What is comely poisons those who have it."[2] The proverb exhorts us to be humble rather than haughty, to identify with the lowly rather than the lofty, the poor rather than the proud.

The late evangelist Ford Philpot once told me that he and Graham planned to be together after a crusade service. They had to elbow their way through thousands of people wanting Graham's autograph. When they finally got to the cab, a reporter said, "Mr. Graham, just give me one minute of your time." Exasperated, Graham said, "Well, get in the front seat and I'll talk to you on the way to the hotel." The reporter said, "With thousands of people reaching for you, are you ever tempted with pride?" Graham replied, "Do you remember the story when Jesus rode the donkey into Jerusalem while all the people on the sidelines shouted his praises? Do you think that donkey was tempted to pride?" The point was made and the lesson was clear.

---

[1] Jon Tal Murphree, *Giant of a Century Trail: Life Story of John L. Brasher* (Apollo, PA: West Pub., 1969) p. 84.
[2] A paraphrase of Shakespeare, *As You Like It,* Act II, Scene 3, lines 10-15.

200 Trusting and Obeying

He who gives attention to the word shall find good, and blessed is he who trusts in the Lord (16:20 NASB).

Assuming the Vulgate is correct that the first line here refers to the word of God, two keys to a happy prosperous life jump up at us. They are obedience and trust.

Genuine faith is not a "blind leap," but it is an open-eyed leap that springs from the point where the factual evidence has led, in the direction that the evidence points. Thus it is an intelligent *faith* that is *founded* on *fact*. Weatherhead said, "It is a faith . . . supported by intellectual discoveries."[1] Whittier wrote: "To one fixed trust my spirit clings; / I know that God is good!"[2]

Trusting entails a willingness to entrust our lives and our future to the God whom we trust, and that means obedience. Chaucer's Marquis said, "I trust in God's great goodness, and therefore / . . . all my ease / I trust to Him to do with as He please."[3] Trusting God means He can trust us to be trustworthy trustees of our responsibility to Him. Goethe's emperor said to his commander-in-chief, "Thy duty, Prince, be trusted to thy hand!"[4]

Trusting and obeying imply each other. Each entails the other. My daughter wrote to me, "A strong arm makes work seem effortless, and a strong faith makes obedience look easy."[5] When they go together, the result is a happy life. Hannah Smith said, "Perfect obedience would be perfect happiness if only we had perfect confidence in the power we were obeying."[6]

---

[1] Leslie D. Weatherhead, *Why Do Men Suffer?* (Nashville: Abingdon Press, 1936) p. 24.

[2] John Greenleaf Whittier, "The Eternal Goodness," Fuller and Kinnick, eds., *Adventures in American Literature* (New York: Harcourt, Brace & World, 1963) p. 620.

[3] Chaucer, "The Clerk's Tale," *Canterbury Tales* (Garden City, NY: Garden City Pub. Co., Inc., 1934) p. 378.

[4] Goethe, *Faust*, Second Part, Act IV, Scene 2, p. 441.

[5] Marisa Murphree Kelly, in a personal letter to me in 2005 commending the faith and obedience of her parents after I had earlier accepted a call to be academic dean at Vennard College in Iowa.

[6] Hannah Whitall Smith, *The Christian's Secret of Happy Life* (Westwood, NJ: Fleming H. Revell, 1952) p. 208.

The Talk and the Talker 201

The wise in heart will be called prudent, and sweetness of the lips increases learning (16:21 NKJV).

Here are two lessons for everybody who attempts to explain anything to anybody. The first is in what you say and the second is in how you say it—the talk and the talker, the substance and the style. Wise persons have something worth saying. They package what they say with clarity, to accommodate the organizing instincts of rational minds.

To communicate, they use a vocabulary that is understandable. C. S. Lewis said, "Any fool can write *learned* language. The vernacular is the real test."[1] The wise talker is soon considered by others to be wise, which adds credibility to what she says.

But the purpose of the talk is not to gain a prudent public image, but to communicate, to inform, to teach, to convince, and even to persuade. This requires the personality of the talker. Without pleasantness of speech ("sweetness of lips"), most messages are not effective, because the personality of the talker is what delivers the message. If the mail carrier fails, the best of messages will not get through. Classroom subjects can become dull and boring with the cold or lifeless personality of a teacher. In a commercial, a dull, dead product comes alive with the brightness of the personality that endorses it. Most people respond or react to people more than to ideas. Warm, winsome personalities are persuasive.

Once something is said in the wrong way with a poor disposition, it will forever have been said that way. Seldom can it be emended. It cannot be resaid to rectify the wrong. Chaucer said, "He who has missaid, I dare explain, / He may not aye recall his words again. / That which is said, is said."[2] Wrong talking is capable of causing much damage because good talk has the ability to produce so much good!

---

[1] C. S. Lewis, *God in the Dock* (Grand Rapids: Eerdmans, 1970) p. 338.
[2] Chaucer, "The Manciple's Tale," *Canterbury Tales* (Garden City, NY: Garden City Pub. Co., 1934) p. 538.

202 Fountain or Folly

Wisdom is a fountain of life to him who has it, but folly is the chastisement of fools (16:22 RSV).

In the 6th century BC, the Pre-Socratic philosophers considered wisdom to be a correct knowledge of the natural universe. A century later the Sophists defined wisdom as virtue, which to them was the ability to be successful and influence others. Then Socrates thought virtue was knowledge, and wisdom consisted in understanding one's lack of knowledge. Later Aristotle said, "Wisdom must be the most finished form of knowledge . . . [It includes] intuitive reason combined with scientific [i.e., factual]."[1] Four centuries before any of those Hellenistic philosophers, Solomon understood wisdom as a combination of knowledge, analytic understanding, and discretion in moral virtue and practical living. (See the Book of Proverbs, Chapters 1-9.)

A paraphrase of this proverb could read: "Wisdom is a fountain to the wise; folly is punishment to fools." The wise are rewarded by their wisdom, and the foolish are punished by their own foolishness. The live fountain of wisdom constantly flows with insight, counsel, direction, and caution to the wise, like an artesian well. Festering in the stale pond of folly are deception, blindness, misdirection, and reckless rashness, from which the foolish continually draw. Wisdom becomes its own reward, and folly its own punishment.

Earlier in the Book of Proverbs, Solomon personified wisdom as crying out: "I am understanding; I have strength; I love them that love me. Those that seek me early shall find me. The Lord possessed me in the beginning. When He prepared the heavens, I was there. I was by Him. I was daily His delight, rejoicing always before Him. Now hearken unto me. Blessed are they that keep my ways. Whoso findeth me findeth life, and shall obtain favor of the Lord."[2]

Gaining wisdom, we gain something very close to God, and in that way become Godlike!

---

[1] Aristotle, *Nichomachean Ethics*, Book VI, Chapter 7, p. 430 in McKeon.
[2] An abridgement of a portion of Proverbs, Chapter 8 (KJV).

A wise man's heart guards his mouth, and his lips promote instruction (16:23 NIV).

A wise heart is not standard equipment for all human models. It is a costly extra that is worth many times its cost. Wisdom reaches beyond knowledge, but it starts with knowledge as a base. J. Ellsworth Kalas spoke of "the accumulation of knowledge, out of which comes at least some measure of wisdom."[1] Standing alone, however, knowledge is inadequate.

Wisdom entails critical analysis that we call reasoning. The human brain contains multiple millions of neuronal cells, each one sending out over ten thousand connecting fibers to contact other nerve cells in a network of trillions of connections. What initially appears to be a chaotic jungle of tangled briars and vines is actually a highly organized network designed to facilitate the reasoning process by networking ideas. Each tidbit in the knowledge fabric interacts with newly observed facts and regularly encountered ideas from other minds. Lord Shaftsbury said, "The mind . . . is a spectator or auditor of other minds."[2] Some of the new notions are bounced off and others are embraced, creating more connections and expanding the network. In the process, unworthy notions are screened out and others are sharpened and refined.

In his prologue to the Proverbs, Solomon included a third ingredient—an ethos for integrity that drives and disciplines us in pursuing wisdom. Charles Colson defined prudence as "a classical virtue that . . . applies moral truth."[3] Solomon attached wisdom and moral discretion to one's relationship with God: "The fear of the Lord is the beginning of wisdom, and knowledge of the Holy One is understanding" (Prov. 9:10 NIV). (Continued in the next essay)

---

[1] Terry Muck, "Interview with President Ellsworth Kalas," *The Asbury Herald* (Wilmore, KY, Summer, 2009) p. 8.

[2] Lord Shaftsbury, "An Inquiry Concerning Virtue and Merit," in Ernest Bernbaum, ed., *Selections from the Pre-Romantic Movement* (New York: Thomas Nelson and Sons, 1929) p. 13.

[3] Charles Colson, "We Need Health-Care Reform," *Christianity Today* (Carol Stream, IL, August 2009) p. 64.

204 Words of Wisdom

CONTINUED FROM PREVIOUS ESSAY

What Solomon calls "a wise heart" is more than knowledge, reason, or moral integrity. Wisdom is a solidarity of all three ingredients in appropriate proportion. When unity converges, wisdom emerges. Standing alone, each ingredient is deficient. When isolated from the other two, even reason is less than wisdom. Pascal said, "The heart has its reasons of which reason knows nothing."[1]

Earlier Solomon defined wisdom as "understanding"[2] which entails all three.

One's heart expresses itself most prominently in what one says. Understanding is spelled out in words of wisdom. Without all three ingredients in harmony, a foolish heart spouts its foolishness, as Shakespeare's Bassanio said to Antonio, "Gratiano speaks an infinite deal of nothing. . . . His reasons are as two grains of wheat hid in two bushels of chaff. You seek all day ere you find them, and when you have them, they are not worth the search."[3] At other times unwise hearts express good ideas that are nevertheless trite. They are stale and stagnant.

When the three ingredients unite into a "wise heart," talk is both intelligent and persuasive. Our blundering conversational goofs sneak out through the cracks in our wisdom. Perhaps wisdom is best expressed in what one does *not* say.

When my son was thinking marriage, he said to me, "I've learned from you a lot of lessons about being married. I have never heard you yell at Mother one time." My "lips were promoting instruction" when I was not aware of it—by what my lips did *not* say. Wisdom is taught by "guarding one's mouth."

Your wise heart "promotes understanding" by both what you say and what you do not say. So Solomon urged us to "get wisdom, and with all thy getting, get understanding" (Prov. 4:7 KJV).

---

[1] Blaise Pascal, *Pensées*, A. J. Krailsheimer, tr. (London: Penguin Books, 1995) p. 127.

[2] Prov. 1:6; 2:2,3,5,6,9; 3:13; 4:1,7; 7:4; 8:5,14; 9:6,10

[3] Shakespeare, *The Mechant of Venice*, Act I, Scene 1, lines 113-118.

Pleasant words are like a honeycomb, sweetness to the soul and health to the body (16:24 RSV).

When honey was used for medicinal purposes, parents had no problem getting children to take their doses. What was good for the body was sweet to the taste. Like drops of honey, pleasant words please the mind and help the body, bringing happiness as well as health. Marilyn McEntyre wrote: When words are "cleaned and polished and placed with a jeweler's precision, [they] . . . surprise us out of our conventionalities and lift us into epiphany and delight."[1]

The human species has tools for dispatching delight that lower orders do not have. Those tools need to be used appropriately. Spoken words have more power for help and healing than written words, because they can be expressed with pleasant voice quality, personal warmth, and facial expression. Some northerners could learn lessons from many southerners and some men from most women in vocal expression. Spoken in the right way at the right time, words can bring the balm of cheerful fragrance to the heavy heart, new energy to the discouraged, and delight to those who are bored. The reverse is also true. Expressing pleasant words improves one's own attitude. It brings health to the one who speaks as well as the one who hears.

Honey, however, must be given in disciplined portions. Too much sweetness becomes sickening. When compliments become flattery, they can damage relationships. Chaucer advised us to speak "advisedly." He said, "Keep your tongue and keep your friend, / A wicked tongue is worse than any fiend. / . . . [The] high God, of His relentless goodness, / Walled up the tongue with teeth and lips and cheeks / That man should speak advisedly when he speaks."[2] Appropriate speaking will sweeten the spirit and strengthen the body with happiness and health.

---

[1] Marilyn Chandler McEntyre, "Why the Care of Language Is More Important than Ever," *Christianity Today* (Carol Stream, IL: September 2009) p. 57.
[2] Chaucer, "The Manciple's Tale," *Canterbury Tales* (Garden City: NY: Garden City Pub. Co., 1934) p. 538.

206 Wrong Seems Right

There is a way that seems right to a man, but its end is the way of death (16:25 NKJV; same as 14:12).

In Goethe's classic work, his character Mephistopheles, representing the devil, enticed Faust to walk the evil way: "Thy steps through life, I'll guide thee, / Will willingly walk beside thee, / Will serve thee at once and forever / With best endeavor." Later Faust rued his being deceived: "And that I might not live alone, unheeded, / Myself at last unto the Devil deeded!" Then as an old man facing death, regretting the road he had taken, he pined aloud: "Now fills the air so many a haunting shape, / That no one knows how best he may escape. / What though One Day with rational brightness beams, / The Night entangles us in webs of dreams."[1]

Literally translated, the proverb reads: "There is a way straight before a man, but the ways of death are the end of it." That is to say, the wrong road is straight ahead when you are headed in the wrong direction. What looks straight looks so right—for you. But the road is a collision course that ends in disaster.

Jesus said many people are on the broad road that leads to death (Matt. 7:13). It is dangerous to walk the road of popular opinion. Paul denounced those who "measure themselves by themselves and compare themselves with themselves" (2. Cor. 10:12). In Chaucer, the dame said to Melibeus, "You have . . . inclined your heart toward the majority, and . . . stooped to folly."[2]

In spite of the lure of contemporary opinion, no one else can trek your road—for you. No one can live your life—for you. Kipling said, "If their souls were your soul, it would be different."[3] Making moral choices is a lonely exercise. Inside, you are isolated from the crowd. In your road to destiny, there is no safety in numbers!

(Continued in the next essay)

---

[1] Goethe, *Faust*, First Part, Scene 4, p. 65; Second Part, Act I, Scene 5, p. 269; Second Part, Act V, Scene 5, p. 480.
[2] Chaucer, "The Tale of Melibeus," *Canterbury Tales* (Garden City, NY: Garden City Pub. Co., 1934) p. 207-208.
[3] Rudyard Kipling, *The Light that Failed* (New York: Books, Inc., n.d.) p. 75.

CONTINUED FROM PREVIOUS ESSAY

Roadways are not built for parking lots, but for going some place. And a journey is not ordinarily taken for its own sake but for its destination, which gives meaning to the trip and makes it worthwhile. Traversing life's road with no eye on the future leaves no purpose beyond the present. Those who live simply for the joy of living eventually lose their reason for living. Without a chosen destination, they meet sudden dead end with an unwanted destiny.

Churchill wrote, "When the notes of life ring false, men should correct them by referring to the tuning fork of death."[1]

From the vantage point of the destination, the journey has renewable meaning. Sir Walter Scott's dying woman said to Fitz-James, "This hour of death has given me more / Of reason's power than years before."[2] Christians want life's journey to be as pleasant as possible, but the inconvenience of the pilgrimage is accepted for the joy of arrival. Kierkegaard exaggerated, but he said, "Christianity . . . issues no checks except those payable in another world."[3]

To Bunyan's pilgrims, Mr. By-Ends exclaimed, "We never strive against wind and tide; we are most zealous when religion goes in silver slippers. We love to walk with [Christ] . . . in the street if the sun shines and the people applaud." The pilgrim replied, "If you go with us, you must go against wind and tide, . . . in His rags as well as His silver slippers, and stand by Him when bound in irons, as well as when He walketh the streets with applause."[4]

Those who chart their odyssey by the biblical roadmap reach a destiny worth every sacrifice. Since we are on the road of life anyhow, let's shoot for a destination worth the journey!

---

[1] Jon Meacham, *Franklin and Winston* (New York: Random House, 2003) p. 35.
[2] Sir Walter Scott, *The Lady of the Lake* (New York: The New American Library, 1962) Canto Fourth, Sec. XXVII, p. 111.
[3] Soren Kierkegaard, *Attack Upon Christendom,* Walter Lowrie, tr. (Boston: The Beacon Press, 1956) p. 112.
[4] John Bunyan, *The Pilgrim's Progress* (Grand Rapids: Zondervan, 1966) pp. 82-83.

208 The Desires that Drive Us

A worker's appetite works for him; his mouth urges him on (16:26 RSV).

Physical and emotional appetites are gifts from the Creator to bless our lives with abundance. Without control, they can drive us to gluttony, dishonest gain, indulgence, illicit love and infidelity. When they are regimented with discipline, they provide personal and social fulfillment. Appetites are tools to work for us.

Without desire we could have no pleasure, either physical, mental or emotional, for pleasure by its nature is derived from the process of gratifying desire. Hunger makes eating a pleasurable experience. Even animals are tamed and trained by fulfilling their appetite for food. For humans, that appetite is an important tool to motivate us to industry. Paul said, "If anyone will not work, neither let him eat" (2 Thes. 3:10 NASB). That assumes, of course, that the person is able and work is available. Goethe wrote, "Waste not a day in vain digression. . . . / Seize every possible impression, / And make it firmly your possession."[1]

Work not only feeds our mouths; it also fulfills the emotional need for self-respect. In our economy, some persons manage to become indulgent without having to work. Easily they can become slovenly sloths and lose the personal self-esteem that comes from honest labor.

Browning's Paracelsus bemoaned, "I trifle while time fleets, and this occasion, lost, will never return."[2]

When our innate desires drive us to industry, the fulfillment of those desires become incentives to engage us in worthwhile activity. Appetites work as motives and their gratification works as incentives. But tools are worthless unless they are employed. And good tools become menacing tools when used for wrong purposes. Thank God for our appetites! Now we must learn to use them in the right way.

---

[1] Goethe, *Faust*, Prelude, pp. 8-9.
[2] Robert Browning, "Paracelsus," *The Complete . . . Works . . .* (Cambridge, MA: Houghton Mifflin, 1895) p. 44.

An ungodly man digs up evil, and it is on his lips like a burning fire
(16:27 NKJV).

The subject of this proverb is more than irreligious. The original wording makes him a vile, depraved scoundrel. Instead of digging to find trash to expose, he devises evil schemes, digging pits to entrap victims, planning and plotting evil acts. He is an arsonist, igniting malicious flames with a tongue of fire and bitter, burning words.

Our population is punctuated with miniature terrorists, culturally inhibited from obstreperous acts of terrorism, but operating from the same mindset, getting a rush of ego satisfaction from targeting innocent people.

Evil persons live in a perpetual process of losing inhibitions for more blatant acts of evil. Vibrations of conscience die out. Eventually they lose the ability to recoil from evil atrocities, and get an adrenaline rush from outrageous barbarism. The instinct for goodness is lost. To them, evil is not only a tool for revenge or an outlet for hatred. It is a sport for fun. It is mischief for the sake of mischief. As Chesterton says, Evil people may not get "wilder and wilder, but [they get] meaner and meaner."[1]

They are not only dangerous to other people, but evil itself is dangerous to them. It encages them like tigers in their own evil cages. Evil is progressive, not static, and if not checked it plunges its participants into a downward spiraling syndrome. Lewis says, "Evil of itself [can] never reach a worst. Evil . . . could never in a thousand eternities find a way to arrest [itself]. If it could, it would [not] be evil."[2] By its nature, evil runs out of other options, endlessly getting worse.

Since we all have participated in evil, our only recourse is to access God's rescue operation initiated by Christ, and to get in His rehabilitation program.

---

[1] G. K. Chesterton, "The Sign of the Broken Sword," *Favorite Father Brown Stories* (New York: Dover Publications, Inc., 1993) p. 43.
[2] C. S. Lewis, *The Pilgrim's Regress* (Grand Rapids, Wm. B. Eerdmans Publishing Co., 1979) p. 181.

210 Disseminating Dissension

A perverse man sows strife, and a whisperer separates the best of friends (16:28 NKJV).

When seed-bits of discord are sowed, they germinate and multiply. Innuendoes are repeated and exaggerated, producing multiple bits of strife. Whisperers are really more damaging than loudmouths, because they are taken seriously when they drop their voice and lift their eyebrows. What they say is propelled by the props. In its effect, a whisper shouts!

Aeneas made a little speech depicting Rumor, the fowl goddess of talebearing: "Rumor is of all pests the swiftest. In her freedom of movement lies her power, and she gathers new strength from her going. She begins as a small and timorous creature; then she grows until she towers into the air. . . . . Rumor is fleet of foot, and swift are her wings; she is a vast, fearful monster, with a watchful eye set under every feather . . . and for every one of them a tongue . . . and an ear ever alert. By night she flies hissing through the dark, . . . repeating alike facts and fiction."[1]

Tabloids and other news agencies feed the public frenzy for the forbidden with verbal peep shows, disseminating stories that should be hushed, devastating reputations, infiltrating the culture with filth. Smut sticks, long after sugar is washed away. Paracelsus said, "Men . . . reject the weak and scorn the false rather than praise the strong and true."[2] Scandal results in disgrace, division and dissension. Relationships are wrecked. Gossip is grossly unfair because it is behind the victim's back. The one who is implicated has no opportunity to defend herself.

Instead of *hurting* people, why not make *helping* people our agenda? Why not broadcast a person's good points rather than bad? It will give the person a fair shake, it will support public mores in the culture, and it will make you feel good about yourself!

---

[1] Virgil, *The Aeneid*, W. F. Jackson Knight, tr. (London: Penguin Books, 1958) Book Four, pp. 102-103.
[2] Robert Browning, "Paracelsus," *The Complete . . . Works . . .* (Cambridge, MA: Houghton Mifflin, 1895) p. 48.

Opportunities and Obligations 211

A violent man entices his neighbor, and leads him into the way that is not good (16:29 NKJV).

Not to be a positive influence is a monumental waste of opportunity. To be a negative influence is even worse. It is one thing to be a neutral bystander, but quite another to join the multiple forces that lead people astray. Not to help others along the road is inexcusably bad. How much worse it is to hinder and hurt our fellow pilgrims on life's journey!

When violent people cannot subdue others by political pressure and public threats, they resort to personal influence, enticing their victims by pretending goodwill and promising favors. Threats are switched to subtle bribes and deception. Shakespeare said, "To win us to our harm, the instruments of darkness tell us truths, win us with honest trifles, to betray [us]."[1]

Unsuspecting people are duped by smiles, compliments, and staged congeniality. Forceful personalities overwhelm those that are weaker. Distinguishing the genuine from the phony is sometimes a formidable challenge. King Duncan, surprised by the thane's treason, said, "There's no art to find the mind's construction on the face. He was a gentleman on whom I built my absolute trust."[2] The first lesson here is not to be sucked in by deceit.

The greater lesson is to guard against the temptation to become "instruments of darkness" for our own favors. Using our personal influence for ulterior purposes reduces us to the emptiest, meanest, most spurious level of superficiality!

People are vulnerable to bad influence, but most are just as responsive to good influence. That gives us the daily privilege to be influences for good, even when we are not aware of it. Our lives, our attitudes, our principles are contagious. Others absorb them. Because people can be influenced, we can be influential. We have enviable opportunities! Those opportunities become our obligations.

---

[1] Shakespeare, *Macbeth*, Act I, Scene 3, lines 123-125.
[2] *Op. cit.*, Act I Scene 4, lines 11-14.

212 Shutting the Eyes and Pursing the Lips

He shutteth his eyes to devise froward things; moving his lips he bringeth evil to pass (16:30 KJV).

The last three proverbs depict evildoers who victimize innocent people, separate neighbors with rumors and gossip, and use trickery and deceit to lead people astray. The present proverb employs imagery to picture those who set their purposes for evil pursuits. Two different interpretations of the imagery both picture those who commit premeditated evil.

The first says they "close their eyes" in deep concentration, shutting out other ideas while concocting their crooked schemes and hatching their plots. When the plot is planned they "constrict their lips," indicating a menacing resolve to move with the plot. The second interpretation says evil people "wink the eye" and "purse the lips," signaling to their cohorts that a secret scheme is in place to entrap an unknowing person. Both show premeditated evil.

David Hume said that both *"reason* and *sentiment* concur in almost all moral determinations." He adds that an "amiable or odious action . . . depends on some internal sense."[1] Premeditated evil suggests the interplay of both one's mind and one's evil disposition. When the two work together, the volition is outnumbered and usually complies.

Marcus Aurelius says that "offenses through desire are more blamable than those committed through anger."[2] He explains that people offend from anger because of the pain they feel, but from desire because of the pleasure they want. In this proverb the evil person seems to commit the more serious sin, simply for the pleasure of doing it. Committing evil from the heat of the moment is abominable. Planning it in advance from the desire for pleasure is atrocious! Righteous persons desire goodness, and they operate from premeditated righteousness.

---

[1] David Hume, *An Inquiry Concerning the Principles of Morals* (New York: The Bobbs-Merrill Co., 1957) p. 6.
[2] Marcus Aurelius, *The Thoughts of the Emperor*, George Long, tr. (New York: John B. Alden, Pub., 1887) p. 53. Aurelius credits Theophrastus with the idea, without giving specific citation.

Physically Old and Morally Strong 213

A hoary head is a crown of glory; it is gained in a righteous life
(16:31 KJV).

The old man helping Orlando said, "My age is as a [vigorous] winter, frosty but kindly."[1] Gray hair belongs to seniors, and it is deemed a crown of splendor when it sits atop a righteous life. Moral character is not acquired in a day; it is developed over a lifetime. Warren Wiersbe says, "A reputation can be made—or lost—overnight, but it takes years to build character."[2]

Christian character is not prefabbed. It is not a collection of precut materials that can be assembled in a single day. The infrastructure of moral strength does not come in a singular spiritual experience. Someone with a checkered lifestyle raises the alibi, "But this is who I am—the way I'm made." But morally, you are not *made*. You are *being made*. God is not finished with you. Aristotle said, "Moral virtue comes about as a result of habit."[3] H. C. Morrison said, "There is no such thing as strong, holy character without sore trial, bitter testing, severe temptation, and positive decision."[4] There are no shortcuts to character.

Every courageous exercise installs new courage. Every strong grip toughens the skin and builds the moral muscle. Stumbling blocks become stepping stones. Eventually, as C. S. Lewis said, "All natures that were your enemies become slaves to dance before you . . . and firmness for your feet to rest on. . . . The strengths that once opposed your will shall be obedient fire in your blood and heavenly thunder in your voice!"[5]

How lamentable it would be to grow physically weak with age without growing morally strong! How gratifying it is to arrive at a senior age with a moral diadem of majestic splendor!

---

[1] Shakespeare, *As You Like It*, Act II, Scene 3, lines 52-53.
[2] Warren Wiersbe, *God Isn't in a Hurry* (Grand Rapids: Baker Books, 1994) p. 12.
[3] Aristotle, *Nichomachean Ethics*, Book II, Chapter 1, p. 331 in McKeon.
[4] H. C. Morrison, *From Sanai to Calvary* (Louisville, KY: Pentecostal Pub. Co., 1942) p. 81.
[5] C. S. Lewis, *The Great Divorce* (New York: Macmillan Pub. Co., 1978 printing) pp. 103-104.

214 Ruling over Rage

He who is slow to anger is better than the mighty, and he who rules his spirit, than he who captures a city (16:32 NASB).

Alexander the Great conquered the vast Persian empire, but in a fit of rage he killed his own best friend Clitus.[1] He conquered the world but could not control himself. For some people, it is easier to take a city than to subdue their own inner beasts.

Certainly biochemical makeup and past conditioning create more formidable problems for some than for others, but when carnality camps with chemistry, the alliance is indomitable. Ruled by rage, people get careless about future consequences. Intemperate anger blinds their minds to the new world of fractured relationships they are creating.

When Scotland's warring chieftain Roderick Dhu was ruled by revenge, the Hermit Monk warned, "'Tis hard for such to view unfurled / The curtain of the future world."[2] Without ruling yourself, you are ruled by your incorrigible self. Losing your present, you lose your future.

If you vent unjustified anger, you become contagious to yourself. Future patterns of expression are infected with the virus of past patterns. Emotional sinuses get congested and clogged. Vehemence is coughed up from moral bronchitis. The fire of ire burns the throat.

When inhibitions are broken down, precedents are set. The man who honks his horn in road rage finds it easier to honk the next time. Snapping at a spouse creates a pattern that is hard to break. Snarling at a colleague is easier the second time around, and automatic the third time. Brake pads cannot stop a steamroller. Without inhibitions, freewheeling persons careen out of control. When they cannot vent, they seethe. Refueling the flames, they boil and stew. They get headaches and ulcers, and lose the joy of living—because they have lost control of themselves!

---

[1] *Compton's Encyclopedia* (Chicago: F. E. Compton & Co., 1952) Vol. I, p. 148-149.

[2] Sir Walter Scott, *The Lady of the Lake* (New York: The American Library, 1962) Canto Fourth, Sec. VI, p. 95.

Casting Lots and Flipping Coins 215

The lot is cast into the lap, but the whole disposing thereof is of the Lord (16:33 KJV). Also 18:18.

Like other ancient people, the Hebrews recognized that many occurrences are beyond human ability to cause or alter. Life itself is determined by a source outside oneself. In *The Odyssey*, Homer quotes the goddess Athena as saying, "Thou wert . . . not born without the will of the gods."[1]   In addition to divine determination, blind chance was acknowledged as a cause of some occurrences.[2] When decisions had to be made for which they had no direction, civil people often resorted to chance as a method that does not require preferential treatment—casting lots, rolling dice, or flipping coins—like the coin toss to start a football game.

The God-conscious Hebrews placed the two outside sources, God and chance, beside each other, affirming a possible connection between the two. They recognized that God Himself was in a position to determine the way the lot would fall—if He should choose to do so—thereby determining occurrences through secondary causes. They did not believe, however, that all random occurrences were divinely determined, but only those that were appropriately referred to God. Then He either caused the lots to fall a certain way, or He caused the chance occurrences to serve His ultimate purposes. Thus they could say, "The disposing of the lot is of the Lord."

Many of our unfortunate situations, however, we have brought on ourselves. We humans demand our independence and then blame God for the effects we ourselves cause. In William Young's novel, God says, "We [the Trinity] carefully respect your choices, so we work within your systems even while we seek to free you from them."[3]   (Continued in the next essay)

---

[1] Homer, *The Odyssey of Homer*, Butcher & Lang, trs. (New York: The MacMillan Co., 1911) Book III, p. 26.
[2] Chance properly means without a cause, either natural or intentional. Here it is used in the popular sense of accident, i.e., unintended yet still by natural or social causation.
[3] William P. Young, *The Shack* (Newbury Park, CA: Windblown Media, 2007) p. 123.

216 Orchestrated Occurrences

CONTINUED FROM PREVIOUS ESSAY
When we create our own dilemmas, we should expect the automatic fallout. Chaucer said, "For whoso makes of God his adversary / To work out anything that is contrary / To what He wills, he'll surely never thrive, / Though he should multiply while he's alive."[1] Nor does God regularly exempt us from the effects of natural causes. Since the natural system is God's system, even ancient pagans understood God's reluctance to interfere excessively with the system. When "the mother of the gods" asked her son Jove to prevent Aeneas' fleet from peril on the sea, he replied, "Are keels made by mortal hands to own immortal privilege?"[2]

Yet God is active through the happenings of life to work through those random occurrences that we regularly face. In Young's novel, God says, "I work incredible good out of unspeakable tragedies."[3] Paul did not say that God purposes everything that happens, but he said that God makes everything that happens "work for good" (Rom. 8:28). For His children He screens the others out. Leslie Weatherhead wrote: "This is a guarded universe. . . . Nothing can break through . . . to smash us or destroy the purpose of our lives."[4] God "disposes the lots!"

Plus(!)—God Himself often originates for us special experiences or alters events. Many, many occurrences in my life that I attributed to chance now seem so obviously to have been orchestrated by God. I can speak from experience that God "disposes the lots." Lon Woodrum's protagonist closed his novel by saying, "It came up out of my inner being . . . [that] life was an adventure, and with God in it, anything *good* could happen!"[5]

---

[1] Chaucer, "The Canon's Yeoman's Tale," *Canterbury Tales* (Garden City, NY: Garden City Pub. Co., 1934) p. 528.

[2] Virgil, *The Aeneid* (London: Penguin Books, 1958) Book Nine, p. 228.

[3] William P. Young, *The Shack* (Newburg Park, CA: Windblown Media, 2007) p. 185.

[4] Leslie D. Weatherhead, *Why Do Men Suffer?* (Nashville: Abingdon Press, 1936) pp. 206-207.

[5] Lon Woodrum, *Stumble Upon the Dark Mountains* (Waco, TX: Word Books, 1956) p. 146.

Contention or Contentment 217

Better is a dry morsel with quietness than a house full of feasting with strife (17:1 NKJV).

Here we have four ingredients composing two sets of opposites—dry bread or a feast, and strife or peace. When you connect the two sets, a feast with peace would be the best, and dry bread with strife the worst. But the proverb aligns them for comparative value rather than superlative and says dry bread with contentment is better than a feast with contention.

Peaceful congeniality rides comfortably with either a cuisine of lamb chops or a dried-out end piece of bread, but banqueting and quarreling do not belong together at the same table. Either good food will dissolve a dispute or the dispute will ruin the good food. The two do not comfortably co-exist.

The reason that peace is better than a feast and contention is worse than dry crust is that contention is *morally* bad while dry bread is only *lousy* bad. Relational evil is stronger than good taste, and relational good is stronger than bad taste.

In the Old Testament, the best meals came when the people made a peace-offering, because they served at the table the portion of the sacrifice that was not consumed on the altar. Thus the Hebrew word for sacrifice was often used for feast.

The irony of this proverb is a parody of paradox. *Contention* can sabotage the very meal that is provided by the *peace*-offering! The peace-offering not only produced no peace, but it provided the occasion for strife. Religious gestures can undermine the religious purpose of the gestures. Dissension preempts harmony. Bickering and backbiting replace tranquillity and repose.

Food flavors are enhanced in a congenial social context. Insipid servings become delicious. Of all times of the day, family mealtime should be the warmest, brightest, and most social. Correcting children's behavior should be postponed. Differences of opinion should be modified. Even if the menu is bland and sparse, eating together can be a cherished social activity. Not only does it improve digestion, but it is also a potent emotional therapy.

218 Servants and Sons

A servant who acts wisely will rule over a son who acts shamefully, and will share in the inheritance among brothers (17:2 NASB).

In ancient Israel, servitude was governed by divine mandates that gave slaves a chance for a better life.[1] Slaves were regarded as something like secondary members of the family. A rebellious son could be sold as a slave, allowing a faithful servant to move into the son's position to claim the inheritance. Even Saul's lazy son lost his inheritance to the good servant (2 Sam. 16:4).

It is ironic that King Solomon's own son did not read or else did not heed this proverb of his father. So the kingdoms of ten tribes were wrested from him and given to the son of Solomon's slave, leaving Rehoboam with only the one tribe of Judah (See 1 Kgs. 11:26 ff.).

The principle is operative in life today. Diligence and faithfulness supersede birthright. Wisdom trumps privilege. Those who read résumés look for more than one's heritage.

The principle extends into God's great redemptive program. God said, "The sons of the stranger . . . will I bring to my holy mountain" (Is. 56:6-7 KJV). Jesus said, "The kingdom of God will be taken away from you and given to a people who will produce its fruits" (Matt. 21:43 NIV). Again He said, "Many that are first shall be last, and the last shall be first" (Matt. 19:30 KJV).

We who were "children of wrath" (Eph. 2:3 KJV) have become "children of God" (1 Jno. 3:10). The point of spiritual rebirth (Jno. 3:3,7,8; 1 Jno. 3:9) is that slaves can become sons! Spiritual birthright replaces natural birthright. We become children of a higher kingdom, with a new inheritance!

When Faust finally entered heaven, Goethe's character Margaret exclaimed: "The spirit-choir around him seeing, / New to himself, he scarce divines / HIS HERITAGE OF NEW-BORN BEING, / When like the Holy Host he shines."[2]

---

[1] Voluntary slavery was allowed for those who wished to transfer to the slave owner a debt they could not pay, and forced slavery was allowed for criminals as reparation for misconduct.

[2] Goethe, *Faust*, Second Part, Act V, Scene 7, p. 505. Capitals added.

The refining pot is for silver and the furnace for gold, but the Lord tests hearts (17:3 NASB).

To say that God *imposes* affliction on humans for *His* purposes is not an adequate answer to a puzzling question. But to say that God can *use* our trials for *our own* good is quite different.

In processing silver and gold, the fires of crucibles and furnaces are used for two purposes, both of which are analogous to our afflictions. First, fire discovers the inferior ingredients by forcing them to separate as dross. Similarly, our trials like fire reveal to us the unworthy elements of our mental, emotional and moral states that need to be eliminated. We never know what is in our character until we observe ourselves in temptation or affliction.

Second, as fire purifies precious minerals by burning out everything that cannot withstand the heat, the Lord can use our trials to purify our lives. Under heat, our values take shape. Unworthy items are identified and dealt with. Trials become redemptive.

Adelaide Proctor wrote: "I thank Thee more that all our joy / Is touched with pain; / That shadows fall on brightest hours, / That thorns remain; / So that earth's bliss may be our guide, / And not our chain."[1] The great Roman Emperor said "a hindrance" can become "a furtherance."[2] Testing can be constructive. Suffering can be sacramental. God intends to sort out the worthless from the priceless, until we are refined like precious gold!

Malachi exclaimed, "And He shall sit as a smelter and purifier of silver, and . . . purify the sons of Levi and purge them as gold" (Mal. 3:3 KJV). While the early Christians were under persecution, the apostle Peter wrote to them: "You have been distressed by various trials, that the proof of your faith, being more precious than gold which is perishable, even though tested by fire, may be found to result in praise and glory and honor" (1 Pet. 1:6-7).

---

[1] A. Proctor, "My God, I Thank Thee," *The Methodist Hymnal* (Nashville: Methodist Pub. House, 1966) p. 50.

[2] Marcus Aurelius, *The Thoughts of the Emperor* (New York: John B. Alden, Pub., 1887) p. 88.

220 Hearing and Heeding

An evildoer listens to wicked lips, and a liar gives heed to a mischievous tongue (17:4 RSV).

Daily we are bombarded with a barrage of high-decibel volume. Most people heed what they like to hear and tune out what is distasteful. You can tell the kind of person someone is by the CDs she listens to, the television programs she watches, and the kind of material she reads.

Depraved minds delight in depraved sounds. Never content with their own depravity, they crave to hear more evil, to see more evil, eliciting help to excite their own debauchery. They delight in profane, obscene, or abusive talk, because their hearts resonate with it. They take pleasure in hearing it. The evil of our culture was exposed when the television networks discovered they could attract more listeners by using course, raunchy language!

Accommodating an inward bias bends a person more and more in the direction toward which he is prone. Evil not only attracts evil people, but it confirms their evil inclinations. They become what they hear and see. Drooling over evil sounds and sights is like submitting voluntarily to massive, merciless tentacles. Reveling in reports of violence or licentious fantasies scars the mind and enslaves the soul. Those who do so become their own prisons to enslave themselves. Mental and moral addiction is more enslaving than chemical addiction. Marcus Aurelius said, "The soul of man does violence to itself when it becomes an abcess."[1]

Similarly, those who hear and heed goodness become better persons. A heart that delights in it becomes more delighted with it. What you take pleasure in becomes a part of your nature. It streams in through your ears and eyes and lodges in your heart. Beholding more beauty makes you a more beautiful person. Inhaling more roses gives you a more fragrant spirit. Experiencing more goodness intensifies the core of goodness at the center of your life.

---

[1] Marcus Aurelius, *The Thoughts of the Emperor* (New York: John B. Alden, pub., 1887) p. 56.

Commendable or Condemnable 221

He who mocks the poor reproaches his Maker; he who is glad at calamity will not go unpunished (17:5 NKJV).

Those who profile all poor persons as lazy. Those who consider themselves superior because they are affluent. Those who get their entertainment by watching news reports of disasters. Those who glory in the tragedies depicted in movies and novels. Both those who make sport of the unfortunate and those who gloat over their misfortune position themselves for condemnation, and will not be acquitted. So says the proverb.

But disregarding the impoverished by contributing to poverty is also making mock of the poor. For a business to sell commodities at lower prices because of increased sales, or because it refuses to price gouge, is commendable. But to do so by underpaying employees or exploiting those who provide raw materials is not only contemptible. It is condemnable! And those that justify price gouging by combining scarcity with human need are despicable!

The phrases "reproach his Maker" and "will not go unpunished" show a connection between our attitudes toward other people and our relationship with God. The horizontal mirrors the vertical. Christ exhorted us to feed the hungry, clothe the needy, attend the ill, visit prisoners. Then in a startling pronouncement, He identified Himself with the people of misfortune: "Inasmuch as ye have done it . . . as ye did it not . . . to one of the least of these, ye have done it . . . ye did it not . . . unto Me" (Matt. 25:35-46 KJV). Our attitudes and actions toward hurting people do not end with those people. We are committing those actions against God! He is the reference point for everything we do! Rejecting His mandate, we face a divine sentence!

When we do, we ourselves will be desperate for mercy. But as the Duke said to Shylock, "How shalt thou hope for mercy, rendering none?"[1] Mercy in, mercy out! We get it when we give it.

---

[1] Shakespeare, *The Mechant of Venice*, Act IV, Scene 1, line 88.

222 Fathers and Children

Children's children are the crown of old men, and the glory of children is their father (17:6 NKJV).

Fathers and children delight in each other like a reciprocal ornament. Mutual delight breaks down when either the children do not give honor or parents do not earn it.

Goddesses like Venus cherished being mothers, but Hellenistic and Roman gods were more interested in power, authority, and control than in being fatherly toward humans. Aeneas even prayed to the god Apollo, "Be to us a father god,"[1] but Aeneas was disappointed.

The notion of God as Father is unique to Judaism and Christianity. In Islam, Muslims have a rosary with 99 beads, each with a different name or title for God, not one of which is "Father." But God is depicted as father throughout the Old Testament,[2] and even more so in the New. Over and over Jesus addressed God as "Father." God said, "I will be a Father to you, and you will be my sons and daughters" (2 Cor. 6:18 NIV). Throughout the epistles of Paul and John, we are called children of God. In His dying hour, Jesus prayed, "Father, into Thy hands I commend my spirit" (Lu. 23:46 KJV). Jesus taught, "When you pray say, Our Father . . ." (Matt. 6:9; Lu. 11:2).

As a rule, children acquire their image of God from their image of their own fathers. Those whose fathers are tyrants usually transfer that image to God. Indulgent fathers give their children an image of God as a pushover. Those who think of their fathers as authority-love easily acquire the biblical image of God. The word "father" connotes more than a sire. It has a nuance of affection, care, and even delight in the child. The psalmist was so bold as to announce that God "delighted in me!" (Ps. 18:19).

When children see God in their own fathers, they are apt to discover a father in God. Then, knowing that God delights in them as children, they delight in Him as Father. With mutual honor and delight, each becomes a crown of glory for the other.

---

[1] Virgil, *The Aeneid* (London: Penguin Books, 1958) Book Three, p. 77.
[2] See Ps. 103:13; Prov. 3:12; Is. 9:6; 63:16; 64:8; Jer. 3:19; 31:9; Hos. 11:1; Mal. 1:6; 2:10.

Excellent speech is not fitting for a fool; much less are lying lips to a prince (17:7 NASB).

This original proverb is laced with delicate subtleties that make it difficult to reduce to a crisp capsule. The word translated "fool" refers to a crude, uncultured person. Attempting to use eloquent speech above his capacity makes him look like an arrogant fool, using "arrogant speech" (see NIV). Those who regularly use street talk thinking they can switch to elegant speech for a job interview, or for talk with a distinguished person, or for public speaking, end up demonstrating both their pride and their folly. Attempting to step out of yourself to become someone you are not leaves you with an awkward clumsiness that you cannot hide. As the damsel said to Peter, "Your speech betrays you" (Matt. 26:73).

Here are two remedies. First, *be what you are* without pretense. Emily Dickinson wrote: "I'm Nobody! Who are you? / Are you Nobody too? . . . / How dreary to be Somebody! / How public, like a Frog, / To tell your name the livelong June / To an admiring Bog!"[1]

Second, *change what you are*. Speaking correctly in your own home enables you to feel comfortable speaking correctly when it is required. You can become what you aspire to be! The term translated "prince" more specifically means an urbane person of nobility, from whom excellent speech is expected. He is so accustomed to vocal style that he feels comfortable with it. He can be the same in public that he is in private. The proverb says you should no more expect rude or deceptive words from a noble than eloquent words from a fool.

Two or three centuries after the proverb was written, Isaiah said, "No longer will the fool be called noble . . . for the fool speaks folly . . . and spreads error. . . . But the noble man makes noble plans, and by noble deeds he stands" (Isa. 32:5-8 NIV).

---

[1] Emily Dickinson, "I'm Nobody! Who Are You?" Gordon N. Ray, ed., *Masters of American Literature* (Cambridge, MA: The Riverside Press of Houghton Mifflin Co., 1959) p. 783.

224 Doing Right and Being Safe

A gift is as a precious stone in the eyes of him that hath it. Whithersoever it turneth, it prospereth (17:8 KJV).

The metaphor is not clear. If it is a gift to placate anger like Jacob's gift to Esau, it is justified. More translators, however, interpret it to be a bribe. And "*it* turns and prospers" (KJV, ASV) connects with the "precious stone," while "*he* turns and prospers" (RSV, NIV, NASB) does not. A lapidary cuts various faces on a gem so that, any way it is turned, at least one facet will sparkle in the light. Similarly, any way a bribe is turned, it "prospers" in favoring both the giver and the receiver with benefits. The proverb is a warning to shun the lure.

Bribery is morally wrong, because the purpose is to corrupt the conduct of the bribed. And it is dishonest, otherwise it would not be deceptive. The transaction is done under the counter. Its success depends on everyone else's ignorance of the matter. Letting the truth be known would blow the cover, so truth is locked in the safe of falsity.

And bribery is dangerous. After the money is given, the briber depends on the bribed to be *honest* enough to keep his commitment to *dishonesty*. Honesty is required to protect dishonesty! But a person who is dishonest in one area is capable of dishonesty in other areas. Those who can be bought off for silence are capable of snitching for a higher price. The bribed can become a double agent. Under pressure, silence from hush money can spring a leak.

And the bribed can always raise the price, blackmailing the briber for repeated layouts. As a quick fix, bribery can lose its power. When Brahanto thought his daughter had deceived him, he said to his unwelcomed son-in-law, "Look to her, Moor, if thou hast eyes to see; / She has deceived her father, and may thee."[1]

Engaging in duplicity for the benefits of duplicity is precarious! It is always right to shun the wrong. It is always safe to do the right.

---

[1] Shakespeare, *Othello*, Act I, Scene 3, lines 293-294.

He who covers over an offense promotes love, but whoever repeats the matter separates close friends (17:9 NIV).

So you want everyone else to think that you are "in the know." Your mind itches to tattle to those who have not heard. You get an ego surge from reporting misdeeds.

But doing so starts a chain of damage to friendships wherever the report is repeated. And when word gets back that you are the informer, you have forever lost that person as a friend. Squelching an offensive matter fosters love and friendship. Squealing over the matter promotes hatred and enmity. The food that feeds your ego is expensive. You will be making time payments on that egotism as long as the friendship is damaged.

But we ourselves have made outrageous mistakes and committed shameful evils. Ancient Roman playwright Horace said, "One who expects his friend not to be offended by his own warts will pardon the other's pimples. . . . One who craves indulgence for failings should grant them in return." Again Horace said, "The lover . . . fails to see the lady's blemishes. . . . I could wish that we made the like mistake in friendship."[1]

Jesus said, "In the same way you judge others, you will be judged, and with the measure you use, it will be measured to you. Why do you look at the speck of sawdust in your brother's eye and pay no attention to the plank in your own eye?" (Matt. 7:2-3).

You and I are not aware of every contributing cause to the other person's mistake. We cannot read her history well enough. Besides, God is the judge. From us, those who have failed need mercy.

Lon Woodrum wrote: "We'd better stick to *mercy* while 'long life's way we trudge; / Fer *we'll* be needing mercy when the *Lord* is come t' judge!"[2]

---

[1] Horace, *Satires, Epistles, Ars Poetica* (Cambridge, MA: Harvard University Press, 1991) Satire III, Book I, pp. 39, 35.
[2] Lon Woodrum, "Judgin'," in Woodrum, *Take My Heart* (Kansas City, MO: Beacon Hill Press, n.d.) p. 10.

226 Directed or Driven

A rebuke goes deeper into one who has understanding than a hundred blows into a fool (17:10 NASB).

The primary lesson is for us *who are given the rebuke*. Being directed by understanding (NASB, RSV) and discernment (NIV), being wise (KJV) and sensible (CEV), is a hundred-to-one times better than being driven by foolishness. Wise persons change courses by one reprimand, and the foolish are still wayward after a hundred lashes. Rejecting reproof, they punish themselves by locking themselves in prison stocks for further punishing. Entailed in wisdom is the humility to accept rebuke, and entailed in folly is the pride to resist it.

The secondary lesson is for us *who give rebuke*. How do we get the attention of those who are driven by the foolishness of pride?

Preferably we first give the gentle rebuke in the form of teaching and explanation. Only after that fails do we resort to threats of punishment. The corrective should precede the judicial. Insofar as possible, behavior modification should be achieved by positive incentives rather than negative motivation. People should be directed rather than driven, with reason rather than threats, appealing to wisdom rather than punishment.

In the dichotomy of wisdom and folly, wisdom marches with reason and folly rides the slippery slope of passion. Kahlil Gibran, the prophet of Lebanon, wrote: "Passion, unattended, is a flame that burns to its own destruction. Therefore let your soul exalt your reason to the height of passion, that it may sing."[1] When passion is disciplined with reason, and reason is proportioned with passion, we have a healthy pride that preempts a sickly pride, enabling us to accept reproof. Onward we go, our lives laughing and our souls singing!

One version translates the proverb, "A sensible person accepts correction, but you can't beat sense into a fool" (CEV).

---

[1] Kahlil Gibran, *The Prophet* (New York: Alfred A. Knopf, 1926) p. 57.

An evil man is bent only on rebellion; a merciless official will be sent against him (17:11 NIV).

Some translators transpose the subject and the predicate to say that rebellious persons seek evil. If either proposition is true, however, both are true, because each implies the other.

Moral evil by nature is rebellion against what is right and good. Evil cannot even be defined on its own, but only by its deviation from the good. Words like "degradation" and "corruption" imply the existence something good to degrade and corrupt. Rebellion and disobedience presuppose authority and law. A lie requires truth to falsify. Goodness exists independently of evil, but evil is dependent on goodness for its existence.[1]

Evil is a reaction against good and therefore against God. C. S. Lewis says, "He is the inventor, we are only the machine. He is the painter, we are only the picture."[2] Evildoers affront other humans because God seems out of reach, but all evil acts are against Him. Precipitating a confrontation with God is suicidal! As civil rebellion triggers a confrontation with the government, violating God's law invites a divine visitation to settle the score.

Lon Woodrum's character Debbie Rogers said to a rebellious youth in jail, "You can't win with your kind of fight. Look at you, stuck in jail. Oh, you're a tiger all right, I can see that. But you're a tiger in a cage. And caged tigers aren't going anywhere."[3] We humans have all been rebellious outlaws in the universe. To avoid incarceration, our only recourse is to surrender to God's authority. It is a tough move even for tigers, but it beats being caged. Dennis Kinlaw said, "Surrender is never a noble gesture; it is the capitulation of a rebel."[4]

---

[1] See Jon Tal Murphree, *Autographed by God* (University Park, IA: Vennard College, 2006) pp. 169-171.
[2] C. S. Lewis, *Mere Christianity* (New York: The MacMillan Company, 1960) 159.
[3] Lon Woodrum, *Eternity in Their Heart* (Grand Rapids: Zondervan Publishing House, 1955) p. 183.
[4] Dennis F. Kinlaw, *Preaching in the Spirit* (Grand Rapids: Francis Asbury Press of Zondervan, 1985) pp. 105-106.

228 Animal Rage or Human Folly

Better to meet a bear robbed of her cubs than a fool in his folly
(17:12 NIV).

So who would prefer to confront an infuriated beast rather than a naïve, simple-minded human? But we do not easily understand what Solomon meant by a fool.

Hebrew scholars remind us that the original term(s) did not refer to mentally challenged persons with inferior intelligence. Solomon's term came nearer meaning those with a worldview based on a warped self-view. Expecting the world to accommodate their own whims and tastes, they see themselves as central figures in their own little worlds, expecting others to feed their self-interests.

Their folly may take the form of pride and stubbornness, refusing to listen or take rebuke. It may be expressed in laziness, refusing to work. Or pleasure seeking for constant thrills. Or casual nonchalance, committing pranks that go beyond jokes. Or even cruelty, gloating over sadistic torture. Folly includes moral insolence, with minds closed toward God.

In a sonnet, Shakespeare deplored the "sin of self-love [that] possesseth / . . . all my every part. . . . / It is so grounded in my heart."[1] The world is so full of foolish self-centered people that Goethe's herald exclaimed, "The world is one enormous fool!"[2]

Problem is that moral fools cannot keep their foolishness to themselves. They find ways to engage others. Virgil said, "Savage passion quickly finds weapons."[3] Humans have ways to cause more damage than monsters. Caught in the sway of some kinds of folly is worse than confronting beastly rage. Human iniquity is more dangerous than animal ferocity. Allowing your soul to be raped is worse than having your body torn to pieces. The point of the proverb: Do not allow yourself to be maneuvered into a vulnerable position to the folly of the world.

Devil-like or Godlike 229

---

[1] Shakespeare, *Sonnets*, # 62.
[2] Goethe, *Faust*, Second Part, Act I, Scene 3, p. 227.
[3] Virgil, *The Aeneid* (London: Penguin Books, 1958) Book One, p. 32.

He who returns evil for good, evil will not depart from his house
(17:13 NASB).

In the forest of Arden, Shakespeare's Amiens sang about the sin of ingratitude to the exiled Duke: "Blow, blow, thou winter wind. / Thou art not so unkind / As man's ingratitude. / Thy tooth is not so keen, / Because thou art not seen / Although thy breath be rude. / Freeze, freeze, thou bitter sky, / That dost not bite so nigh / As benefits forgot. / Though thou the waters warp, / Thy sting is not so sharp / As friends remembered not."[1]

David complained that Nabal had given him *evil for good* (1 Sam. 25:21), but then David did the same thing to Uriah, and God said, "The sword will never depart from your house" (2 Sam. 12:10). And it never did! Returning evil for good is more than a foible. It is a serious sin, with serious effects! Woodrum's protagonist said, "There's a kind of gravity of justice that holds life together—keeps it from falling apart. [An evil man] hasn't got a chance in a divinely arranged universe. . . . There is nothing so pitiable as a big tyrant when he stands at dead end!"[2]

Both Peter and Paul went further than Solomon and exhorted us not to return *evil for evil* (Rom. 12:17; 1 Thes. 5:15; 1 Pet. 3:9). And Jesus went still further, declaring an ethic that turned traditional values upside down! He said to return *good for evil*! "Whosoever shall smite thee on the right cheek, turn to him the other also. . . . Love your enemies, bless them that curse you, do good to them that hate you, and pray for them which . . . persecute you" (Matt. 5:39-44 KJV).

Years ago I learned an old adage that said: "To return evil for good is devil-like. To return evil for evil is animal-like. To return good for good is human-like. To return good for evil is Godlike." Solomon said not to return *evil for good*. Jesus said to return *good for evil*! The king of Israel said not to be devil-like. The King of kings said to be Godlike!

---

[1] Shakespeare, *As You Like It*, Act II, Scene 7, lines 174-189.
[2] Lon Woodrum, *Stumble Upon the Dark Mountains* (Waco, TX: Word Books, 1956) pp. 111, 128.

230 Quit the Quarrel

The beginning of strife is like letting out water; so abandon the quarrel before it breaks out (17:14 NASB).

Human relationships require adjusting to all kinds of people. Some are more comfortable in negative converse. Some crave control. Some have developed defensive patterns. Some can only speak with a sneer. Someone is perfectionistic about minute incidentals, expecting others to line up their ducklings with her ducks. She is picky over what is ludicrously dinky!

Bellicose persons are by nature competitive, leaping at every opportunity for combat, and sparing no feelings to achieve victory. Chaucer's dame said, "It is madness . . . to strive with one who is stronger . . . ; to strive with a man of equal strength is dangerous, and to strive with a weaker man is foolish. [So] . . . avoid all strife. . . . If a man of greater power does you an injury, make it your business to study how to stop the cause of it, rather than how to avenge it."[1]

It is better to win a friend than to win an argument. President Lyndon B. Johnson quipped, "I'd rather win a convert than a fight."[2] Marcus Aurelius said, "Suppose any man should hate me. Let him look to that himself. I will look to this, that I not . . . do or say anything deserving of contempt."[3] We can best communicate ideas as we communicate personal warmth.

The proverb says to stop the tiniest water leak in the dike or dam, before it becomes a deluge of desolation! Do not enter an argument with acrimonious persons who attempt to win by increased volume, emotional put-downs, and personality force. Keep your arguments academic and cerebral, never emotional, without accusatorial overtones. Keep the other person disarmed, respecting her view. Quit the quarrel before it begins. Protect the relationship. Paul said, "If it be possible, as much as lieth in you, live peaceably with all men (Rom. 12:18 KJV).

---

[1] Chaucer, "The Tale of Melibeus," *Canterbury Tales* (Garden City: NY: Garden City Pub. Co., 1934) pp. 218-219.

[2] Bob Dole, *Great Political Wit* (New York: Doubleday, 1998) p. 160.

[3] Marcus Aurelius, *The Thoughts of the Emperor* (New York: John B. Alden, publisher, 1887) p. 170.

Acquitting and Accusing 231

*Acquitting the guilty and condemning the innocent—the Lord
detests them both* (17:15 NIV).

Pointing out the irony of popular opinion, Alan Paton said:
"If a law is unjust, and if a judge judges according to the law, that
is justice, even if it is not just."[1] Paton's point is that real justice
transcends law, because only justice can determine whether a law
is just or unjust. Congress enacts laws, but the judiciary judges
those laws. "Justice that is not just" is, of course, not justice. If
legal justice is not morally just, what is called legal justice is not
justice at all.

The proverb is referring to jurisprudence, but the principle
also applies personally, in justifying what is wrong or condemning
what is right. The Lord does not "detest" *those who do it*, but He
does detest *what they do*. To be like Him, we should embrace
equitable fairness and abhor partiality and favoritism. Entailed in
goodness itself, justice carries a moral mandate. Exonerating the
guilty is as much evil as convicting the innocent. Being tender
toward and concerned for evil people is a far cry from excusing
their wrongdoing. Failing to deplore immorality in our culture is
no less evil than sanctioning false accusations of those who are
innocent. The gutless cowardice of both is abominable to God and
should be abhorrent to us! Those who so indulge are
mollycoddlers and milksops!

The proverb does not specifically say to condemn the
wicked and to praise the righteous. It says we should *not* condone
evil or disparage the good. Remaining morally neutral, however,
amounts to both offenses. Refusing to censure is to sanction, and
failing to approve is to reprove. We need to oppose what is wrong
and champion what is right. Our culture needs the cumulative
effect from all who are good. The Kingdom of God needs it.
Others need to see our example and influence. And for our own
sake, we need to be persons who take a stand.

---

[1] Alan Paton, *Cry, the Beloved Country* (New York: MacMillan Pub. Co., 1948)
p. 158.

232 Full Hands and Empty Heads

Of what use is money in the hand of a fool, since he has no desire to get wisdom? (17:16 NIV). Or, "*. . . in the hand of a fool to get wisdom, seeing he hath no heart to it?* (KJV).

Those of us who are in education have seen many students enter college with money "in hand" for tuition, but who are short on motivation. They want the campus social life without classroom assignments. Without the will for wisdom, financial resources to pay instructors and buy textbooks are wasted. When students want to purchase a college degree without having to earn a college education, they settle for being what Shakespeare called "deliberate fools," and the investment is squandered.

When the prince of Arragon chose the silver casket hoping to find Portia's picture to gain the right to claim her in marriage, he found the portrait of a blinking idiot with a note that said, "Some there be that shadows kiss; / Such have but a shadow's bliss." Then Portia opined, "O, these deliberate fools! When they do choose, / They have the wisdom by their wit to lose."[1]

The old *Scottish Hymnal* translates a line from Solomon into rhyme: "[Wisdom] has treasures greater far / Than east or west unfold; / And her rewards more precious are / Than all their stores of gold" (Prov. 3:14-15).[2] A financial fund can buy more wisdom than its worth in gold. But money cannot buy motivation. Without the will to be wise, the investment is lost.

What may be inferred from the proverb is sadder than what is stated. Multiple persons have paid a heavy price in suffering and sacrifice, and are no wiser for it. Goethe wrote: ". . . tis wise to use the chance, / And draw some profit from each circumstance."[3] To endure the suffering and be no wiser for it, to pay the price and gain no profit from it—that is not the mark of a wise person. To have a chance for wisdom and waste the opportunity is the mark of a fool.

---

[1] Shakespeare, *The Merchant of Venice*, Act II, Scene 9, lines 66-67, 80-81.

[2] *The Book of Psalms in Metre: The Scottich Hymnal* (Edinburgh: Thomas Nelson and Sons, 1882) p. 164.

[3] Goethe, *Faust*, Second Part, Act IV, Scene 1, p. 431.

Formal Friends or Blood Brothers 233

A friend loves at all times, and a brother is born for adversity (17:17 RSV, NASB, NKJV, NIV).

Being a formal friend entails subscribing to expectations, fitting the role, and following the script, like playacting. Little more is required. Genuine relationships are a lot messier, but a million times more meaningful—

—especially in times of adversity. In the trials of life, authentic friends show up. Then you see who your real friends are. Formal, casual friendships keep crumbling in adversity. Trials and difficulties tear them apart. They keep coming unglued. Horace asked, "Does your friendship, like a wound ill-stitched, close vainly and tear open once more?"[1]

Genuine love functions "at all times," in the shadows as well as the bright lights. On rough terrain as much as on superhighways. In poverty as well as in wealth. Chaucer said, "And poverty's an eye-glass, seems to me, / Through which a man his loyal friends may see."[2]

Not only are real friends exposed *by* adversity, but they become more than friends *in* adversity. They become closer than blood brothers. Genuine brotherhood is "born" in adverse situations. When superficial friendships are torn apart by painful problems leaving open wounds, real friendships restitch the new wounds. Brothers and sisters walk into the world of suffering with their friends, hurt with them, hold their hands, and pour the balm of healing. In some ordeals, nothing short of brotherhood provides the therapy needed. Hurting people provide opportunities for deep-level relationships that should not be wasted. In the vocabulary of one Native American tribe, the word for friend meant "one-who-carries-my-sorows-on-his-back."[3]

---

[1] Horace, *Satires, Epistles, Ars Poetica* (Cambridge, MA: Harvard U. Press, 1991) Epistle III, Book I, p. 273.
[2] Chaucer, "The Tale of the Wife of Bath," *Canterbury Tales* (Garden City, NY: Garden City Pub., 1934) p. 343.
[3] Paul Lee Tan, compiler, *Encyclopedia of 7700 Illustrations* (Rockville, MD: Assurance Publishers, 1979) p. 462. Quoted from *United Church Observer*, without further documentation.

234 Victim of the System

A man lacking in judgment strikes hands in pledge and puts up security for his neighbor (17:18 NIV).

Perhaps striking hands was something between a high five and a fist bump. In ancient times, contracts were closed by striking hands after the oral promise had been made, thus ratifying the commitment and ensnaring the man with the words of his own mouth.

Since responsible people were reticent to borrow money, Jewish moneylenders specialized in making loans to prodigals expecting them to default. Their security came from foreclosing on the collateral of the second party who stood surety for the loan. The system was corrupt. One time a creditor claimed a man's own two sons as slaves to cover a debt (2 Kgs. 4:1). Jesus condemned the system that looked clean on "the outside" but was filled with "extortion and excess" (Matt. 23:25). In this proverb Solomon warns against becoming a victim of the system.

Earlier Solomon elucidated the moral dimension of wisdom (Prov. 1-9), and that means business prudence is a moral matter. And the entire Bible embraces moral ethics as an essential part of religion. If business ethics are moral ethics and moral matters are religious issues, it shakes out to mean that financial matters are religious matters. Throughout the New Testament, responsible control of one's monetary affairs is depicted as a religious responsibility.

The previous proverb (vs. 17) accents the importance of honoring friendships. Lest that should be pushed too far, this proverb follows, warning against allowing others to use our friendship carelessly.

In *Hamlet*, Polonius advised Ophelia, "Neither a borrower nor a lender be; for loan oft loses both itself and friend."[1] When the one whose bank note you countersigned defaults, you lose as much as he owes. As bad as that would be, you also stand to lose the person as a friend. That is too costly a price to pay for "lacking judgment." Solomon advises caution.

---

[1] Shakespeare, *Hamlet*, Act I, Scene 3, lines 75-76.

Resolved and Dissolved 235

He who loves transgression loves strife; he who raises his door seeks destruction (17:19 NASB). Also 28:25.

Transgression is rebellion that produces conflict.[1] *Inter*personal problems are precipitated by *intra*personal problems. Conflict between neighbors, races, or nations reflects the inner conflict a person has with herself. Cultural and ethnic animosity is nonexistent except as it exists in individual minds and hearts. Since society is the composite person, a social norm is merely the mean ethos of those who compose society. The subject of the proverb is singular. It reduces social confrontations to personal conflicts. The institutional can be changed by the individual. When human heart problems are *resolved*, global conflicts are more easily *dissolved*.

In Solomon's day, neighboring tribal people would enter homes on horseback to sack and loot the goods, seldom dismounting. So doorways were generally made very low to prevent predatory horsemen from pillaging and plundering the home. High doors were often decorated with ornaments in an ostentatious act of pride. Those who did so were risking disaster.

Here we have two proverbs in one—rebellion causes war and pride invites defeat. The second is an expansion of the first, implying that pride causes rebellion,[2] which causes conflict, which results in destruction. It is the domino theory. What starts with pride ends in disaster. A later proverb connects the two and gives the solution: *An arrogant man stirs up strife, but he who trusts in the Lord will prosper* (28:25). Trusting God indicates dependence, which means humility, which resolves rebellion, preempts strife, and prevents defeat. The domino theory works in reverse. Humility resolves both strife and defeat. The result is both peace and security.

---

[1] In the original of the first clause, distinguishing the subject term and the predicate term is confusing. If the two are reversed as some translate it ("he who loves strife loves transgression"), the two are still linked together. Conflict and rebellion are reciprocally producing, each causing the other.
[2] To have pride is to replace God's role in one's life with one's own agenda, which amounts to rebellion.

236 Crooked Minds and Turned Tongues

He who has a crooked mind finds no good, and he who is perverted in his language falls into evil (17:20 NASB).

To find no good is no good, but to fall into evil is even worse. The danger of falling into the pit of evil is breathtaking. The precipice is stark, and merciless. To tweak the truth is to tiptoe too close to the edge. Disaster grabs for you!

A "crooked mind" is a "perverse heart" (NIV), or a "wayward heart" (ASV), or a "contrary heart" (Jerus). The phrase, "who is perverted in his language," literally translated says "whose tongue is turned," meaning to be untruthful.

To talk with an upside-down tongue is to pervert truth into falsehood. An old legend says that the ancient philosopher Diogenes walked midday with a lantern through the streets of Athens looking for an honest man.

Truth is not always attractive, especially when we calculate an advantage by evading it. When truth frowns at us with furrowed brow, the temptation to twist it into something more attractive can be appealing. Hamlet said, "The power of beauty will sooner transform honesty [into] a bawd than the force of honesty can translate beauty into its likeness."[1]

Those with warped minds and wayward hearts seek their own good by adjusting truth to their utility, and they get the opposite of what they want. They find no good and are deluged with the bad.

An ancient sage asked the Lord, "Who may abide in Thy tent? Who may dwell in Thy holy hill?" The Lord's answer came in a psalm, "He who walks in his integrity . . . and speaks truth in his heart. . . . who . . . swears [i.e., tells the truth] to his own hurt, and does not change" (Ps. 15:1-2, 4).

As Lon Woodrum says, "Some men *accept* the Truth. They rejoice in it. They would not alter it one whit; rather will they change their own lives to live by it."[2]

---

[1] Shakespeare, *Hamlet*, Act III, Scene 1, lines 111-114.
[2] Lon Woodrum, *The Rebellious Planet* (Grand Rapids: Zondervan Pub. House, 1965) p. 46.

To have a fool for a son brings grief; there is no joy for the father of a fool (17:21 NIV). Also 17:25; 27:11.

Virgil's Aeneas braved horrible hazards, and then was carried for a visit through the pitfalls of the infernal world. Finally he came to the fair haven of the disembodied spirits in the Land of Joy. There he met his deceased father who was overjoyed that his son had cleared the obstacle course. Aeneas replied, "Father, it was ever the vision of yourself . . . which compelled me to make my way to the threshold of this world." Later, before going into a perilous battle, Aeneas embraced his own son and said, "From me, my son, you may learn what is valor and strenuous toil. . . . But in due time when your own age ripens to maturity. . . . do not forget . . . the examples set before you. . . . Your father is Aeneas. . . . Let that be your inspiration."[1]

The second part of the proverb is a restatement of the first, but slightly different. Both words translated "fool" mean impiety. But the first has a shade of coarseness and the second dullness. Both connotations might grieve a father, but neither so much as the impiety itself.

When a child is young, the parents are overjoyed with every little progress he makes. Part of their joy is borrowed from the future they expect of him. When those expectations are betrayed, the disappointment is painful. The grief is worse because the joy had been a chimera, based on an illusion. They have invested a big portion of their lives in futility. The sorrow is often complicated with guilt, the parents wondering whether they were adequate parents.

Every child wants a parent to cherish, and every parent wants to be cherished by the child. And every parent wants a child to cherish, and every child wants to be cherished by the parent. The construct is accompanied with overwhelming joy for both parent and child. The collapse of the construct wreaks heaviest grief on both.

---

[1] Virgil, *The Aeneid* (London: Penguin Books, 1958) Book Six, p. 168, and Book Twelve, p. 322.

238 Happy Heart or Barren Bones

A merry heart does good like a medicine, but a broken spirit dries the bones (17:22 NKJV).

Long before the science of psychology was born, Solomon enunciated psychosomatics. Anxiety, stress, grief, and guilt can wreck one's health. Conversely, chronic pain can throw one's mind into deep depression, which in turn inhibits the healing process. The downward spiral gains momentum, with mind and body each accelerating the problems of the other. Somewhere in the syndrome, mind-control needs to kick in. Mental gears need to shift into forward. When a little operating leverage is secured, life can take a turn for the better. A merry heart is medicinal! Nehemiah said, "The joy of the Lord is your strength" (Neh. 8:10).

A few days after the horrendous Haitian earthquake in 2010, my nephew Tom Corson was in Haiti on a relief mission.[1] A lad with both arms amputated flashed a smile and said, "But I can still play soccer!" Baseball and basketball were out. But soccer was still in! Adelaide Procter prayed: "I thank Thee, too, that Thou hast made/ Joy to abound, / So many gentle thoughts and deeds / Circle us round, / That in the darkest spot on earth / Some love is found."[2]

Here is a puzzling phenomenon: Love is purer against the background of mistreatment. Good things are appreciated more when one has experienced privations. Tidbits of joy are more passionately seized in predicaments of sorrow. Scott wrote: "Hope is brightest when it dawns from fears; / The rose is sweetest washed with morning dew, / And love is loveliest when embalmed in tears."[3] Broken spirits can become merry hearts! Gibran said, "The deeper sorrow carves into your being, the more joy you can contain."[4] We must not allow the added space to go to waste.

---

[1] Tom Corson is Director of SIFAT, a Christrian overseas training organization based in Lineville, Alabama.
[2] A. Procter, "My God, I Thank Thee," *The Methodist Hymnal* (Nasville: Methodist Pub. House, 1966) p. 50.
[3] Sir Walter Scott, *The Lady of the Lake* (New York: The New American Library, 1962) Canto Fourth, Sec. I, p. 92.
[4] Kahlil Gibran, *The Prophet* (New York: Alfred A. Knoph, 1926) p. 35.

A wicked man receives a bribe from the bosom to pervert the ways of justice. / A gift in secret subdues anger, and a bribe in the bosom, strong wrath (17:23; 21:14 NASB). Also 18:16.

In these two proverbs, the phrase "from (or in) the bosom" probably has a double meaning. First, it is a monetary bribe, for Asians in that day carried their purses high on their torso, above the abdomen. Second, it is a secret bribe, covered by a coat to conceal from view.

The second proverb distinguishes between a *gift* and a *bribe*. The first term used is rather mild, but the second is strong. A gift to mitigate anger is justified as an indication of goodwill, as the gifts Jacob sent by his sons to Egypt to mollify the feigned wrath of Joseph (Gen. 43:11 ff.). A goodwill gift is not attached to an agreement. It only commits the giver to the personal warmth that the gift expresses. Reciprocation may be hoped for, but it is not a part of the arrangement.

A bribe is quite different in that response is agreed upon, at least implicitly. And it is given to a person in a position of trust to corrupt his/her conduct to provide an advantage or a loophole for escape. The judicial process is twisted and wrested. By quibbles and equivocation, evenhandedness is undermined. Impartiality is perverted. When the trustees that are entrusted with the common good are untrustworthy, justice becomes unjust.

Pockets of corruption in government violate an ethic embraced by the human race from its beginning. In the cultural psyche of pagan polytheists, the ethic of impartial justice was ordinarily connected to their concept of God. Through the words of Nisus, Virgil referred to "Jupiter, or however we should name the one who looks on our deeds with impartial eyes."[1]

Several hundred years before Solomon, Moses declared the word of Jehovah God: "You shall not distort justice; you shall not be partial, and you shall not take a bribe, for a bribe blinds the eyes of the wise. . . . Justice, and only justice, you shall pursue" (Deut. 16:19-20).

---

[1] Virgil, *The Aeneid* (London: Penguin Books, 1958) Book Nine, p. 231.

240 Sharp Sight or Dancing Eyes

A man of understanding sets his face toward wisdom, but the eyes of a fool are on the ends of the earth (17:24 RSV).

Wisdom or folly becomes a guiding principle in life that plays out in various ways. Wise persons "keep wisdom in view" (NIV); they "are thoughtful and absorbed in wisdom" (Mof); they "set their face toward wisdom" (RSV). They keep their eyes focused, not letting wisdom out of sight. It gives them composure and gravity, seen in a steady face with a resolute countenance.

Foolish people, largely controlled by folly, are visionary in the bad sense. They aim at unfeasible impossibilities with desires that are scattered abroad. With roving, wandering eyes, their interests flit from place to place, "roaming far and wide" (Mof), as Beowulf said, "[with] dancing eyes like spearpoints."[1] They are volatile and impulsive, pushed around by wind gusts of popular opinion, by the influence of others, or by their own fantasies. Their purposes keep flying loose, leaving them unsteady, unsettled, and unstable. For foolish persons, Macbeth was surely right: "Life is but a walking shadow, a poor player that struts and frets his hour upon the stage . . . It is a tale told by an idiot, full of sound and fury, signifying nothing."[2]

Those people with unfocused eyes, straying from one fantasy to another, need the wisdom to "center down," as the Quakers used to say. They need to shift from fantasy to realism and concentrate their forces on feasible possibilities. They need to centralize their interests, as the people, Dante said, who "sharpened their sight, as keen as an old tailor at his needle's eye."[3]

In the context of needing wisdom, the New Testament says, "A double-minded man is unstable . . . (Ja. 1:8 KJV). He that wavereth is like a wave of the sea, driven with the wind and tossed (vs. 6). If . . . you lack wisdom . . . ask of God . . . in faith, nothing wavering" (vss. 5-6).

---

[1] *Beowulf the Warrior*, Ian Serraillier, tr. (New York: Hanry Z. Walck, Inc., 1961) p. 39.
[2] Shakespeare, *Macbeth*, Act V, Scene 5, lines 24-28.
[3] Dante, *The Divine Comedy*, Henry F. Cary, tr. (no city given: A. L. Burt Co., n.d.) "Hell," Canto XV, p. 66.

It is also not good to fine the righteous, nor to strike the noble for their uprightness. / It is not good to be partial to a wicked man, or to deprive a righteous man of justice. / To show partiality is not good . . . (17:26 NASB; 18:5 RSV; 28:21 RSV).

The first proverb makes specific the general principle given in the other two.   At first glance, they seem to state a trite platitude. Closer scrutiny, however, will uncover some cunningly contrived nuances.

First, by making injustice specific, the lines leave room for a broader bias that is not condemned.   A characteristic temperament or outlook is not a judicial matter. In the sense of favoring, we *should be* biased toward goodness and truth, and partial toward our spouses.

Second, the first proverb implies it is evil enough to punish those who are not bad, but even worse to punish those who are outstandingly good. "The noble" are specifically occupied with doing good. It is not right to impose even a simple fine on those who do not deserve punishment, but it is even worse "to strike" (RSV: "to flog") those who deserve reward.

Third, the evil act of partiality is an affront, an insult, an offense, to the very highest standard of ethics. Instead of using strong phrases like "mercilessly cruel" or "unthinkably atrocious," Solomon used the simply phrase "is not good." That, however, is a herculean act of evil that defies an absolute, unalterable principle. Evil cannot be stated more strongly than by its contrast with good. Shaking one's fist at eternal goodness is like gambling one's life on the odds that the sun will not rise tomorrow. Violating goodness is inexpressibly evil simply because goodness is indescribably good. C. S. Lewis spoke of "golden goodness."[1] God said, "You shall do no injustice in judgment; you shall not be partial to the poor or defer to the great" (Lev. 19:15 RSV). Isaiah warned, "Woe to those who . . . deprive the needy of justice" (10:1-2 NASB).

---

[1] C. S. Lewis, *The Magician's Nephew*, Bk. 6 in The Chronicles (New York: Macmillan, Collier Bks., 1978) p. 178.

242 Sober or Shallow

A man of knowledge uses words with restraint . . . / Even a fool is thought wise if he keeps silent, and discerning if he holds his tongue (17:27, 28 NIV). Also 18:13; 29:20.

Naturally fluent people are gifted with a blessing that can quickly become a bane. Reserved people need an active mind to speak, but expressive people speak too easily. When the mouth goes into overdrive, the mind shifts into neutral. A freewheeling vehicle gets out of control! Silence indicates sobriety, and chatter communicates shallowness. Chaucer's fox said to the cock, ". . . God shall never cease to plague the chattering tongue."[1]

Natural wordsmiths require more self-discipline than word bunglers. They lose both respect and influence by talking too much. The ability to refrain from speaking has more virtue than the ability to speak. Too few of us know when to keep silent.

Dante was an artisan of language, but he said, "[I] curb my genius . . . lest it run where virtue guides it not."[2]

In other proverbs, Solomon said it is folly and shame to answer before listening (18:13), and there is more hope for a fool than for one who speaks hastily (29:20). When President Lyndon Johnson was senator, he displayed in his office a sign that said, "You ain't learnin' nothin' when you're talking'."[3] So, says Solomon, shut up! Zip your lip. Be sober rather than shallow. Do more listening than talking. "Use words with restraint."

And there is a bonus benefit: "Even a fool is thought wise if he keeps silent." Shakespeare's Gratiano spoke of those who "are reputed wise for saying nothing."[4] In areas where you are ignorant, others will think you are smart. Where you are foolish they will think you are prudent—because you are wise enough to conceal your folly!

---

[1] Chaucer, "The Nun's Priest's Tale," *Canterbury Tales,* in Priestley and Spear, eds., *Adventures in English Literature* (New York: Harcourt, Brace & World, Inc., 1963) 93.
[2] Dante, *The Divine Comedy* (New York: Random House, 1932) "The Inferno," Canto XXVI, p. 139.
[3] Bob Dole, *Great Political Wit* (New York: Doubleday, 1998) p. 157.
[4] Shakespeare, *The Merchant of Venice*, Act I, Scene 1, lines 96-97.

He who . . . seeks his own desire . . . quarrels against all sound wisdom. / The soul of the wicked desires evil . . . / Hell and destruction are never full; so the eyes of man are never satisfied
(18:1 NASB; 21:10 NKJV; 27:20 NKJV).

Evil begins with self-centered desires that lead to a pattern of placating those desires. Robert Browning wrote: ". . . As is your sort of mind, / So is your sort of search: You'll find / What you desire . . ."[1] Desires can be dangerous! Shakespeare's Laertes pleaded with his sister Ophelia, "Keep [yourself] within the rear of your affection, out of the shot and danger of desire."[2]

From preconditioned patterns, some people sin from weakness. Worse still is to sin from desires for the benefits or advantages of the act (first proverb above). Worst of all is to sin from the desire for evil itself (second and third proverbs). The human soul was made with antenna toward God, desiring His presence and fellowship. Isaiah prayed, "My soul yearns for you in the night; in the morning my spirit longs for you" (Is. 26:9 NIV). But in this proverb, "the soul" of the wicked, that very noblest part of a person where desires aspire toward God, is prostituted with evil desires.

The words translated "hell and destruction" generally refer to the unseen netherworld. At times they seem to refer to death, destruction, or the grave, and at other times to perdition. Because of the confusion, some translations simply anglicize the Hebrew terms as Sheol and Abaddon. Isaiah said, "Sheol has enlarged its throat . . . without measure" (Is. 5:14 NASB). The proverb says Sheol is never full, and in the same way, evil desires "are never satisfied." The soul with noble potential can be so perverted that it is compared with death and perdition! As the grave and hell can never be filled, the depraved soul can never be satisfied! The soul becomes its own hell! Ungratified desires burn with unquenchable fires of frustration, tormenting the soul with unthinkable torture! It is the precarious hazard of undisciplined desires!

---

[1] R. Browning, "Easter-Day," *The Complete . . . Works* (Cambridge, MA: Houghton Mifflin, 1895) Sec. VII, p. 328.
[2] Shakespeare, *Hamlet,* Act I, Scene 3, lines 34-35.

244 To Love to Learn

The fool has no delight in understanding, but in expressing his own heart. / The heart of the prudent acquires knowledge, and the ear of the wise seeks knowledge (18:2, 15 NKJV).

The Hebrews often spoke of the mind as we sometimes do today, in its broader sense to include volition along with intellect. That is why some versions translate "mind" as "heart." In this proverb, those who have no heart for knowing and understanding are foolish. Many of them acquire knowledge to boost their egos by putting it on display—"delights in airing his own opinions" (NIV). Getting an education in order to parade it before the public is the cheapest reason for getting it. It is a matter of a bad heart.

The second proverb suggests that acquiring knowledge is one of the priorities of prudent people. Wisdom and knowledge-getting go together. The more you learn, the more you learn there is to be learned. Gaining knowledge whets the appetite to gain more knowledge. Those who have little inquisitiveness do not know enough to make them hunger for more. Socrates said, "All I know is that I know nothing."[1] Though he overstated his point, the greatest human minds have been acutely aware of their ignorance, giving them appetites for more knowledge. With the ear to hear, they have a heart that heeds. They love to learn.

By ascribing knowledge to the hearts of prudent people, Solomon makes its acquisition a moral and religious responsibility. Einstein said, "Science without religion is lame; religion without science is blind."[2] Solomon himself prayed for "wisdom and knowledge" (2 Chr. 1:10), and God was pleased and gave him blessing beyond his prayers (vss. 11-12). Charles Wesley put his prayer into a Christian hymn: "Unite the pair so long disjoined, / Knowledge and vital piety; / Learning and holiness combined, / And truth and love let all men see."[3]

---

[1] Manuel Velasquez, *Philosophy: A Text with Readings* (Belmont. CA: Wadsworth Pub. Co., 1999) p. 349.

[2] William C. Ringenberg, *Letters to Young Scholars* (Upland, IN: Taylor University Press, 2003) p. 323.

[3] Charles Wesley, "Come, Father, Son . . . ," *The Methodist Hymnal* (Nashville: Meth. Pub. House, 1964) p. 344.

With wickedness comes contempt, and with dishonor comes disgrace. / He who sows iniquity will reap vanity, and the rod of his fury will perish (18:3 AAT; 22:8 NASB).

Wickedness never sneaks into town alone. Contempt, dishonor and disgrace like hoboes go along for the ride. When their damage is done on others, they turn on the engineer. In the end, a wicked person's fury will fail, and his own evil will come back on him. He is detested even by wicked people. By abusing others, he ends up punishing himself.

Marcus Aurelius said, "He who does wrong does wrong against himself. He who acts unjustly acts unjustly to himself, because he makes himself bad."[1] Acts of evil become a part of the one who commits them. What you do becomes who you are. You become your own victim.

Whittier wrote, ". . . from those great eyes / The soul has fled; / . . . when honor dies / The man is dead."[2] Those who experiment with evil, thinking they can retain a foothold of respectability and a self-image of integrity, do not understand how human nature works. Commenting on Silas Marner, George Eliot said, "Our consciousness rarely registers the beginning of a growth within us. . . . There have been many circulations of [bad] sap before we detect the smallest sign of a [bad] bud."[3] The cancer becomes terminal before its symptoms are noted. These proverbs accent the dangers of circulating bad sap.

Just as glory is the side effect of holiness, dishonor and disgrace are side effects of evil. Some may lose all desire for public esteem, but when wickedness reaches complete cycle, they lose all self-esteem. Their contempt is turned back on themselves. They hate themselves both for hating themselves and for being hated by themselves. Their souls are suffocated with shame.

---

[1] Marcus Aurelius, *The Thoughts of the Emperor* (New York: John B. Alden, publisher, 1887) p. 140.
[2] John G. Whittier, "Ichabod," McQuade, *The Harper Amer Lit* (No city: Addison-Wesley, 1994) V. I, p. 2131.
[3] G. Eliot, *Silas Marner*, Loban, ed., *Adventures in Appreciation* (New York: Harcourt, Brace . . . , 1963) p. 660.

246 Deep Fountains or Surface Runoff

Words . . . are deep waters; the fountain of wisdom is a gushing stream. / A fool's lips bring strife, and his mouth invites a flogging. / A fool's mouth is his ruin.../ The words of a whisperer are like delicious morsels; they go down into the inner parts of the body (18:4, 6, 7, 8 RSV). Also 26:22.

These last three proverbs elucidate some negative effects of careless talk. Verse 6: It brings strife, provoking reaction. Verse 7: It is a snag for one's own soul, bringing ruin. President Calvin Coolidge said, "I have never been hurt by anything I didn't say."[1] Verse 8: Simple gossip becomes damaging slander. What seems to be a dainty morsel to be easily swallowed with great relish becomes toxic venom deep down, causing suspicion and distrust. "Tasty trifles" (NKJV) cause stomach cramps. Gossip unfairly discriminates against the one who is not present to defend herself.

Horace wrote of one whose "stream runs muddy, and often carries more that you would rather remove."[2] Muddy streams are usually shallow because they carry surface runoff. Ordinary gossip, muddy with innuendoes, is surface runoff from shallow minds.

The first proverb (vs. 4) uses the same metaphor that Horace used, but rather showing the value of good talk. Wise words from a wise person are like "deep waters" that flow from "a fountain of wisdom." Deep streams are usually clear. Oceans are not muddy. The flow of wisdom from an inexhaustible fountain shows a depth that cannot be fathomed. Tennyson wrote: "I sometimes hold it half a sin / To put in words the grief I feel; / For words, like Nature, half reveal / And half conceal the Soul within."[3]

Words are more than words. They carry shiploads of meaning beyond themselves. A load of explosives can deliver destruction. A shipment of humanitarian cargo delivers life!

---

[1] Bob Dole, *Great Political Wit* (New York: Doubleday, 1998) p. 153.
[2] Horace, *Satires, Epistles, Ars Poetica* (Cambridge, MA: Harvard U. Press, 1991) Satire X, Book I, p. 121.
[3] Alfred Lord Tennyson, "In Memoriam," Poem 5, M. H. Abram, ed., *The Norton Anthology of English Literature* (New York: W. W. Norton & Co., 1968) p. 1881.

One who is slack in his work is brother to one who destroys (18:9 NIV). Also 19:24; 26:15.

Neglecting to produce and destroying what is already produced both add up to the same thing. Adding nothing to nothing amounts to nothing, and adding destruction to something results in nothing. Subtracting ends on the same figure. Subtracting what *could be* from what *could be* ends in nothing, and subtracting what *is* from what *is* gives the same answer. Figure it either by addition or subtraction, the sum and the remainder are the same. Arithmetic works both ways. The consequent of each is zero. One who is too lazy to produce is blood brother to him who wastes what is produced. The sluggard and the spendthrift both end with zero balance.

Proverbs 19:24 and 26:15 use a sarcastic hyperbole to make the point. Some are too lazy to feed themselves—they will not even go to the trouble to eat—much less to plow their fields and raise their crops. The return is many times greater than the investment, but they will not invest the energy. Living, for the lazy, is not worth getting out of bed to go to work.

In his preface to Proverbs, Solomon uses the ant as a model of productive diligence (6:6ff.), and it has been translated into Scottish verse: "Ye indolent and slothful, rise, / View the ant's labors, and be wise; / Yet see with what incessant cares / She for the winter's storm prepares. / In summer she provides her meat, / And harvest finds her store complete. / But when will slothful man arise? / How long shall sleep seal up his eyes? / Sloth more indulgence still demands; / Sloth shuts the eyes, and folds the hands. / But mark the end; want shall assail, / When all your strength and vigor fail. . . ."[1] Often we look up to those we admire and wish to emulate.

Here Solomon says to look up to the ant. Learn its lessons. Be motivated by its industry. Get off your stool. Get on your feet. Walk on stilts! Get to work and learn to live!

---

[1] *The Book of Psalms in Scottish Metre: The Scottish Hymnal* (Edinburgh: Thomas Nelson & Sons, 1882) p. 164-5.

248 Possibilities not Impossible

The name of the Lord is a strong tower. The righteous runneth into it, and is safe. / . . . safety is of the Lord. / . . . whoso putteth his trust in the Lord shall be safe (18:10; 21:31; 29:25 KJV).

When *trust* hangs loose, without anchor in *belief, faith* is foolish. Skeptics believe that God either may not exist or may not be trustworthy. When details do not fit smugly into a mathematical equation, they do not see the bigger picture. Gibran said, "If you would know God, be not a solver of riddles. Rather . . . see Him walking in the cloud outstretching His arms in the lightning and descending in rain . . . See Him smiling in flowers, then rising and waving His hands in trees."[1] Genuine faith is more than philosophical or practical, but it is not less.

Unjustified trust should be avoided. Depending on God to do what He has not committed Himself to do is presumptuous. Even Virgil a pagan, speaking of the sacking of Troy, announced: "Trust in heaven is forbidden when heaven itself declines the trust."[2]

These proverbs invite us to rely on God for security—temporal security unless God has other plans for us, and certainly ultimate security. The psalmist assures us, "Under His wings you will find refuge" (Ps. 91:4 NIV). We have an emotional nest! The Lord Himself is a fortress above danger, a high citidel out of reach to attackers. The Most High is our refuge! We have a security pocket! He is our bomb shelter! We can face the danger of battle without retreat because we are already *in* our retreat center. We can even be killed, and we will not die!

Some naïve people are easily deluded with superstitious faith. We all know that. We also know that some are too focused on particulars to see the big picture. Big-time possibilities look impossible! Goethe's Helena, about to be killed but hoping to be spared, said, "Unto the wide-seeing mind is verily shown / The impossible is oft possible."[3] And Helena was spared.

---

[1] Kahlil Gibran, *The Prophet* (New York: Alfred A. Knoph, 1926) p. 89.

[2] Virgil, *The Aeneid* (London: Penguin Books, 1958) Book Two, p. 63.

[3] Goethe, *Faust*, Second Part, Act III, p. 382.

A rich man's wealth is his strong city, and like a high wall is his own imagination (18:11 NASB). Also 28:11; 28:26.

The metaphor in the first clause is explained by the simile in the second. Wealth is the fortress of a rich man *only* in his imagination. In the previous proverb, the righteous person finds security in God, and here a person looks for safety in wealth. But one is real and the other is in the imagination. Most of us know that reality is safer than fiction. Another proverb says a wise, poor person can spot the fancy (28:11). Another says he who trusts his own fantasy is a fool (28:26).

The materialist's god of money is just as unreliable as the mythical goddess Juno who complained, "My divine power is . . . exhausted."[1] Wealth does not protect a home from burglary, or a daughter from a sex crime, nor a son from being kidnapped for hostage. A savings account cannot cushion an accident to prevent a broken, mangled body. A padded wallet does not guarantee a good education, moral character, or reliable friendships. A bullish stock market is powerless to generate genuine love or meaningful relationships. No amount of health coverage can deliver immortality.

A fortified city gives no cover for missiles or bombs or meteorites or space aliens. Against an onslaught of nuclear warheads, fortress walls collapse. Job cried, "If I have put my confidence in gold, . . . if I have gloated because [of] my wealth, . . . I have denied God above" (Job 31:24-28). Paul wrote to Timothy, "Instruct those who are rich . . . not to . . . fix their hope on the uncertainty of riches, but on God" (1Tim. 6:17). Earlier Solomon personified wisdom as the voice of God, saying, "Whoso hearkeneth unto me shall dwell safely, and shall be quiet from the fear of evil" (Prov. 1:33 KJV).

When the false and flimsy fortresses of fortune have foreclosed, He is still our security. God has signed our mortgage, and He will not default.

---

[1] Virgil, *The Aeneid* (London: Penguin Books, 1958) Book Seven, p. 184.

250 Character Conditioning

Before his downfall a man's heart is proud, but humility comes before honor (18:12 NIV).

Here is a principle that runs throughout all of life—every performance has a staging area. You have to make the journey and get in position before the big move.

The proverb opens up the principle in two lessons. First, *move into position*. The journey precedes the arrival. You must get on the porch before you enter the house. Humility comes before honor. Menial work comes before accomplishment, practice comes before ability, rehearsal before performance, and study before making a good grade. Before becoming a good leader, one must learn how to be a good follower. A good teacher is first a good student; a good speaker is first a good listener; a good writer is first a profuse reader. To reach the top you must begin at the bottom. The way up is down.

Arriving where you wish to go is a process rather than a quantum leap. When the opportunity calls, you will be ready. When the door opens, you have already arrived in the staging area. Brutus said to Cassius: "There is a tide in the affairs of men / Which, taken at the flood, leads on to fortune."[1]

Second, *beware of your position*. Be cautious about getting in the wrong staging area. Pride is too near humiliation to be comfortable. If you get on an unreliable scaffold, you are apt to crash. When you park on the wrong launching pad, you may be sent where you do not wish to go. Make sure you are journeying toward the right staging area. No one ever got lost who did not make a first wrong turn. No one ever got hooked on tobacco who did not drag for a first puff. Undisciplined fantasies move one dangerously close to their actuality.

The journey conditions a person's mind and character for a certain destination, even when the person is unaware. Once the character is conditioned, you are at the brink.

---

[1] Shakespeare, *Julius Caesar*, Act IV, Scene 3, lines 218-219.

The spirit of a man will sustain him in sickness, but who can bear a broken spirit (18:14 NKJV)?

The notion of "spirit" is vaporous and difficult to grasp. Attitude is what a person *has*, but spirit is more like what she *is*. A healthy spirit usually has fortitude to bear physical illness. But if the spirit is wounded with deep hurt, disappointment or guilt, inner resources are diminished or depleted. Goethe wrote of the one who is "Perfect in external senses, / Inwardly his darkness dense is; / And he knows not how to measure / True possession of his treasure."[1]

We petition God for health and healing to prop up a slumping spirit. Equal concern should be given to emotional and spiritual health, to sustain a life that is otherwise ill. God often does grant physical help, but He specifically operates in the department of healing hurting hearts. Whether sick or well, we all need renewed spirits that are regularly replenished. Sir Walter Scott said, "Some feelings are to mortals given / With less of earth in them than heaven."[2]

Jesus Christ at the cross, with one hand toward God and the other to us, plugged us in to God. The circuit breaker was flipped back on. The short-circuited connection was restored. The divine current can flow into our spirits, recharging dead batteries. God becomes a Father Companion. Thomas Gray wrote of the one who ". . . gave to misery (all he had) a tear, / He gained from Heaven ('twas all he wished) a Friend."[3]

The human spirit is designed to host the Divine Spirit. Occupied by His Spirit, we can say with Marcus Aurelius, "Happy am I, though this has happened to me, because I . . . [am] neither crushed by the present nor fearing the future."[4]

---

[1] Goethe, *Faust*, Second Part, Act V, Scene 5, p. 482.
[2] Sir Walter Scott, *The Lady of the Lake* (New York: New American Library, 1962) Canto Second, Sec. XXII, p. 58.
[3] Thomas Gray, "Elegy: The Epitaph," Ernest Bernbaum, ed., *Anthology of Romanticism* (New York: Thomas Nelson & Sons, 1929) Volume Two, p. 157.
[4] Marcus Aurelius, *The Thoughts of the Emperor* (New York: John B. Alden, publisher, 1887) p. 78.

252 Critical or Gullible

The first to present his case seems right, till another comes forward and questions him (18:17 NIV).

Argument is an art that can be both helpful and harmful. It is useful in convincing others of truth. It is beneficial in detecting falsehood that is presented as truth.

Those who are good in argument know the difference between reason and rhetoric, between the logical and the psychological, between what a statement implies and what someone infers. They can detect "informal fallacies" like hasty generalization, the appeal to popular sentiment, and the genetic fallacy. They see through political spin, and recognize popular opinion polls that are padded by the way the questions are worded, like stacking the deck.

We need to be critical in a healthy sense. The term "criticize" really means to "cut through" the conglomerate. We need to dissect issues, to distinguish between subcategories, to disentangle complications. In a complex situation, problems must be broken down into chunks that can be handled, so that falsehood is not allowed to ride piggyback on bits of truth.

Gullible people easily believe what initially seems plausible or what is presented with personality force or appeal. Or they believe what they wish to be true because, as Beowulf said, their "minds are choked with hatred"[1] or prejudice or desire.

Also, argument can be harmful to the arguer when she is deluded by her own arguments. We can deceive ourselves to believe what we want to be true. To us, our own reasons or excuses become plausible. Practicing deceit victimizes oneself. The deceiver is deceived by her own deception. With courageous candor, Paul said, "I do not even judge myself." Then he added, "It is the Lord who judges me" (1 Cor. 4:3-4).

The point of the proverb is for us not to arrive at knee-jerk conclusions, but to access optional opinions, and weigh carefully all the evidence.

---

[1] *Beowulf the Warrior*, Ian Serraillier, tr. (New York: Henry Z. Walck, Inc., 1961) p. 32.

A brother offended is harder to win than a strong city, and contentions are like the bars of a castle (18:19 NKJV).

Some ancient manuscripts read, "A brother assisted by a brother," while others say, "A brother offended by a brother." Either reading shows the strong and delicate feeling between brothers. In concord, they are invincible, and in animosity they are irreconcilable.

Both predicaments are like a fortified city. One is indomitable and the other is implacable.

Small offenses build inveterate hostilities, and small gestures of goodwill build venerable fraternity. Both are products of family feeling. When love works, it unites friends, but when it is betrayed it creates pain. Thus Dante wrote: "Love is the seed of every virtue and every [sin]."[1]

To feel hurt is a primary emotion, but if you are not big enough to accept the hurt, a secondary emotion like self-pity or anger kicks in to mitigate the hurt. But the secondary is harder to handle than the primary. Thus forgiveness helps the forgiver more than the forgiven.

The proverb is a statement of fact, but the lesson cannot be missed. As much as possible, offenses must be avoided and camaraderie must be built. But Goethe said, "While man's desires and aspirations stir, / He cannot choose but err."[2] Therefore attitudes of acceptance and support must be consistently worn, and the disposition of forgiveness constantly carried as a buffer zone to cushion any offense.

"Pardon" is a legal term, meaning that you will not hold the guilty culpable. Forgiveness includes that, but it adds the relational touch. Forgiveness means, "I am willing to restore the relationship. I accept you into my life again as a friend." Genuine forgiveness can break the iron bars on the castle gate. Family feuds can dissolve, and a family can be a family again.

---

[1] Dante, *The Divine Comedy* (New York: Random House, 1932) "Purgatorio," Canto XVII, p. 291.
[2] Goethe, *Faust*, Prologue in Heaven, p. 13.

254 Delicious or Distasteful

From the fruit of his mouth a man's stomach is filled . . . / The tongue has the power of life and death, and those who love it will eat its fruit. / . . . Lips that speak knowledge are a rare jewel. / A word aptly spoken is like apples of gold . . . " (18:20, 21; 20:15; 25:11 NIV).

Here is a paradox. Physically a person is affected by what goes into the mouth, but morally and spiritually by what comes out. Jesus concurred with Solomon: "Not what goes into the mouth defiles a man, but what comes out" (Matt. 15:11 NKJV). Eating apples and oranges is optional, but eating your own words is unavoidable. You can, however, control the words you speak, and give health to your soul. Hearing what you say helps shape your own self-image. Kindly words make you kind and gentle. Acrid talk makes you sour and bitter. Your words turn on you. You become what you speak. You catch the effect of what you say.

Words are juicy or bitter, delicious or distasteful, nutritious or toxic. They deliver enzymes, antioxidants, and omega-3 fats, or cholesterol, trans fats, and concentrated starches. They give fresh-fruit nutrition or synthetic foodstuffs that are sickening. Words provide pleasure or make you gag with nausea. They deliver food that can enrich life or corrupt life. Wise words of knowledge are like "apples of gold" from "lips that are rare jewels."

In the original, the phrase "aptly spoken" is a graphic metaphor that literally says "spoken upon its wheels." The metaphor pictures both the spontaneity and the easy flow of word-talk, not scripted, but spinning off the wheels in existing situations, fitting smoothly into the flow.

Referring to Billy Graham's relationship with a former president, *Time* magazine writers said, "Where [the president] was stiff and awkward, Graham was liquid charm [with] disarming grace . . . [He] could talk to anyone about anything."[1] Millions of souls have been nourished to health by his spoken words, both public and personal. We need to be sure that our talk is nutritional.

---

[1] Gibbs and Duffy, *The Preacher and the Presidents* (New York: Center Street, Hatchette, 2007) pp. 58-59.

Reciprocal Relationship 255

He who finds a wife finds a good thing, and obtains favor from the Lord (18:22 NKJV, RSV, NASB).

Why not also say that she who finds a husband finds a good thing? Perhaps the proverbialist did not consider a man to be as good a catch as a woman. Generally speaking, a woman is more self-contained and is better able to live a single life than a man. Without a spouse, most men are both domestically and emotionally lost.

What is called a functional or dysfunctional marriage is reducible to a relational matter. Oneness "in the flesh" (Gen. 2:24) is symbolic of a relational oneness in spirit (Eph. 5:31 RSV). Portia said to Bassanio, "One half of me is yours, and the other half . . . is mine. . . . But if mine, then yours, and so all is yours."[1] When that is reciprocal, it is a relationship of mutual oneness.

Relational unity requires sacrificing those self-centered interests that would preempt or sabotage the oneness. Faust said to his lover Helena, "All we seek has therefore found us; / I am thine and thou art mine! / So we stand as love hath bound us: / Other fortune we resign."[2]

Social doors to other people may be kept open, but privacy doors are open only to your spouse. Emotional intimacy is closed to everyone else. All other attractive "fortunes" you reject. Any feeling of romance for another is immediately sacrificed for the sake of the spousal relationship.

You and your spouse have entered a world of mutual intimacy on the deepest level of the human spirit, where two personalities are bonded into oneness. It is a world that belongs only to the two of you. To all others, that door must be locked with dead bolt!

No human relationship approximates ones relationship with Christ, and no marriage equals the joys of heaven. But with spousal oneness, you may have a heavenly relationship which in kind is like heaven itself.

---

[1] Shakespeare, *The Merchant of Venice,* Act III, Scene 2, lines 16-17.
[2] Goethe, *Faust*, Second Part, Act III, p. 410.

256 The Plight of Poverty

The poor man uses entreaties, but the rich answers roughly. / . . .
his friends go far from him! He may pursue them with words, yet
they abandon him (18:23; 19:7 NKJV).

Chaucer said, "Just as from riches come many good things, so from poverty come many ills and evils."[1] In Bolivia, Sarah Corson had "meals" in thatch-roofed huts where the people squatted on dirt floors to drink their daily cup of soup, a soup that consisted of hot water with half an onion and a garlic clove for the entire family. Nothing more. All around them people were dying from malnutrition.[2] The world's overfed minority can hardly imagine the poverty of the majority.

Paralyzed with privation, hard-workers sometimes survive penury while their sense of self-worth depreciates with despair. Thomas Gray wrote, "Some heart once pregnant with celestial fire . . . penury repressed . . . and froze the genial current of the soul."[3] Many noble spirits have been squelched and their souls squandered by scarcity. Destitute of basic human needs, their grandest and most elevated desires are dissipated and depleted. Their human will withers, and its strength is wasted. Their dilemma is made unbearable when their friends forsake and their pleas are rebuffed. Alone in an uncaring world, they are immobilized by abandonment. Shakespeare's character Orlando said to the two princesses, "If I [die] . . . , I shall do my friends no wrong, for I have none to lament me. . . . Only in the world I fill up a place, which may be better supplied when I have made it empty."[4]

Instead of being competitive, we humans are in this thing together. The plea of the proverb is not to abandon the deprived. Those of us who have survival supply must help those who do not.

---

[1] Chaucer, "The Tale of Melibeus," *Canterbury Tales* (Garden City, NY: Garden City Pub. Co., 1934) p. 222.

[2] Jon Tal Murphree, *The Road to SIFAT* (Columbus, GA: Quill Publications, 1990) p. 136.

[3] Thomas Gray, "Elegy Written in a County Churchyard," Richard Aldington, ed., *The Viking Book of Poetry* (New York: The Viking Press, 1958) Vol. I, p. 560.

[4] Shakespeare, *As You Like It*, Act I, Scene 2, lines 199ff.

Some friends bring ruin on us . . . / . . . a poor man's friend deserts him. / . . . everyone is the friend of a man who gives gifts (18:24 NAB; 19:4 NIV: 19:6 NIV).

The notion of unstructured relationships has attracted many proponents. Rigid rules restrict relationships. William Young said, "Rules . . . will never love you."[1] By nature, relationships reject rigorous regimentation. They need the freedom to function.

By definition, however, relationships entail a measure of regulation. They may be overstructured, but they cannot be unstructured. Without any structure at all, they cease to exist. The word "friend" itself entails both love and loyalty. Desertion exposes relationships that are not authentic. Faithfulness is so inherent in friendship that without it the relationship crumbles. Polonius said to his son, "Grapple [thy friends] to thy soul with hoops of steel."[2]

Staged friendships for personal favors are not friendships. Presumed friendships can be expensive and injurious because they can be exploited. Exorbitant monetary or material claims can be made on the one who is deceived. To accommodate the friendship, he signs the note or mortgages the home, and suffers financial ruin. Morals are compromised and lifestyles realigned for the sake of a relationship that proves to be phony. When the friendship is pillaged and plundered, the beguiled person is emotionally ravaged. "Some friends bring ruin."

Real friendships are to be enjoyed, but not to be used. Shaw's character said, "I [was] a fugitive, a beggar, and a starving man. You accepted me. You gave me your hand . . . your bed . . . and your roof."[3] Friendship is focused on the friend, not on oneself. You use *your* friendship to help the friend, but never *her* friendship for your advantage. When each defers to the other in mutual friendship, you both grow richer than you can be alone.

---

[1] William P. Young, *The Shack* (Newbury Park, CA: Windblown Media, 2007) p. 198.

[2] Shakespeare, *Hamlet*, Act I, Scene 3, line 63.

[3] George B. Shaw, *Arms and the Man*, Act III, Abrams, *Norton Anthology* (New York: Norton, 1962) V 2, p. 1338.

258 Faithful Friends

. . . But there is a friend who sticks closer than a brother. / Do not forsake your own friend or your father's friend . . . (18:24; 27:10 NKJV).
Also 20:6.

First, friendships have to begin, usually triggered by a common interest, personal relating and respect. They are created by taking the initiative, overcoming inhibitions, and chancing rebuff. Then they have to develop naturally and easily, without excess regimentation. Friendship is a desirable plant that yields beautiful blossoms and luscious fruit, but it requires cultivation. Then the fruit we get from it is better than what give to it.

The first part of the proverb (previous essay) says some friends can betray you and ruin you, but this last part says some friends are faithful and true. They will defend you, cover your faults, and put the best face on whatever you do. Sir Walter Scott says a friend's "affection rises like a light on the canvass, improves any favorable tints . . . and throws its defects into the shade."[1]

Jane Merchant's poem reads: "She cannot drive a nail / Nor put a shelf together / Nor even assist with castles / In child-and sea-shore weather; / But her rebuilding talent / Yields endless satisfactions; / She puts the best construction / On other people's actions."[2]

Friendship need not be blind, but it overlooks little faults and failures, and makes excuses for blemishes and blunders. A friend is a venue where you can be safe—and where your name is safe when you are not there. Another proverb (20:6) says many may proclaim their loyalty, but the person is fortunate who finds a trustworthy friend. Real friends are faithful friends.

The most exalting experiences in life come from relationships that are noble and clean—beginning with one's relationship with God. Heaven itself is all about relationships, and those relationships can begin on earth.

---

[1] Sir Walter Scott, *The Lady of the Lake* (New York: The New American Library, 1962) "Introduction," p. 19.
[2] Jane Merchant, "Builder," *Because It's Here* (Nashville: Abingdon Press, 1970) p. 70.

Better . . . integrity than . . . perverse in speech. / . . . He who lies will perish. / He . . . disguises with his lips . . . / [and] covers . . . with guile. (19:1; 19:9; 26:24; 26:26 NASB). Also 19:5; 21:23; 26:25.

Here the stroke is on honesty. "Perversity in speech" is sometimes translated crooked (AAT) or twisted (Bas) or doubletalk (Jerus). The precept is not to tell all the truth you know, but to be truthful in what you do say.

Twisting the truth until it is crooked is a common inclination among many who have integrity in other areas. Too easily we can slip into a pattern of warping and distorting truth with little cover-ups, or spinning the truth with selective anecdotes, juggled figures, and subtle implications. Or fabricating minor alternate scenarios. The hazard should take our breath! At this point, scripture is strong! It declares, "All liars shall have their part in the lake which burns with fire and brimstone" (Rev. 21:8 NKJV). That is frightening, and should be sobering![1]

In addition to the moral mandate, these proverbs warn about the consequence to the deceiver. "Will perish" is sometimes translated "lost," as in a wilderness. False talk laces together a network of inconsistent pronouncements that entangles falsifiers in their own mesh. They get lost in their own wilderness. The jungle is matted with thick vines and prickly brambles. Bees buzz. Fowl fiends swoop in with frightening calls of clashing discords. Snakes slither in the dense undergrowth. Impenetrable darkness suffocates like a blanket. Sir Walter Scott wrote: "Oh! What a tangled web we weave / When first we practice to deceive!"[2]

Solomon said, "He who guards his . . . tongue, guards his soul from troubles" (Prov. 21:23 NASB).

---

[1] Conceivably, two moral principles can come into conflict, as the biblical injunction not to lie and the edict to intervene to spare innocent persons from being unjustly slaughtered (Prov. 31:8). In that circumstance, a "consequential ethic" should apply, and a person should opt for the one lower on the scale of consequence. When you are forced into a decision between two values, "the lesser of two evils" ceases to be evil under the circumstance.

[2] Sir Walter Scott, *Marmion* (New York: The Macmillan Co., 1901) Canto VI, Stanza 17, p. 192.

260 Knowing *About* God and Knowing God

It is not good for a man to be without knowledge, and he who
makes haste with his feet misses his way (19:2 RSV).

The second clause relates both to the previous proverb (19:1) and to the first clause of the present one. The other spoke of "walking in integrity" and this one of "hasty walking." Fast feet make missteps. Deliberate footfalls take time for consideration and reflection. To be hasty with the feet indicates nervousness, anxiety, and a lack of confidence. Jittery feet dance the jitterbug. The jitters can indicate lack of either moral direction or moral willingness to have integrity. Appropriate knowledge restores confidence and steadies the footstep.

Note two kinds of important knowledge—propositional and personal. It is the difference between knowing *something* and knowing *someone*, between being *aware of* and being *acquainted with*. One is cognition and the other is association. Biblical-rational theology emphasizes knowing the truth, while Neo-orthodox theology emphasizes knowing God as a person, the first through objective revelation and the second by a subjective "encounter."

When the two are together, as in historic theology, we have a double motive for integrity, from both the mind and the heart. We walk straight because we have *direction* for what is right and because we have *delight* to please Him whom we know and love. But the second must be based on the first, otherwise it becomes soft as quicksand, with nothing solid to walk on. In Dante's fantasy, Aquinas appears to him and says, "Let [my theological explanation] ever be lead to thy feet, to make thee more slow . . . Swift-formed opinions lean the wrong way."[1]

We need knowledge *about* God, and we need knowledge *of* God—to know about Him, and to know Him! We need both a good roadmap and good friend to guide. On our odyssey from birth to death, from time to eternity, "it is not good to be without knowledge."

---

[1] Dante, *The Divine Comedy* (New York: Random House, 1932) "Paradiso," Canto XIII, p. 486.

A man's own folly ruins his life, yet his heart rages against the Lord! / Stone is heavy and sand a burden, but provocation by a fool is heavier than both (19:3; 27:3 NIV).

Angry people make other people angry. They ruin their own lives with folly and blame it on others. Uncontrolled wrath is often misfocused on those closest by, family members, spouses, neighbors, simply because they are closer by. Angry people kick at anyone that gets in the way. Handling their provocation is a heavier burden than lifting boulders and sandbags.

Too often God Himself becomes the easy scapegoat to blame. Not wanting to comply with God's order, foolish folk target Him for recrimination. They crash into Him, and then blame Him for being there, like blaming the stone they stumble over or the power pole they run into. Isaiah said those who seek ungodly direction will be "hard-pressed and famished, . . . [and] will be enraged and curse their king and their God" (Is. 8:21 NASB).

In *Paradise Lost*, John Milton's description of the apostate archangel depicts the form that evil often takes. After he was banished from heaven for orchestrating an ancient mutiny of angelic renegades, Satan raged in rancor and declared to His sidekick Beelzebub, "All is not lost . . . revenge, immortal hate. . . . We [will] resolve to wage by force or guile eternal war. . . . Ever to do ill [will be] our sole delight."[1] Festering with venom like those described in the Apocalypse, some have "cursed the name of God . . . [and] refused to repent" (Rev. 16:9 NIV).

Complaining to God for the evil we bring on ourselves is an exercise in both futility and stupidity. Folly is too blind to recognize that we have no leverage. We have no hand to play. Lamentations says, "Why should any living mortal . . . offer complaint in view of his own sins" (Lam. 3:39 NASB)? Our only cushion is God's mercy, and that is not activated by accusatorial complaints or raging insanity. It comes by humility and soul-searching repentance.

---

[1] John Milton, *Paradise Lost* (Indianapolis: ITT Bobbs-Merrill, 1962) BK I, pp. 9-10, lines 106-107, 120-121, 160.

262 Living Liberated Lives

He who gets wisdom loves his own soul; . . . / A prudent man sees danger and takes refuge, but the simple keep going and suffer for it (19:8; 22:3 NIV). Also 27:12.

In what way should we "love our own souls?" Exorbitant self-love is sickly, but proper self-love is healthy. C. S. Lewis says it is appropriate to love oneself "with charity instead of partiality."[1] To esteem ourselves *worthy* is narcissistic and corrupt, but self-esteem based on the *worth* God ascribes to us through creation and redemption is wholesome.

Sickly self-love is self-centered, while appropriate self-love sees oneself in relationship with God and other humans. Since our value is bestowed rather than intrinsic, it is in a relational context. That frees us from the tyranny of selfish love to live liberated lives beyond our self-interests. So the two "greatest commandments" are to love God and other people" (Matt. 22:36-39).

Here is the problem. Self-centered love is warped to fulfill immediate desires without respect for one's future. It is shortsighted, borrowing from the future what cannot be repaid. Never seeing future danger, selfish love is compulsive, taking dares, heedless of warning alerts. In a present spending spree, future peace and prosperity are bartered for present pleasures. Checks are drawn on eternal joys for temporary thrills. It is like a person who goes through an inheritance with no thought of the future. Having buried future assets in present excess, one faces the future, bankrupt and broken. To play fast and loose with folly is suicidal!

To focus our love on Someone bigger than ourselves disentangles us from our present selves to preserve our future intact. God has not given us knowledge of the future, but He has given the option of wisdom to avert future disasters. Liabilities can be recognized. Wisdom climbs into the bomb shelter and closes the door. Solomon's preface to the proverbs quotes wisdom as saying, "Whoever finds me finds life. . . . All who hate me love death" (Pro. 8:35-36 NIV).

---

[1] C. S. Lewis, *God in the Dock* (Grand Rapids: Eerdmans, 1970) p. 194.

Wandering into Waywardness 263

Luxury is not fitting for a fool . . . / A man who wanders from the way of understanding will rest in the congregation of the dead. / A wise man scales the city of the mighty, and brings down the trusted stronghold (19:10; 21:16; 21:22 NKJV).

Dante pictures himself as a young man wandering into dark woods and losing his way. He comes to the foot of a steep hill splashed with sunlight from the heavenly body that "leads men straight on every road." When he attempts to abandon his waywardness and climb the mountain of God, he confronts a leopard of worldly pleasure, then a lion of ambition, then a she-wolf of greedy avarice that drive him back into the dark valley.[1]

A taste of luxurious living for simpletons can become an overpowering temptation for more of the same. Inundated with a deluge of inordinate desire, they follow their fantasies into unfathomable folly.

Wanderlust leads to waywardness. Indulgence turns wise persons into fools, and fools into moral addicts. Hamlet said to Horatio, "Give me that man that is not passion's slave, and I will wear him in my heart."[2] Foolish people cannot afford the luxury of indulgence. It does not sit well on them. They cannot handle it. Eventually, libertines lose their liberty, and the wayward wander into a wilderness.

What a difference with wise persons! They are disciplined, and committed to goals beyond self-centered interests. They scale mighty fortresses and bring down strongholds. Wisdom is more workable than mighty power. Heavy metal beams succumb to demolition skills. Fortified garrisons collapse before sagacity. Walls crumble before the wisdom of the wise! Foolish people first lose their way and then lose their mobility in the "congregation of the dead." They dead-end. All the while, the wise move with spontaneity, flexing their muscles, whetting their skills, sharpening their wits. And running over with surging streams of wisdom!

---

[1] Dante, *The Divine Comedy* (New York: Random House, 1932) "Inferno," Canto I, pp. 11-12.

[2] Shakespeare, *Hamlet*, Act III, Scene 2, lines 72-74.

264 To Act or to React

It is prudent for a man to restrain his anger; it is his glory to overlook an offense (19:11 Ber). Also 20:3.

To Beowulf's palace came the dragon, ". . . flying by night, scorching the dark on wings of fire! . . . Riotous with rage he went forth in flame, breathing out ruin, snorting hurricanes! Villages he burned, he laid waste the land; the palace of Beowulf . . . he swamped in waves of fire—O terrible was the king's anger—in his heart the wrathful embers flared!"[1]

Beowulf had reason for anger that we seldom have. These days, wrathful embers flare in hearts with inadequate reason. Minor provocations cause major eruptions. Virgil said that anger is like lightning—"darting wrath wrapped in vindictive flames."[2]

Negative reaction becomes a pattern that is difficult to break. We easily get sucked into the action-reaction syndrome. Others' actions trigger in us an attitude. Their dissipation determines our disposition. Our *actions* are *reactions* to their *actions*. Then our attitude gets out of tune and plays discordant notes. We become disharmonious with ourselves.

To "overlook an offense" is to be magnanimous, which means you are *big* enough to be willing to look *little*. You are *somebody* enough, in the bigger context of God's universe, to be willing to look like a *nobody* in the world. You have an outside source for your self-esteem. You are playing for the Coach and not for the fans. You have credentials for your self-image in another kingdom! You are marching to a different drumbeat! Refusing to react to an offense arrays your life with beauty and crowns your head with glory!

And it will equip you for handling greater wrongs that *cannot* be rectified or avenged. Kipling said, "A wrong which admits of no reparation . . . is best to forget."[3]

---

[1] *Beowulf the Warrior*, Ian Serraillier, tr. (New York: Henry Z. Walck, Inc., 1961) pp. 37-38.

[2] Virgil, *The Aeneid* (London: Penguin Books, 1958) Book Eight, P. 214.

[3] Rudyard Kipling, *The Light That Failed* (New York: Books, Inc., n.d.) p. 208.

A king's rage is like the roar of a lion; . . . / . . . he who angers him forfeits his life (19:12; 20:2 NIV).

Of course, when a moral issue requires public opposition to a despotic policy, a stand must be taken.   But with our cultural emphasis on individual rights, disgruntled people daily badmouth dignitaries as a popular pastime. Public office has become a target where officials are pierced and pulverized without protection. In some ways, we are becoming dehumanized.

We all rejoice in our constitutional protection from petty tyrants, but it creates a mood for refractory people to feel comfortable shaking their fists in the face of Almighty God and daring Him to react! Irreverence on talk shows has become a "virtuous" sport.   God is daily insulted by the verbal and behavioral lifestyles of those who attempt to make themselves gods over God!

Forest animals tremble at the roar of a raging lion, and people are horror-stricken with the frown of a tyrant who operates a genocide machine. Yet they systematically flout the laws of an Omnipotent God. John Milton described how Lucifer with his legions gambled their future on a miscalculation of God's power.[1] Yet without fear we have dethroned God from our lives. Russian roulette is a dangerous game!

In Narnia, Aslan the lion personified Christ. Mrs. Beaver told Susan that no one "can appear before Aslan without their knees knocking." Lucy queried, "Then he isn't safe?" Mr. Beaver replied, "Of course he isn't safe! . . . He's the King, I tell you!"[2]

God does not roar. He does not need to. One trace of His frown will strike eternal panic on those who have "forfeited their lives!" The apostle John got a glimpse of future judgment and wrote: "I saw Him that sat on [the throne], *from whose face* the earth and the heaven fled away . . ." (Rev. 20: 11 KJV, italics added).

---

[1] John Milton, *Paradise Lost* (Indianapolis: ITT Bobbs-Merrill, 1962) Bk. I, pp. 24-25, lines 626-646.
[2] C. S. Lewis, *The Lion, the Witch and the Wardrobe* (New York: Collier Books, Macmillan, 1978) pp. 75-76.

266 Decree of the Decalogue

A foolish son is destruction to his father . . . / . . . a shameful and disgraceful son. / Cease listening, my son, to discipline, and you will stray . . . (19:13; 19:26; 19:27 NASB) Also 20:20; 28:7; 28:24; 29:3.

When the pastor of the far-out village visited Johannesburg, he talked proudly of the beautiful mountains and rivers near his home, and the mists that covered the hills. Then Kumalo thought of his lost son who had left home, rejecting his father. Author Alan Paton wrote: "[Immediately] the hills with the deep melodious names stood out waste and desolate beneath the pitiless sun, the streams ceased to run, the cattle moved thin and listless over the red and rootless earth. . . . His voice would falter and die away, and he would fall silent."[1]

With the birth of a child, most parents are flooded with heavenly exhilaration. Goethe wrote: "Love, in human wise to bless us, / In a noble pair must be; / But divinely to possess us, / It must form a precious three."[2] But daring to love a child makes a parent vulnerable to the pain of rejected love. By loving, parents leave their hearts unguarded, allowing their feelings to be crucified. When King David's son Absalom was killed in rebellion, the king went to his chamber over the gate, sobbing and chanting like a liturgical dirge: "O my son, Absalom, my son, Absalom! Would God I had died for thee, O Absalom, my son, my son" (2 Sam. 18:33 KJV).

Today many parents are placed in professional care facilities and cut off from the outside world. Their children, busy with their own schedules, spend too little time with them. The parents are hurt with neglect. Feeling abandoned, they are silent, without complaining.

The decree of the Decalogue rings with clarion clarity: "Honor your father and mother" (Ex. 20:12)! It is one of the cardinal commandments of God. To transgress is to handle parental love selfishly. And it is to deal with divine law recklessly!

---

[1] Alan Paton, *Cry, the Beloved Country* (New York: MacMillan Pub. Co., 1948) p. 61.
[2] Goethe, *Faust*, Second Part, Act III, p. 409.

Listless or Spirited 267

Laziness casts into a deep sleep, and an idle man will suffer hunger. / Do not love sleep, lest you become poor; open your eyes. . . . / As the door turns on its hinges, so does the sluggard on his bed (19:15; 20:13; 26:14 NASB).

Of course, we all need adequate sleep. Those who consistently deprive themselves are reckless stewards. But like gluttony, indulging a utility can become a curse. That is the burden of these proverbs. Browning wrote, "Life is to wake, not sleep / . . . But press . . . to heaven's height, far and steep."[1]

Probably Solomon was using sleep as a metaphor for lethargic complacency. While you are asleep you cannot work, or make plans, or accomplish. Apathetic people are nonproductive. Groggy people are a drag on company time. A "door turns on its hinges," but it cannot move away from its hinges. Sluggards turn on their beds, but do not move away. Dante, attempting to climb out of one of the deepest circles of the inferno, became so exhausted that he sat down to catch his breath. His guide said to him, "Free thyself from sloth, for sitting down . . . leaves such vestige of [oneself] as smoke in air or foam in water. Therefore rise! Conquer thy panting!"[2] Apathetic people can become energetic, like pure air and water, free of smoke and foam.

Wide-awake people are alert. They leave their beds and get on their feet. They get out of their nests. They are on the cutting edge. They become creative and productive. Listless people waste opportunities, but spirited people can be a blessing to humankind.

Goethe wrote: In "happiness or sorrow, / He who postpones it till tomorrow / To the future only cleaveth. / Nothing, therefore, he achieveth."[3] Again, "What's left undone today, tomorrow will not do. / . . . With resolute, courageous trust / . . . Work on because you must!"[4]

---

[1] Robert Browning, "Asolando," *The Complete . . . Works . . .* (Cambridge, MA: Houghton Mifflin, 1895) p. 1006.

[2] Dante, *The Divine Comedy* (New York: Random House, 1932) "The Inferno," Canto XXIV, p. 129.

[3] Goethe, *Faust*, Second Part, Act V, Scene 5, p. 482.

[4] *op. cit.,* Prelude, pp. 8-9.

268 Disgusted or Delighted

He who keeps the commandment keeps his soul, but he who is careless of his ways will die. / Those who forsake the law praise the wicked . . . (19:16; 28:4 NASB, NKJV).

Yes, your soul can be saved by being good—*if* you are good enough! But because God and heaven are holy, if you are anything less than absolute moral perfection you will not qualify for heaven. We have all violated the principle of goodness, so our only recourse is mercy. Keeping the commandments will not save us, but flouting God's commandments can doom us!

Many who outwardly attempt to keep the commandments nevertheless delight in iniquity, "praising the wicked." Vulgarity is relished in stand-up comedians under the cover of comedy. Evil is savored in others by those who are not brave enough to do it themselves. They "have pleasure in" (Rom. 1:32 KJV), "give hearty approval to" (NASB), those who do it.

Those whose hearts are changed find evil disgusting and good delightful. They are not opposed to the commandments. Senior souls who never drive over 25 miles-an-hour have no problem with the 60-mph speed limit. If the law against stealing were rescinded for 24 hours, nonthieves still would not steal. When the Trojans finally arrived in Italy, King Latinus sat on his ancestral throne and announced, "Latins . . . need no bond of law to keep them just, but are just by their own free will and hold to the way of their ancient God."[1] Paul said, "The law is made not for the righteous, but for . . . rebels, the ungodly and sinful" (1 Tim. 1:9 NIV).

The speed limit is binding over those who would speed, the law against theft is operative for thieves, and all of God's commandments stand as a warning to those who would transgress, white collar, blue collar, or common criminal. Chaucer said, "Between a tyrant or usurping chief / And any outlawed man or errant thief, / It's just the same, there is no difference."[2]

---

[1] Virgil, *The Aeneid* (London: Penguin Books, 1958) Book Seven, p. 181.
[2] Chaucer, "The Manciple's Tale of the Crow," *CanterburyTales* (Garden City, NY: Garden City Pub. Co., 1934) p. 535.

Discipline your son while there is hope . . . / A . . . man who walks
in his integrity—blessed are his sons . . . / Train up a child in the
way he should go . . . (19:18; 20:7; 22:6 RSV). Also 22:15; 29:15; 29:17.

A startling line leaps up from one of Wordsworth's poems:
"The child is father of the man."[1] The idea is that the child you
once were is still a part of you. What a child feels and thinks is
brain-recorded to be played back throughout life. The way the
child is shaped determines in varying degrees the adult it will be.
In this way, the child produces the adult.

To rear children is to program them for later life, and it
requires a delicate act between three proportional ingredients. The
first is *discipline*. Children gain self-control from learning parental
control. Responsibility is developed. When authoritarian control
is overbearing, however, the reverse effect is produced. Rebellion
kicks in. Children must be allowed the freedom to be children, to
act like children, and to make childhood mistakes.

The second is *love relationships*. The proverb says to steer
and shape a child "while there is hope." Teenage years are too
late. An advance relational reservoir is imperative. Because each
child is different, the way you relate with each is different. Much
of the relating should be in the child's own areas of interest. As a
father, I had to play house with my daughter. My son would not
watch news programs or ball games with me, so I had to watch his
children's shows with him. Even discipline needs to be in the
context of a love relationship.

The third ingredient is *example*. Children screen their
parents' actions and motives with a fine-toothed comb. In some
ways, they know us better than we know ourselves. The emperor
of Rome said, "From my father [I learned] modesty and a manly
character. From my mother . . . beneficence."[2] Those children are
fortunate whose parents model integrity!

---

[1] William Wordsworth, "My Heart Leaps Up," Richard Aldington, ed., *The
Viking Book of Poetry* (New York: The Viking Press, 1958) Volume 2, p. 655.
[2] Marcus Aurelius, *The Thoughts of the Emperor* (New York: John B. Alden,
publisher, 1887) p. 41.

270 Penalty of Pain

A man of great anger shall bear the penalty . . . (19:19 NASB).

Milton said, "No pain can equal anger."[1] An angry person bears the pain of anger, and that should elicit our sympathy. What is called "the penalty" is built into its nature as a consequence. The pain can be worse for the one who has it than for the one who gets it, worse for its subject than its object. That is true whether the anger is righteous indignation or evil rage. To agitate a person's anger is to compound the pain. To do it for sport is an act of cruelty.

We sometimes think that love is the antidote to anger, so the more we love we have the less anger. Actually, however, the antithesis of love is indifference. Wrath is its corollary. When Queen Dido of Carthage felt her love betrayed, Virgil said, "Her torment redoubled; her love came back again and again, and heaved in oceantides of rage."[2]

When love and wrath are directed toward the same person, one's pain is complicated. The pain of anger is intensified by the measure of the love. The more you love someone, the greater the potential for pain. In a person's heart, love and anger clash in conflict. They grind and grate. They are conflicting corollaries—moral corollaries, but emotionally conflicting.

The incarnate Jesus took on human nature while retaining divine nature. As God, He was the subject of God's righteous wrath toward sinners. As man, He was the object of that wrath. As both subject and object of the wrath evoked by our betrayal of infinite love, the pain of anger was excruciating beyond our ability to conceive! He bore the pain of anger both ways—by having it and receiving it.   In His death, Jesus not only *made the payment* for our sins, but He *took the pain* of the payment. Christ had the resources to make the payment by taking the pain![3]

---

[1] John Milton, *Paradise Lost* (Indianapolis: ITT Bobbs-Merrill, 1962) BK. IV, pp. 109-110, lines 915-916.

[2] Virgil, *The Aeneid* (London: Penguin Books, 1958) Book Four, p. 113.

[3] The death of Christ was *morally* required from God's *justice*, not *emotionally* required from His *wrath*. But since His wrath is moral wrath, the pain of anger was included in Christ's death.

Present Counsel for Future Wisdom 271

Listen to counsel and receive instruction, that you may be wise in your latter days. / Every purpose is established by counsel; by wise counsel wage war (19:20; 20:18 NKJV). Also 25:12.

The God of all worlds has ways to direct us earthlings. Chaucer said, "You shall first . . . meekly pray to the high God that He will be your advisor."[1] One way He guides is through the advice of human counselors. Here we must hit a happy medium between taking everybody's advice and refusing to take anybody's advice. Lady Prudence gave to her husband a lot of advice about taking advice. "The truth," she said, ". . . is found rather among a few folk who are wise and reasonable than among the multitude, where every man cries and gabbles as he likes."[2]

The first proverb urges the need for counsel to become wise. Younger people acquire knowledge more easily than older, and Solomon says to get instruction while you are young if you wish to be wise when you are old. Childish folly seen in seniors is disdained, but the wisdom of age is soon recognized and venerated.

The second proverb insists on counsel for those in positions of leadership. Counselors should be chosen with cautious discretion. It is dangerous to surround oneself with yes-men who tell you only what you wish to hear. Prudence said, "Counselors are commonly flatterers . . . inclining toward the lord's desire."[3] Wise leaders seek wise counselors with courage to disagree.

Rather than advising war, the proverb says that weighty issues like war-waging deserves wisest counsel. Most wars in world history have been unjust wars of aggression and ambition with inadequate counsel. Blood is spilled, economies crash, millions of lives are lost, and some soldiers are turned into beasts of brutality. The worthy goals of many wars could more easily be obtained by favor than by force. This proverb directly addresses war-making warmongers.

---

[1] Chaucer, "The Tale of Melibeus," *Canterbury Tales* (Garden City, NY: Garden City Pub. Co., 1934) p. 199.

[2] *op. cit.*, p. 196.

[3] *op. cit.*, p. 201.

272 Wells of Wisdom

Many are the plans of a man's heart, but the counsel of the Lord, it will stand. / A plan in the heart of a man is like deep water, but a man of understanding draws it out (19:21; 20:5 NASB).

In the inner secret self, most persons harbor hopes that are concealed from their closest companions—ideas never intimated, plans that never prevail. Our imaginations grind out fantasy fiction, as Poe said of himself, "dreaming dreams no mortal ever dared to dream before."[1] "The counsel of the Lord will stand," but those ill-advised plans in the first proverb will falter and fail. It is appropriate for them to be concealed, but . . .

. . . the worthy plans in the second should be revealed. Some hearts are profuse with plans and purposes, copious with concepts, deep with ideas and ideals. Those without creative thoughts are often quick to express themselves, but those rich in ideas are more reticent. To unload what they have without being invited would breach their own modesty. While simple people chatter on in shallow palaver, those rich with ideas are hesitant to crash the party.

But friends and acquaintances would profit from picking their ticking thoughts. Sneaking a peak at their clicking minds could make a delightful experience. Someone needs to open the door to allow rich souls to express themselves without violating modesty. Someone needs to take the initiative to tap their subterranean streams. Sagacious people, in appropriate social contexts, should pose germane inquiries, not as a quiz, but in a relational, nonthreatening way.

What most of us have to say is more boring than we know. A break with a new voice would be welcomed. Good social fellowship is more than one-way sharing. It includes getting the other person to share. Learning to listen is more important than vocal verbosity.

By genuine interest and gentle inquiry, thoughtful people can draw water from the deep wells of wisdom.

---

[1] Edgar Allan Poe, "The Raven," Aldington, ed., *The Viking Book of Poetry* (New York: The Viking Press, 1958) Vol. II, Stansa 5, p. 866.

*The fear of the Lord leads to life, so that one may sleep satisfied,
untouched by evil* (19:23 NASB).

Insomnia comes from multiple sources. Living under strain and stress takes its toll. Anxiety intercepts sleep. Fear keeps one wide-awake. Concern over one's unchecked moral condition and final destiny *should* frighten a person out of slumber. But a Christian relationship with God absolves us from guilt and exempts us from future punishment. In that way we are "untouched by evil." If you have *His* life, you need not fear *your* death. And that should improve your sleep! A psalmist said, "I will lie down and sleep in peace" (Ps. 4:8 NIV).

Though God has not promised to prevent all our troubles, we are "untouched by evil" in two other senses. First, His therapeutic presence is with us in trouble (Isa. 41:10) and gives us resources to handle it (Phil. 4:13, 19). Second, God brings good out of every bad experience (Rom. 8: 28), making the bad work for our good. William Young says that God is not attempting to "justify suffering." Instead He is working to "redeem it."[1] One way is that He uses it to make us stronger for future trials and to prepare us to appreciate future relief. When Aeneas' crew made landfall after a relentless storm, he told his ragtag crew, "One day you will enjoy looking back on what you now endure. . . . Hold hard, therefore. Preserve yourselves for better days."[2]

Another way is that God uses our tears to make us tender and our suffering to give us sympathy. As affliction strengthens our character, it softens our souls. Queen Dido said, "My own acquaintance with misfortune has been teaching me to help others who are in distress."[3]

In these ways, suffering is redeemed with values and benefits that wear well in life. We can "be quiet from the fear of evil, . . . [and] sleep shall be sweet" (Pr. 1:33; 3:24 KJV).

---

[1] William P. Young, *The Shack* (Newbury Park, CA: Windblown Media, 2007) p. 127.

[2] Virgil, *The Aeneid* (London: Penguin Books, 1958) Book One, p. 33.

[3] *op. cit.,* p. 47.

274 Empty Head or Open Mind

*Flog a mocker, and the simple will learn prudence; rebuke a
discerning man, and he will gain knowledge. / A whip for the
horse, a halter for the donkey, and a rod for the backs of fools* (19:25;
26:3 NIV). Also 21:11.

Mockers have scorched brains, simple fools have empty
heads, and discerning people have open minds. The first may not
be helped, but the second will learn some lessons by seeing the
first punished.   Only the third will profit by a simple rebuke.
Naive people are motivated by fear.   The wise need only
admonition.

Scornful, close-minded mockers may not respond to
anything.   Their punishment is remedial in society, used as a
preventive move for foolish simpletons to see. It is educative for
the culture. But the punishment is nevertheless deserved by those
who are punished. Retributive justice prevents false charges from
being fabricated for public examples.

Traditional literature sees the human species as distinct
primarily at the point of rational reasoning.   Animals have
empirical intelligence, discerning causal relationships between
cause and effect.   But they are without rational intelligence to
discern logical relationships between premises and conclusions. A
psalmist said, "The horse or the mule . . . [has] no understanding"
(Ps. 32;9). Adam Barkman says the human race is an animal-angel
hybrid, like both beasts and seraphim.[1] Jude says some people are
"like unreasoning animals" (Ju. 10).   The second proverb says
corrective punishment is as befitting for a fool as a whip for a
horse and a halter for a donkey. Those who will not respond to
counsel need reproof. Those who reject rebuke need punishment.
Polonius advised, "Take each man's censure."[2]

The lesson for us is this: Gain wisdom every way possible.
Turn advice, reproof and punishment into wisdom. Doing the first
two will make the third unnecessary.

---

[1] Adam Barkman, "A New Philosophy of Darkness," *Christian Scholar's
Review*, Spring 2010, p. 265.
[2] Shakespeare, *Hamlet*, Act I, Scene 3, line 69.

*A corrupt witness mocks at justice . . . / . . . a sly tongue brings
angry looks. / Like a thornbush in a drunkard's hand is a proverb
in the mouth of a fool. / Like a coating of glaze over earthenware
are fervent lips with an evil heart* (19:28; 25:23; 26:9; 26:23 NIV).

If everyone were a perjurer, civilization would disintegrate
into anarchy.   Oath-breakers are self-servers who score only
because most other people are *not* perjurers. Like thieves, they
succeed only as parasites. A deceiver's talk may be smooth as silk,
but it is only a thin and superficial glaze to conceal a heartless
heart. Fabricators refine their style to emulate sincerity, enhancing
their ability to deceive. Some are so adept at falsehood that they
are clumsy with truth, like an inebriated person attempting to
handle a bramble bush.

On the short run, falsehood can have more force than truth
because it can be embellished for appeal, while truth stands naked
without camouflage. That enables false reports to do more damage
than truth can immediately correct.

Flippant   chatterboxes   readily   leave   false   insinuations
because their talk is out of control. Innuendoes with accusatorial
overtones can do irreparable damage. Chaucer said, "Speaking
little and advisedly, / Is no man harmed, to put it generally / . . .
My son, of too much speaking, ill advised, / Where less had been
enough and had sufficed, / Much harm may come."[1]

Freewheeling   speakers   spit   out   multiple   droplets   of
meaningless trivia, usually mixing negative hints with positive.
The negative always strikes harder and is remembered longer
simply because it is negative. Horace said, "Think often what you
say. . . . The word once let slip flies beyond recall."[2] Paul said,
"Do not let unwholesome talk come out of your mouths, but only
what is helpful for building others up . . . , that it may benefit those
who listen" (Eph. 4:29).

---

[1] Chaucer, "The Manciple's Tale," *Canterbury Tales* (Garden City NY: Garden
City Pub. Co., 1934) p. 538.
[2] Horace, *Satires, Epistles, Ars Poetica* (Cambridge, MA: Harvard U. Press,
1991) Epistle XVIII, Book I, p. 375.

279 Righteous Retribution

Penalties are prepared for mockers, and beatings for the backs of fools. / The violence of the wicked will drag them away, because they refuse to act with justice. / If a man digs a pit, he will fall into it; if a man rolls a stone, it will roll back on him (19:29 NIV; 21:7 NASB; 26:27 NIV).

Mephistopheles, representing the devil, considered Faust to be his prize catch. But when he lost him to heaven, he declared he had worked hard to make him evil, and regretfully complained: "My rare, great treasure they have perculated, / The lofty soul to me hypothecated. / . . . But unto whom shall I appeal my justice? / Who would secure to me my well-earned right? / . . . And I deserve it, this infernal spite! / I've managed in a most disgraceful fashion; / . . . By lowest lust seduced [him] in senseless passion."[1]

In earlier essays, I have enunciated the automatic connections between causes and their effects, showing that calamity can be a consequence of moral evil. While these proverbs underscore the same point, they add the judicial element, and clarify that consequences come also in the form of punishment. Penalties "are prepared." Mephistopheles had no claim on justice because he is the victim of his own injustice, having "refused to act with justice."

Righteous retribution is often "in kind." Trap setters are caught in their own traps. Stone rollers are rolled over by their own stones. Arsonists are burned in their own fires. Jesus said, Those "who draw the sword will die by the sword" (Matt. 26:52 NIV). He said, "In the same way you judge others, you will be judged" (Matt. 7:1 NIV).

Macbeth devised a scheme to have assissins kill King Duncan, and instructed them how to do it. Then he ominously reminded himself of the possible pending aftermath: "Bloody instructions . . . being taught, return to plague the inventor."[2] Wherever moral choice is available, retributive justice is operative. Macbeth discovered it to be true!

---

[1] Goethe, *Faust*, Second Part, Act V, Scene 6, p. 496.
[2] Shakespeare, *Macbeth*, Act I, Scene 7, lines 9-10.

Wine is a mocker, strong drink is raging, and whosoever is deceived thereby is not wise (20:1 KJV).

Two specific effects of alcoholic beverage spin out multiple problems. The first is *inebriation*, in varying degrees. It breaks down moral inhibitions, throwing off restraint and arousing lust. Chaucer said, "A lecherous thing is wine."[1] It inflates emotion and impairs reason, endangering highways, damaging relationships, and provoking rage. Being "under the influence" is a dangerous condition in any situation!

The second is *addiction*. Twenty million alcoholics live in America today, and millions of others are on the edge. When moderate drinkers face traumatic problems, most start drinking more. When any consumer item combines intoxication and addiction, red flags fly high. More than twenty thousand people die each year in alcohol-related highway accidents, and thousands of others are broken and mangled for life! Tens of thousands of marriages are destroyed, and thousands of children are abused! Medical and auto insurance rates skyrocket. Taxes increase for law enforcement. Alcohol is a major contributor to most of our social problems—crime, vice, divorce, disease, highway deaths, fatherless children, spouse abuse, betrayed love and broken hearts! Any other such social evil would be outlawed immediately! Shakespeare's Cassio exclaimed, "O thou invisible spirit of wine, if thou hast no name to be known by, let us call thee devil!"[2]

First the church needs to be actively involved in rescuing and helping recovering addicts. And second, the church should take a strong preventative stand in denouncing consumption! No one ever got hooked who did not take a first drink. Teetotal abstinence is not passé. While doing the evangelistic and priestly functions of spiritual ministry, the church must not skirt ethical social issues. On this matter, the church needs a prophetic voice!

---

[1] Chaucer, "The Pardoner's Tale," *Canterbury Tales* (Garden City, NY: Garden City Pub. Co., 1934) p. 299.
[2] Shakespeare, *Othello*, Act II, Scene 3, lines 282-284.

278 Winnowing the Wicked

A king who sits on the throne of justice disperses all evil with his eyes. / A wise king winnows the wicked, and drives the threshing wheel over them (20:8; 20:26 NASB).

Sir Walter Scott said that any public figure "is sure to encounter abuse and ridicule. . . . As he gallops through a village," he will be "followed by curs in full cry." If the rider attempts to swipe at all the yappers, he is sure to have a bad fall. "Nor is an attempt to chastise a malignant critic attended with less danger."[1]

A discreet, judicious leader does not need to swat at critics. His very presence on a judicial throne winnows the wicked and crushes them with a threshing wheel. His eyes are like a sieve through which they are sifted. Evil critics scatter in all directions to avoid popping up on the judge's radar screen. They do not want to appear in his eyes.

The principle applies to God. A Hebrew psalmist sang, "Thou dost sit on the throne judging righteously" (Ps. 9:4). Many people wonder why God tolerates the daily abuse that He gets. Does His silence imply an infant god who is too immature to react, or a senile god who dotes on the attention? God does not need to eliminate His opposition and silence His critics. Simply by being the God that He is, evil people destroy themselves by striking against Him. A friend told President Woodrow Wilson "never to murder a man who is committing suicide."[2]

Queen Orual in Lewis' novel said, "The Divine Nature wounds and perhaps destroys us merely by being what it is. We call it the wrath of the gods; as if the great cataract . . . were angry with every fly it sweeps down in its green thunder."[3] Evil people who oppose righteousness oppose themselves. Those who defeat God's rightful role in their lives end up defeating themselves. Eventually all evil opposition will be eliminated—because God is God!

---

[1] Sir Walter Scott, *The Lady of the Lake* (New York: The New American Library, 1962) "Introduction," p. 27.
[2] Bob Dole, *Great Political Wit* (New York: Doubleday, 1998) p. 153.
[3] C. S. Lewis, *Till We Have Faces* (Grand Rapids: William B. Eerdmans Pub. Co., 1966) p. 284.

Divine Detergent 279

Who can say, "I have made my heart clean, I am pure from my sin" (20:9 NKJV)?

When Lady Macbeth was wringing her hands in guilt, the king instructed the physician to use "some sweet oblivious antidote [to] cleanse [her] of the perilous stuff which weighs upon the heart." The doctor replied, "Therein the patient must minister to [her]self."[1]

Both were mistaken. The physician could not cleanse her heart, and she could not do it for herself. The proverb is a rhetorical question whose answer is intended to be obvious. No one can cleanse herself of sin! But millions have verified by personal experience the apostle's declaration that "the blood of Jesus Christ . . . cleanses from all sin" (1 Jno. 1:7).

Two kinds of sin are covered by the death of Christ. The *act* of sin can be forgiven, which absolves a person of her guilt. The *condition* of sin—motives and dispositions—can be cleansed away. In no way is a person exonerated from ever having sinned. That is the reason the atonement was necessary to redeem people from the penalty of sin, operating on mercy without bypassing justice, allowing them to appear before God *as if* they had never sinned.

Many forgiven persons, however, are miserably frustrated by a residual condition of self-centered motives. James speaks of "a double-minded man, unstable in all his ways" (Ja. 1:8). Horace said, "Unless the vessel is clean, whatever you pour into it turns sour."[2] Marcus Aurelius, a pagan, wanted a "purified" mind where one will "find no corrupted matter, nor impurity, nor any sore skinned over."[3] Calvary grace can lead a person into pure motives. Sanctification is included with salvation in the provisions of the Cross. Our hearts can be bathed in the divine detergent and our deepest motives made pure in the efficacious blood of Christ!

[1] Shakespeare, *Macbeth*, Act V, Scene 3, lines 43-45.
[2] Horace, *Satires, Epistles, Ars Poetica* (Cambridge, MA: Harvard U. Press, 1991) Epistle II, Book I, p. 267.
[3] Marcus Aurelius, *The Thoughts of the Emperor* (New York: John B. Alden, publisher, 1887) p. 63.

280 Tricks of Trade

Differing weights and differing measures—the Lord detests them both (20:10 NIV).   Also 20:23.

For millennia, the human race has used deception in business deals to gain unfair advantage. Now market tricks are refined with subtlety to bamboozle unsuspecting victims.

In Hebrew the proverb literally says, "A stone and a stone; an ephah and an ephah." Stone is a weight and ephah is a measure. The line is saying there are true weights and measures, and then there are false ones. The standard is used by the dealer for purchasing, and the below-standard is used for selling. Thus the customer gets less than she pays for.

But everybody hates cheating, especially when it is done by the other person. Yet many otherwise respectable persons have a fraudulent character quirk for taking secret advantage of trusting people. Imposters have indulged the practice until it has become a science. They have cut the corners of conscience until they have no more compunction. Their feelings toward the victims are as arid as a desert. Inwardly they have lost all sense of shame, but outwardly they have to hide behind false fronts. A ten-percent good deal is used to cover for a ninety-percent bad. Bassanio said, "There is no vice so simple but assumes some mark of virtue."[1]

"Everybody does it" does not even impress the Senate Investigating Committee, much less God! All alibis fail in the presence of Him who "detests differing weights and measures." Kierkegaard asserts that sinners become blind to the point of thinking God is blind to their sins.[2]

Yet there live today millions of character-controlled people who could not live with themselves behind false masks. The cost of guilt is too expensive to pay for gaining a deceitful advantage. They can honestly say with Shakespeare, "I lack iniquity . . . to do me service."[3]

---

[1] Shakespeare, *The Merchant of Venice*, Act III, Scene 2, lines 81-82.
[2] Soren Kierkegaard, *Attack Upon Christendom*, Walter Lowrie, tr. (Boston: The Beacon Press, 1956) p. 252.
[3] Shakespeare, *Othello*, Act I, Scene 2, lines 3-4.

Motives and Actions 281

It is by his deeds that a lad distinguishes himself if his conduct is pure and right (20:11 NASB).

Jesus validated the truth of the proverb when He said, "You will know them by their fruits" (Matt. 6:16). It is Aquinas' "cosmological argument" for the existence of God. You infer the cause from the effect. You can read a person's motives by his actions. Children are seldom hypocritical. Their conduct betrays their disposition. They give advance indication of the kind of adult they may become. When parents observe the virtues and vices a child may be inclined toward, they can tweak his motivations with stimuli, incentives, and reinforcement.

Children, like most adults, want to feel distinguished. They want to stand out from the ordinary and be someone special. When they are praised for their virtues, they will naturally adjust their behavior for the distinction. The child that is constantly accused of being bad may increase his badness in order to accent the distinction of being bad.

By complying with our more ethical motives, we intensify and fortify them. Then they help direct our lifestyle. What we *are* and what we *do* support each other.

With Christ in our hearts we have a dynamo that generates an even greater dynamic. Our entire lives should be spent reinforcing our higher motives and starving out the inferior ones. We do not have to settle for mediocrity! We can rise above the status quo! We can all be special—to God! Horace said, "Beware of doing anything unworthy of yourself."[1] Again he said, "I will not fail myself."[2]

Because motives largely control actions and what we are determines what we do, Polonius advised his daughter: "This above all: to thine own self be true, and it must follow, as the night the day, thou canst not then be false to any man."[3]

---

[1] Horace, *Satires, Epistles, Ars Poetica* (Cambridge, MA: Harvard U. Press, 1991) Satire III, Book II, p. 157.
[2] Horace, *op. cit.,* Satire I, Book II, p.129.
[3] Shakespeare, *Hamlet*, Act I, Scene3, lines 78-80.

282 Talking Right and Walking Wrong

"Bad, bad," says the buyer; but when he goes his way, then he boasts. / Better is the poor who walks in his integrity, than he who is crooked though he be rich (20:14; 28:6 NASB).   Also 28:18.

Chaucer wrote: "The word must needs accord well with the deed."[1] Two hundred years later Shakespeare said, "Suit the action to the word, the word to the action."[2]

The term here translated "crooked" means "in two ways"—talking in the right way and walking in the wrong way. The other proverb applies it to commerce, disparaging a commodity to get a lower purchase price or unduly extolling its value for a higher sale price. Covering deceit with the notion of "a business deal" is morally reprehensible. And the consequences can be perilous. Turning and shifting on a crooked walk, with double-dealing and duplicitous talk, the faker trips and falls. James spoke of the instability of "a double-minded man" (Ja. 1:8).

Professing one thing and practicing another is hypocrisy! Augustine St. Clare admitted, "It's up and down with me—up to heaven's gate in theory, down in earth's dust in practice."[3]

Granted, it is harder to walk it than to talk it. Shakespeare's character said, "I can easier teach twenty what [is] good to be done, than to be one of the twenty to follow mine own teaching."[4] S. E. Kiser wrote: "To keep my standards always high, / To find my task and always do it; / This is my creed—I wish that I / Could learn to shape my action to it."[5]

Solomon did not allow the difficulty as an excuse. But Jesus does what Solomon could not do. He provides the resources to walk the talk and live the life. Paul declared, "His power . . . is at work within us" (Eph. 3:20 NIV).

---

[1] Chaucer, "The Manciple's Tale," *Canterbury Tales* (Garden City, NY: Garden City Pub. Co., 1934), p. 535.

[2] Shakespeare, *Hamlet*, Act III, Scene 2, lines 18-19.

[3] Harriet Beecher Stowe, *Uncle Tom's Cabin* (New York: Everyman's Library, A. Knoph, Inc., 1994) p. 261.

[4] Shakespeare, *The Merchant of Venice*, Act I, Scene 2, lines 17-19.

[5] S. E. Kiser, "My Creed," Alexander, *Poems That Touch the Heart* (Garden City, NY: Hanover House, 1958) p. 88.

Take the garment of one who puts up security for a stranger; hold it in pledge if he does it for a wayward woman (20:16 NIV). Also 27:13.

Much of western economy is built on advance financing for future payment. Lending to poor risks caused the 2008-2010 collapse of big loan companies and the government bailouts.

In the day of this proverb, garments were cherished property that people could not live without. Those who loaned money often required clothing for collateral security.

The lesson is addressed to creditors. Greater caution should be used for loaning to people of high risk, which include unknown persons who have not established credit and also those who are unethical in other areas. Sexual ethics often parallel financial ethics. Lending is precarious enough for those with good credit ratings and character credentials.

To many borrowers, paying a debt is a legal burden but not a moral responsibility. They can always bankrupt and be cleared. Chapter Eleven is an easy way out. Most of the few to whom I have loaned small sums of money have defaulted and subsequently avoided me.

When you advance cash, you are not only hazarding your assets; you are bartering your friendship for nothing in return. Losing a friend is a bigger thing than losing the cash. Now I prize my friendships too much to sign for many of them. The risk is too great. Antonio advised Shylock, "If thou wilt lend this money, lend it not as to thy friends. . . . But lend it rather to thine enemy, who, if he break, thou mayest with better face exact the penalty."[1]

Addendum: When Benjamin Franklin lent a man ten dollars, he said, "When you meet another man in distress, you must pay me by lending this sum to him, requiring him to discharge the debt in like action. . . . I hope it may go through many hands before it meets with a knave who will stop its progress. This is a trick of mine for doing a deal of good with a little money."[2]

---

[1] Shakespeare, *The Mechant of Venice*, Act I, Scene 3, line 133-138.
[2] William Elson, *Elson Readers* (New York: Scott, Foresman and Co., 1912) Book Four, p. 278.

284 Verbal Venom

A gossip betrays a confidence, so avoid a man who talks too much.
/ Without wood a fire goes out; without gossip a fire dies down
(20:19; 26:20 NIV).

Idle talkers who specialize in the affairs of others easily become malicious. At best, frivolous, futile talk is useless. At worst, it betrays confidences, creates dissension, puts the honor of others in disrepair, and irreparably damages future lives.

Once spoken, a word is not over with. It will forever have been spoken. A word is active. It lives on. The idea may lie latent in some mind for years before it is reactivated. Then it darts about from person to person, pillaging the reputation of someone who has long since risen above a checkered past. Ordinarily the story snowballs, accumulating negative nuances every time it is repeated. Gibran said, "Words are timeless. You should utter them . . . with a knowledge of their timelessness."[1]   Emily Dickinson wrote: "A word is dead / When it is said, / Some say. / I say it just / Begins to live / That day."[2]

Words are packed with dynamite! They detonate with explosives! They splatter ideas across a large terrain. They can soothe like balm, and help and heal. They can also stab like swords and shred like shrapnel! Horace, a prominent ancient Italian author, said, "Both my dagger and my pen shall never of my free will assail any man."[3]

Too many who would never stab with a sword or pull the trigger of a handgun are quick to sting with the tongue and wound with the lips. Multitudes are poisoned with verbal venom. We humans are all on this little planet together, and we need to protect each other. While the children of Israel were still in the wilderness, God gave them explicit social laws, one of which was, "Thou shalt not go up and down as a talebearer among thy people" (Lev. 19:16 KJV).

---

[1] Kahlil Gibran, *Sand and Foam* (New York: Alfred A. Kropf, Inc., 1926) p. 21.
[2] Dickinson, "A Word," Fuller, ed., *Adventures in American Literatue* (New York: Harcourt, Brace, 1963) p. 753.
[3] Horace, *Satires, Epistles, Ars Poetica* (Cambridge, MA: Harvard U. Press, 1991) Satire I, Book II, pp. 129-131.

An inheritance gained hastily at the beginning will not be blessed at the end. / A man with an evil eye hastens after riches . . . (20:21; 28:22 NKJV). Also 21:5; 28:20.

An inordinate desire for wealth—either for its own sake, or for an indulgent lifestyle in the fast lane, is different from hoping for adequate reserves for a comfortable retirement.

Our human problem is that we are not emotionally or morally equipped for sudden surplus assets. Pride kicks in, then indolence, then idleness. "Hastily" implies not diligent. Get-rich-quick schemes lead to haphazard planning and slipshod work. Then greed gets a foothold, causing us to desire even more. What is hurriedly gained is often greedily gained. "An evil eye hastens after wealth," leading to covetousness, unjust gains, and fraud. Paul said, "Those who want to get rich fall into . . . many foolish and harmful desires which plunge men into ruin" (1 Tim. 6:9 NASB). Chaucer said, "It is better to lose goods with honor than to win them by shame."[1]

Dante lost his way in dark woods where he confronted the bestial she-wolf of avarice, the greedy desire for gain. Then the ghost of Virgil warned him, "[Avarice] has a nature so perverse and vicious, that she never satiates her craving appetite; and after feeding, she is hungrier than before." This beast "lets not men pass by, but entangles them [and] slays them."[2]

Then comes the letdown. What comes quickly usually goes quickly. Assets become liabilities. A bullish market turns bear, and gains become losses. Chaucer's Prudence advised, "You should get [wealth] . . . gradually, and not over eagerly."[3] God's general plan is for gradual gain, a process of diligent calculations, and hard work. That is a program that accommodates our emotional needs and supports our moral values. It is a plan God chooses to bless. And He is the one who audits the books.

---

[1] Chaucer, "The Tale of Melibeus," *Canterbury Tales* (Garden City, NY: Garden City Pub. Co., 1934) p. 234.

[2] Dante, *The Divine Comedy* (New York: Random House, 1932) "The Inferno," Canto I, p. 13.

[3] Chaucer, *op. cit.*, p. 223.

286 Burning or Warming

Do not say, "I will repay evil" . . . / If your enemy is hungry, give him food to eat; and if he is thirsty, give him water to drink; / For you will heap burning coals on his head, and the Lord will reward you (20:22; 25:21-22 NASB).

Virgil spoke of "the dark instincts of revenge."[1] When Beowulf's hideous monster caused havoc among the Danes, he "made riot in their brains."[2] Coleridge wrote, "Giddiness of heart and brain / Come seldom save from rage and pain."[3] We are so vulnerable to the hurt that others bring on us. A surge of bile rises in our throat. We develop an acidic esophagus. Our skull seethes with rioting brains. Our tongue becomes a flame-thrower!

The proverbs say we can keep our equilibrium in spite of relational conflicts. Aurelius said, "Let the wrong which a man has done stay where the wrong was done."[4] Turn loose the person's throat! It takes two people to be enemies. One person cannot achieve it alone. I may have enmity toward you, but in order to be a *successful* enemy, I must engage your enmity. If you refuse to reciprocate, my enmity fails.

If you have been wronged, you have the offender precisely where you want her. She is in your hands. You have opportunity to demonstrate the love of Christ. "Heaping burning coals" is not to hurt the person with spite. The burning coals warm her and melt her into kindness. Paul repeats this proverb and adds, "Do not be overcome with evil, but overcome evil with good" (Rom. 12:20-21).

"Repaying evil" is God's department, not ours. He reads all the evidence that we overlook. If you want to even the score, a good way to begin is by getting even with all those who have *helped* you. That way, you will never get around to those who have *hurt* you.

---

[1] Virgil, *The Aeneid* (London: Penguin Books, 1958) Book Two, p. 61.
[2] *Beowulf the Warrior*, Ian Serraillier, tr. (New York: Henry Z. Walck, Inc., 1961) p. 12.
[3] Samuel Coleridge, "Christabel," Abrams, ed., *Norton Anthology* . . . (New York: Norton, 1962) V. 2, p. 215.
[4] Marcus Aurelius, *The Thoughts of the Emperor* (New York: John B. Alden, publisher, 1887) p. 113.

A man's steps are directed by the Lord. How then can anyone understand his own way? / The king's heart is in the hand of the Lord; He directs it . . . wherever He pleases (20:24; 21:1 NIV).

Moral direction is given through scripture and the moral code that God has put in place. Guidance in practical areas comes through scripture (like Solomon's proverbs), through rational wisdom, and through providentially arranged circumstances. Those who have close fellowship with Christ may receive promptings and impressions in their inner spirits. Jesus said, "The Spirit of truth . . . will guide you" (Jno. 16:13). No one can read the future well enough to "understand his own way." God has a plan and procedure for each life. A blueprint for each person is drawn up in heaven, no two of them precisely alike. Instead of rejoicing over the blueprint, we are tempted to change it. But direction is available for those who sincerely wish to safeguard their future.

On occasion God moves the hearts of pagan potentates for His purposes. Unknown to them, they are pieces of God's puzzle, working His will when they are least aware of it. It seems that God has used a Marxist regime in the People's Republic of China to break down the ancient clan system that precluded effective Christian evangelism. Today Sino-people are responding daily to the Christian gospel. Dante's guide said to the infernal judge, "It is willed where what is willed can be done. Ask no more."[1] And the judge relented. God can be King over kings!

Why then does God not control all rulers' hearts to prevent genocide? Here are two answers. First, He may have done so more than we know. Directly or indirectly, He has had a strong hand in legislating civil liberties and human rights, negotiating arms control, and freeing Eastern Europe from puppet dictators. Second, human hearts are most difficult to direct in moral areas. Divine influence that is strong enough to effect moral repentance of hardened hearts would effectively neutralize their moral freedom, which God is committed to protect.

---

[1] Dante, *The Divine Comedy* (New York: Random House, 1932) "Inferno," Canto V, p. 31.

288 To Perjure and to Profane

It is a snare for a man to devote rashly something as holy, and afterward to reconsider his vows (20:25 NKJV).

The judiciary considers an oath to be a weighty matter, and is committed to keeping it inviolate. To debase a solemn commitment is to perjure oneself for severest consequences.

It must be puzzling to the outsider that the church requires public marriage vows and church membership vows, and then so easily overlooks their violation as if it is a small matter. Taking the vow becomes a perfunctory ritual. They cannot be expected to realize its dire importance when the church that gave the vows is nonchalant about their fulfillment. Persons take their vows lightly when the church gives them lightly.

To make a casual vow "in the name of the Father, the Son, and the Holy Spirit" is to take God's name in vain (Ex. 20:7). It is to profane oneself in breaking a cardinal commandment of God.

Some scholars interpret this proverb to mean we should not appropriate ("devour," KJV) for ourselves what is dedicated to God. What is sacred should not be used for personal benefit or self-glory. More scholars think the proverb means we should not default on a sacred promise, and therefore we should be totally committed before we take the vow. Both interpretations condemn disrespect toward God. Speaking of righteous Repheus, Aeneas said, "The gods regarded not his righteousness."[1] What is true of pagan gods is not the case with Jehovah God. He regards righteousness and disdains unrighteousness. Writing of Christ, Milton said, "His countenance [was] too severe to behold."[2] Milton's angelic choir sang of "the terror of His voice."[3]

Profaning oneself before the Supreme Court Judge of all the world is more serious than perjuring oneself before a judicial magistrate. All second thoughts should be taken in advance

---

[1] Virgil, *The Aeneid* (London: Penguin Books, 1958) Book Two, p. 64.
[2] John Milton, *Paradise Lost* (Indianapolis: ITT Bobbs-Merrill Educational Pub. Co., 1962) Book VI, p. 160.
[3] Milton, *Paradise Regained,* Bush, ed., *The Portable Milton* (New York: Penguin Books, 1949) Book IV, p. 609.

The Lamp of the Lord 289

The spirit of man is the lamp of the Lord, searching all his innermost parts (20:27 RSV).

C. S. Lewis' queen of Glome said, "There must, whether the gods see it or not, be something great in the mortal soul. . . . Our capacity [is] without limit"[1]

Some have surmised that a major difference between humankind and lower animals is the difference between self-consciousness and sense-consciousness. The latter includes pain, tastes, sounds, awareness of sense experience. Consciousness of oneself includes intelligence and conscience—knowing one's thoughts and knowing the moral quality of one's thoughts.[2] Some understand this as a part of the *imago Dei*, the image of God in us. Woodrum's protagonist says, "We never . . . become so vile but what we somehow remember the shape of good, the vague outline of God . . . perhaps hand-written on the filing cards of our being."[3]

This intelligent-moral-spiritual personality center is "the lamp of the Lord" through which He shines His light into our lives. But the lamp has to be lit with God's presence, His truth, and His Spirit. Left alone, our spirits are dark. Without His moral guidelines, our consciences ring a false signal. Without His Spirit, our spirits are empty. What was intended as His residence can become the abode of selfishness, harshness, and hostility.

Milton caricatured Satan as saying to an assemblage of his comrades, "[You have] a mind not to be changed by place or time. The mind is its own place, and in itself can make a heaven of hell, a hell of heaven."[4] Milton was both wrong and right. The mind cannot turn real hell into real heaven. But it can turn good into bad bad into good. With God's light, our souls can search our souls.

---

[1] C. S. Lewis, *Till We Have Faces* (Grand Rapids: William B. Eerdmans Pub. Co., 1966) p. 277.
[2] Descartes' c*ogito*, "I think," and Kant's sense of duty, "The Categorical Imperative."
[3] Lon Woodrum, *Stumble Upon the Dark Mountains* (Waco, TX: Word Books, 1980) p. 86.
[4] John Milton, *Paradise Lost* (Indianapolis: ITT Bobbs-Merrill Educational Pub. Co., 1962) Book I, p. 13.

290 Principle without Partiality

Loyalty and truth preserve the king, and he upholds his throne by righteousness. / When the righteous are in authority, the people rejoice; but when a wicked man rules, the people groan (20:28 NASB; 29:2 NKJV). Also 28:28; 29:12.

Regardless of how evil they themselves may be, people want to see virtue in government and public life. Except for those special-interest groups that expect illicit favors, they expect to get a better break from fair leadership than from corrupted government. Successful leaders consolidate their powers by the consent of the people to be led. If the leaders are qualified for leadership, they gain public consent by their commitment to righteous government.

A sympathetic disposition toward all the people is an admirable attitude, but the sympathy must function inside the context of constitutional law, ethical principles, and moral standards. Outside those objective principles, subjective sentiment is dangerous. By operating from principles without partiality, government secures public respect.

Criminals should fear good government more than bad. Good judges cannot be bought off. Felons can placate a leader's anger more easily than they can appease a principle. A just law can be harsher than wrath. Good leaders are committed to what is right. The good Roman emperor Marcus Aurelius said, "Whatever anyone does or says, I must be good, just as if the . . . emerald were always saying, I must be emerald and keep my color."[1]

Good leaders are responsible for what is best for *all* the people. Speaking of leadership, Aurelius also said, "That which is not good for the swarm, neither is it good for the bee."[2] Each person must find her own place as a part of the populace and "rejoice" that "the righteous are in authority." God declared, "You have gone far enough, O princes of Israel! Give up your violence and oppression, and do what is just and right" (Ez. 45:9 NIV).

---

[1] Marcus Aurelius, *The Thoughts of the Emperor* (New York: John B. Alden, publisher, 1887) p. 110.

[2] *op. cit.*, p. 106.

Glory and Gray Hair 291

The glory of young men is their strength, gray hair the splendor of the old (20:29 NIV).

England's 17th century poet laureate John Dryden wrote, "Youth, beauty, graceful action, seldom fail."[1] Shakespeare wrote of "the morn and liquid dew of youth."[2] Goethe spoke of ". . . the old emotion, / The bliss that touched the verge of pain, / . . . love's deep devotion, / O, give me back my youth again!"[3] Remembering his youth, Faust sang, "Sound on, ye hymns of heaven, so sweet and mild! / My tears gush forth. The earth takes back her child!"[4]

The best and the worst of one's youth projects itself into the adult. Horace said, "The jar will long keep the fragrance of what it was once steeped in when new."[5] While in prison, Woodrum's character Chris Jaggard returned to his earlier faith in Christ, and "the youthful dreams he had caught at had not vanished; they returned to him, cleansed, meaningful."[6]

Though many young men are motivated for academic success, perhaps more focus on physical strength and dexterity. And older men take pride in their experience and wisdom. Lack of appreciation in each for the other becomes a wedge that drives open the generation gap. The excellence of each should be accepted without envying the other's specialty. The proverb bridges the two, giving glory to one and splendor to the other. The aged should "glory" in the abilities of the young, and the young should honor the "splendid" wisdom of age. For progress with continuity, the church and the world need the strength, vision and zeal of youth and young adults and the sobering, steadying wisdom of the aged. With mutual respect, both are enriched!

---

[1] John Dryden, "Absalom and Achitophel," *John Dryden: Selected Poems* (London: J. M. Dent Ltd., 1993) p. 115.
[2] Shakespeare, *Hamlet*, Act I, Scene 3, line 41.
[3] Goethe, *Faust*, Prelude, pp. 7-8.
[4] Goethe, *op. cit.*, First Part, Scene 1, p. 33.
[5] Horace, *Satires, Epistles, Ars Poetica* (Cambridge, MA: Harvard U. Press, 1991) Epistle II, Book I, p. 267.
[6] Lon Woodrum, *Eternity in Their Hearts* (Grand Rapids: Zondervan Pub. House, 1955) p. 209.

292 Strikes and Stripes

Blows that hurt cleanse away evil, as do stripes the inner depths of the heart (20:30 NKJV).

Note a distinction between two kinds of evil. Utilitarian evil is pain, discomfort, or sorrow. Moral evil is vice, wickedness, sin. Both are bad, but only the second is morally bad.[1]

To cause pain maliciously for spite is an act of wickedness. But under certain conditions, producing utilitarian evil to correct moral evil is justified. That is one purpose of penalties, traffic tickets, and correctional institutions.

God said to Jeremiah, "It may be they will listen, and . . . turn from [their] *evil* way, that I may repent of the *evil* which I intend to do to them because of their *evil* doings" (Jer. 26:3 RSV, italics added). Here God threatens utilitarian evil (calamity, disaster) hoping to prevent moral evil. A sluggish conscience can often use such a stimulus.

In the proverb, "blows that hurt" and "stripes" may include inner strikes—heart wounds, disappointments, and conscience smites. Whether outward or inward, utilitarian evil can have a cleansing, purging effect on moral evil. Though God *can* bring about corrective discipline, the proverb does not say that God *initiates* our problems. Rather He *uses* many bad situations to purify our motives and make us better persons.

If we fail to allow our pains and problems to work for our moral good, our moral evil will eventually bring its own utilitarian evil. Sin has detrimental effects. Hell itself is primarily characterized by wickedness and secondarily by its effect, which is pain. In this life, God attempts to use pain to prevent a more fatal pain—by cleansing the inner depths of our hearts.

He also uses the pain of another Person to heal our souls in a way the proverb does not mention. Predicting a Suffering Savior, Isaiah said, "He was wounded for our transgressions, He was bruised for our iniquities . . . By His stripes we are healed" (Is. 53:5).

---

[1] Counterpart terms are utilitarian and moral goodness. The first is pleasure or happiness; the second is virtue, innocence, or righteousness.

Symbol and Substance 293

*To do righteousness and justice is more acceptable to the Lord
than sacrifice* (21:3 NKJV).

The Old Testament sacrificial system was set up as a tangible way for the people to express (1) their faith in God's redemptive system, though not knowing it would involve the Redeemer's sacrifice, and (2) their commitment to obey God's precepts in living righteous lives. Those ceremonial regulations were only vaguely symbolic of God's moral precepts on which He placed greater import. Samuel said to Saul, "To obey is better than sacrifice" (1 Sam. 15:22). God said, "I desire steadfast love and not sacrifice" (Hos. 6:6 RSV). Jesus said, "I desire compassion and not sacrifice" (Matt. 9:13 NASB). The difference is between the symbol and the substance.

Playing obedience with a scripted form is less troublesome than moral obedience from the heart. When the symbol becomes perfunctory, the sacrifice becomes a useless surrogate for the substance. Preferably, submission to God comes from a relationship of love and respect, rather than from a chain of command. But if the love breaks down, the moral imperative is still in place. God is authority, and you and I are His servants in righteousness. If we fail, our sins may be forgiven, but they are never excused. Righteousness is basic.

Complying with religious forms can even be detrimental when it is used as a substitute for the substance. Props are intended to accent the real, not replace it. What should be a help can become a hindrance. God exclaimed, "I have had enough of burnt offerings" (Is. 1:11)!

Genuine Christian faith and commitment go into action in the nitty-gritty grind of daily life. Until the symbols are activated in righteousness, they have no substance. Jane Merchant wrote: ". . . Until we put our faith into our actions / We cannot know how much our faith is worth, / As mustard seed can never grow and flourish / Until it is committed to the earth."[1]

---

[1] Jane Merchant, "Though It Be Little," *Because It's Here* (Nashville, Abingdon Press, 1970) p. 113.

294 Elated Mind and Dilated Eyes

Haughty eyes and a proud heart, the lamp of the wicked, are sin
(21:4 NIV).

Today we think of the wicked as those who are vilest and most corrupt. But the scripture includes pride as a state of wickedness. C. S. Lewis said, "Pride leads to every other vice: it is the complete anti-God state of mind."[1] Some theologians think evil first originated when the "son of the dawn" said in his heart, "I will ascend to heaven, I will raise my throne above the stars of God. I will sit enthroned . . . on the utmost heights of the sacred mountain. I will ascend above the tops of the clouds. I will make myself like the Most High" (Is. 14:13-14).

To condemn carnal pride, of course, is not to condemn a healthy self-esteem. Humble people can honestly recognize their own merits and feel good about themselves. Aristotle spoke of a proper pride when he said the "proud man" is the ideal. "The man who falls short of him is unduly humble, and the man who goes beyond him is vain."[2] The "unduly humble" are the spineless weaklings who have an apologetic attitude about their own existence.

A "lamp" is what motivates a person, what one glories in, what keeps the spring in his step and the brightness in her eyes. A "proud heart" is a lamp that fires one's motives, bathes the face in stage light, and shoots strobe lights through the eyes. It expresses itself in "haughty eyes" or "showy splendor" (Mof). Pride elates the mind and dilates the eyes. The lamp sparkles a splatter of temporary joy and twinkles the eye. And it rankles others who see!

When you are your own biggest fan, you cannot live up to your expectations, and you disappoint yourself. No one has adequate resources to sustain the glow. The human lamp that was made to blaze with God's Spirit cannot continue to burn synthetic fuel. Sooner or later, the flame flickers out, and the lamp goes dark. Focused on oneself, midday can become midnight!

---

[1] C. S. Lewis, *Mere Christianity* (New York: The Macmillan Co., 1960) p. 94.
[2] Aristotle, *Nichomachean Ethics*, Book IV, Chapter 3, p. 387 in McKeon.

Fabricating and Prevaricating 295

The getting of treasures by a lying tongue is a fleeting vapor and a snare of death. / Bread gained by deceit is sweet to man, but afterward his mouth will be full of gravel. / . . . a poor man is better than a liar (21:6; 20:17; 19:22 RSV).

Malcolm declared that he as a king would be even more murderous than Macbeth, and would destroy the good and loyal people to loot their wealth. Within minutes he flip-flopped and said, "I . . . scarcely have coveted what was mine own, at no time broke my faith, would not betray the devil to his fellow, and delight no less in truth than life."[1] Somewhere in these contradictory claims is a prevaricating tongue. Both caricatures were false characterizations in order to achieve his wishes. The first was a threat and the second more like a bribe.

Daniel Webster is quoted as saying, "Falsehoods not only disagree with truths, but usually quarrel among themselves."[2] Truths are never at odds, because they are determined by objective reality. Falsehoods center in people's wishes, and are rarely the same. The proverb warns that the person who attempts to snare an advantage by deceit will be ensnared by death.

The other proverb concedes that bread of deceit is more attractive to some people than delectable dishes that are honestly earned. But stolen apples become like the grit of gravel in the mouth, with a nauseating aftertaste. Illicit sex appeals to one's lowest nature, but the hangover is rotten to the conscience and self-esteem. The fantasyland appeal is only phantom pleasure, and it turns into an illusory shadow with no substance.

The third proverb makes a sobering announcement. Economic poverty, with its appalling privation, is not as bad as moral poverty. Fabricating lies and equivocating truth are obscenely evil. Prevaricators become morally bankrupt! But honest people who labor long and hard to sustain a meager living can be healthy in mind, strong in character, and rich in spirit!

---

[1] Shakespeare, *Macbeth*, Act IV, Scene 3, lines 78-84, 122-130.

[2] Paul Lee Tan, ed., *Encyclopedia of 7,700 Illustrations* (Rockville, MD: Assurance Publishers, 1979) p. 563.

296 Saddled with Sin

The conduct of a guilty man is full of turnings; but the pure is straightforward . . . / A man who is laden with the guilt of human blood will be a fugitive . . . (21:8 Sprl; 28:17 NASB).

Guilty persons often develop a pattern of evasion, imperceptibly turning and twisting, darting and deviating, subconsciously attempting to avoid confronting the consequences of their actions. Those who are guilty "of human blood" are even more fearful of facing revenge. Any wrong move could be disastrous. Now they are fugitives to themselves because no place allows them the comfort of being who they are. After he murdered King Duncan, Macbeth said, "I am afraid to think what I have done . . . To know my deed, 'twere best not know myself."[1]

Apart from objective guilt, subjective feelings of guilt weigh heavily on the conscience. Temporary relief is short-lived. The burden keeps returning. Laden with the load of guilt, a person teeters and totters, wavers and wobbles, staggering with unsteady steps. The load is too heavy. Attempting to walk straight, he stumbles. When Lady Macbeth came on stage sleepwalking, wringing her hands, attempting to wipe away her bloodstain of guilt, the gentleman said, "I would not have such a heart in my bosom for the dignity of the whole body."[2]

Psychological guilt is devastating, but it can be beneficial in driving one to rectify her deeds and leading her to God's forgiveness. False guilt needs to be dealt with appropriately, but genuine guilt should be allowed to do its work. Hawthorne said, "There can be no outrage . . . more flagrant than to forbid the culprit to hide his face in shame."[3]

To the person who is saddled with sin and bowed under its load, the appeal of divine forgiveness has great incentive. The sinner needs to follow the guilt trail to repentance and forgiveness. At the cross of Christ, where we see ourselves at our worst, we see God in His loving and forgiving best!

---

[1] Shakespeare, *Macbeth*, Act II, Scene 2, lines 51, 73.
[2] *op. cit.*, Act V, Scene 1, lines 61-62.
[3] Nathaniel Hawthorne, *The Scarlet Letter* (New York: Books, Inc., n.d.) p. 44.

It is better to live in a corner of the housetop than in a home shared with a contentious woman. / . . . A prudent wife is from the Lord (21:9; 19:14 RSV). Also 21:19; 25:24; 27:15-16.

"Don Jòse and Donna Inez led / For some time an unhappy sort of life, / Wishing each other, not divorced, but dead; / They lived respectably as man and wife. / Their conduct was exceedingly well-bred, / And gave no outward signs of inward strife, / Until at length the smothered fire broke out, / And put the business past all kind of doubt."[1]

These lines from *Don Juan* depict the concealed tension in many marriages. The proverbs were born in a paternalistic culture, but even then what was said about a wife could be said for either spouse. Relational harmony is sparse when a wife is contentious or a husband is stubborn, inconsiderate, and implacable. In Shakespeare, Hermia declared, ". . . all the vows that ever men have broke, / In number more than ever women spoke."[2]

In western culture, many marriages ride in on the sensationalism of infatuation, and rapidly disintegrate. The Duke said, "Lovers and madmen have . . . seething brains."[3] Instead of choosing to love, they become willing slaves to a feeling. In Chaucer, when the lord put his wife away for another, she said, "But truth be said—at least I find it true / . . . Old love is not the same as when it's new."[4] We all know that "the course of true love never did run smooth."[5] But in the gritty grind of committed love, irritations are minimized and quickly absorbed.

Prudent spouses are big enough and humble enough to take little hurts and humiliations, and let them dissolve. When affection and commitment are reciprocal, moving both ways, living together is a delight worth every sacrifice many times over!

---

[1] Lord Byron, *Don Juan*, Canto I, Stanza 26, *The Norton Anthology . . .* , V. 2 (New York: Norton, 1962) p. 288.

[2] Shakespeare, *A Midsummer Night's Dream*, Act I, Scene 1, lines 175-176.

[3] Shakespeare, *op. cit.*, Act V, Scene 1, line 4.

[4] Chaucer, "The Clerk's Tale," *Canterbury Tales* (Garden City, NY: Garden City Pub. Co., 1934) p. 398.

[5] Shakespeare, *op. cit.*, Act I, Scene 1, line 134.

298 Righteousness or Ruin

The Righteous One takes note of the house of the wicked and brings the wicked to ruin. / He who pursues righteousness and loyalty finds life, righteousness and honor. / Like a sparrow in its flitting, like a swallow in its flying, so a curse without cause does not alight. / He who leads the upright astray in an evil way will himself fall into his own pit, but the blameless will inherit good (21:12 NIV; 21:21 NASB; 26:2 NASB; 28:10 NASB).

These proverbs juxtapose evil people and good, to contrast their outcomes. Sinners will come to ruin (21:12), but the righteous will find the fruits of righteousness (21:21). If innocent people are imprecated, the curse may flit around like a sparrow, but soon it will migrate away like a swallow (26:2). Guilty people will meet mishap, but the blameless will find good (28:10).

The law of just retribution functions. Dante heard a messenger of heaven asking, "What profits it to butt against the Fates?"[1] In classical mythology, Jupiter convened an assembly of gods in Olympus and declared: "To each man shall his own free actions bring both his suffering and his good fortune."[2] The principle works both ways. Those who align with badness will be losers, and those who identify with goodness will be winners.

Evil cannot compete with eternal goodness. It cannot even handle itself; it has to defer to itself. Buddha is quoted as saying, "Hatred does not cease by hatred . . . ; hatred ceases by love—this is an eternal law."[3] C. S. Lewis said, "Bad cannot succeed even in being bad as truly as good is good."[4] In principle, it is true in the little subplots of life, but it will be absolute in the end. When the war of the ages is over, goodness will emerge triumphantly over badness! On that day, all persons will have either eternal loss or eternal gain, determined by the side they have embraced.

---

[1] Dante, *The Divine Comedy* (New York: Random House, 1932) "The Inferno," Canto IX, p. 51.

[2] Virgil, *The Aeneid* (London: Penguin Books, 1958) Book Ten, p. 254.

[3] Douglas J. Soccio, *Archetypes of Wisdom* (Belmont, CA: Wadsworth/Thomson Learning, 2001) p. 46.

[4] C. S. Lewis, *The Great Divorce* (New York: Macmillan Pub. Co., 1946) p. 123.

When justice is done, it brings joy to the righteous but terror to evildoers (21:15 NIV).

A corrupt city government takes payoffs to protect executives in hiring discrimination, looks the other way while the police chief gets kickbacks from commercialized vice, winks at racial injustice, and promotes cronyism for political support.

When the profligates are swept out of office, righteous people rejoice, but those who have profited from the corruption are terrorized. Not only do they face reprisal but they also lose the benefits of injustice. In the Bible, justice often means strict retribution, but sometimes it is used for impact as a heavyweight word that is broadly synonymous with righteousness. The threat of justice strikes terror to the unrighteous on both counts. While the righteous rejoice, evildoers lose their advantages from unrighteousness, and they face prosecution from justice.

God's justice assures a future that is free from corruption, and that is cause for joy. But it means retribution proportionate to the gravity of sin, and that is frightening to those who are profanely foul. It may be a long time coming, but Kierkegaard argues that justice itself requires God to postpone punishment. "If capital crime needs a whole lifetime to come into existence, it cannot be punished in this life. [That] would not be to punish it, but to prevent it." And that would not be justice.[1] The sinful may be surprised to learn that they were never flying under the radar. While they think they are outwitting justice, they are steadily marching into it. If they realize the future justice they face, they should have an advance taste of the terror . . .

. . . just as the righteous today taste the joy of an anticipated kingdom of justice. The appetizer presages the eternal banquet. We do not have to wait for the dinner bell. Emily Dickinson wrote: "Instead of getting to heaven at last, I'm going all along!"[2]

---

[1] Soren Kierkegaard, *Attack Upon Christendom* (Boston: The Beacon Press, 1956) p. 252.
[2] E. Dickinson, "Some Keep the Sabbath ," *Modern American Poetry* (New York: Harcourt, Brace, 1950) p. 104.

300 Pleasure and Poverty

He who loves pleasure will be a poor man; he who loves wine and oil will not be rich (21:17 NKJV).

Plato is known for insisting that one's "appetitive" nature be controlled by the "spirited" nature—the physical appetites by the rational spirit. He disdained "a life taken up with . . . banquets, . . . filling oneself twice a day, never sleeping alone at night. . . . No man on earth . . . in self-indulgence could ever grow to be wise." He extolled "holding virtue dearer than pleasure."[1] Horace advised, "Scorn pleasures; pleasure bought without pain is harmful. The covetous is ever in want. Aim at a fixed limit to your desires. The envious man grows lean."[2]

The Christian faith does not condemn pleasure to be enjoyed, but it denounces the wrong kind of pleasure and warns against prioritizing pleasure. The most satisfying pleasures are by-products of other worthy ends rather than ends in themselves. Jesus said those who sacrifice to follow Him will "receive a hundred-fold now in this time . . . and in the world to come eternal life" (Mk. 10:30 KJV). They become rich with eternal life. Marcus Aurelius said, "Work . . . at keeping the divine part [in you] pure. . . . expecting nothing, . . . [and] thou wilt be happy."[3]

"Loving pleasure" goes much further than enjoying pleasure. It allows pleasure to become a passion that controls one's life. When you live for boating, or golfing, or attending the ladies' bridge club, not to mention casino gambling, carousing, and call girls, you are wasting your money, your time, your potential, your character, and your soul. You become an impoverished person. You "will not be rich." The apostle John wrote: "Do not love the world or the things in the world. . . . the lust of the flesh, the lust of the eyes, . . . The world is passing away, and the lust of it; but he who does the will of God abides forever" (1 Jno. 2:15-17).

---

[1] Plato, *Epistle VII*, Albert B. Hakim, ed., *Historical Introduction to Philosophy* (Upper Saddle River, NJ: Prentice Hall, 2001) pp. 83-84.

[2] Horace, *Satires, Epistles, Ars Poetica* (Cambridge, MA: Harvard U. Press, 1991) Epistle II, Book I, p. 267.

[3] Marcus Aurelius, *The Thoughts of the Emperor* (New York: John B. Alden, publisher, 1887) p. 64.

Devouring or Sharing 301

Precious treasure remains in a wise man's dwelling, but a foolish man devours it (21:20 RSV).

Thinking that all poor people are helpless victims of exploitation is just as fallacious as thinking they are all indolent sloths. From irresponsible behavior or simple laziness, some have wasted their opportunities and squandered their supplies. Frittering their time away in idleness, chattering in chitchat rooms, or surfing the web for fun, they are barren of basic human needs.

We are accountable for what we do with what we have, little as it may be. God can never trust us with something big until He can trust us with something small. The renowned inner-city mission worker, "Brother Bryan" of Birmingham, gave a barefoot man a pair of shoes and said, "God gave you these shoes . . . and He is taking notes on the places your feet take these shoes."[1]

Sometimes we have overreacted against spiritualizing a text like this, until we miss a principle that runs through all possessions, spiritual as well as material. Treasures can be lost or never gained because of neglect, indulgence, or indolence.

Mr. Wickfield continued to grieve for his deceased wife, lavishing all his love on his daughter. Then when she married an unworthy young man, he was devastated. He said to David Copperfield, "Indulgence has ruined me. . . . My grief . . . and love . . . turned to disease. I thought . . . I could love one creature . . . and mourn one creature, and not love the rest [or] have some part in the grief of all who mourned. Thus the lessons of my life have been perverted!"[2] We can withdraw and get turned in on ourselves, and the treasure of our hearts will dwindle. Or we can open up to others, and our hearts will enlarge with love and sympathy to embrace a world of happy and hurting people. And we will be wealthy with the treasures of love! Devouring what we have leaves us empty. Sharing with others fills us full!

---

[1] Hunter B. Blakely, *Religion in Shoes* (Richmond, VA: John Knox Press, revised 1953) p. 50.
[2] Charles Dickens, *David Copperfield* in *Best Loved Books* (Pleasantville, NY: Reader's Digest Ass'n., 1966) p. 360.

302 Parading Pride

A proud and haughty man—"Scoffer" is his name; he acts with arrogant pride (21:24 NKJV).

The original wording suggests a combination of anger and pride—"proud wrath" (KJV), "insolent pride" (NASB), "mocker . . . overweening pride" (NIV). Derek Kidner uses the terms "aggressive insolence," "pride boiling up," "an insubordinate spirit."[1] When pride and passion conjoin, you have a stubborn scoffer. "When Haman saw that Mordecai did not bow down or do obeisance to him, Haman was filled with fury" (Esth. 3:5 RSV).

Pride is competitive. It drives wedges into human relationships and separates friends. C. S. Lewis said: "It is because I wanted to be the big noise at the party that I am so annoyed at someone else being the big noise . . . We say that people are proud of being rich, or clever, or good-looking, but they are not. They are proud of being richer, or cleverer, or better-looking than others. . . . Pride . . . is enmity. . . . It eats up the very possibility of love."[2]

When name-calling begins, the relationship has already crumbled. When the label of scoffer is earned, the friendship has been forfeited. Labels are shorthand for prominent ignominy; they encapsulate contempt. They are symbols of a person's obnoxious predicates. Calling a person a name is like cracking his reputation with a sledgehammer.

The more arrogance we have, the more detestable we become. Most of us withdraw in disgust from conceited persons, and most likewise recoil from those of us who are conceited. Condemnation comes in proportion to the commendation we seek. Reaching for praise, we get disdain. Self-deprecation keeps the friends that self-aggrandizement loses. To parade our pride for praise comes at the cost of a warm relationship. It is an ill-conceived reach for respect at the sacrifice of friendship. The effort is lost. We end up losing both.

---

[1] Derek Kidner, *Proverbs*, Wiseman, ed., *Tyndale O.T. Commentaries* (Downers Grove, IL: IVP, 1964) pp. 145, 90.
[2] C. S. Lewis, *Mere Christianity* (New York: The Macmillan Co., 1960) pp. 95, 96, 97.

The desire of the slothful kills him, for his hands refuse to labor.
He covets greedily all day long, but the righteous gives and does
not spare (21:25-26 NKJV).

In Solomon's day, most work was done by hand in either farming or crafting, or both. The proverb pictures the sluggard who substitutes *wishing* for *working* and starves to death desiring ease, attempting to circumvent hard labor. Lazy living negates living.

The phrase "covets greedily," literally translated, is "desires a desire." That was a common Hebrew turn-of-a-phrase to intensify the meaning of the term. Lazy persons *crave and long* for daily sustenance for survival. But they have conflicting desires for effortless comfort, leisure, and ease. When desire confronts desire, they have civil war inside. If the shiftless indolence is stronger, they are filled with greed, covetousness, and envy. Then they resort to shortcuts for survival, like begging, or stealing, or fraud. The last line draws a connection between righteousness and labor, implying a relation between wickedness and laziness

Lack of motivation may be physiologically based, or it may be habitual from past conditioning. Often it is from purposelessness. Some hardworkers also are driven by unworthy self-interests like power, possessions, or glory. When Faust wanted land to work, he exclaimed, "Power and estate to win, inspires my thought! / The deed is everything, the glory naught."[1]

Righteous people have yet a higher motive for work: It is the right thing to do. They are driven with "desiring a desire" to do what is right. They crave it. In stark contrast to the indolent, they keep pouring energy into their work without sparing themselves. Then they have enough to share with others. Not having to wish for themselves, they do not brush off those in need with mere wishes.

Paul said, "He who has been stealing must steal no longer, but must work . . . that he may have something to share with those in need" (Eph. 4:28 NIV).

---

[1] Goethe, *Faust*, Second Part, Act IV, Scene 1, p. 420.

304 Listen to Speak

A false witness will perish, but the man who listens to the truth will speak forever. / The hearing ear and the seeing eye, the Lord has made both of them (21:28; 20:12 NASB).

Postmodernism is not postmodern, because it has been around a long time. A hundred fifty years ago, Robert Browning's character said, "I feel, am what I feel, know what I feel; so much is truth to me."[1] Thus truth and value were predicated on emotional moods, determined by the weather, or bodily biorhythms, or changing circumstances.

But when a court witness "swears to tell the truth," the judge and jury are thinking something different from the way she feels. The witness takes an oath to report *actual, factual reality*, regardless of her feeling. The proverb says a false witness will be banned from court, but the witness who listens (and looks) and reports what she has heard (and seen) is allowed freedom to speak, and her words will be enduring.

The Lord gave us two ears and two eyes, and only one tongue. The ratio of hearing and seeing to talking should be four-to-one. And the appropriate sequence is to see and hear first, and talk last. Speaking before we have listened, studied, and researched our subject, we hardly know whereof we speak. The world will listen to those who first have "listened to the truth." Isaiah declared, "The Sovereign Lord has given me an instructed tongue, to know the word [to speak]. . . . Morning by morning [He] wakens my ear to listen like one being taught" (Is. 50:4 NIV).

The disciples of Jesus sat at His feet, listened to every word and observed all that He did. They did not report human ideas and opinions, or mystical revelation. They claimed empirical evidence for what they said. John declared, "That . . . which we have heard, [and] seen with our eyes . . . declare we unto you" (1 Jn. 1:1-3 KJV). The lesson in the proverb is capsulated in a line from James: "Take note of this: Everyone should be quick to listen, slow to speak" (Ja. 1:19 NIV).

---

[1] Robert Browning, *Sordello*, in *The Complete . . . Works* (Cambridge, MA: Houghton Mifflin, 1895) p. 124.

A wicked man shows a bold face, but as for the upright, he makes his way sure (21:29 NASB). Also 22:5; 25:26; 29:16; 29:27.

It is the case of the two "Arthurs." The young priest Arthur Dimmesdale did not "make his way sure." For years, Hawthorne's character concealed the skeletons in his closet that his congregation did not know, and endured the guilt in private. Years later he said to Hester, who had been his partner in the affair, "I have laughed, in bitterness and agony of heart, at the contrast between what I seem and what I am! And Satan laughs at it!" He spoke of wishing he had "thrown off these garments of mock holiness," and added that his guilt "burns in secret."[1]

Paton's character Arthur Jarvis *did* "make his way sure." After he was an innocent victim of racial murder, his half-finished essay was discovered that said, "I shall not ask . . . if [something] is expedient, but only if it is right, . . . because I cannot do anything else. . . . I am lost when I ask if this is safe, [or] if men will approve. . . . I [cannot] aspire to the highest with one part of myself, and deny it with another. . . . I would rather die than live like that."[2] The difference between the two was integrity, uprightness, and nobility!

Pity those who walk a tenuous way. Under pressure, they are diverted. They forfeit their future. They gamble their honor, their integrity, their character—and lose!

There *are* those, however, who affirm their resolve, and walk with steady footstep. They guard themselves from thorns and snares (22:5), and refuse to compromise (25:26), until the thoughts of evil become distasteful (29:27). They stand taller than those dropouts who collapse under the weight of sin (29:16).

Some may bluff their way with impudence and a bold front, but their way is shaky. Others have "made their way sure," and they journey with confidence into the future.

---

[1] Nathaniel Hawthorne, *The Scarlet Letter* (New York: Books, Inc., n.d.) p. 157.
[2] Alan Paton, *Cry, the Beloved Country* (New York: MacMillan Pub. Co., 1948) p. 175.

306 Lifelong Lobbyists

There is no wisdom, no insight, no plan that can succeed against the Lord. / Humility and the fear of the Lord bring wealth and honor and life (21:30; 22:4 NIV).

When we first heard that God answers prayer, many of us became lifelong lobbyists. We attempted to manipulate God by mastering proper protocol. We programmed our prayers like a word processor for the desired printout. Even Virgil's pagan prophetess was wise enough to proclaim, "Cease to imagine that divine decrees can be changed by prayers."[1]

When we discovered prayer is not a tool for maneuvering fate, we set out to implement our own plans and purposes, bypassing God. But then we crashed against an invincible obstacle and were thrown back on God. Again we started politicking with God, making wild promises for favors on a credit, vowing to pay later. We attempted to plea bargain for a special break, asking Him to look the other way "just this one time." Again we discovered we have no negotiating leverage. God will not lower His standards in response to a curtsy. He holds the cards. We are empty-handed. The eternal, immutable God is not a pushover.

God has His own program that dwarfs our programs in size and importance. If our plans violate His, we are boll weevils in the cotton field, or bean beetles in the garden. We risk extermination! Martin Luther King, Jr., said, "The end of life is not to be happy . . . [but] to do the will of God, come what may."[2] Marcus Aurelius said, "Neither wilt thou do anything well that pertains to man without at the same time having a reference to things divine."[3]

Sneaking our insidious programs in on God's turf is like being illegal aliens. Company employees adhere to company practice, building contractors conform to zoning codes, and wise humans in God's world plan their programs to comply with divine mandates.

---

[1] Virgil, *The Aeneid* (London: Penguin Books, 1958) Book Six, p. 158.
[2] Quoted by Douglas J. Soccio, *Archetypes of Wisdom* (Belmont, CA: Wadsworth/Thomas Learning, 2001) p. 535.
[3] Marcus Aurelius, *The Thoughts of the Emperor* (New York: John B. Alden, publisher, 1887) p. 65.

A good name is more desirable than great riches; to be esteemed is better than silver or gold (22:1 NIV).

The Queen of the Danes bubbled to Beowulf, "In the farthest corners of the earth your name shall be known. Wherever the ocean laps the windy shore. . . , your praise shall be sung."[1]

Note, however, the difference between fame and honor. Al Capone and Adolf Hitler are famous for their *dis*honor. Some swollen egos want to be well-known for any reason, even if it is disgraceful. The proverb speaks of a good name rather than a big name. Beowulf had both.

A name is a badge of character, whether good or bad. Whatever a person is or does attaches to one's name because it stands for the person. In our day, through publicity gimmicks and promotion gizmos, the names of unworthy persons can be blown up for idol worship. Conversely, names of good persons can be sullied with slander, and their reputations ruined. Iago said, "Who steals my purse steels trash; 'tis something, nothing; / 'Twas mine, 'tis his, and has been slave to thousands. / But he who filches from me my good name / . . . Makes me poor indeed."[2] Its loss is more fatal than the loss of riches. It cannot be protected by a liability policy. Yet it is better than a savings account or the money market. Chaucer said one should "keep a good name and impose on himself the constant task of renewing it."[3] Even God Himself said, "I will not let them pollute my holy name any more" (Ez. 39:7 KJV).

A good reputation, earned by good character, gives a platform for good influence on others that nothing else can give. Those who say they do not care what people think of them are saying they care nothing for other people or for helping them be better persons. If for no other reason, we should retain honor and keep respect for the sake of those who trust us.

---

[1] *Beowulf the Warrior*, Ian Serraillier, tr. (New York: Henry Z. Walck, Inc., 1961) p. 16.

[2] Shakespeare, *Othello*, Act III, Scene 3, lines 157-161.

[3] Chaucer, "The Tale of Melibeus," *Canterbury Tales* (Garden City, NY: Garden City Pub. Co., 1934) p. 234.

308 The Stuffed and the Starved

The rich and the poor have a common bond; the Lord is the maker of them all. / The poor man and the oppressor have this in common: the Lord gives light to the eyes of both (22:2; 29:13 NASB).

The pendulum swings, and social values vary. In some cultures and periods of history, the accepted standard is an education, in some it is pedigree, in others, an elegant style. In some, it is notoriety or popular prominence. Unfortunately, material wealth is often the bottom line.

In *our* cultural order, capital and labor, professionals and artisans, specialists and generalists, physicians and patients, complement each other by mutual dependence. But the chasm between the stuffed and the starved should not be tolerated.

We all have so much in common that class distinctions should rate no more than a trivial trifle. We share finitude, human weakness, and disease. We desire worth and significance and love. We have comparable hopes and aspirations. We breathe the same recycled air, drink the same recycled water, and share the same sunlight from the same Lord. We all have happiness and hurt, and pleasure and pain. We all face the destiny of death.

Beyond those common bonds, God Himself steps in to level our footing. Speaking of poverty and the birth of Jesus, Chaucer said, ". . . there dwelt a man / Who was considered poorest of them all; / But the High God of Heaven . . . can / Send His grace to an ox's stall."[1]

As a divine equalizer, the Christian faith places the highest and richest treasures within reach of the poorest pauper. In the Narnian fantasies, Roonwit the centaur, felled in a noble battle, asked Farsight to give King Tirian his dying message: "Noble death is a treasure which no one is too poor to buy."[2] Beyond death, the society of the redeemed has no class distinctions based on wealth.

---

[1] Chaucer, "The Clerk's Tale, *Canterbury Tales* (Garden City NY: Garden City Pub. Co., 1934) p. 380.
[2] C. S, Lewis, *The Last Battle: Book 7 in the Chronicles* (New York: Collier Books, Macmillan, 1978) p. 91.

Bound by the Bent 309

*He who has a bountiful eye will be blessed, for he gives of his
bread to the poor. / He who gives to the poor will not lack, but he
who hides his eyes will have many curses* (22:9; 28:27 NKJV).

King Evander told of a despot who bound "together the
living and the dead with hands tied to rotting hands and faces to
rotting faces," destroying "many victims by protracted death in this
harrowing embrace."[1] That seems to be what Paul alluded to in
depicting his own self-centered nature before he described his
release in the following chapter. He lamented, "O wretched man
that I am! Who will deliver me from this body of death" (Rom. 7:24)?

Here we have an age-old theological issue that is in the
confession of most churches, including Catholic—we are all born
with a self-centered bias that is like rot attached to our lives.
Pascal said, "The will is . . . depraved. . . . No religion except our
own has taught that man is born sinful."[2] Aurelius said, "I have
often wondered how every man loves himself more than all the
rest."[3] Whittier spoke of our "common inheritance of frailty."[4]

The self-centered bias is a twist or bent toward ourselves in
our deepest love-motive, a motive that should be straight toward
God. The bent of such a major motive is enslaving. Scott said,
"He who stems a stream with sand, / And fetters flame with flaxen
band, / Has yet a harder task to prove, / By firm resolve to conquer
love!"[5] How can we conquer our twisted love? Kierkegaard said,
"That man is a rarity who . . . can *will* what is not pleasant to him,
hold that it is truth although it does not please him, and then . . .
commit himself to it."[6]   (Continued in next essay)

---

[1] Virgil, *The Aeneid* (London: Penguin Books, 1958) Book Eight, p. 215.
[2] Blaise Pascal, *Pensées* (London: Penguin Books, 1995) p. 126.
[3] Marcus Aurelius, *The Thoughts of the Emperor* (New York: John B. Alden,
publisher, 1887) p. 180.
[4] John Greenleaf Whittier, in a note explaining his writing of "Ichabod." Donald
McQuade, ed., *The Harper American Literature* (No city: Addison-Wesley
Educational Publishers, 1994) Vol. I, p. 2130.
[5] Sir Walter Scott, *The Lady of the Lake* (New York: New Amer. Library, 1962)
Canto Third, Sec. XXVIII, p. 89.
[6] Soren Kierkegaard, *Attack Upon Christendom* (Boston: The Beacon Press,
1956), p. 151.

310 Suffering and Sympathy

CONTINUED FROM PREVIOUS ESSAY

When by God's Spirit, with our cooperation, our deepest love-motive is straightened toward God, the bent is automatically eliminated, purifying our hearts (Acts 15:9), cleansing away the bias (1 Jno. 1:9), filling us with love for God (Eph. 3:19). Having our love focused on an object as big and beautiful as God, is both purifying and liberating. Purified of self-centered love, we are liberated from its tyranny.

Living with ourselves is more fun when the self we live with is not a tyrant. The Holy Spirit transposes our lives into a dynamo when we abandon ourselves to Christ.

Released from the sickly, enslaving self-love, we are free to love others. Jesus attached the second commandment to the first—loving your neighbor to loving God (Matt. 22:37-39). When we refocus our love from self to those beyond ourselves, we get unhooked from ourselves. The big boulder that obstructs us from others is rolled away. Those around us rate higher importance.

The contemporary tendency to translate "a bountiful eye" as simply "being generous" is a reduction that loses some of the richness of Solomon's imagery. The bountiful eye sees the poor with pity and is moved with sympathy. Those who are self-biased "hide the eyes," preferring not to see and pretending not to know. In some ways, the eyes *are* the windows of the soul, letting the poverty and suffering in and letting the love and sympathy out.

Self-biased people are afraid to give, for fear they will lack what they need. Actually, the reverse is true. The generous "will be blessed" in many ways and "will not lack." But those who refuse "will have many curses."

When the beneficent king of Sicily was asked what he kept for himself, Alfonso answered, "I keep what I give. The rest I do not count mine."[1]

Jesus said, "Give to the poor, and you will have treasure in heaven" (Matt. 19:21).

---

[1] Jamieson, Fausset and Brown's *Commentary* (Grand Rapids: Wm. B. Eerdmans, 1945) Vol. III, p. 504.

The Manner and the Message 311

Drive out the mocker, and out goes strife; quarrels and insults are ended. / An angry man stirs up dissension, and a hot-tempered one commits many sins (22:10; 29:22 NIV).

Most strife comes more from what a person *is* than from what the person *does*. Both proverbs show that attitudes stir up contention more than the facts that are stated. The manner does more damage than the message. Unfortunately, troublemakers do the church a greater favor by leaving than by staying. The two proverbs speak of two different kinds of antagonists.

The first are the mockers who either do not have the intelligence or the will to go to the trouble to argue their point. They simply scoff and scorn other positions. The only answer some classroom teachers have to a contrary view is a sneer. To intelligent people, popular put-downs reflect on those who do it more than on the positions they oppose.

The second are the hot-tempered, angry persons whose attitudes beget like attitudes in others. Dissension and discord follow. Caught in the crosscurrents of conflicting weather patterns, they are tornadoes looking for a place to touch down. Obsessed with indignation, they have a meltdown. Fury drives them into "many sins." Horace said, "Anger is short-lived madness. Rule your passion, for unless it obeys, it gives commands. Check it with a bridle."[1] Radioactive with rancor and rage, angry people are driven with insane boldness.

Refusing to be drawn into a nasty dispute, civil people sometimes have to withdraw from the social into the personal. Aurelius said, "It is in thy power to retire into thyself. For nowhere either with more quiet or more freedom from trouble does a man retire than into his own soul. . . . Give to thyself this retreat. . . . Retire into this little territory of thy own."[2] That will allow dissension to dissipate, and disharmony will dissolve.

---

[1] Horace, *Satires, Epistles, Ars Poetica* (Cambridge, MA: Harvard University Press, 1991) Epistle II, Book I, p. 267.
[2] Marcus Aurelius, *The Thoughts of the Emperor* (New York: John B. Alden, publisher, 1887) p. 67

312 Falling for Flattery

The mouth of an adulteress is a deep pit; he who is cursed of the Lord will fall into it (22:14 NASB).

Chaucer denounces male lust with a rhyme: "For men have aye a lickerish appetite / On lower things to do their base delight / Than on their wives, though they be ne'er so fair / And ne'er so true and ne'er so debonair." His analogy to a well-fed cat would be comical if it were not so sadly true: "Let [the cat] see a mouse by the wall; / And anon he leaves the milk and flesh and all / And every dainty that is in the house, / Such appetite has he to eat a mouse."[1]

Introducing his proverbs, the sage refers to "the smooth tongue of the adulteress" (Prov. 6:24) "who flatters with her words" (2:16). He says, "A young man, void of understanding, . . . went the way to her house . . . as an ox to the slaughter. . . . Her house is the way of hell, going down to the chambers of death" (Prov. 7:7-8, 22, 27 KJV). Falling for the flattery is like falling into "a deep pit." Forming licentious habits to feed one's lust triggers the trap from which one cannot escape. God's generosity in allowing personal evil is here conceived of as a curse. God said, "My people would not hearken unto my voice. . . , so I gave them up unto their own hearts' lust" (Ps. 81:11-12 KJV). Paul said, "God gave them over to a depraved mind" (Rom. 1:28 NASB). Moral freedom is a blessing that enables us to develop virtue. When the blessing is misused, it becomes a curse!

The warning is to a man about being enticed by a loose woman. But many otherwise innocent women have been seduced by smooth-talking men. Millions of devious men can effectively impersonate a gentleman. Listening to their pitch is like attempting a balancing act on the edge of a precipice. The bottomless pit of iniquity yawns open for both sexes.

In what may seem to be a feasible situation, those who are not committed to stand for principle will fall for the cheapest line. Solomon's point: Protect the blessing. Prevent the curse!

---

[1] Chaucer, "The Manciple's Tale of the Crow," *Canterbury Tales* (Garden City, NY: (Garden City Pub. Co., 1934) p. 534.

He who oppresses the poor to increase his riches . . . will surely come to poverty. / Like a roaring lion and a charging bear is a wicked ruler over the poor (22:16; 28:15 NKJV). Also 22:7; 28:16.

Economic exploitation takes two forms—the personal and the institutional. Personal oppression of the poor in the first proverb leads to institutional oppression in the second.

Economic corruption operates in three spiraling cycles of cruelty, beginning on the personal level. Getting what one covets drives him to covet more. The more he gets, the more he wants, and the more he wants the more he gets. The second cycle comes in clustering for cumulative control. Like-minded persons partner to institutionalize their covetousness for each to hide behind. Adding more people adds power, and additional power attracts more people. Whether big corporations or big governments, institutions can become formidable. The third cycle completes the triad. Economic exploitation gives control, and control increases the exploitation for more control. Power empowers power, and power is empowered by power. Heavy wheels roll with increasing speed, crunching and crushing their victims.

In our world, competitive capitalism is more workable than other economic systems, but it requires government control to prevent exploitation. When it grows powerful enough to control the government, fascism results. Over 2,000 years ago Horace wrote: "Set bounds to the quest for wealth . . . There are fixed bounds, beyond and short of which right can find no place."[1]

The entire syndrome could be preempted on the personal level where the motives begin. Aurelius exhorted, "Take care that thou dost not [become] so pleased with [wealth] to be disturbed if ever thou shouldst not have [it]."[2] Horace warned, "If you set your heart on aught, you will be loath to lay it down."[3] Moral values must control our motives even in commerce.

[1] Horace, *Satires, Epistles, Ars Poetica* (Cambridge, MA: Harvard U. Press, 1991) Satire I, Book I, pp. 11, 13.
[2] Marcus Aurelius, *The Thoughts of the Emperor* (New York: John B. Alden, publisher, 1887) p. 113.
[3] Horace, *op. cit.*, Epistle X, Book I, p. 317.

314 Concealing and Revealing

It is the glory of God to conceal a matter . . . / The eyes of the Lord preserve knowledge . . . (25:2; 22:12 NKJV).

Somewhere we got the idea that we have the right to know every reason for everything God does. He is expected to run it by us before He activates a plan or program. We easily overlook that God is God, which itself means that He is accountable only to Himself.

Dante got a sneak peek of God, and exclaimed, "Eternal Light, in Thyself only dwelling . . . for Thou . . . art fully comprehended by Thyself alone!"[1] Concealing the details of our future makes life for us a daily adventure, and preserving His own mysteries facilitates our daily worship. We may spend eternity exploring more and more of God's mysteries and never exhaust them—for He is infinite! Moses declared, "The secret things belong to the Lord" (Deut. 29:29).

Yet He has revealed in scripture and in nature all we need to know about Him for our lives and for our journey to the next life. And He will "preserve that knowledge" for us.

The 20th century saw a careless scramble to initiate new theologies. In my lifetime, I have seen the fall of Classical Liberalism, the rise and wane of Neo-orthodoxy, Secular Theology, Radical Theology, Theology of Hope, Process Theology, Latin Liberation Theology, Black Theology, Feminist Theology, African Indigenous Theology, Reconstructionism, Creation Spirituality, the Postmodern Theology of Deconstructionism, and other lesser movements. Most of them made an initial splash, and soon lost their zip and zing.

Dennis Kinlaw wrote: " The graveyard of history has many stones to mark the passing of various ideologies. One marker, though, is missing. There is no gravestone for historic biblical faith. It lives and will continue to do so, for its word is eternal."[2]

---

[1] Dante, *The Divine Comedy*, Bergin, tr. (New York: Meredith Pub. Co., 1955) "Paradise," Canto XXXIII, p. 108.
[2] Dennis F. Kinlaw, "Behind Scholars' Closed Doors," *Chtistianity Today*, April 29, 1991, P. 11.

. . . The heart of kings is unsearchable. / Do not exalt yourself in the presence of the king, and do not stand in the place of great men (25:3; 25:6 NKJV). Also 25:7.

The American public appreciates a president who identifies with common people by rolling up his sleeves and getting his fingernails dirty. They also want their leader to carry an imperial ambience like an aura of royalty. If he has the second, it makes the first noteworthy.

A distinctive mystery about most national leaders gives them a fascinating mystique. Their world is "unsearchable" by Joe Plumber because the complexities of state are unknown. A delicate linkage system connects every presidential move and every spoken word to a variety of situations in a complicated network that most of us cannot conceive. Respect is appropriate.

Those who wish to hobnob with royalty come in two forms. Some attempt to prop up an inferior self-image by associations that will prop up their public image. Someone said, "To reveal a superior exterior is to conceal an inferior interior." Those people are simply using a coping mechanism. Others have an exaggerated opinion of themselves, and they wish to educate others about their own superiority by embellishing their public image. The first are attempting to nourish an impoverished self-esteem, and the second are trying to feed their inflated lust for acclaim. In the New Testament, James describes a similar situation and says that association by discrimination makes you "judges with evil thoughts" (Ja. 2:4).

Both situations foster a self-centered pride that is disgusting. Those in the first group need to be encouraged with honest approbation. Most of those in the second will be reduced to reality by the experiences of life. When those with low self-regard are lifted and those with distended self-regard are lowered, they arrive as colleagues of life on a common level of healthy self-respect. They both can accept their respective areas of inferiority and superiority without being either unduly deflated or inflated. The word for that ideal ego state is humility.

316 Tarnished or Burnished

Take away the dross from silver . . . / Take away the wicked from before the king, and his throne will be established . . . / Because of the transgression of the land, many are its princes . . . / The king establishes the land by justice, but he who receives bribes overthrows it. / The king who judges . . . with truth, his throne will be established forever (25:4,5; 28:2; 29:4,14 NKJV).

The previous proverb (25:3) speaks of the mystery of a king's heart. If it is the "mystery of iniquity" (2 Thes. 2:7 KJV) that conceals and camouflages evil, it is more disturbing than evil that is exposed. Isaiah shouts to the sinful city, "Your silver has become dross" (Is. 1:22).

When a nation's values are corroded with bribery, underhanded deals, preferential treatment, reprisals and political payoffs, you often have a rapid succession of rulers ("many are its princes") with military coups d'etat and counterrevolutions. From ancient history into the present, despots retain power by flexing military muscles against their own people and by using underhanded fraud. In America the legislative and executive branches of government with their multilevel bureaucratic complexes are vulnerable. A volatile government gives its people no stability.

When honesty and integrity trump selfish gain and fraud, the dross is taken from the silver, and a nation gleams and glows with new luster. What was tarnished is burnished. A primary provision of the Magna Carta (article 40) reads: "To no one will we sell . . . or refuse justice."[1] Horace said, "I am not one to hunt for the votes of a fickle public at the cost of suppers and gifts."[2] When backroom bargaining and undercounter gifts are eliminated from all levels of the political process, "the land will be established by justice" and the government "will be established forever." The people are given stability and security, God is honored, and future generations will be the designated beneficiaries.

---

[1] *The New Book of Knowledge* (New York: Grolier, Inc., 1967) Vol. 12, p. 22.
[2] Horace, *Satires, Epistles, Ars Poetica* (Cambridge, MA: Harvard U. Press, 1991) Epistle XIX, Book I, p. 383.

Do not go hastily to court; for what will you do in the end, when your neighbor has put you to shame? / Debate your case with your neighbor himself, and do not disclose the secret to another; / Lest he who hears it expose your shame, and your reputation be ruined (25:8,9,10 NKJV).

Jesus said to go first to the one who offends you and attempt to resolve the problem in private (Mat. 18:15). To duck out and go to court is to dodge the responsibilities of relationship.

The matter should be kept between the two of you. To violate a confidence is treachery. To divulge something that is private is to indict oneself. Putting yourself up by putting the other person down is morally wrong. And attempting to gain public esteem by sacrificing another's public image has rebound effect. You ruin your own reputation. The shame is on you.

If we reach impasse, we are still in a position to cut the person some slack. The Christian heart is a cushion to absorb considerable injustice. We become bigger and better persons by letting the issue drop. Aurelius said, "Does another do me wrong? Let him do it. He has his own disposition."[1] We can be big enough to rise above the matter.

Relational problems easily arise in dealing with repugnant personalities. Odious attitudes are interpreted as offensive acts. We allow what is distasteful to become disagreeable. What is objectionable becomes obnoxious. And other people may find our own personalities loathsome as well. In one of Lewis' novels, King Trom's daughter said: "Where my father could give only a Yes or No . . . , [the slave] could pare the Yes to the very quick and sweeten the No till it went down like wine."[2] Softening our attitude and improving our relational style will take us a long distance in neighborly relations. Paul said, "If it be possible, as much as depends on you, live peaceably with all men" (Rom. 12:18).

---

[1] Marcus Aurelius, *The Thoughts of the Emperor* (New York: John B. Alden, publisher, 1887) p. 89.
[2] C. S. Lewis, *Till We Have Faces* (Grand Rapids: William B. Eerdmans Pub. Co., 1966) p. 19.

318 Refreshing and Rewarding

Like the cold of snow in time of harvest is a faithful messenger to those who send him, for he refreshes the soul of his masters. / Confidence in an unfaithful man in time of trouble is like a bad tooth and a foot out of joint (25:13; 25:19 NKJV).

Without texting, voice mail, or even snail mail, ancient leaders depended on fleet-footed couriers to transport important messages. Once the runner strikes off, the communication is exclusively in his hands. He can be irresponsible with the trust, taking leisure time and distorting the message. The sender's only assurance rests on his confidence in the courier's integrity.

Placing confidence in an unfaithful person is like chewing on a toothache or walking on a sprained ankle. The sandwich remains uneaten, the stroll ends before you arrive, and you incur acute pain. The undependable runner hurts you like an abscessed tooth or a broken foot.

Betrayal by those you trust not only gives you great problems. It causes great pain. Those who discredit their promise to return a phone call not only cause inconvenience and frustration. They produce disappointment and distrust. The national epidemic of infidelity causes more acute heart-hurt than bad teeth or cracked ankles ever gave! The human race has misused its freedom and betrayed God's trust, causing pain in His soul that is only symbolized by the Cross of Christ. Our unfaithfulness is pandemic! The fallout can never be measured.

Without freezers or icemakers, the Hebrews used snow for cooling their drinks as we use ice today. Winter snow was packed and stored away for use in summer seasons. Knowing the trusted messenger had honored the trust by faithfully delivering the message was a refreshing relief to the leader, like a snow-cooled drink in the heat of harvest. Jesus intimated that He will someday look at those who have honored His trust and say, "Well done, good and faithful servant; you have been faithful" (Matt. 25:23). Making that announcement will be as refreshing and rewarding to Him as to those who hear! The psalmist exulted, "He delighted in me" (Ps. 18:19)!

Like clouds and wind without rain is a man who boasts of gifts he does not give (25:14 NIV).

For the farmer whose crops are dry with drought, heavy dark clouds with strong winds that bring no rain are disappointing. False forecasts are fakes and frauds. To withhold gifts from those in need is bad enough, but to trick and dupe with empty promises to raise false hope is a cruel hoax. Such impostors were identified and condemned by Solomon 3,000 years ago.

Both Peter and Jude picked up Solomon's simile and applied it to theological charlatans who promised what God had not promised to give. They were merchants of souls, winning followers for personal gain by reducing the requirements of God (2 Pet. 2:3, 14). They turned God's grace into a license to sin and a cover for crimes, making it safe to sin (Ju. 4). Teachers without truth to teach, seed sowers with only weed seed to sow, they were "springs without water, mists driven by a storm" (2 Pet. 2:17), "clouds without rain, blown along by the wind" (Ju. 12).

Today we have a new breed of religionists who exploit the needs of hurting people for personal profit (2 Pet. 2:3), and others "who change the grace of God into a license for immorality" (Ju. 4). Overreacting against a false salvation-by-works theology, they have watered down the requirements of Christ until anything goes! Instead of "denying self, taking up the cross" (Mat. 16:24), obeying Christ (Lu. 6:46), and keeping God's commandments (1 Jn. 2:3), we are made free for sex outside marriage, living in luxury without helping the poor, and undisciplined lives of self-centered indulgence. They make promises for God that He has not made, "boasting of gifts" that will never be delivered—"for whom blackest darkness has been reserved" (2 Pet. 2:17; Ju. 13).

How different the humility and respect of Whittier who said, "I bow my forehead to the dust, / I veil mine eyes for shame, / And urge, in trembling self-distrust, / A prayer without a claim."[1]

---

[1] John Greenleaf Whittier, "The Eternal Goodness," Fuller and Kinnick, eds., *Adventures in American Literature* (New York: Harcourt, Brace & World, 1963) p. 620.

320 Persuaded by Patience

With patience a ruler may be persuaded, and a soft tongue will break a bone (25:15 RSV).

It violates the laws of physics. Sledgehammers, not soft tongues, break bones. But we are not talking tongues and bones. We are talking patience and persistence. An old German proverb says, "Patience breaks iron."[1] When our requests are not honored, it is easier to vent frustration than to "keep our cool." Then we become victims of our own impatience. Robinson Crusoe said, Something within us "hurries us on to be the instruments of our own destruction."[2] Victories are not won by confrontational weapons, because they precipitate confrontation. They are won by disarming strategies and attitudes that promote congeniality.

As a rule, situations are too complex to be changed by the snap of a finger, and obstinate minds are not altered by a simple request. They are changed by a soft tongue rather than a clenched fist. Of course, a request should be strong rather than weak, but it should be soft rather than harsh. Aurelius said to be "neither violent . . . nor torpid."[3] When a request is made to an official who is a part of a system, we have to wait until it is sifted through the sluggish sieve of a bungling bureaucracy. The offended widow was faced with discouragement, but she refused to accept defeat (Lu. 18). James said, "Let patience have its perfect work" (Ja. 1:4 NKJV).

Paul's key to patience is love: "Love is patient, love is kind . . . It always trusts, always hopes, always perseveres" (1 Cor. 13:4, 7). Browning said, Patient love is "like a chance-sown plant which, cast on stubborn soil, puts forth buds and softer stains, unknown in happier climes. [It] endures . . . and is oppressed . . . , suffering much and much sustaining, . . . oft-failing, yet believing, . . . the heir of hopes too fair to turn out false."[4]

---

[1] Daniel D. Whedon, ed., *Whedon's Commentary* (New York: Phillips and Hunt, 1885) Vol. VI, p. 442.

[2] Daniel Defoe, *Robinson Crusoe* (Garden City, NY: Doubleday, 1945) p. 15.

[3] Marcus Aurelius, *The Thoughts of the Emperor* (New York: John B. Alden, publisher, 1887) p. 120.

[4] Robert Browning, "Paracelsus," *The Complete . . . Works . . .* (Cambridge, MA: Houghton Mifflin, 1895) p. 46-47.

*Have you found honey? Eat only what you need, lest you have it in
excess and vomit it* (25:16 NASB).

In Solomon's day, locating a comb of honey in a rock cavity or hollow tree was a celebrated find. The immediate temptation was to gorge and glut until regurgitating. The proverb is a caution against indulgence and a plea for moderation even in legitimate pleasures.

Aristotle said, "Self-indulgence . . . is concerned with the kind of pleasures that . . . animals share in. . . . These are touch and taste—food, . . . drink, . . . and sex."[1] Indulgence is dangerously detrimental. The mind has the same problem with concentrated pleasures that the body has with concentrated sweets. It can become hooked. Patterns are formed that become habits. People become mentally addicted to their desires until they lose control of themselves. They become runaway vehicles with no brakes. The rational will loses control of the body.

Roderigo's romantic infatuation became uncontrollable lust. He admitted, "It is my shame to be so fond; but it is not in my virtue to amend it." Iago advised: "Our bodies are our gardens . . . I take this that you call love to be . . . merely a lust of the blood and a permission of the will. Come, be a man!"[2] This is our problem. We can fertilize our hormones with indulgent imagination until they grow as uncontrollable weeds in our gardens. The will can defer to the desires until it becomes lethargic. When our wills atrophy, they lose control.

If we are ill from gluttony, the best thing we can do is to regurgitate. We need to get the problem out of our system. The theological term is repentance. We need to gag on our glut until we heave. Nauseated with excessive pleasures, we become sick and tired of being sick and tired of ourselves. Sick of sin, we vomit it up. We turn loose of our enslaving desires. Our wills are recaptured, re-empowered, and placed back in control. Next time, we go slow on the honey.

---

[1] Aristotle, *Nicomachean Ethics*, Book III, Chapter 10, p. 370 in McKeon.
[2] Shakespeare, *Othello*, Act I, Scene 3, lines 319-324, 336-341.

322 Regular or Rare

Seldom set foot in your neighbor's house—too much of you, and he will hate you. / If a man loudly blesses his neighbor early in the morning, it will be taken as a curse (25:17; 27:14 NIV).

The shells of these compact kernels must be cracked for us to get the goody. First, taking friendships for granted comes too easily. Thoughtlessness can damage a relationship. Too much of a good thing turns it bad. What is regular becomes commonplace, and what is rare is considered precious. Some people need to work hard at making themselves absent.

Engaged persons are eager to be married because they cannot get enough of each other. But after they are together both day and night, each starts unpacking the other's personality. When they discover faults and flaws, some of the appeal is lost. Even a soul mate must not be suffocated. The proverb says not to wear out your welcome. Do not suck the sap out of friendship. Goodwill can be abused. Do not leech the liaison. Make your visits rare enough to be valued. Do not allow yourself to be a pest. Let your presence be appreciated.

The proverb may also suggest that intrusiveness is resented. Too frequent visits to borrow items, or to ask for help, or to pry into family matters, can turn a friend into a nuisance. Using another person's time to talk about yourself, or your feats, or your grandchildren, can give a friend the earache! Fellowship over the backyard fence leaves each person free to bow out. But a hostess can hardly leave an uninvited guest that is parked in a chair at her kitchen table.

The second proverb says ill-timed or extravagant praise can be "taken as a curse." An old Italian proverb states: "He who praises you more than is customary has either deceived you or is about to do so."[1] Excess adulation makes your sincerity suspect.

Together the proverbs underscore the delicate fabric of human relationships, and the importance of modesty and caution to protect and strengthen them.

---

[1] Adam Clarke's *Commentary* (New York: Eaton and Mains, 1883) Vol III, p. 779.

*A man who bears false witness against his neighbor is like a club,
a sword, or a sharp arrow* (25:18 NKJV).

Mauls, swords, and arrows were the most dangerous weapons in ancient times. Even today they are more analogous to false witnesses than switchblades or handguns, because they evoke the picture of a body that is deeply stabbed, slashed with deep lacerations, and broken to pieces. The word for "club" literally means "something that scatters in pieces."

False witnesses include all who discolor others' reputations by falsely interpreting their motives or actions. Or by giving selective information for false impressions. Or by insinuating dishonor by subtle vocal nuances. They are not limited to court scenes. They are found on cell phones, at the club meeting over tea, on the city transit system, or in the private office.

Helena said, "Things base and vile, . . . love can transpose to . . . dignity."[1] The reverse is just as true. Envy can transpose honor and dignity into things base and vile. If bad acts can be dressed up with good faces, good acts can be dressed down with bad faces. Using a negative spin is like lacerating a person's reputation or smashing her name into smithereens!

It works by a peculiar dynamic. Putting another person down positions you as superior. You are placing the other person in contrast to yourself. You are posing as the better person. Bassanio said, "The world is still deceived with ornament. . . . What plea so tainted but . . . with a gracious voice . . . some sober brow will bless it with a [Bible] text."[2]

But when the cover is blown and the pretension is exposed, the dishonor you assigned to the other person will rebound on you. The roles will be reversed. Wielding swords and shooting arrows are dangerous activities. Jesus said, "All who take the sword will perish by the sword (Matt. 26:52).

---

[1] Shakespeare, *A Midsummer Night's Dream*, Act I, Scene 1, lines 232-233.
[2] Shakespeare, *The Merchant of Venice*, Act III, Scene 2, lines 74-80.

324 Sing or Sob?

Like one who takes away a garment on a cold day, or like vinegar poured on soda, is one who sings to a heavy heart (25:20 NIV).

Waterman wrote, "Life has so many hidden woes, / So many thorns for every rose."[1]

When a person is hurting, we often stand by helplessly, not knowing how to approach. When we do venture, we say the wrong thing. This proverb gives an important directive: Do not make an effort to heal the hurt too soon. Attempting to impose a bright mood on a grieving person is to belittle her sorrow. Implying she should not grieve is demeaning. Jane Merchant wrote: "Shelter sorrow / In shimmering pride / Lest friend deplore, / Lest foe deride. / But weep, weep well / When you're all alone, / Lest your heart congeal / To a cold small stone."[2]

Hurting people do not need to be forced into our happy mood. They need a friend to walk into their sorrow and share their grief. Procter prayed: "I do not ask that flowers should always spring / Beneath my feet; / I know too well the poison and the sting / Of things too sweet."[3] Those who hurt must be allowed the leverage to hurt. The human mechanism is structured so that time itself heals many wounds, and much good is gained from the process. Queen Dido requested extra time so that her misfortune could "teach [her] submission and the art of grieving."[4] Slow recovery is better than a quick fix.

Solomon said, There is "a time to weep, and a time to laugh; a time to mourn and a time to dance" (Ecc. 3:4). Singing and laughing belong to their own time. But this is the time for an empathizing friend to weep. When Mary told Jesus her brother had died, "Jesus wept" (Jno. 11:35).

---

[1] Nixon Waterman, "To Know All Is to Forgive All," Richard C. MacKenzie, ed., *The New Home Book of Best Love Poems* (Garden City, NY: Garden City Books, 1946) p. 114.

[2] Jane Merchant, "Prescription for Pride," *Because It's Here* (Nashville, Abingdon Press, 1970) P. 112.

[3] A. Procter, "Per Pacem Ad Lucem," *English Sacred Lyrics* (U. of Calif. Library, YA 01604) Selection 133, p. 261.

[4] Virgil, *The Aeneid* (London: Penguin Books, 1958) Book Four, p. 110.

As cold waters to a thirsty soul, so is good news from a far country
(25:25 KJV).

Those who sip on soda pop in air-conditioned offices do not feel the impact of this simile. The thirsty wayfarer trudging barefoot across hot barren deserts understood. If we multiply exponentially the meaning of "refreshing" several times, we will come nearer understanding.

Ancient Jews were not provincial. They were acutely aware of neighboring nationalities, with which they had considerable interchange. But news came slowly by foot and was generally sparse. The news could be from a friend or family member in a distant land, or from a political or military situation that could affect one's life back home. Much of the news that did come was bad news. Good news was rare, which made it even more refreshing!

The greatest good news for us earthlings came two millennia ago in a breaking story from an angelic reporter: "Behold, I bring you good tidings of great joy . . . to all people" (Lu. 2:10). God had initiated a rescue operation for the human race. He had invaded our planet from outer space!

Gospel good news, however, presupposes bad news, without which the gospel would not be good news. Sympathy has no value unless there is suffering. Insurance coverage is futile unless there is the possibility of liability. Pursuing an education is meaningless unless there is ignorance. Forgiveness, salvation, and liberation are good news only against the backdrop of sin, lostness, and enslavement. Forgiveness would have no value to anyone without sin.

Human souls are charbroiled in the heat of iniquity. They are parched, sin-scorched, and arid, like living in desert sand. Their thirsting souls are dry. Word of an oasis is a welcome relief! The good news of the Christian gospel is for those who realize their need for the gospel. Paul said Christ came to save sinners (1 Tim. 1:15). Jesus said He came to save the lost (Lu. 19:10). To us who have been lost sinners, the good news from heaven is enormously refreshing!

326 Gorging on Glory

It is not good to eat much honey, so to seek one's own glory is not glory (25:27 NKJV).

Who wants to be groggy and queasy and sick with sweets? Too much of a good thing is not good. The sweeter it is, the more nauseating it can become. Personal honor like honey is a good thing, but too much honor is heavy to carry. Having a public image you cannot live up to puts you under too much pressure. With too much stardom you get sick of yourself. It is not good for you emotionally, morally, or spiritually. Gorging on glory is shamefully inglorious.

Glory is coy and evasive. It hides when sought. Seeking it, you lose it. The search is frustrating rather than fulfilling, because it is elusive. It is futile to seek glory that you do not have. Glory seeks you when you do not seek it. It attaches to those who have not sought it. Glorying in God gives a taste of glory because He is glorious. We glory in His glory!

When Satan offered to Jesus the glories of the world (Matt. 4:8-9), Milton has Jesus answering, "If there be in glory [any] good, it may by means far different be attained without ambition . . . by deeds of peace, by wisdom eminent, by patience, temperance . . ."[1]

The dialog continued, and Jesus said, "Glory is false glory [when] attributed to things not glorious, [to] men not worthy of fame." Then He said, "Why should man seek glory who of his own hath nothing, and to whom nothing belongs but condemnation and shame? . . . Yet to himself would take that which to God alone of right belongs; yet so much bounty is in God, such grace, that [those] who advance His glory, not their own, he himself to glory will advance."[2]   The permanence we seek is beyond death. We are not in life for the short-distance run. We are in it for the long stretch. To seek our own glory is not glorious. But those who glory in His glory, God intends to advance to permanent glory!

---

[1] John Milton, *Paradise Regained,* in *The Portable Milton* (New York: Penguin Books, 1949) Book III, p. 581.
[2] *op. cit., p. 580, 582.*

Cracked and Crumbling 327

Whoever has no rule over his own spirit is like a city broken down, without walls (25:28 NKJV).

Cities were walled to protect them from invasion, but when the walls were broken, the people had no protection. This analogy quickly arrests our attention with an unexpected angle. Here the danger is not from outside invasion, but from an inside job. We need protection from ourselves. Matthew Arnold wrote of "the mystery of this heart which beats so wild, so deep."[1]

Our untamed spirits are like a two-year-old thoroughbred, prancing, pawing and snorting inside the gate at the Kentucky Derby, ready for the races. Our spirits need to be bridled. Dickinson wrote, "How frugal is the chariot that bears a human soul."[2] Like a jockey, we must ride our spirits with a tight rein. We must rein in fantasies and focus on worthy goals. Wordsworth exclaimed, "What fond and wayward thoughts slide into a lover's head"[3] In Milton, Adam spoke about our "wandering thoughts" and how "apt the mind and fancy is to rove unchecked."[4]

After our pristine parents ate the forbidden fruit, Milton says, "They sat down to weep," and "high winds . . . within began to rise, high passion, anger, suspicion."[5] With our cracked and crumbling character, high winds rise from inner tempers we did not know were there. We seem defenseless against ourselves! The unstated warning is not veiled: Get control of yourself! Alert security! Repair the citadel! We will either control ourselves or be controlled by ourselves. Given free rein, the human spirit is ruthless. Under restraint, it is an obedient child. With God's help, excuses run out. The ball is in our court.

---

[1] Matthew Arnold, "The Buried life," *Norton Anthology of English Lit* (New York: W. W. Norton, 1968) p. 2043.

[2] Emily Dickinson, "There Is No Frigate Like a Book," *Modern American Poetry* (New York: Harcourt, Brace and Co., 1950) p. 97.

[3] William Wordsworth, "Strange Fits of Passion," *The Viking Book of Poetry* (New York: Viking Press, 1958) Volume II, p. 656.

[4] John Milton, *Paradise Lost* (Indianapolis: ITT Bobbs-Merrill Educational Pub. Co., 1962) Book VIII, p. 189.

[5] Milton, *op. cit.*, Book IX, p. 232.

328 Fit for a Fool

Like snow in summer or rain in harvest, honor is not fitting for a
fool (26:1 NIV).

Genuine honor is based on merit for meritorious persons. Applauding the unworthy is as incongruous as unseasonable weather. Public honor is not a good fit for fools. They wear it sloppily, like a suit two sizes too large. If it is an ill fit, those who wear it are misfits. Honor is only suitable for those who can wear it comfortably. All others are clumsy with it.

Getting honor simply for honor's sake is cheap, and not worthy of the sacrifice to get it. Bloated egos drive eccentrics to meaningless acts of artificial heroism in order to win recognition. But the sacrifice is awkward, and recognized as a ludicrous absurdity. Virgil's Turnus said, "Let me bargain death for honor."[1] Eurylus said, "Mine is . . . a temper to scorn the light of life and count it a cheap price to pay for . . . honor."[2] James Fitz-James said, "Yet life I hold for idle breath, / When . . . honor is weighed with death."[3] To die voluntarily for nothing more than honor does not wear well. When honor is worn by one to whom it does not belong, that person is as laughable as a circus clown. If it does not fit, it should not be donned. Fools wear borrowed honor that does not belong to them.

Worthy honor is based on character and righteous actions, which cannot be bargained for and must not be bartered away. Some principles *are* worth dying for. Those persons who honor the principles are honorable persons. They have honor even if they do not receive honor. Perhaps Iago was referring to those who *have honor* and are *not honored* when he said, "Honor is an essence that's not seen; they have it very oft that have it not."[4] Some have it without wearing it. Fools wear it but do not have it. They are misfits.

---

[1] Virgil, *The Aeneid* (London: Penguin Books, 1958) Book Twelve, p. 310.
[2] Virgil, *op. cit.*, Book Nine, p. 231.
[3] Sir Walter Scott, *The Lady of the Lake* (New York: New American Library, 1962) Canto Fourth, Sec. XVII, p. 104.
[4] Shakespeare, *Othello*, Act IV, Scene 1, lines 17-18.

Do not answer a fool according to his folly, lest you also be like him. / Answer a fool according to his folly, lest he be wise in his own eyes (26:4, 5 NKJV). Also 26:8.

These two proverbs were positioned together to point out a distinction, otherwise they would have been separated to conceal the apparent contradiction. The two refer to separate sets of circumstances that require different responses. The phrase "according to" in the first means "in the same way that the fool argues," and in the second, "in the way that the fool deserves."

If a fool uses sarcasm, insults, and ridicule, we should not emulate his mode. Never make a fool of yourself by fooling with a fool! Another proverb (26:8) supports the first, saying it is pointless to honor foolish fools with a reply. They cannot be changed.

But wise fools can be changed. If they foolishly attempt a rational explanation, they deserve a rational response. Illogic can only be corrected by real logic. C. S. Lewis said, "Good pholosophy must exist . . . because bad philosophy needs to be answered."[1] Showing the foolishness of an argument by using its own principles will promote humility. Wise fools can learn from the reasoning of the wise, and become less foolish. Chesterton's fake priest argued, "There may well be wonderful universes above us where reason is utterly unreasonable?" The real priest replied, "Reason is always reasonable, even in the last limbo, in the lost borderland."[2]

Refusing to answer *with* folly keeps you from being foolish, and giving answer *to* folly prevents the fool from being "wise in his own eyes." Here is the principle of the proverbs: Keep silent when response would make you foolish, but give response when silence would make him arrogant. It is a formula for fiddling with the foolish. Elsewhere Solomon said there is "a time to be silent and a time to speak" (Eccl. 3:7 NIV).

---

[1] C. S. Lewis, *The Weight of Glory,* Grand Rapids: Eerdmans Pub. Co., 1977) p. 50.
[2] G. K. Chesterton, "The Blue Cross," *Favorite Father Brown Stories* (New York: Dover Pub., 1993) pp. 12-13.

330 Messengers with a Message

Like cutting off one's own feet or drinking violence is the sending of a message by the hand of a fool. / Like an archer who wounds at random is he who hires a fool or any passer-by (26:6, 10 NIV).

Without stating the word, these proverbs use the notion of responsibility in two separate ways. The two definitions are *accountability* and *dependability*. A person is irresponsible who employs an irresponsible person—by which I mean, one is not accountable who employs one who is not dependable. Accountable employers employ dependable employees.

Expecting fools and passers-by to be prompt and discreet in delivering your message is like crippling yourself with lameness or drinking poison that you think is benign. Wise persons do not employ foolish helpers. Before managerial crash-courses and Business Administration majors, this proverb was apropos for those working in human resources. It still addresses nepotism, favoritism, and bribe-taking.

God had an urgent message to be delivered to the world, but He did not have an ideal resource pool to draw from. Initially He did not choose academicians, entertainment celebrities, or political power brokers. He bypassed the greatest brains with great talent and good looks. He chose fishermen who were inferior enough to be committed beyond themselves, weak enough to depend on Him, and wise enough to be taught. Through the centuries, Christ has added to that confused and disorganized band of disciples millions of others, and "entrusted them with the gospel" message (1 Thes. 2:4). The question today is whether we are trustworthy messengers.

Today the church has joined the world in debating the dependability of God. In writing his classic, John Milton stated that one of his purposes was to "justify the ways of God to man."[1] More important, however, is to "justify the ways of man to God." Our dependability is what is questionable, not His! The big question is whether He can depend on us with His message.

---

[1] John Milton, *Paradise Lost* (Indianapolis: ITT Bobbs-Merrill Educational Pub. Co., 1962) Book I, p. 6.

*Like a lame man's legs . . . is a proverb [to] a fool. / As a dog
returns to its vomit, so a fool . . . / Though you grind a fool in a
mortar, . . . you will not remove his folly* (26:7; 26:11; 27:22 NIV).

In our culture, this first simile is crude and insensitive, and
the second is grossly distasteful, but the imagery of all three is
sharp and striking. The first says that wisdom is unusable for those
who are handicapped with folly. The second suggests that one's
innate foolish nature subdues the intellect that initially responds to
wisdom. The third metaphor intimates that some fools never learn
from experience, excruciating as it may be. They operate on
impulse, or desire, or the inclinations of ingrained patterns.

These analogies elucidate Solomon's repeated point that
folly, as he uses the term, is a matter of the heart as well as the
head. It is moral as well as mental. Marcus Aurelius quizzed,
"Hast thou reason? Why then dost thou not use it?"[1] The answer
is that the heart with its evil passions overwhelms intelligent
reason. The heart needs to be aligned with the head.

In his epistle, Peter quotes this second proverb and adds
another: "A sow that is washed goes back to her wallowing in the
mud" (2 Pet. 2:22). Billy Sunday illustrated the importance of a
changed heart by pointing to the difference between a hog and a
sheep. They both may fall into the mud, but a sheep "hates it and
scrambles out. A hog loves it and wallows in it."[2] When the
inclinations of the heart are changed, the patterns can be redirected.

Dante says that God like the sun gives equal measure of
heat and light, love and intelligence, emotion and insight.[3] Moral-
emotional-will and mental-intelligent-reason are two primordial
forms of God's energy. Spiritual rebirth can give a new heart that
will converge with intelligence to direct one's life. The synergism
is what Solomon called wisdom.

---

[1] Marcus Aurelius, *The Thoughts of the Emperor* (New York: John B. Alden,
publisher, 1887) p. 70.
[2] William T. Ellis, *Billy Sunday: The Man and His Message* (Chicago: Moody
Press, 1959) pp. 94-95.
[3] Dante, *The Divine Comedy* (New York: Random House, 1932) "Paradiso,"
Canto XIV, p. 497.

332 Hope for a Half-wit

Do you see a man wise in his own eyes? There is more hope for a fool than for him (26:12 NKJV, NASB, NIV).

"Wise in his own eyes" strongly hints of arrogant conceit, so much so that one version translates it as "wise in his own conceit" (KJV), and another as "a man of self-conceit" (Mof).

Over and over in these proverbs, the fool is pilloried in public scorn. One might get the idea that a fool is the most hopeless of all persons. But here we learn that an arrogant egotist is more hopeless than a mere fool. Proverb 26:3 says an ordinary fool can learn some remedial lessons (Essay 274), but conceit is more difficult to crack. Cockiness precludes correction. It closes the gate on improvement. Those who think they are wise are superlatively unwise. The proverbialist had more hope for a half-wit and more faith in a fool. Paul said, "If any man among you thinks that he is wise . . . , let him become foolish that he may become wise" (1 Cor. 3:18 NASB).

In an Aesop fable, a stag admired its antlers in a pool of still water, but its legs looked frail and scrawny. When a lion pursued, the stag outran the predator on open ground, but when it went into the forest its rack was snagged in branches, and it was killed. As the stag was dying, it thought, "These pitiable legs almost saved me, but my noble antlers proved my undoing."[1]

The lesson about conceit and wisdom applies to conceit in other areas. Whatever we admire most in ourselves can hook our egos and cause our downfall. Being "wise in our own eyes" keeps us from seeking counsel to become wiser. Thinking we are healthy keeps us from aerobics and healthy eating habits. Admiring our safety record blinds us to caution. Applauding our abilities keeps us from making improvements.

Recognizing our inadequacy in any area enables us to advance in that area. Progress comes not from self-sufficiency, but from awareness of a need. Some of us foolish people know we are limited in wisdom. For us there is hope!

---

[1] Aesop, *The Fables of Aesop* (New York: Dorset Press, 1975) p. 42.

Wise in the Eyes 333

The sluggard is wiser in his own eyes than seven men who answer discreetly. / A sluggard does not plow in season; so at harvest time he looks but finds nothing (26:16; 20:4 NIV).

Emotional problems can contribute to indolence, but the reverse is also true. In a chain reaction, each continues to make the other worse. But if the cycle is broken, body and mind can boost each other in an upward spiral. Patterns are broken by replacing them with better ones.

Mentally lazy persons do not see themselves in this proverb, because they do not know they are lazy. They often become conceited over the little knowledge they do have, leaving them without motivation to reach for more. By study, lifelong students constantly face their ignorance, which motivates them to study more. When the brain is allowed to atrophy, brain cramps occur. C. S. Lewis says, "The laziest boy in the class is the one who works hardest in the end,"[1] cramming for final exams! When he finally wakes up, he becomes envious of those sharp minds that have worked hard. Horace said, "If you don't call for a book and light before daybreak, . . . envy . . . will keep you awake in torment."[2]

Excuses abound. Lazy farmers are deterred by unfavorable weather. Small difficulties make big alibis. But, *If you are too lazy to plow, don't expect a harvest* (CEV). Indolence freezes us in mediocrity. Spiritual laziness is most dangerous of all. People use the most insignificant reasons to procrastinate their being squared away with God. Horace said, "Why . . . , if aught is eating into your soul, [do] you put off the time of cure till next year? [It] is like the bumpkin waiting for the river to run out. Yet on it glides."[3] Eventually, many will join in Israel's lamentable dirge, sighing, "The harvest is past, the summer is ended, and we are not saved" (Jer. 8:20)!

---

[1] C. S. Lewis, *Mere Christianity* (New York: Macmillan, 1960) p. 153.
[2] Horace, *Satires, Epistles, Ars Poetica* (Cambridge, MA: Harvard U. Press, 1991) Epistle II, Book I, p. 265.
[3] *Ibid.*

334 Their Actions and Our Attitudes

Like one who seizes a dog by the ears is a passer-by who meddles in a quarrel not his own. / Like a madman shooting firebrands or deadly arrows / is a man who deceives his neighbor and says, "I was only joking!" / As charcoal to embers and as wood to fire, so is a quarrelsome man for kindling strife (26:17, 18, 19, 21 NIV).

The ancient sage uses three similes to depict three kinds of strife-makers—the meddler, the madman, and the miffer. The meddler pushes his way into quarrels, like one who takes a bulldog by the ears enraging the dog. That is different from a would-be mediator who attempts to bring peace. This person gets in the fracas for the fun of it, and gets gashed by canine tusks.

The madman deceives a neighbor for sport, getting his giggles by enraging the neighbor, and defending himself by pretending it was in jest. Paul condemned "silly talk and coarse jesting" (Eph. 5:4 NASB). Peter denounced those who "revel in their deceptions" (2 Pet. 2:13 NASB). Shakespeare's Brabanto describes our appropriate response to deception: "So let the Turk of Cyprus us beguile; / We lose it not so long as we can smile."[1]

The miffer is miffed at the world and attempts to miff everybody else. Rather than rushing into existing strife or creating strife for sport, he "kindles strife," not for fun but from anger. His rage ignites raging fires and fuels the flames to keep them blazing. He gets sickly satisfaction from doing to others the injustice that has been done to him. Granted he has been hurt and needs to be healed, but being cantankerous to others does not heal the hurt.

Among all the nuisances, handling ourselves is a challenge. Aurelius remarked, "To fly from one's own badness is possible, but to fly from another man's badness is impossible."[2] We feel like Portia who said, "There is not one among them but I dote on his very absence."[3] One thing is sure: Controlling our own attitude is easier than controlling everybody else's actions.

---

[1] Shakespeare, *Othello*, Act I, Scene 3, lines 210-211.
[2] Marcus Aurelius, *The Thoughts of the Emperor* (New York: John B. Alden, publisher, 1887) p. 121.
[3] Shakespeare, *The Merchant of Venice*, Act I, Scene 2, lines 120-121.

. . . a flattering mouth works ruin. / . . . deceitful are the kisses of an enemy (26:28; 27:6 NASB). Also 28:23).

The ideal is to be genuinely complimentary. It is even okay to use hyperbole—to exaggerate either to make your point or for playful jesting—*if it is recognized* as hyperbole. Inhibited persons are too tightly scripted to give spontaneous praise. They need to break out of social inhibitions. The world needs encouragers. Millions of people are plagued with inferiority, and they need support props. Every person can be a minister of encouragement. It can begin by giving an honest compliment. We need to be unselfish enough to have real interest in the accomplishments of other persons.

Problem is, most of us are vulnerable to compliments. Even when it is recognized as flattery, most of us would prefer to hear people brag on us than brag on themselves. And therein lies its danger. Flattery has enormous power, especially over those with anemic egos. It can be used to win a favor, to get a vote, or to make a sale. We need to be cautious of receiving compliments that have a veiled agenda attached.

These proverbs not only warn of the danger of *receiving* fake flattery, but also of *giving* counterfeit compliments. We must be sure we are not exploiting a person's emotional needs for our own agenda.

Phony flattery is flat-out falsehood! It is hypocritical because it is under the guise of sincerity. Shakespeare's Antonio exclaimed to Shylock, "The devil can cite scripture for his purpose. An evil soul producing holy witness is like a villain with a smiling cheek, a goodly apple rotten at the heart. O, what a goodly outside falsehood hath!"[1]

Selfishness alone is evil enough. But to exploit other persons by manipulating their psychological needs with blatant falsehoods for selfish gain is to stand in the shoes of Judas Iscariot! To "deceive with the kisses of an enemy" is shameful sham!

---

[1] Shakespeare, *The Merchant of Venice*, Act I, Scene 3, lines 99-103.

336 Vanishing Vapor

Do not boast about tomorrow, for you do not know what a day may bring forth (27:1 NKJV, and others).

Time is slippery. We cannot get a grip on it. Golden moments of opportunity slide through our fingers, like Poe's "grains of golden sand" that "creep / Through my fingers to the deep, / While I weep—while I weep!"[1] Gibran said, "Yesterday is but today's memory and tomorrow is today's dream."[2] On time's continuum, the present moment is all that we can claim as our own. Aurelius said we "cannot lose either the past or the future, for . . . a man cannot lose a thing if he has it not."[3] As the moments click by, we lose exactly one moment for every new one we gain. Scott said, "Time rolls his ceaseless course."[4] Swinburne wrote, "Laurel is green for a season, and love is sweet for a day; / But love grows bitter with treason, and laurel outlives not May."[5] William Cullen Bryant mused, "The long train of ages glides away."[6]

When Uncle Tom was taken from his family in chains, a line of Holy Writ kept running through his mind, "We have here no continuing city" (Heb. 13:14).[7] Time's rapid speed is a blessing in difficult circumstances, but it can be a bane. At every moment, we must be ready to live without the past, and either *with* the future or *without* the future, whichever comes first. Longfellow spoke of "tomorrow" as "the mysterious, unknown guest."[8]

---

[1] Edgar Allan Poe, "A Dream Within a Dream," Gordon N. Ray, ed., *Masters of American Literature* (Boston: Houghton Mifflin, 1959) p. 153.

[2] Kahlil Gibran, *The Prophet* (New York: Alfred A. Knoph, 1926) p. 70.

[3] Marcus Aurelius, *The Thoughts of the Emperor* (New York: John B. Alden, publisher, 1887) p. 56.

[4] Sir Walter Scott, *The Lady of the Lake* (New York: New American Library, 1962) Canto Third, Sec. I, p. 70.

[5] Algernon Charles Swinburne, "Hymn to Proserpine," Abrams, ed., *The Norton Anthology . . .* (New York: W. W. Norton Co.., 1962) Vol. 2, p. 1044.

[6] W. C. Bryant, "Thanatopsis," *Adventures in American Lit* (New York: Harcourt, Brace & World, 1963) p. 510.

[7] Harriet Beecher Stowe, *Uncle Tom's Cabin* (New York: Everyman's Library, 1994) p. 135.

[8] Henry Wadsworth Longfellow, "Tomorrow," in Longfellow, *Best Loved Poems* (Chicago: The Spencer Press, 1949) p. 301.

To Glory in God's Glory 337

Let another praise you, and not your own mouth, a stranger, and not your own lips (27:2 RSV, NASB).

Everyone knows that everyone is partial toward himself, so self-commendation is not convincing. Since strangers are impartial toward strangers, their compliments ring true.

When we brag on ourselves, our imaginations spin heroic scenarios. We pad our résumés without even knowing it. We make up our faces for the cameras. Soon we get to believing our own exaggerations. And the persons we really *are* sit alone, isolated, with no identity. Goethe wrote: "Why, on the whole, thou'rt what thou art. / Set wigs of million curls upon thy head. To raise thee / Wear shoes an ell in height—the truth betrays thee, / And thou remainest—what thou art."[1] What we are is really diminished by pretending to be what we are not. We do better to build on what we are, for others to recognize our value, than to build air castles that burst.

The first item in the Shorter Catechism reads: "Man's chief end is to glorify God and to enjoy Him forever."[2] Attempting to glorify ourselves is disappointing because others recognize that we are not glorious. When Dante took a fictitious visit to the area of purgatory where the arrogant were punished, he met a man who exclaimed, "O empty glory!"[3] The self-glory of arrogance is so empty! Only God is glorious enough to thrill us with His glory. He glorifies us by giving us the glory of glorifying Him. God so wishes to share His glory with us that He glories in our glorying in Him. We glory in His glory, and He glories in our glorying in His glory. Not because He is vain, but because His glory is so real! By allowing us to glory in His glory, He demonstrates the value He places on us! When we bow out of the crusade to win glory for ourselves and learn the thrill of glorifying God, we will "enjoy Him forever."

---

[1] Goethe, *Faust*, First Part, Scene 4, p. 70.

[2] G. I. Williamson, *The Shorter Catechism* (no city: Presbyterian and Reformed Publishing Co., 1976) Vol. I, p. 1.

[3] Dante, *The Divine Comedy* (New York: Random House, 1932) "Purgatorio," Canto XI, p. 254.

338 Primeval Evil

Wrath is cruel and anger a torrent, but who is able to stand before jealousy (27:4 NKJV)?

"The more I see pleasures about me, so much more I feel torment within me. . . . Only in destroying [do] I find ease from my relentless thoughts. . . . [I hope] to taste of pleasure, but all pleasure to destroy, save what [comes] in destroying."[1] That soliloquy, placed in Satan's mouth by Milton, speaks of the potent power of jealousy as a primeval evil.

The word has two definitions, a good and a bad. Good jealousy refers to zeal in guarding one's worthy possessions with vigilance. In that sense, God said, "I am a jealous God" (Ex. 20:5). To be jealous *for* something or someone indicates it is held in high esteem or affection.

Bad jealousy is different. It means to be jealous *of* something or someone that you wish belonged to you. It is a grudging attitude of rivalry that grows with animosity until it becomes viciously malicious. In the proverb, its evil is accented in contrast to the very strongest anger. Wrath can become impetuous like a rushing, raging torrent, but jealousy sweeps cleaner than a flood. Anger can be appeased, but jealousy grows more intense. Angry people let you know how they feel, but jealous people conceal their feelings while scheming devious designs for revenge. Jealousy creeps along craftily, gaining momentum and intensity. It penetrates deeply, driving a person with vengeance. Anger can be mollified, but jealousy is as relentless as a bulldozer! Before its blade, no one can stand. Earlier in Proverbs, Solomon said, "Jealousy enrages a man, and will not spare in the day of vengeance" (6:34 NASB). That ancient disposition is a modern danger. Primeval evil becomes primetime evil!

Much of jealousy is self-torture from imagined scenarios. Shakespeare said, "Jealous souls . . . are not jealous for the cause. . . . 'Tis a monster begot upon itself, born on itself."[2]

---

[1] John Milton, *Paradise Lost* (Indianapolis: ITT Bobbs-Merrill Educational Pub. Co., 1962) Book IX, p. 206, 215.
[2] Shakespeare, *Othello*, Act III, Scene 4, lines 159-162.

Open rebuke is better than love carefully concealed (27:5 NKJV).

How can anyone tolerate those who are sticky with sentimental syrup? Some of us recoil from those who melt and run all over you, like southern sorghum in July!

With that disclaimer, however, I sympathize with those many persons who are inhibited from expressing affection. Imprisoned in their relational patterns, they are more socially comfortable, even in the home, when couched inside their inhibitions. Some of them love, but their spouses and children do not feel it—because they cannot express it.

Many people are freezing for lack of love. Gibran said, "Life is divided into two halves, one frozen, the other aflame; the burning half is love." Then he prayed, "Make me, O Lord, nourishment for the blazing flame. Make me, O God, food for the sacred fire."[1]

Of course, nonverbal expression is included. The verbal rides in on facial expression, and is authenticated be consistent action and attitude, otherwise the words are empty. Looking a person in the eye with softness, rather than harshness, speaks volumes. Shakespeare's Lysander, referring to the eyes, warned you can "overlook love's stories written in love's richest book."[2]

One way love is expressed is by candid rebuke. But the spirit in which it is given reveals whether it comes as a put-down from vindictiveness or as a genuine concern from camaraderie. Reproof should be given solicitously rather than harshly. It can be strong as needed, without apology, but still given in a supportive way with personal warmth—"speaking the truth in love" (Eph. 4:15). Love has a moral dimension that entails rebuking in urgent circumstances, but only from someone who has won the right to give reproof. When a friend needs strong admonition from a friend, keeping quiet communicates a lack of concern. Silence is no indication of love.

---

[1] Kahlil Gibran, *Thoughts and Meditations* (New York: The Citadel Press, 1960) pp. 89-90.
[2] Shakespeare, *A Midsummer Night's Dream*, Act II, Sc. 2, lines 121-122.

340 Deceptive Delicacies

A man full-fed refuses honey, but even bitter food tastes sweet to a hungry man (27:7 NEB).

Human personality works in strange ways. Eating chocolate sharpens the appetite for chocolates. Getting more makes you want more. Indulgence becomes addictive

Barring chemical addiction, however, *over*indulgence works the opposite way. Full stomachs reduce appetite and empty stomachs produce appetite. Pampered epicures do not get the pleasure from exquisite cuisine that a hardworker gets from a hamburger. In Jesus' story, the well-fed elder brother refused to eat veal cutlets and the hungry brother grabbed at pods of pig food (Lu. 15). Overeating for pleasure reduces the pleasure of eating. Self-control is rewarded with good appetite.

For sensate persons, appetite-control is generally basic to handling greater temptations. The world's first recorded temptation was about food (Gen. 3), after which, said Milton, "Sensual appetite . . . , usurping over reason, claimed superior sway."[1] Jesus was assaulted with temptation for food at a moment after He had fasted 40 days (Matt. 4). The easiest way to handle temptation is to give in. Oscar Wilde's character said, "I can resist everything except temptation."[2] Refusing temptation can intensify it. Jesus resisted to the end. Milton says His temptation was like "surging waves against solid rock."[3]

Gibran said, "Your soul is . . . a battlefield, upon which your reason . . . wages war against your . . . appetite."[4] Office workers should remove the dish of candy from the office desk. Another wise man said, "Do not crave . . . delicacies, for that food is deceptive. / Put a knife to your throat if you are given to gluttony" (Prov. 23:3, 2 NIV). And that is strong language!

---

[1] John Milton, *Paradise Lost* (Indianapolis: ITT Bobbs-Merrill Educational Pub. Co., 1962) Book IX, p. 233.

[2] Oscar Wilde, "Lady Windermere's Fan," *The Works of . . . Wilde* (Cambridge, Eng.: Blitz Editions, 1990) p. 373.

[3] John Milton, *Paradise Regained* in *The Portable Milton* (New York: Penguin Books, 1949) Book IV, p. 592.

[4] Kahlil Gibran, *The Prophet* (New York: Alfred A. Knoph, 1926) p. 57.

Homeless at Home 341

Like a bird that wanders from her nest, so is a man who wanders from his home (27:8 NASB).

At one time, the majority of Americans lived in small communities that had their own social ethos and cultural mores that gave social support for good behavior and social stigma to bad. When we became a mobile society, social roots were cut and emotional ties were broken, creating the temptation for moral discontinuity. The dazzling lights of the city outshone the values of the small community. God was often left behind, along with religious values.

Many kinds of employment require domestic mobility, not least of which is Christian ministry. Some persons, however, crave novelty that gives a roving instinct. Pastures always look greener across the creek. The proverb is a caution against a fickle mindset for hasty change. Wandering from home gives a person a wandering mind that those who remain in place may not have. Moral and emotional change often comes with the new venue.

The lesson is amplified to include those who leave home emotionally while remaining in the same house. An imagination in overdrive fabricates fantastic scenarios to be explored. Synthetic relationships in chat rooms isolate one emotionally from the family. At best, they are counterfeit relationships. Others get started on internet pornography and live phony lives of pretension as homeless persons in their own homes. Pornography is addictive! It will clutch you with its tentacles until your life is choked out! Jude speaks of those who morally roam and rove, like "wandering stars, for whom blackest darkness has been reserved" (Ju. 13 NIV).

Marcus Aurelius said, "The soul is dyed by the thoughts."[1] Paul said, "Whatever is true, whatever is noble, whatever is right, whatever is pure . . . think about such things" (Phil. 4:8 NIV). The proverb is a plea: Pack up your wandering thoughts, and bring them back home.

---

[1] Marcus Aurelius, *The Thoughts of the Emperor* (New York: John B. Alden, publisher, 1887) p. 87.

342 Impelling Influence

As iron sharpens iron, so one man sharpens another. / . . . a man's counsel is sweet to a friend. / . . . not . . . by words alone (27:17 NIV; 27:9 NASB; 29:19 NASB). Also 22:11.

Like "force fields" in outer space, human personalities emit a field of influence that is hard to resist. In a commercial, the person that promotes the product has more marketing value than the product itself. The entertainment industry depends on a constant parade of pleasing personalities. Churches want pastors with powerful pulpit personalities. Good leadership requires a person with a relational personality. Those who bury their personal qualities in meticulous control or academic pedantry do not make good leaders or good instructors.

We humans are enamored, almost enchanted, by other pleasing personalities. We become voluntary slaves to their influence. That is the peril of bad influence and the profit of good. Iron can either dull iron or sharpen it. We need to wear raincoats to shed bad influence while emitting good influence. In Paradise, Dante was enthralled by a good "spirit shade" and said to him, "You so lift me that I am more than I!"[1] The company we keep will either drag us down or boost us up. Virgil in Limbo said to Dante, "Love, kindled by virtue, hath ever kindled other love."[2] That is to say that good love produces good love in others.

Roy Croft wrote: "I love you, / Not only for what you are, / But for what I am / When I am with you. / . . . Not only for what / You have made of yourself, / But for what / You are making of me. / . . . You are helping me to make / Of the lumber of my life / Not a tavern / But a temple. / . . . You have done it / By being yourself."[3] Our influence is impelling! We are contagious! Being with us, others get either worse or better. We are either a perilous liability or a priceless asset!

---

[1] Dante, *The Divine Comedy* (New York: Random House, 1932) "Paradiso," Canto XVI, p. 502.
[2] Dante, *op. cit.,* "Purgatorio," Canto XXII, p. 321.
[3] Roy Croft, "Love," MacKenzie, ed., *Best Love Poems* (Garden City, NY: Garden City Books, 1946) pp. 15-16.

He who tends a fig tree will eat its fruit, and he who guards his master will be honored (27:18 RSV).

The point is that regular righteousness will be rewarded. Goodness is primarily a relational matter, and diligence in relationships will generally be honored. But the diligence is not for the purpose of rewards, but for the persons with whom we relate. Otherwise it would be neither goodness nor genuine relationships. In appreciation to his faithful general, King Duncan said, "Let me . . . hold thee to my heart." Banquo responded, "There if I grow, the harvest is your own."[1] Such a double-knit fabric of relationship is its own reward to both participants.

Tending an orchard and attending a superior are alike in that both will be honored. But the honor at times is intrinsic rather than overt. Serving Christ is sometimes belittled as a reward-focused activity. Servants are called opportunists, like cozying up to the boss for a bonus benefit. But real servants share in their master's honor by contributing to it. They have abandoned making a name for themselves. They are honored when their master is honored.

Beyond that, seeing the Master's smile of approval is its own reward. Christian servants are pleased when the Master is pleased. That reward is focused on Christ's feeling rather than their own. It is not stained with self-interest. It is clean! Hearing Him say "Well done, faithful servant" (Matt. 25:21 NIV) will be sweeter reward than the sweet luscious taste of a fresh ripe fig!

As Beowulf lay dying, he said, "I abode by the lot assigned, . . . courted no quarrels, swore no false oaths. And now for all this . . . my heart is glad."[2] As Saint Paul awaited his own execution at Nero's bloody block, he could say more than Beowulf: "I have finished my course, I have kept the faith. Henceforth there is laid up for me a crown of righteousness" (2 Tim. 4:7-8 KJV). Jesus said, "If anyone serves Me, the Father will honor him" (Jno. 12:26).

---

[1] Shakespeare, *Macbeth*, Act I, Scene 4, lines 31-33.
[2] *Beowulf the Warrior*, Ian Serraillier, tr. (New York: Henry Z. Walck, Inc., 1961), p. 87.

344 Face to Face

As in water face reflects face, so the heart of man reflects man (27:19 NASB).

This translation may accommodate two interpretations of this puzzling proverb. The first is that *a person's heart reveals what the person really is*—"a man's heart reflects the man" (NIV, NKJV). Unfortunately, we often reverse the phrase to mean a person's face reflects the heart. We have judged people by their worst faults and failures, refusing to look beneath the crude exterior. Paracelsus bemoaned, "I saw no good in man to overbalance all the wear and waste . . . In my own heart love had not been made wise."[1] Attempting to see the good behind their callous expressions will shape our own attitudes. You only know people when you know their hearts.

The second interpretation is that *the attitudes you express toward others will be reflected back to you*—". . . so are the hearts of men to one another" (Bas); ". . . so one man's heart answers another's" (NEB). Hawthorne said both love and hate are alike in that "each . . . supposes a high degree of . . . heart-knowledge."[2] When others read your heart, they respond in like attitude.

Smile into a mirror and it will smile back at you. Frown and you will be frowned upon. People reflect back the attitudes you project—sarcasm for sarcasm, hate for hate, love for love. If your first move in relating with a person is simply proper, you allow him or her to set the relational tone as either warm or cool. If you break out of the gate with personal warmth, you get the jump on the other person. You get a head start. You have set the initial mood for the relationship. Every new face should be met with a warm heart. An unknown person wrote, "I went out to find a friend, / But could not find one there. / I went out to be a friend, / And friends were everywhere!"[3] Face-to-face encounters can become heart-to-heart relationships.

---

[1] Robert Browning, "Paracelsus," *The Complete . . . Works . . .* (Cambridge, MA: Houghton Mifflin, 1895) p. 48.
[2] Nathaniel Hawthorne, *The Scarlet Letter* (New York: Books, Inc., n.d.) p. 211.
[3] Paul Lee Tan, ed., *Encyclopedia or 7,700 Illustrations* (Rockville, MD: Assurance Publishers, 1979) p. 464.

Compliments and Criticism 345

Gold and silver are tested in a red-hot furnace, but we are tested by praise (27:21 CEV).

The noble lord married a worthy young commoner and brought her into a life of luxury and popular esteem. After awhile, the nobleman abandoned her for a woman with a higher social pedigree. Deeply disappointed but without complaining, the forsaken woman went back to a life of poverty. The clerk commented, "No wonder, though, for while in high estate, / Her soul kept ever full humility."[1] Chaucer's point is well made: If you do not prioritize the applause, you can lose it without sustaining a loss. You cannot lose the pride that you do not have.

The praise test is like a furnace for testing precious minerals. Impurities and dross will rise to the top, or else a character of pure gold! C. S. Lewis points out that "pleasure in being praised is not pride" when the pleasure comes from pleasing "someone you wanted to please." But when you start delighting in yourself rather than in pleasing another, it is self-centered.[2]

Attaching our egos to the praise we receive places us in a perilous position. When the props fall, we have no back-up support. We collapse, and are exposed. Many people can handle criticism better than compliments. They can suffer pain without complaining but cannot get praise without bragging. Being a good winner is more difficult than being a good loser. But a poor winner is fragile. Blown-up egos can be punctured. Only inflated egos can be deflated!

If we are committed to Christ, we do not belong to ourselves. Since we belong to Him, the good that comes to us goes to Him, and the bad that comes, He is willing to take. We are His rather than our own, so we have nothing to lose! Our gains are His gains and our losses His losses. What a way to live! We desperately need to get our emotions attached to that kind of commitment!

[1] Chaucer, "The Clerk's Tale," *Canterbury Tales* (Garden City, NY: Garden City Pub. Co., 1934) p. 400.
[2] C. S. Lewis, *Mere Christianity* (New York: The Macmillan Co., 1960) p. 97.

346 Prosperity Projects

Be sure you know the condition of your flocks, give careful attention to your herds. / . . . The lambs will provide you with clothing, and / . . . you will have plenty of goats' milk to feed you and your family (27:23-27 NIV). Also 22:13; 26:13.

This beautiful idyllic scene should be read in its entirety from the scripture. The verses here omitted say that some things like riches and even ruling crowns are by nature impermanent. But cattle and crops can be extended indefinitely for human support. They require, however, constant vigilance and careful attention to seasonal cycles.

We humans have the tendency to maneuver and manipulate for huge financial returns, while allowing economic continuity to collapse. Some score big, while others do not survive. Most successful businesspersons, however, succeed by precise planning and careful calculation. Most survival systems do not run themselves. They require attention to details and frequent tweaking. Economic survival is not for sluggards.

Of the young commoner whom Chaucer's lord chose for a wife, the clerk said: "She knew work well, but knew not idle ease. / . . . A few sheep grazing in a field she kept, / For she would not be idle till she slept."[1] Successful shepherdesses fall into seasonal rhythms.

When work is available, joblessness comes not from fears of failure or feelings of inadequacy as much as from indolence. Work-shy people fabricate all sorts of fancied difficulties to keep them idle, like "imagining lions in the street" (22:13; 26:13). Then they are plagued with financial failure and simultaneously bored with nothing to do. St. Clare, dull from inactivity, complains, "What on earth is the use of time to a fellow who has twice as much of it as he knows what to do with?"[2] Relief from poverty comes from work. The remedy for slothfulness is self-motivation.

---

[1] Chaucer, "The Clerk's Tale," *Canterbury Tales* (Garden City, NY: Garden City Pub. Co., 1934) p. 380.

[2] Harriet Beecher Stowe, *Uncle Tom's Cabin* (New York: Everyman's Library, A. Knoph, Inc., 1994) p. 238.

Courage or Cowardice 347

The wicked flee when no one pursues, but the righteous are bold as a lion (28:1 NKJV).

In Homer's *Odyssey*, the goddess Athena said to Odysseus, "Fear not in thine heart, for the dauntless man is the best . . ."[1] Emerson said, "The hero is not fed with sweets, / Daily his own heart he eats."[2] Goethe decried the spineless multitudes who go with popular influence: "Awhile with halting minds the masses go, / Then ride the stream, wherever it may flow."[3]

Of course, many evil people have brazen audacity, which is more folly than courage. Impious people have legitimate reasons to fear. Shadows of guilt stalk their footsteps. Ghouls of their past can haunt their breath. Without cover, their backs are bare. Hamlet said, "Conscience does make cowards of us all."[4] Virgil's Queen Dido said, "An ignoble spirit is always revealed by fear."[5] God said, "The sound of a shaken leaf shall cause them to flee" (Lev. 26:36). Shakespeare said, "Cowards die many times before their deaths; the valiant never taste of death but once."[6]

Devout believers do not have to look over their shoulders. God said, "Fear not, for I am with you" (Is. 43:5). He's got our backs, so confidence can dispel fear. Many evil persons are brave without a basis. Fearlessness comes from folly. The righteous have a basis for boldness. They can be gallant from God's grace.

After Beowulf died in a valiant struggle with the fire dragon, Wiglaf, the one helper who did not defect, pondered the crowd's cowardice in light of the hero's death and exclaimed, "Better a man should die than live a coward's life."[7]

[1] Homer, *The Odyssey of Homer*, Butcher & Lang, trs. (New York: The MacMillan Co., 1911) Book VII, p. 78.
[2] Ralph Waldo Emerson, "Heroism," *The Viking Book of Poetry* (New York: Viking Press, 1958) Vol. II, p. 807.
[3] Goethe, *Faust*, Taylor, tr. (New York: The Macmillan Co., 1937) Second Part, Act IV, Scene 2, p. 437.
[4] Shakespeare, *Hamlet*, Act III, Scene 1, line 83.
[5] Virgil, *The Aeneid* (London: Penguin Books, 1958) Book Four, p. 97.
[6] Shakespeare, *Julius Caesar*, Act II, Scene 2, lines 32-33.
[7] *Beowulf the Warrior*, Ian Serraillier, tr. (New York: Henry Z. Walck, Inc., 1961) p. 46.

348 Justice and Mercy

Evil men do not understand justice, but those who seek the Lord understand it fully (28:5 NIV).

What is called "cognitive fluency" is a hot topic in psychology. Grasping difficult concepts does not come easily for those who are negatively affected. I have talked with criminals in state correctional institutions who think incarceration is a matter of mistreatment deserving sympathy. They have little concept of retributive justice. Cognitive roadblocks divert them from the principle of rectitude. People lose ethical discernment in proportion to their evil.

Because we have sinned, we detest the judgment of justice and love the notion of mercy. We even get the idea that justice is something bad while mercy is good. Forgetting that both are entailed in the notion of moral goodness, we get the idea that God is a cushy softy. Actually, however, without embracing both justice and mercy, God would be less than morally good. Milton depicts God as saying, "In mercy and justice both . . . shall my glory excel, but mercy . . . shall brightest shine."[1] When Dante approached purgatory, his guide said, "The height of justice is not abased [when God shows mercy], because the fire of [His] love fulfills in one moment" what justice owes those who have sinned.[2] Pascal said, "God's justice toward the [lost] is . . . less startling to us than His mercy toward the [saved]."[3]

Most Christians understand that God's mercy did not impede His moral justice. Rather God's mercy *fulfilled* His justice for those who turn to Him in repentance. At the crucifixion the sinless Son of God became the Savior. Human sins separated Christ from God, vicariously inflicting on Him the judgment of human sins. Mercy met justice's terms. Now justice bows to mercy in full support. For those who refuse His mercy, however, God's justice still functions.

---

[1] John Milton, *Paradise Lost* (Indianapolis: ITT Bobbs-Merrill Educational Pub. Co., Inc. 1962) Book III, p. 64.
[2] Dante, *The Divine Comedy* (New York: Random House, 1932) "Purgatorio," Canto VI, p. 224.
[3] Blaise Pascal, *Pensées* (London: Penguin Books, 1995) p. 121.

One who increases his possessions by . . . extortion gathers it for him who will pity the poor. / Whoever shuts his ears to the cry of the poor will also cry himself and not be heard (28:8; 21:13 NKJV).

Making money the wrong way and using it the wrong way are both condemned. Both are caused by poor attitudes from overvaluing material possessions. Good attitudes determine good actions, resulting in ethical acquisition of income, and frugality and generosity in its use.

Chaucer said, "Whoso will be content with poverty, I hold him rich, though not a shirt has he."[1] Good attitudes can better handle bad economic situations. Keeping control of oneself can help get the situation under control. Marcus Aurelius said, "Think not of what you have not, but of what you have. And think how eagerly you would have sought it if you did not have it."[2] An attitude of gratitude can make an unfortunate person happier than some with greater fortune.

Many large-income people are miserable, and need an attitude check.   Shakespeare said, "They are as sick that surfeit with too much as they that starve with nothing."[3] The wise Roman Emperor advised, "Receive [wealth] without arrogance, and be ready to let it go."[4] Detach your emotions from the possessions that will eventually detach themselves from you. Adjust your values and realign your attitudes. That will free you to be liberal toward those in need, and make you happy for making them happy!

The proverb says those who get it the wrong way will lose it. And God will not hear the cry of those who will not hear the cry of the poor. Those are weighty warnings!

---

[1] Chaucer, "The Tale of the Wife of Bath," *Canterbury Tales* (Garden City, NY: Garden City Pub. Co., 1934) p. 342.

[2] A paraphrase of Marcus Aurelius, *The Thoughts of the Emperor*)New York: John B. Alden, 1887) p. 112.

[3] Shakespeare, *The Merchant of Venice*, Act I, Scene 2, lines 6-7.

[4] Marcus Aurelius, *op. cit.*, p. 130. Brackets are included in the editor's translation.

350 Selfish Pleas or Sterling Prayer

If anyone turns a deaf ear to the law, even his prayers are detestable (28:9 NIV).

God responds to the prayers of His servants, not to those who pretend loyalty hoping to gain an advantage. The proverb connects grace with law, fellowship with obedience, special favors with servanthood. God does not read second-class letters of appeal. He does not open junk mail. He does not respond to spam! He is interested in a personal relationship. Milton says, "Prayer against His absolute decree no more avails than breath against the wind . . . Therefore to His great bidding I submit."[1]

Prayer is fellowship with God, and self-centered petitions are less than genuine prayer. Prayer plugs into God's purposes more than into our pleasures. Othello said, ". . . Heaven, I therefore beg it not / To please the palate of my appetite."[2]

All of God's laws are wrapped up in the two great commandments to love God and other people (Matt. 22:36-40). To want God to hear us without wanting to hear Him is to love ourselves more than God. To march into His presence with little concern for other people is presumptuous. Jane Merchant wrote: "My gratitude for good is small / Unless I ask Thy good for all."[3] Coleridge wrote: "He prayeth well who loveth well. . . . He prayeth best who loveth best."[4]

Those who refuse to hear deserve no more help than those who hear and refuse to heed. Ignorance of the law will not preempt the penalty. Those who decline to hear God cannot expect to be heard by God. All talking tongue and no hearing ear makes for poor fellowship God! He detests selfish pleas. He delights in sterling prayer.

---

[1] John Milton, *Paradise Lost* (Indianapolis: ITT Bobbs-Merrill Educational Pub. Co., 1962) Book XI, p. 273.

[2] Shakespeare, *Othello*, Act I, Scene 3, lines 262-263.

[3] Jane Merchant, "Unless I ask," *Every Good Gift* (Nashville: Abingdon Press, 1968) p. 29.

[4] Samuel Taylor Coleridge, "The Rhyme of the Ancient Mariner," Part VII, in Richard Aldington, ed., *The Viking Book of Poetry* (New York: The Viking Press, 1958) Vol. II, p. 697-698.

When the righteous triumph, there is great elation; but when the wicked rise to power, men go into hiding. / The sacrifice of the wicked is detestable—how much more so when brought with evil intent! (28:12; 21:27 NIV).

Some may wonder why Solomon keeps juxtaposing the wicked and the righteous, as if everyone is in one category or the other. Surely there are varying degrees of goodness and badness, and many people are near the borderline. Solomon, however, does not commit the fallacy of the excluded middle. The truth is that each person ultimately is on one side or the other. The line is severe, showing an infinite difference between the two sides.

Shakespeare's character said, "There's no bottom, none, in my voluptuousness. Your wives, your daughters, your matrons and your maids, could not fill up the cistern of my lust."[1] Evil is a bottomless pit, not because it is an equal opposite to the good, but because it is an aberration from goodness which itself is infinite. Goodness is the universal norm. Evil hides behind the good in a way that good does not hide behind the bad. An evil mask is only used in jest, but a good mask is seriously used to cover evil. People attempt to justify bad deeds, but never attempt to vilify good deeds. Morally, ours is not a dualistic universe.

Goodness has value quite apart from its good consequences. Because goodness is the norm, existing absolutely in the nature of God, its value is intrinsic, for its own sake. The righteous person identifies with the good for no greater *moral* reason than that goodness is good.[2] An unknown Greek poet long ago wrote: "For virtue only of all human things / Takes her reward not from the hands of others. / Virtue herself rewards the toils of virtue."[3] Righteous people love righteousness, bask in it, glory in it! Virtue is its own reward.

---

[1] Shakespeare, *Macbeth*, Act IV, Scene 3, lines 60-63.
[2] For *relational* and *affectionate* reasons, righteous people identify with goodness because they love God.
[3] Quoted by George Long, ed., "Introduction," Marcus Aurelius, *The Thoughts of the Emperor* (New York: John B. Alden, publisher., 1887) p. 39

352 To Cover or to Confess

He who covers his sins will not prosper, but whoever confesses and forsakes them will have mercy (28:13 NKJV).

A judge cannot pardon a person for what she has not done. To plead innocent is to reject mercy and plead for justice. Concealing our wrongs from public view may be advantageous until the truth comes out. But only a guilty plea to God positions one for pardon. Then God does better than a reduced sentence. He gives a full pardon! Every sin is erased from the record!

Beatrice said to Dante, "When self-accusation of sin bursts from the cheeks . . . , the grindstone is turned back against the edge."[1] That is, the sharp sword of justice is blunted. Mercy prevails.

Then the crushing implication of confession is replaced with a catharsis, an emotional cleansing, that is not possible when the guilt is suppressed. Getting it out, the guilt is absolved.

A willingness to renounce and forsake sin authenticates the sincerity of the confession. Forgiveness is not a license for indulgence. Isaiah said, "Let the wicked forsake his way . . . and the Lord will have mercy . . . and abundantly pardon" (Is. 55:7). Walking away from sin is called repentance, which is the condition in which "regeneration" (new birth and new life) takes place.

The next proverb (28:14, Essay 353) speaks of those whose hearts are hardened. But C. S. Lewis speaks of the attitude that "had nothing of the conspirator in it. It did not defy goodness. It ignored it . . ."[2] That nonchalant disposition toward God requires repentance as much as an antagonistic attitude. To accept forgiveness means you are willing to enter into a forgiven relationship with Christ. That requires more than acknowledging your sin. It means you are willing to turn from attitudes and activities that would hinder or damage the relationship.

The Hebrew psalmist sang, "Blessed is he whose transgression is forgiven (Ps. 32:1)!

---

[1] Dante, *The Divine Comedy* (New York: Random House, 1932) "Purgatorio," Canto XXXI, p. 379.
[2] C. S. Lewis, *Perelandra* (New York: Macmillan Pub. Co., 1944) p. 110.

Blessed is the man who always fears the Lord, but he who hardens his heart falls into trouble (28:14 NIV).

Aesop has a funny fable about a cat that fell in love with a young man. So Aphrodite changed the cat into a young woman to marry. On the wedding night, the goddess let loose a mouse in the nuptial chamber, and immediately the bride leaped out of bed to chase the mouse![1] In her heart, the bride was still a feline. Relating with God requires an inner change of heart . . .

. . . which includes what scripture calls repentance (See Matt. 3:2; 4:17; Lu. 13:3; Acts 3:19). In our natural state, C. S. Lewis says we are "opaque" to "the white light" of God, "molten to (our) desire."[2] We are chasing mice. Self-centered instead of God-centered, we need to do an about-face. Our focus needs a 180-degree shift

Repentance means more than feeling remorse or regret. It means we are willing to change. Remorse makes you hate yourself while you still love your sin. Repentance can make you hate your sin while you can respect yourself. Dante said, "The nettle of repentance . . . so did sting me that . . . [what had] turned me most to love it became most hateful to me."[3]

Milton's angelic choir sang to Satan, "Learn with awe to dread the Son of God."[4] For the unrepentant soul, to "fear the Lord" means no less. But for the regenerate soul, it means filial fear, the loving respect that leads a child to obedience. In the proverb, the "fear" of God's child stands out in stark contrast to the impudent defiance of the hard-hearted rebel. That childlike attitude of respect must continue through life. Dwight L. Moody said, "I have repented more since I came to Christ than before."[5]

---

[1] Aesop, *The Fables of Aesop* (New York: Dorset Press, 1975) p. 28.

[2] C. S. Lewis, *The Pilgrim's Regress* (Grand Rapids: Wm. B. Eerdmans Pub. Co., 1943) p. 177.

[3] Dante, *The Divine Comedy* (New York: Random House, 1932) "Purgatorio," Canto XXXI, p. 380.

[4] John Milton, *Paradise Regained* in *The Portable Milton* (New York: Penguin Books, 1949) Book IV, p. 609.

[5] Arthur Percy Fitt, *The Shorter Life of D. L. Moody* (Chicago: Moody Press, 1900) p. 44.

354 Resisting Reproof

[He] who hardens his neck after much reproof will suddenly be broken beyond remedy (29:1 NASB).

What we call volition, or will, can be either beneficial beyond belief or detrimentally destructive, determined by the way it is conditioned and what it is focused on. Turned toward self instead of God, it is the basis of sin. Presumably, evil first emerged when the "star of the morning" asserted five times against God, "I will" (Is. 14:12-14). Milton depicts Satan as gloating over his "unconquerable will . . . and the courage never to submit" to God.[1]

The hardened neck is a figure from an ox that tries to shake off the yoke until its neck is hardened. It speaks of those whose wills are stubborn, obstinate, and calloused, "estranged from all morality and full of corruption," said Dante.[2] Your will adjusts to the patterns you set. If the patterns are self-centered, your self-centered will takes control. You become a slave to yourself. You *cannot* break out of the syndrome simply because you *will not*. You still have will, but it is *controlled* will, not *free* will. Dante said, "Where . . . mind is joined to evil will, men can make no defense against it."[3] Eventually, your ration of reproofs is used up, your quota of second chances runs out, and you end in catastrophe. The proverb states the urgency of heeding reproof.

But some do heed reproof before it is too late. They take reproof, they repent, and grace kicks in. They get going in a life with God. They are redeemed! Like Charles Dickens' protagonist Sydney Carton. After a wasted life, the profligate got in gear with God, and sacrificed his life in an act of undaunted heroism to spare the man whose wife he loved. As he approached the guillotine, the final thought kept burning in his mind: "It is a far, far better thing that I do, than I have ever done. It is a far, far greater rest that I go to, than I have ever known."[4]

---

[1] John Milton, *Paradise Lost* (Indianapolis: ITT Bobbs-Merrill Educational Pub. Co., 1962) Book I, p. 9.

[2] Dante, *The Divine Comedy* (New York: Random House, 1932) "Inferno," Canto XXXIII, p. 179.

[3] *op. cit.*, Canto XXXI, p. 165.

[4] Charles Dickens, *A Tale of Two Cities* (New York: Books, Inc., n.d.) p. 374.

A man who flatters his neighbor spreads a net for his feet (29:5 RSV, NKJV).

On the second or third date with the girl I later married, I made a flattering remark, to which she placed a finger on my nose and warned, "Flattery will get you everywhere!"

As different from a sincere compliment, flattery is excessive and specious, and it portrays someone, or a feature of someone, too favorably. Note, however, the difference between innocent flattery and empty flattery. Innocent flattery is usually in jest and is intended to be understood as hyperbole. Sometimes it is used in sarcasm to make the opposite point.

Empty flattery is intended to *please* with the purpose to *deceive*—in order to profit oneself. It is the act of a schemer pretending to be an admirer, attempting to set a trap for personal advantage. It is the insidious strategy of a crafty conniver with devious designs to exploit those who are naïve. The flatterer spreads a network of words to trick the feelings and trip the feet of the victim. Though it cannot be proved in court, flattery is a fraud!

In the proverb, the first "his" refers to the flatterer and the second presumably to the flattered. But if the second "his" refers back to the flatterer, it highlights a more subtle principle, that trappers are trapped in their own traps. Exploiters are exploited by their own exploitation. Net-spreaders are tripped up in their own nets. Haters will be doomed by their own hatred. Marcus Aurelius said, "Does anyone do wrong? It is to himself that he does wrong."[1]

This rule of recompense sometimes works in even more subtle ways. Flatterers get to flattering themselves for their successful flattery. Soon they get to believing their own opinion of themselves. Their egos swell, filled with hot air, waiting to be punctured. When the collapse occurs and the ego slumps, flattery becomes flavorless—and flat!

---

[1] Marcus Aurelius, *The Thoughts of the Emperor* (New York: John B. Alden, publisher, 1887) p. 73.

356 A Snare or a Song

By transgression an evil man is snared, but the righteous sings and rejoices (29:6 NKJV).

Exercising the freedom to sin snares a person into bondage, but restricting oneself from sinning opens the gate to the road of freedom. Freedom and bondage work off each other. Violating freedom gives bondage, and voluntary bondage gives freedom. Down the road, the one who *uses* the freedom to sin *loses* the freedom *not* to sin. Sinning snares the soul in slavery.

In the "Inferno," Dante found evil souls that took root in the ground and became stunted trees, unable to move out of position, gnarled and knotted, with withered leaves, producing poison. Virgil queried, "Tell me how the soul gets bound up in these knots."[1] The answer is found in the human personality's delicate vulnerability to what Paul called "the mystery of lawlessness" (2 Thes. 2:7). The soul's freedom to be good provides its liability to be bad.

Created dependent rather than independent, we humans are made to be mastered. Freedom without boundaries is a false notion. If we refuse voluntary servitude to God, we become servants of self. With the awesome potential to be mastered by goodness, we carry the frightening vulnerability to the bondage of evil. Made to be *love*-slaves to God, we become *bond*-slaves to ourselves. Sin is enslaving! Freedom to sin is not freedom from the consequence of sin! Rudyard Kipling said, "Only the free are bound, and only the bound are free."[2] In Milton, the angel warned Adam, "Remember [the fallen angels], and fear to transgress."[3]

Peter wrote, "By what a man is overcome, by this he is enslaved" (2 Pet. 2:19 NASB). The choice is between a snare and a song, between slavery and singing. Real freedom comes in the willingness to be the right kind of slave, to the right Master, in the right way.

---

[1] Dante, *The Divine Comedy* (New York: Random House, 1932) "Inferno", Canto XIII, p. 73.
[2] Rudyard Kipling, *The Light that Failed* (New York: Books, Inc., n.d.) p. 59.
[3] John Milton, *Paradise Lost* (Indianapolis: ITT Bobbs-Merrill Educational Pub. Co., 1962) Book VI, p. 163.

The righteous is concerned for the rights of the poor . . . / He who is gracious to a poor man lends to the Lord, and He will repay him for his good deed (29:7; 19:17 NASB). Also 28:3.

Depicting the wealthy as industrious and the poor as lazy, or vice versa, is a fallacious reductionism. Groupings are not uniformly aligned. Both the "Haves" and the "Have-nots" include hardworkers and sluggards, and both categories include people who are both good and bad. Another proverb (28:3) speaks of poor people who are guilty of oppressing other poor people.

Attitude and character are more important than economic groupings. C. S. Lewis says we should love our belongings "enough to enrich our lives while we have them—not enough to impoverish our lives when they are gone."[1] Whatever economic category, people who are righteous are concerned with the needs of the poor. George Bernard Shaw is quoted as saying, "You have no right to consume happiness [or] wealth without producing it."[2]

When we help the poor, the proverb promises a return on our investment. When we favor the needy, we are favoring God (Matt. 25:45). When we give, God considers us His creditors. He makes Himself debtor for what is given. He credits the benefactor. "He will repay . . ." Jesus said, "Give and it will be given to you. A good measure, pressed down, shaken together and running over will be poured into your lap" (Lu. 6:38 NIV). The more you give, the more you are given. But if the motive for giving is getting, as a good business deal, the giver is not "gracious" and "concerned for the poor." Then the condition for benefits is not met. The return, however, may or may not be "in kind." When the compensation is not monetary, it could be meaningless to the miser with only entrepreneurial interests. A psalm says, "How blessed is he who considers the helpless" (Ps. 41:1)! Part of the blessing is the sheer joy of helping those who hurt.

---

[1] C. S. Lewis, *The Pilgrim's Regress* (Grand Rapids: Eerdmans Pub. Co., reprint 1979) p. 83.

[2] Manual Velasquez, *Philosophy: A Text with Readings* (Belmont, CA: Wadsworth, 7th edition 1999) p. 614.

358 Hotheads or Level Heads

Scorners set a city aflame, but wise men turn away anger (29:8 NASB).

Easily excitable people are easily excited by scorners and scoffers who play to public emotion more than rational wisdom. Cynical minds automatically oppose whatever is vilified by cynics and whatever is praised by optimists. Negative people resonate with negative ideas.

Irresponsible politicians appeal to cynics with fallacies of accent and straw man, buzzing out buzzwords for popular appeal. Soundbytes are calculated for maximum impact. Partisan politics has become a science that can be used to incite public clamor. In Solomon's day, cities were smaller, and word spread by mouth. Today, mass media can arouse the rancor of masses with the single surly snarl of a scorner. Aspiring leaders that are political beasts pounce on discontent for political advantage. They seize conflict to exploit it.

In America, our freedom from anarchy reflects the intelligence of the electorate and the wisdom of national leaders. Yet we need more politicians who are into conflict management and fewer into conflict manipulation. When uncontrolled scorn blazes out of control, we need level heads to counter hotheads. Virgil spoke of those with "savage passion" who chance to meet someone "whose character and record commands respect. . . . He will speak to them, calming their passions and guiding their energies."[1] We need more responsible leaders who can abate anger, allay passion, and extinguish the emotional flames that can torch a city.

James said, "Who among you is wise and understanding? . . . The wisdom from above is first pure, then peaceable, gentle, reasonable, full of mercy and good fruits, unwavering, without hypocrisy. And the seed whose fruit is righteousness is sown in peace by those who make peace" (Ja. 3:13, 17-18).

Jesus said, "Blessed are the peacemakers" (Matt. 5:9).

---

[1] Virgil, *The Aeneid* (London: Penguin Books, 1958) Book One, p. 32.

*If a wise man contends with a foolish man, whether the fool rages
or laughs, there is no peace* (29:9 NKJV).

The preponderant opinion is that this refers to litigation, but
there is likewise "no peace" in *personal* disputation with a person
of folly. Also some scholars think the "rage and laugh" refers to
the wise man rather than the fool, since the original only uses the
pronoun "he." If the wise person uses anger, the fool reacts with
more anger, and if he opts for pleasant congeniality, the fool takes
him as a pushover and laughs at him. Either way, the wise man
loses.

Probably the scenario does refer to a court scene and the
"rage and laugh" applies to the foolish person. If the fool loses the
suit he rages, and if he wins he laughs and taunts. So if the wise
man wins, he faces abuse, and if he loses he faces derision.
Whether heads or tails, "there is no peace." Either rage or
mockery will continue long after the suit is settled. Being daily
pricked by a disgruntled loser or a gloating winner creates clashing
relational discords like disharmonious music. Litigation can raise
greater problems than it solves.

Of course, the gravity of the offense must be factored into
the equation. But in most civil suits, peace should rate a higher
priority than winning a court decision. Othello said to his enemies,
"Keep up your bright swords, for the dew will rust them . . . You
shall more command with your years than with your weapons."[1]
Time itself corrects many problems. It should be given a chance.
Other strategies should be exhausted before resorting to litigation.
Paul said, "If it is possible, as much as depends on you, live
peaceably with all men" (Rom. 12:18).

Being willing to compromise can free your future from
facing rage. Being unwilling can freeze your future in derision.
Dealing with fools requires wisdom. Those who have it use it.
Paul said, "Live in peace, and the God of . . . peace will be with
you" (2 Cor. 13:11).

Jesus said, "Have peace" (Mk. 9:50).

---

[1] Shakespeare, *Othello*, Act I, Scene 2, lines 59-61.

360 Upside Down or Right-side Up

Bloodthirsty men hate a man of integrity and seek to kill the upright (29:10 NIV).

The scripture says Cain murdered Abel "because his actions were evil and his brother's were righteous" (1 Jno. 3:12). Both evil and righteousness are highlighted in contrast to the other. The human race embraces various worldviews, but the most diametrical positions are those of good and evil. Morally, righteous people are right-side up while evil people are upside down. But upside-down people think they are right-side up. So they see right-side-up people as upside down. To them, their moral position is the norm and all others are aberrations.

Unless worldviews entail principles of righteousness, groups with antithetical positions automatically fall into tension, competition, and antipathy. When nominal Christians claim the Christian worldview without embracing its moral code, they can slip easily into hostility.

Jesus embodied righteousness absolutely, and became the victim of a bloodthirsty socio-religious system of worldly evil that crucified Him. He said to His followers, "The world . . . hated Me before it hated you. If you were of the world, the world would love its own. Yet because you are not of the world, . . . the world hates you" (Jno. 15:18-19 NKJV).

At this point, a committed Christian has two responsibilities. The first is never to be an enemy to worldlings over their presuppositions. A thoroughly righteous position deplores evil without detesting evil people. The second is to take a forthright stance for righteousness even when persecuted for your position. Our commitment is not proved in public approval but in opposition. We are citizens of a higher kingdom, and we have a retreat center in the heart of God that the world does not have. Isaac Watts sang, "Should earth against my soul engage, / And fiery darts be hurled, / Then I can smile at Satan's rage / And face a frowning world!"[1]

---

[1] Isaac Watts, "When I Can Read My Title Clear," *Baptist Hymnal* (Nashville: Convention Press, 1956) p. 468.

A fool always loses his temper, but a wise man holds it back (29:11 NASB).

Referring to an obnoxious man, Portia said, "When he is best, he is a little worse than a man, and when he is worst, he is little better than a beast."[1] Mephistopheles said humans are "far beastlier than any beast."[2] When life deals bad breaks, some have no haven for resort, nothing positive to accent, no personal friendship with Christ, no resources for rising above the situation. Their only resort is rage. Queen Orual admitted she "had never been . . . in so much sorrow that my burning indignation did not rise above it."[3]

Expressing anger can give emotional release, but often at the cost of establishing an enslaving pattern. You lose good social inhibitions and start hurling verbal grenades. You have a short fuse. At the slightest provocation, tongues of angry flames leap out of the mouth like a blowtorch. Acting like a fool makes you a fool, and being a fool makes you act like a fool.

One option is to sit on the lid to keep all the crap inside. But then it erupts in the form of hostility or violence. Keeping it inside can cause a meltdown of the entire human mechanism.

Wise persons can "hold it back" because they have a resort. They have something bigger and better to which they can retreat. And they have developed the raw courage and tough character to throw the circuit breaker on the anger and switch off to higher purposes and values. Instead of feeding the feeling, they starve it out. If you vent a fire, the flame will flare. If you close the damper it will go out. In a temper tantrum, to make instant analysis for immediate resolution is too much to ask. A principle of conflict management is to back off. Horace said, "The wise man . . . is lord over himself . . . who bravely defies his passions."[4]

---

[1] Shakespeare, *The Merchant of Venice*, Act I, Scene 2, lines 94-96.

[2] Goethe, *Faust*, Prologue, p. 12.

[3] C. S. Lewis, *Till We Have Faces* (Grand Rapids: William B. Eerdmans Pub. Co., 1966) p. 247.

[4] Horace, *Satires, Epistles, Ars Poetica* (Cambridge, MA: Harvard U. Press, 1991) Satire VII, Book II, p. 231.

362 Communicated Commandments

Where there is no revelation, the people cast off restraint; but happy is he who keeps the law (29:18 NKJV).

The term "revelation" is a complement to "the law" in the second clause. It is sometimes translated "prophetic vision," referring to divine moral direction. God's moral guidance is for our benefit, both individually and collectively. What He requires of us is precisely what we need for living meaningful lives. "The commandment is a lamp, and the law is light" (Pr. 6:23).

But God gave us the moral option to obey or disobey. Good *behavior* can be imposed on a person, but *being* good is a matter of obedience that requires our choice. C. S. Lewis pointed out that we are subject to all sorts of natural laws like gravitation, inertia, biochemistry that control much of our lives. But moral law "is the one [we] can disobey if [we] choose."[1] By obeying or disobeying, we comply with or violate a higher law that makes us good or bad.

God's commandments are various expressions of the higher principle of moral value. Something is not wrong because God forbids it, but He forbids it because it is wrong. Rules are not the criteria for righteousness; rather righteousness is the criterion for the rules. They do not *determine* what is right or wrong. Rather they *describe* what is right or wrong.

The commandments are codified laws to communicate to us moral values we otherwise might miss. The Trojan Ilioness rebuked Queen Dido: "If you have no respect for mortal men, . . . you should at least remember that there are gods who know right from wrong."[2]

Not only has God communicated commandments to us, but He has given multiple signs and symbols as props for moral laws. Lon Woodrum wrote: "The stars marching endlessly on galactic night are shouting neon-signs that the Almighty is Author of Law and Order."[3]

---

[1] C. S. Lewis, *Mere Christianity* (New York: The Macmillan Co., 1960) p. 4.
[2] Virgil, *The Aeneid* (London: Penguin Books, 1958) Book One, p. 44.
[3] Lon Woodrum, *The Rebellious Planet* (Grand Rapids: Zondervan, 1965) p. 30.

He who pampers his servant from childhood will have him as a son in the end (29:21 NKJV).

A puzzling proverb. Most Old Testament scholars, rather than disagreeing about its meaning, simply admit they are not sure. The 3,000-year transition from Solomon to the "postmodern person" is laced with ambiguities. The last word of the text is variously translated "son," "weakling," "heir," "a bringer of grief." Most commentators agree that the proverb refers to something bad rather than good, as a son who is expensive and demanding.

Whatever the specifics, however, the underlying principle has been vigorously enunciated throughout the 20th century—that childhood conditioning presages the adult-to-be, as "morning shows the day."[1] Granting many additional variables, including the person's own free choice, adults are ordinarily products of the way they react or respond to childhood rearing. Adult life can grow and blossom or be stunted and twisted by the seedling experiences of childhood.

Pampered and petted with permissiveness, the child can become an indulgent and intemperate adult. Children who are given responsibility become responsible adults more easily. Milton said, "Who best can suffer best can do; [he] best [can] reign who first well hath obeyed."[2]

The principle behind the proverb suggests more than the proverb states. Children who are made to feel personal, relational love more easily learn to grow and thrive in love. If they are allowed to reciprocate love when small, they can become comfortable initiating love. Loving increases by loving, but it begins easily in the heart of a child who is loved. When Dante visited the fourth heaven, he came upon the spirit of Thomas Aquinas, who spoke to him of "the ray of grace, whereat true love is kindled, and then doth grow by loving, multifold."[3]

---

[1] John Milton, *Paradise Regained* in *The Portable Milton* (New York: Penguin Books, 1949) Book IV, p. 597.

[2] *op. cit.*, Book III, p. 584.

[3] Dante, *The Divine Comedy* (New York: Random House, 1932) "Paradiso," Canto X, p. 464.

364 Humility or Hostility

A man's pride will bring him low, but a humble spirit will obtain honor (29:23 NASB).

As soon as I start parading myself, I am in competition with all the others attempting to parade themselves. They fall out of my favor and I fall out of theirs. We become major-league opponents. Speaking of pride, C. S. Lewis said, "There is no fault which makes a man more unpopular. . . . The more we have it ourselves, the more we dislike it in others."[1] My pride keeps me from liking them, and my pride keeps them from liking me! Between us, all honor is lost.

In Paradise, Dante met a woman who had been assigned an inferior position, and he asked, "Do you desire a more lofty place?" To Dante, her answer was "so joyous that she seemed to burn in love's first flame." Piccarda answered, "Brother, . . . love maketh us long only for what we have, and giveth us no other thirst." Dante explained that we do not desire a different food while we are being satisfied by the food we are eating.[2]

Love relationships are satisfying, preempting the desire for superiority. Humble spirits have no problem with inferiority in relationships that are characterized with love. Humility is included in the nature of love. Pride precipitates hostility. Love fosters humility.

Our lives in the next life will be an extension of the lives we live in this life. John made clear that the new venue will be remarkabl y different (Rev. 22:3-5), but our lives will be surprisingly the same (vs. 11). The humility in love relationships begins today. In an old classic, Rebecca Springer wrote: "We cannot be selfish and unloving in one life and generous and loving in the next. The two lives are too closely blended—one but a continuation of the other."[3] Our pride will degrade and disgrace us, or our humility will exalt and extol us. Both here and hereafter!

---

[1] C. S. Lewis, *Mere Christianity* (New York: The Macmillan Co., 1960) p. 94.

[2] Dante, *The Divine Comedy* (New York: Random House, 1932) "Paradiso," Canto III, pp. 416-417.

[3] Rebecca Ruter Springer, *My Dream of Heaven* (Tulsa, OK: Harrison House, n.d.) p. 21. Originally published in 1898 as *Intra Muros*.

Cheated and Defeated 365

If you take part in a crime, you are your worst enemy, because even under oath you can't tell the truth (29:24 CEV).

Telling a lie is bad enough, but lying under the oath to tell the truth in order to cover another lie complicates the dilemma. The rogue is forced to perjure himself to keep from implicating himself. Shakespeare wrote of "a brave man, [who] . . . swears brave oaths and breaks them bravely."[1] Hamlet's queen said "guilt . . . spills itself in fearing to be spilt."[2]

From the first step in the wrong direction to being an accomplice in a crime to stonewalling the evidence with a cover-up, people wind themselves up in a maze with no outlet. Connecting the ominous dots from sin to sin creates an inextricable convolution! The journey charges full steam ahead, increasing momentum on a collision course. Each step becomes more daring, dashing headlong into catastrophe. The nature of evil is progressive!

Sinners are no less criminal to God than criminals are to the court. There can be no covert act against God. At the moment of our very first sinful act, we are apprehended.

When you lose yourself as a friend, you become "your worst enemy." You walk in the shoes, wear the face, and bear the guilt of the one you hate! You have to live twenty-four/seven with the person who has deceived you, cheated you, and defeated you! Contemptible, you become only the shell of the human that God made you to be. The problem should have been dealt with far upstream, long before it got here. Now you are carried downstream to the precipice.

An eternity of difference stands between those who force themselves into dishonesty and those who are honest with themselves. Those who have nothing to cover stand in league with Brutus who said, "I am so armed with honesty that [all threats] pass by me like the idle wind."[3]

---

[1] Shakespeare, *As You Like It*, Act III, Scene 4, lines 42-44.
[2] Shakespeare, *Hamlet*, Act IV, Scene 5, lines 19-20.
[3] Shakespeare, *Julius Caesar*, Act IV, Scene 3, lines 67-68.

366 Pandering for Partiality

Many seek the ruler's favor, but justice for man comes from the Lord (29:26 NASB, NKJV).

Here is Mephistopheles' riddle: "What's cursed and welcomely expected? / What is desired, yet always chased? / What evermore with care protected? / What is accursed, condemned, disgraced?" The answer came from the chancellor: "'Tis Justice!"[1]

Abused persons demand justice, but when they become abusers they do not want justice. The riddle shows how we vacillate between seeking the favorable side of justice and shunning its unfavorable side. But the positive and the negative are flip sides of each other. Having one without the other is not justice at all. It is partiality. Unfairness is opposite justice.

By law, Shylock could take a pound of Antonio's flesh because Antonio could not pay his debt. But by law, no one could shed another person's blood, and Shylock could not get the flesh without shedding blood. Insisting for justice to get the flesh, he brought justice on himself. In pushing for the positive side for himself, he became victim of the negative.[2] Justice, in order to be justice, has to work both ways. Shylock got more justice than he wanted.

Cozying up to a ruler or a judge for favors is an attempt to avoid the justice deserved. But for a judge to be unfair would not be right. God cannot show partiality without violating His nature of righteousness. "He cannot deny Himself" (2 Tim. 2:13). He is not influenced by threats or flattery. God cannot be bought off.

Wanting God to have good positive justice without good negative justice is asking God to be only half-good. The victim of God's justice who complains that God is not good is really upset that God is *too* good to be partial! An unjust judge may be influenced for favors, but God's *justice* is always *just*![3]

---

[1] Goethe, *Faust*, Second Part, Act I, Scene 2, pp. 216-217.
[2] Shakespeare, *The Merchant of Venice*, Act IV, Scene 1, lines 299ff.
[3] How then can God be just and forgive sins? The answer is found in the crucifixion of Christ, where God extended mercy by meticulously fulfilling justice.

Desires and Delicacies 367

Do not eat the bread of a selfish man or desire his delicacies. / For as he thinks within himself, so is he. He says to you, "Eat and drink!" But his heart is not with you. / You will vomit up the morsel you have eaten, and waste your compliments (23:6, 7, 8 NASB).
<u>These are not Solomon Proverbs.</u>

Dainties and delicacies can become decoys to draw one into disaster. When desires are hooked, they blunt one's taste for the ordinary. Common pleasures lose their fizz.

Horace said: "The chiefest pleasure lies not in costly savor. . . . The man who is bloated and pale with excess will find no comfort in oysters. . . . Aim at a fixed limit to your desires. The envious man grows lean while his neighbor waxes fat."[1]

The stingy miser in the proverb who says one thing while closely calculating the opposite is a microcosm of a deceitful world system that seems to be mathematically orchestrated by deception. Those without caution become mentally addicted to pleasure thrills that cannot be sustained. Then they are nauseated to realize they were duped.

In the inferno Dante came upon Ulysses' spirit in a flame of fire. At Dante's inquiry, the fire flickered and murmured "like a flame that struggles with the wind." Then Ulysses' voice came out of the flame bemoaning his "foolish flight" to "experience the world . . . and human vice."[2]

We can align our desires with the higher values of love, beauty, goodness, integrity, truth, devotion, and service, and eternity for us will be filled with pleasure beyond our ability to anticipate. Those desires will continually intensify by continual gratification, providing increasing pleasure! The psalmist sang, "In thy presence is fullness of joy. At thy right hand are pleasures for evermore" (Ps. 16:11 KJV). And—with those desires, heaven's pleasure begins in this life, with heaven in our hearts!

---

[1] Horace, *Satires, Epistles, Ars Poetica* (Cambridge, MA: Harvard U. Press, 1991) Satire II, Book II, pp. 137, 139; Book I, Epistle II, p. 267.
[2] Dante, *The Divine Comedy* (New York: Random House, 1932) "The Inferno," Canto XXVI, p. 140.

Index of Essay Titles

A

A Bribe in the Bosom   239
Accountable Adulthood   363
Acquitting and Accusing   231
A Crown or a Curse   64
Acted or Acted Upon   50
Adored or Abhorred   6
An Endless Hope or
    a Hopeless End   36
Animal Rage or
    Human Folly   228
Arousing Strife or
    Allaying Strife   165
A Shrinking Life or
    an Expanding Life   88
A Snare or a Song   356
Assertion or Affection   297
Association by
    Discrimination   315

B

Bad Days but
    Glad Hearts   162
Bad Wrath or Good Wrath   53
Bane or Blessing   19
Body Language or
    Verbal Language   9
Bound by the Bent   309
Bountiful Wisdom
    or Barren Folly   136
Bowing and Submitting   131
Brute Cruelty and
    Human Kindness   70
Built Up or Torn Down   39
Burning or Warming   286

C

Casting Lots and
    Flipping Coins   215
Cautious or Careless   128
Character Conditioning   250
Cheated and Defeated   365
Children and Parents   269
Clean Cribs or
    Stocked Stalls   117
Closed Minds or
    Open Ears   42
Commendable or
    Condemnable   221
Commended or Despised   68
Communicated
    Commandments   362
Compliments and Criticism   345
Concealing and Revealing   314
Conscience and
    Commandments   181
Consultation and Courage   169
Contention or Contentment   217
Correction and Reproof   157
Courage and Cowardice   347
Cracked and Crumbling   327
Critical and Gullible   252
Crooked Minds and
    Turned Tongues   236
Crude or Cultured   223

D

Damaging Deception   275
Dangerous Desires   243
Deceptive Delicacies   340
Decree of the Decalogue   266
Deeds and Destinies   109

Deep Fountains or
        Surface Runoff   246
Defense or Defeat   26
Delicious or Distasteful   254
Desires and Delicacies   367
Destination or Dead End   207
Destroyed or Delivered   38
Detestable or Delightful   29
Devil-like or Godlike   229
Devouring or Sharing   301
Diligent to Discipline   112
Directed or Driven   226
Disciplined with Diligence   3
Disgraced or Praised   106
Disguise with Guile   259
Disgusted or Delighted   268
Dispatching Delight   205
Disseminating
        Dissension   210
Distant Silence or
        Close Fellowship   176
Divine Detergent   279
Divine Displeasure
        and Delight   156
Doing Right and
        Being Safe   224

E

Earning without Burning   188
Economic Exploitation   313
Elated Mind and
        Dilated Eyes   294
Empty Head or Open Mind   274
Entrapped or Enlightened   66
Everything Seen,
        Nothing Concealed   150
Evil and Its End   184
Evil Sacrifices or
        Upright Prayers   155

F

Fabricating and
        Prevaricating   295
Face to Face   344
Failed Hope or
        Fulfilled Hope   100
Faithful Friends   258
Faithful Witness or
        False Witness   118
Fakes and Frauds   319
Falling for Flattery   312
False Friendships   257
Father of a Fool   237
Fathers and Children   222
Favor or Disfavor   62
Fearing but Fearless   138
Fear of Future or
        Hope of Heaven   21
Fight or Flight   86
Fit for a Fool   328
Fooling with a Fool   329
Foolish and Foodless   71
Foolish Tongue
        and Wise Lips   116
Folly Fun or Wise Walk   168
Formal Friends or
        Blood Brothers   233
Fountain of Life and
        Snares of Death   139
Fountain or Folly   202
Fraudulent Flattery   355
Friend or Fake   132
Friends and Finances   283
From Foes to Friends   187
Frozen or Flaming   339
Fulfilled or Foolish   107
Full Hands and
        Empty Heads   232
Futility and Stupidity   261
Futility or Utility   18

G

Gag on Glut 321
Giving and Receiving 55
Giving Out and
    Getting Back 90
Glory and Gray Hair 291
God's Purpose
    and Our Plans 180
God's Wisdom
    for Leadership 190
Good Desires
    or Bad Desires 52
Good Sport or Bad Sport 20
Gorging on Glory 326
Grace and Grit 44
Gracious Giving 357
Great Opportunity and
    Grave Obligation 15
Grief and Joy 125

H

Happy Heart and
    Barren Bones 238
Harsh Reaction or
    Gentle Response 148
Hasty Assets or
    Solid Gains 285
Hateful Hurts and
    Healing Help 78
Hating and Loving 11
Hating Bribes and
    Loving Bribers 174
Haughty Scoffing or
    Humble Seeking 119
Healing Hope or
    Wounding Words 151
Hearing and Heeding 220
Heart and Head 331
Heart Seeking and
    Mouth Feeding 161
Heavy Hearts and
    Helpful Words 85
Held Together or
    Torn Apart 114
Helping Talk or
    Hurting Talk 10
Helping the Hapless 143
Heritage Received,
    Heritage Given 110
Hidden but Visible 158
Higher Highway 197
Home and Family 58
Homeless at Home 341
Honor and Shame 31
Hope for a Half-wit 332
Hope of Heaven 25
Hostility or Fraternity 253
Hot Heads and
    Heartless Hearts 129
Hotheads or Level Heads 358
Humble or Haughty 199
Humility and Honor 179
Humility or Hostility 364
Hungry Spirits or
    Healthy Souls 92

I

Impelling Influence 342
Indolence or Industry 23
Inebriation and Addiction 277
Initial Salvation and
    Final Salvation 186
Input and Ouput 74
Inspiration and Motivation 177
Integrity and Duplicity 32
Intellect and Integrity 203
Isolated or Inhabited 122

J

Joyful Heart or
  Broken Spirit 160
Joyous Light or
  Doleful Dark 97
Justice and Mercy 348

K

King over Kings 287
Knowing *about* God
  and Knowing God 260

L

Laboring Hands
  and Lazy Hands 84
Lazy Living 303
Leadership and
  Servanthood 147
Learning to Labor 166
Learning to Live 247
Liabilities of Litigation 359
Liabilities of Love 167
Life Fountains or
  Death Traps 102
Lifelong Lobbyists 306
Lifestyle and Life Length 24
Listening and Learning 61
Listen to Speak 304
Listless or Spirited 267
Living Flesh or
  Rotting Bones 142
Living Liberated Lives 262
Loathing Lying and
  Loving Truth 93
Loss and Profit 2
Lovely or Lustful 51
Lying Lips and
  Delightful Dealings 82

M

Making Mischief 209
Marginalized Millions 111
Material Values
  and Moral Values 14
Messengers with
  a Message 330
Moral Distinction,
  not Moral Dualism 351
Moral Evil and
  Utilitarian Evil 34
Moral Goodness and
  Utilitarian Goodness 35
Morally Righteous and
  Factually Right 65
Motives and Actions 281

N

Natural Pride and
  Human Pride 98
Noble Nation or
  Crumbling Culture 146
Nutritious Talk and
  Noxious Talk 28

O

Opportunities and
  Obligations 211
Orchestrated Occurrences 216
Outer Props or Inner Roots 72

P

Pandering for Partiality 366
Parading Pride 302
Partiality and Justice 241
Payoff or Penalty 178

Penalty of Pain 270
Personal Piety and
        Political Policy 193
Persuaded by Patience 320
Physically Old and
        Morally Strong 213
Pleasure and Poverty 300
Plotting Evil or
        Planning Good 134
Plotting Evil or
        Promoting Good 80
Possibilities not Impossible 248
Precarious or Secure 63
Present Counsel for
        Future Wisdom 271
Preserve It to Retain It 87
Pride and Humility 185
Primeval Evil 338
Principle without Partiality 290
Problems with Pride 198
Profuse Populace or
        Sparse Society 140
Prosperity and Poverty 96
Prosperity Projects 346
Protecting the Pattern 183
Prudence or Folly 104
Prudent Hesitation or
    Foolish Proclamation 83
Punishment and
    Consequences 12

Q

Quit the Quarrel 230

R

Rebellion or Surrender 227
Reciprocal Relationship 255
Refreshing and Rewarding 318
Regular or Rare 322

Remorse or Repentance 353
Renewed and Replenished 251
Reprovers and Scoffers 159
Rescued or Abandoned 37
Resisting Reproof 354
Resolved and Dissolved 235
Resort to Court? 317
Resort to Rage 361
Respect the Rage 194
Response and Reaction 76
Resting Wisdom and
        Growing Wisdom 45
Retribution or
        Rehabilitation 191
Reversed Roles 323
Rewards and Retribution 60
Rewards of Righteousness 343
Riches and Righteousness 33
Riches or Respect 307
Rich Treasure or
        Great Treasure 163
Righteous Heart
        or Evil Mouth 175
Righteousness or Ruin 298
Righteous or Removed 27
Righteous Retribution 276
Ruin or Reward 101
Ruling over Rage 214
Ruling with Righteousness 192

S

Saddled with Sin 296
Safe or Shaky 305
Safe or Sorry 43
Safe Tread or Slick Soles 94
Satisfied Sleep 273
Seeking and Finding 56
Self-Hate or Self-Love 126
Selfish Pleas or
        Sterling Prayer 350
Servants and Sons 218

Sharp Sight or
 Dancing Eyes   240
Shutting the Eyes and
 Pursing the Lips   212
Silent or Sorry   17
Sing or Sob?   324
Sin-scorched Souls   325
Slippery Slope or
 Solid Support   67
Sober or Shallow   242
Source of Safety   249
Sowing and Reaping   5
Straight or Crooked   8
Strikes and Stripes   292
Stuffed Egos and
 Starved Stomachs   69
Sudden Wealth or
 Incremental Gains   99
Suffering and Sympathy   310
Suffocated with Shame   245
Symbol and Substance   293

T

Talking Right and
 Walking Wrong   282
Tarnished or Burnished   316
The Abomination
 of Transgression   48
The Battle for the Mind   173
The Desires that Drive Us   208
The Face with Favor   195
The Fickle and the Stable   22
The Heart Devises
 and God Revises   189
The House and the Home   123
Their Actions and
 Our Attitudes   334
The Joy of Justice   299
The Lamp of the Lord   289
The Law of Love   133

The Manner and
 the Message   311
The Plight of Poverty   256
The Poor Rich and
 the Rich Poor   95
The Proud and the Poor   172
The Roar of Rage   265
The Seed and the Grain   54
The Shame of Sham   335
The Simple and
 the Prudent   130
The Stuffed and
 the Starved   308
The Talk and the Talker   201
The Way of Life and
 the Pursuit of Death   47
The Work and the Reward   46
The Wrong Road and
 the Right Road   124
To Act or to React   264
To Believe or to Disbelieve   127
To Bruise or to Bless   1
To Cover or to Confess   352
To Deride or to Defer   40
To Give and to Get   45
To Glory in God's Glory   337
To Go on or to Turn Back   103
To Hide and to Harm   16
Toil or Talk   135
To Injure or to Inspire   73
To Listen or to Scoff   89
To Love to Learn   244
To Mock and
 to Be Mocked   121
To Pain Him or
 to Please Him   49
To Pamper or to Temper   113
To Perjure and to Profane   288
To Reject or to Regard   152
To Reveal or to Conceal   41
To Squelch or to Squeal   225

Transparency
 and Deception 4
Treasures or Troubles 153
Trials of Testing 219
Tricks of Trade 280
Trusting and Obeying 200
Truth and Justice 77
Truthful Lips and
 Lying Tongues 79
Truth or Treachery 137

U

Unworthy or Trustworthy 105
Upright Walk or
 Underhanded Ways 115
Upside Down or
 Right-side Up 360
Upward or Downward 171
Useful or Futile 81
Using Wisdom or Gushing
 Foolishness 149

V

Vanishing Vapor 336
Vegetable Plate or
 Stall-fed Steak 164
Verbal Venom 284
Victim of the System 234
Victim or Victor 144
Vocal or Silent 13

W

Walk with the Wise 108
Wandering into
 Waywardness 263
Weights and Balances 30
Weighty Warnings 349
Wells of Wisdom 272

Winnowing the Wicked 278
Wisdom and Knowledge 75
Wisdom and Righteousness 59
Wisdom and Wealth 196
Wise Hearts or
 Foolish Mouths 7
Wise in the Eyes 333
Wise Lips and
 Foolish Hearts 154
Wise Reaction or
 Foolish Rage 141
Wise Wisdom of
 Foolish Folly 120
Words of Wisdom 204
Words that Work 170
World Wealth or
 Other-World Wealth 57
Wrong Seems Right 206

Y

Your Plans with
 God's Help 182

Z

Zip the Lip 91

Index of the Proverbs
With Chapter, Verse, and Essay Number

10:1	1	11:1	29, 30	12:1	61
:2	2	:2	31	:2	62
:3	3	:3	32	:3	63
:4	3	:4	33	:4	64
:5	3	:5	34, 35	:5	65
:6	4, 5	:6	34, 35	:6	66
:7	6	:7	36	:7	67
:8	7	:8	37	:8	68
:9	8	:9	38	:9	69
:10	9	:10	39	:10	70
:11	10	:11	39	:11	71
:12	11	:12	40	:12	72
:13	12	:13	41	:13	73
:14	13	:14	42	:14	74
:15	14	:15	43	:15	75
:16	14	:16	44	:16	76
:17	15	:17	45	:17	77
:18	16	:18	46	:18	78
:19	17	:19	47	:19	79
:20	18	:20	48, 49	:20	80
:21	18	:21	50	:21	81
:22	19	:22	51	:22	82
:23	20	:23	52, 53	:23	83
:24	21	:24	54	:24	84
:25	22	:25	55	:25	85
:26	23	:26	55	:26	86
:27	24	:27	56	:27	87
:28	25	:28	57	:28	88
:29	26	:29	58		
:30	27	:30	59	13:1	89
:31	28	:31	60	:2	90
:32	28			:3	91

13:4	92	14:17	129	15:20	167
:5	93	:18	130	:21	168
:6	94	:19	131	:22	169
:7	95	:20	132	:23	170
:8	96	:21	133	:24	171
:9	97	:22	134	:25	172
:10	98	:23	135	:26	173
:11	99	:24	136	:27	174
:12	100	:25	137	:28	175
:13	101	:26	138	:29	176
:14	102	:27	139	:30	177
:15	103	:28	140	:31	178, 179
:16	104	:29	141	:32	178, 179
:17	105	:30	142	:33	178, 179
:18	106	:31	143		
:19	107	:32	144	16:1	180
:20	108	:33	145	:2	181
:21	109	:34	146	:3	182
:22	110	:35	147	:4	183, 184
:23	111			:5	185
:24	112	15:1	148	:6	186
:25	113	:2	149	:7	187
		:3	150	:8	188
14:1	114	:4	151	:9	189
:2	115	:5	152	:10	190
:3	116	:6	153	:11	191
:4	117	:7	154	:12	192
:5	118	:8	155	:13	193
:6	119	:9	156	:14	194
:7	120	:10	157	:15	195
:8	120	:11	158	:16	196
:9	121	:12	159	:17	197
:10	122	:13	160	:18	198
:11	123	:14	161	:19	199
:12	124	:15	162	:20	200
:13	125	:16	163	:21	201
:14	126	:17	164	:22	202
:15	127	:18	165	:23	203, 204
:16	128	:19	166	:24	205

16:25	206, 207	18:1	243	19:15	267
:26	208	:2	244	:16	268
:27	209	:3	245	:17	357
:28	210	:4	246	:18	269
:29	211	:5	241	:19	270
:30	212	:6	246	:20	271
:31	213	:7	246	:21	272
:32	214	:8	246	:22	295
:33	215, 216	:9	247	:23	273
		:10	248	:24	247
17:1	217	:11	249	:25	274
:2	218	:12	250	:26	266
:3	219	:13	242	:27	266
:4	220	:14	251	:28	275
:5	221	:15	244	:29	276
:6	222	:16	239		
:7	223	:17	252	20:1	277
:8	224	:18	215, 216	:2	265
:9	225	:19	253	:3	264
:10	226	:20	254	:4	333
:11	227	:21	254	:5	272
:12	228	:22	255	:6	258
:13	229	:23	256	:7	269
:14	230	:24	257, 258	:8	278
:15	231			:9	279
:16	232	19:1	259	:10	280
:17	233	:2	260	:11	281
:18	234	:3	261	:12	304
:19	235	:4	257	:13	267
:20	236	:5	259	:14	282
:21	237	:6	257	:15	254
:22	238	:7	256	:16	283
:23	239	:8	262	:17	295
:24	240	:9	259	:18	271
:25	237	:10	263	:19	284
:26	241	:11	264	:20	266
:27	242	:12	265	:21	285
:28	242	:13	266	:22	286
		:14	297	:23	280

20:24	287	22:1	307	25:16	321
:25	288	:2	308	:17	322
:26	278	:3	262	:18	323
:27	289	:4	306	:19	318
:28	290	:5	305	:20	324
:29	291	:6	269	:21-	
:30	292	:7	313	22	286
		:8	245	:23	275
21:1	287	:9	309, 310	:24	297
:2	181	:10	311	:25	325
:3	293	:11	342	:26	305
:4	294	:12	314	:27	326
:5	285	:13	346	:28	327
:6	295	:14	312		
:7	276	:15	269	26:1	328
:8	296	:16	313	:2	298
:9	297			:3	274
:10	243	(Proverbs 22:17		:4	329
:11	274	through 24:34		:5	329
:12	298	are thought not		:6	330
:13	349	to be Solomon's		:7	331
:14	239	proverbs. Other		:8	329
:15	299	than 23:6-8, they		:9	275
:16	263	are not treated in		:10	330
:17	300	this volume.)		:11	331
:18	37			:12	332
:19	297			:13	346
:20	301	23:6-8	367	:14	267
:21	298			:15	247
:22	263	25:2	314	:16	333
:23	259	:3	315	:17	334
:24	302	:4-5	316	:18-	
:25-		:6-7	315	19	334
26	303	:8-		:20	284
:27	351	10	317	:21	334
:28	304	:11	254	:22	246
:29	305	:12	271	:23	275
:30	306	:13	318	:24	259
:31	248	:14	319	:25	259
		:15	320		

26:26	259	28:4	268	29:7	357
:27	276	:5	348	:8	358
:28	335	:6	282	:9	359
		:7	266	:10	360
27:1	336	:8	349	:11	361
:2	337	:9	350	:12	290
:3	261	:10	298	:13	308
:4	338	:11	249	:14	316
:5	339	:12	351	:15	269
:6	335	:13	352	:16	305
:7	340	:14	353	:17	269
:8	341	:15	313	:18	362
:9	342	:16	313	:19	342
:10	258	:17	296	:20	242
:11	237	:18	282	:21	363
:12	262	:19	71	:22	311
:13	283	:20	285	:23	364
:14	322	:21	241	:24	365
:15-		:22	285	:25	248
16	297	:23	335	:26	366
:17	342	:24	266	:27	305
:18	343	:25	235		
:19	344	:26	249		
:20	243	:27	309, 310		
:21	345	:28	290		
:22	331				
:23-		29:1	354		
27	346	:2	290		
		:3	266		
28:1	347	:4	316		
:2	316	:5	355		
:3	357	:6	356		

(The proverbs in chapters 30 and 31 in the biblical book of The Proverbs are not Solomon's proverbs, and are not treated in this volume.)

Index of Subjects

A

Abandoned to Christ 96
Achievement 117
Adversity, misfortune, trials
    37, 215, 216, 219, 232,
    233, 238, 249, 273, 324
Ambassadors 105
Anger 76, 129, 141, 148,
    165, 194, 214, 261, 264,
    270, 302, 311, 338, 358,
    361
Animal cruelty 70
Atonement, The 30, 184,
    251, 270, 279, 348

B

Beauty, personal 51
Belief and doubt/unbelief
    101, 119, 124, 127, 200,
    248
Benevolence, charity 45, 54,
    55, 133, 221, 256, 283,
    301, 310, 349, 357
Blood of Jesus 279
Bondage and freedom 47,
    107, 157, 220, 309, 356
Bribery 174, 224, 239, 316
Business
    ethics 29, 99, 191, 280,
        282, 283, 285, 349
    loans and security 43,
        234, 283

C

Chance 183, 215
Change and permanency 27,
    63, 336
Character 213, 220
Commandments 24, 101,
    181, 268, 319, 350, 362
Commitment to God 345
Communication 9, 28, 149,
    154, 201, 204, 362
Conscience 2, 32, 181, 280
Consequences, good and bad
    34, 35, 56, 60, 74, 80, 90,
    94, 109, 116, 118, 134,
    198, 250, 276
Conversion, life change 103,
    156, 175
Counsel, counselors 42, 169,
    179, 271
Courage and cowardice 86,
    169, 231, 347, 360
"Crucified with Christ" 47
Crucifixion of Christ 251,
    270
Cynicism/cynics 119, 121,
    152, 358

D

Deception 4, 9, 16, 29, 38,
    46, 62, 65, 66, 73, 82, 93,
    118, 137, 174, 224, 236,
    252, 275, 280, 282, 295,
    319, 323, 335

Deferring to others 40
Dependability 105, 147, 218, 318, 330
Desires 20, 21, 32, 52, 90, 107, 208, 212, 243, 300, 310, 321, 367
Destiny(ies) 26, 189, 197, 206, 207
Divine help and direction 19, 37, 182, 272, 287, 306

E

Economic philosophy 111
Economy 54, 113
Eschatology 27, 172
Evil, evil persons 2, 22 34, 62, 63, 73, 80, 184, 197, 209, 220, 227, 229, 245, 278, 292, 298, 312
Evil thoughts 34, 62, 173, 220, 341
Exploitation 111, 143, 172, 313, 319

F

Family relationships 58, 64, 114, 123, 167, 222, 237, 253, 255, 266, 269, 297, 341
Fantacies/dreams 100, 169, 173, 240, 249, 272, 327, 341
Fatherhood of God 222
Fear and anxiety 85
Fearing or not fearing God 138, 265, 288, 353

Flattery 312, 335, 355
Folly 116, 121, 329. Also see: Wisdom and folly.
Forgiving others 11, 225, 253, 264, 286, 317
Friendship(s) 66, 132, 177, 225, 230, 233, 257, 258, 322, 324, 339
Future 21, 336

G

Generation gap 291
God's favor 62, 348
God's forgiveness 352
God's glory 326, 337
God's moral disposition 48, 156
God's secrets 314
God's system 183, 216
God's vigil 158
Good and evil 67, 131, 298, 351, 360
Goodness, principle of 21, 93, 131, 174,184, 220, 241, 298, 351
Gossip 38, 41, 210, 225, 246, 284, 323
Graciousness 44
Guilt 2, 181, 280, 296

H

Happiness 133, 195
Hate, hostility 16, 40

Health and length of life 24, 92

Heart 142, 161, 175, 184, 244, 331, 344, 353
Heaven and/or hell 25, 36, 94, 144, 243
Heritage 110
Holy Spirit 251, 289, 310
Honesty/dishonesty 4, 77, 79, 82, 93, 118, 137, 224, 236, 259, 275, 282, 295, 323, 335, 365
Honor and shame 4, 6, 31, 69, 179, 245, 307, 312, 317, 326, 328
Honoring parents 1, 167, 237, 266,
Hope 25, 36, 100, 162
Human relations or relationships 98, 147, 164, 185, 187, 194, 195, 217, 221, 230, 235, 253, 257, 258, 272, 286, 302, 308, 310, 317, 322, 323, 334, 335, 343, 344, 359, 360, 361
Humans and animals 98, 228, 274
Human spirit 251, 289, 327
Hurtfulness 78, 80

I

Incarnation 270
Incentives 102
Indulgence 263, 319, 321, 340

Influence 15, 59, 86, 108, 120, 177, 211, 342

Instruction, accepting or rejecting 7, 15, 61, 89, 106, 159
Integrity 8, 12, 82, 259, 305, 312

J

Jealousy 338
Journey, The (path of life) 26, 94, 104, 124, 128, 168, 171, 189, 197, 206, 207, 260, 305, 365
Joy and sorrow 97, 125, 160, 162, 195, 238
Judging 225
Judgment of God 21, 181, 221, 225, 265, 278, 288, 298, 299, 312
Justice and injustice 29, 30, 77, 184, 191, 231, 239, 241, 274, 276, 298, 299, 348, 352, 359, 366

K

Keeping a confidence 41
Knowing God 260
Knowledge 7, 13, 61, 75, 83, 104, 119, 130, 161, 202, 203, 244, 260, 304, 314

L

Laziness 3, 19, 23, 84, 87, 99, 166, 247, 267, 301, 303, 333

Leadership, leaders 39, 42,
140, 147, 190, 192, 193,
271, 290, 342, 358
Life and death 94, 102, 139,
144,157, 207
Light and Darkness 97, 289
Love 133, 141, 156, 253,
262, 301, 339
and hostility 11, 164
in family 58, 123, 363
vulnerability of 1, 167
Lust 51, 312, 321

M

Magna Carta 316
Material Values 14, 33 57,
163, 285, 303, 313, 349,
357
Mind 173, 327, 341
Moneymaking 19, 33, 99,
188, 285, 346, 349
Moral values 14, 88, 188,
213, 319
Motherhood 114
Motives and actions 181,
281, 310, 343

N

National evil 146, 193, 316
Natural system 183
Nco-orthodox Theology 260,
314
Netherworld 158, 243
New birth; new life 47, 218,
251, 331, 352

O

Obedience 200, 268, 293,
362
Occupied by Christ 122, 251
Omnipresence of God 150,
176

P

Pain and suffering 70, 81,
270, 292, 318, 324
Pascal's wager 124
Patience 320
Peace, personal 273
relational 359
social 358
Persistence 250, 320
Plans 182, 272, 306
evil 212
Pleasing God 49, 156, 187,
195
Pleasure 20, 300, 321, 367
Pornography 173, 341
Postmodernisn 6, 75, 304,
314
Prayer 155, 176, 180, 306,
350
Preparation(s) 250
Pretense 65, 337
Pride and/or humility 7, 31,
68, 69, 83, 98, 172, 179,
185, 198, 199, 226, 235,
250, 294, 302, 315, 326,
328, 332, 337, 344, 364
Private self 32
Psychosomatics 3, 142, 160,
238, 333

Public speaking 149, 154, 201

Punishment and consequences 12, 89, 112, 221, 276

Purpose(s) 169, 180, 240, 272, 306
conflicting 7
evil 212
single 7

R

Rationality 124, 203, 252
Reality 79
Rearing children 1, 58, 112, 123, 222, 269, 281, 363
Rebellion 227, 235
Redemption 186, 279, 325, 354
Religion, superficial 155
Religious experience 92, 115, 122
Repentance 155, 186, 227, 261, 296, 321, 352, 353
Reproof, receiving and giving 61, 106, 152, 157, 159, 178, 226, 274, 339, 354
Reputation, good or bad 6
Response and reaction 76, 141, 148, 194, 229, 264, 317, 329, 334, 344
Responsibility 50, 318
Retribution 73, 74
Righteousness, rewards of 5, 59, 65, 88, 113, 115, 192, 197, 293, 343

Roots, foundation, anchor 63, 103

S

Salvation 124, 186, 209, 325, 342
Sanctification 52, 186, 279, 310
Scoffing, scoffers 89, 119, 159, 302, 311, 358
Security 94, 138, 248, 249, 305
Self-centeredness 47, 52, 140, 228, 262, 309
Self-discipline 71, 141, 165, 166, 173, 194, 214, 263, 321, 327, 334, 340, 341
Self-esteem 4, 69, 281, 315
Self-love 126, 262, 309, 310
Senior age 213
Sentiment 156
Servanthood 147, 343
Sin, consequences of 2, 5, 103, 121, 134, 209, 245, 312
Slander 16, 73, 246
Slaveholding 218
Social creatures 108
Social service 45, 143, 256
Spiritual food 92
Spiritual riches and poverty 95, 136
Stability/instabiity 22, 27, 138, 240, 305
Strength 26

Strife and contention 164,
   165, 217, 230, 235, 311,
   334, 358, 360, 361
Success 182

T

Talk, good and bad 28, 175,
   246, 254
  helpful and hurtful 10, 16,
   18, 85, 137, 151, 170, 205,
   210, 275, 284
  idle 7, 9, 13, 17, 73, 78, 91,
   170, 242, 275, 304
  wise and foolish 13, 104,
   116, 135, 148, 149, 154,
   201, 204, 223, 242, 259
Temperance 277
Temptation 86, 139, 263,
   312, 340
Terrorism 165
Theologies, various 314
Tribal morality 39
Trust 200, 248
Truth and falsehood 65, 73,
   77, 79, 101, 252, 275, 288,
   295

U

Usefulness 117

W

War 271

Wealth and poverty,
  attitudes toward 33, 44,
   57, 95, 96, 111, 153, 163,
   196, 249, 285, 301, 349
  attitudes toward the poor
   111, 221, 256, 308, 313,
   349
Will, volition 107, 184, 212,
   309, 310, 321, 354
Wisdom 59, 61, 68, 119,
   203, 244
  and folly 7, 12, 17, 18, 20,
   31, 71, 75, 76, 83, 89, 104,
   120, 128, 136,145, 149,
   161, 168, 196, 202, 204,
   218, 226, 232, 240, 261,
   262, 263, 331, 332, 361
Words 91, 170
Work ethic 3, 19, 23, 46, 71,
   84, 87, 96, 99, 135, 166,
   208, 247, 267, 285, 301,
   303, 333, 346
Wrath of God 53

Index of Names
In Addition to Listings in Works Cited

Alfonso 310
Aristotle 118

Brasher, John L. 199
Bryan, J. A. ("Brother Bryan") 301
Buddha, Guatama the 298
Burton, Lady 154

Carver, George Washington 83
Chesterton, G. K. 170
Churchill, Sir Winston 48, 76, 207
Coolidge, Calvin 104, 246
Corson, Sarah 256
Corson, Tom 238
Crosby, Fanny J. 160

Dante Alighieri 172
Descartes, René 289
Diogenes 236

Elliot, Jim 33
Einstein, Albert 244
Erasmus 130

Finney, Charles G. 126
Frederick the Great 175

Goldwater, Barry 91
Graham, Billy 199, 254

Heraclitus 63
Hoover, Herbert 42
Humphrey, Hubert 91

Joan of Arc 176
Johnson, Lyndon Baines 140, 230, 242

Kalas, J. Ellsworth 203
Kant, Immanuel 289
Kelly, John 170
Kierkegaard, Soren 200
King, Martin Luther King, Jr. 306

Lao-tzu 149
Leibniz, Gottfried Wilhelm von 133
Lincoln, Abraham 105, 146

Martin, Civilla 150, 170
Miller, Joaquin 133
Moody, Dwight L. 353
Murphree, Marisa 200

Nightingale. Florence 59

Philpot, Ford 199
Poe, Edgar Allan 151
Pre-Socratic philosophers 202

Reagan, Ronald, 23, 58
Roosevelt, Colonel 68
Roosevelt, Franklin Delano
    197
Roosevelt, Theodore 68

Saadi 108
Shaw, George Bernard 357
Socrates 244
Sophists, The 202
Sophocles 188
Spurgeon, Charles H. 137
Sunday, Billy 331

Tertullian 130
Twain, Mark 173

Washington, George 127
Watts, Isaac 130
Webster, Daniel 38, 295
Wesley, John 130
Wilde, Oscar 152
Wilson, Woodrow 27, 278
Xenocrates of Chalcedon 17

Index of Works Cited
With Essay Numbers

Aesop. *The Fables of Aesop*. New York: Dorsett Press, 1975.
— 166, 182, 196, 332, 353

Allen, Elizabeth Akers. "Rock Me to Sleep." Richard C. MacKenzie,
ed. *The New Home Book of Best Loved Poems*. Garden City, NY:
Doubleday & Co., Inc., 1946. — 1

Anderson, Maxwell. *Lost in the Stars*. Henry Hewes, ed. *Famous
American Plays of the 1940s*. New York: Dell Publishing Co.,
1960. — 122

"Ann Landers" (advice column). *Pittsburgh Post-Gazette*. Daily
newspaper. Pittsburgh, PA, 17 Feb. 1969. — 163

Anonymous. — 44, 120, 344, 351

Aristotle. *Nicomachean Ethics*. Richard McKeon, ed. *Introduction to
Aristotle*. New York: Random House, Inc., 1947. — 74, 75, 80,
89, 129, 156, 202, 213, 294, 321

Arnold, Matthew. "The Buried Life." M. H. Abrams, ed. *The Norton
Anthology of English Literature*. New York: W. W. Norton &
Co., 1968. — 327

Atlanta Journal-Constitution, The. Daily newspaper, Associated Press
article. Atlanta, GA, May 3, 2007.
Quoting: Ronald Reagan — 58

Aurelius, Marcus. *The Thoughts of the Emperor*. George Long, tr.
New York: John B. Alden, Publisher, 1887. — 212, 219, 220,
230, 245, 251, 269, 279, 286, 290, 300, 306, 309, 311, 313, 317,
320, 331, 334, 336, 341, 349, 351, 355

Barkman, Adam. "A New Philosophy of Darkness." *Christian
Scholar's Review*. Spring 2010. — 274

Belmonte, Kevin. "Greatness Upon Greatness." *Christian History* magazine. Carol Stream, IL, Issue 53, n.d.— 26

Beowulf the Warrior. Ian Serraillier, tr. New York: Henry Z. Walck, Inc., 1961. — 31, 240, 252, 264, 286, 307, 343, 347

Blakeley, Hunter B. *Religion in Shoes: Brother Bryan of Birmingham*. Richmond, VA: John Knox Press, 1953. — 301

Bright, Bill, ed. *Teacher's Manual*. Campus Crusade Publishers, n.d. — 95

Browning, Robert. In Horace E. Scudder, ed. *The Complete Poetic and Dramatic Works of Robert Browning.*Cambridge, MA: Houghton Mifflin Company, 1895.
"Asolando" — 267
"Easter Day" — 243
Paracelsus — 150, 171, 190, 208, 210, 320, 344
Sordello — 304

------. "Andrea del Sarto," in *The Poems of Robert Browning*. London: Oxford University Press, 1928. — 171

Bryant, William Cullen. "Thanatopsis." Edmund Fuller and B. Jo Kinnick, eds. *Adventures in American Literature*. New York: Harcourt, Brace & World, Inc., 1963. — 336

Bunyan, John. *The Pilgrim's Progress*. Grand Rapids: Zondervan, 1966. — 207

------. *The Pilgrim's Progress*. Philadelphia: Universal Book and Bible House, 1933. — 94

Burns, Robert. "To a Louse." Richard Aldington, ed. *The Viking Book of Poetry*. New York: The Viking Press, 1958. Vol.I. — 15

Butler, Joseph. *Analogy of Religion*. New York: Eaton and Mains, 1847. — 178

Byron, George Gordon, Lord. *Don Juan*. M. H. Abrams, ed. *The Norton Anthology of English Literature*. New York: W. W. Norton & Co., 1962. Vol. 2. — 297

Cervantes, Miguelde. *Don Quixote of the Mancha.* New York:
P. F. Collier & Sons, 1909. — 151

Chaucer, Geoffrey. *Canterbury Tales.* J. U. Nicolson, tr. Garden
City, NY: Garden City Publishing Co., 1934.
"The Canon's Yeoman's Tale" — 216
"The Clerk's Tale" — 200, 297, 308, 345, 380
"The Manciple's Tale of the Crow" — 201, 205, 268, 275, 282,
312
"The Miller's Tale" — 169
"The Pardoner's Tale" — 32, 187, 277
"The Tale of Melibeus" — 175, 179, 206, 230, 256, 271,285,
307
"The Tale of the Wife of Bath" — 194, 233, 349

------. *Canterbury Tales.* J. B. Priestley and Josephine Spear, eds.
Adventures in English Literature. New York: Harcourt, Brace &
World, Inc., 1963.
"The Nun's Priest's Tale" — 242

Chesterton, G. K. *Favorite Father Brown Stories.* New York: Dover
Publications, Inc., 1993.
"The Blue Cross" — 124, 146, 329
"The Sign of the Broken Sword" — 209
"The Sins of Prince Saradine" — 30, 180

------. *Robert Browning.* Teddington, Middlesex, UK: Echo Library,
n.d. — 72

Clarke, Adam. *Clarke's Commentary.* New York: Eaton and Mains,
1883. Vol. III.—19, 322

Coleridge, Samuel Taylor. "Christabel." M. H. Abrams, ed. *The
Norton Anthology of English Literature.* New York: W. W.
Norton & Co., 1962. Vol. 2. — 286

------. "The Rhyme of the Ancient Mariner." Richard Aldington, ed.
The Viking Book of Poetry. New York: The Viking Press, 1958.
Vol. II. — 136, 350

Colson, Charles. "We Need Health-Care Reform." *Christianity Today.*
Carol Stream, IL, August 2009. — 203

Compton's Encyclopedia. Chicago: F. E. Compton & Co., 1952. Vol. I.
— 214

Croft, Roy. "Love." Richard Charlton MacKenzie, ed. *The New Home Book of Best Loved Poems.* Garden City, NY: Garden City Books, 1946. — 342

Dante Alighieri. *The Divine Comedy.* Carlyle-Wicksteed translation. New York: Random House, 1932.
"Inferno" — 7, 242, 263, 267, 285, 287, 298, 354, 356, 367
"Purgatorio" — 253, 337, 342, 348, 352, 353
"Paradiso" — 10, 260, 331, 342, 363, 364

------. *The Divine Comedy.* Henry Francis Cary, tr. No city: A. L. Burt Co., n.d. "Hell" — 240

------. *The Divine Comedy.* Thomas G. Bergin, tr. New York: Appleton-Century-Crofts of Meredith Publishing Co., 1955. "Paradise" — 314

Davidson, John. "A Ballad of Hell." Louis Untermeyer, ed. *Modern British Poetry.* New York: Harcourt, Brace and Co., 1950. — 137

Defoe, Daniel. *Robinson Crusoe.* Garden City, NY: Doubleday, 1945. — 14, 33, 50, 125, 150, 320

Dickens, Charles. *A Tale of Two Cities.* New York: Books, Inc., n.d. — 88, 100, 122, 354

------. *A Tale of Two Cities.* New York: J. J. Little & Ives Co., Inc., 1941. — 103, 131

-----. *David Copperfield.* In *Best Loved Books.* Pleasantville, NY: The Reader's Digest Association, 1966. — 84, 99, 128, 163, 301

Dickinson, Emily. In Gordon N. Ray, ed. *Masters of American Literature.* Cambridge, MA: The Riverside Press of Houghton Mifflin Co., 1959. "I'm Nobody! Who Are You?" — 223

------. In Louis Untermeyer, ed. *Modern American Poetry*. New York: Harcourt, Brace and Co., 1950.
"Some Keep the Sabbath" — 299
"There Is No Frigate Like a Book" — 327

Dole, Bob. *Great Political Wit*. New York: Doubleday, 1998.
Quoting: Calvin Coolidge — 246
Sir Winston Churchill—48
Barry Goldwater — 91
Herbert Hoover — 42
Lyndon Baines Johnson — 230, 242
Woodrow Wilson — 27, 278

Dryden, John. "Absalom and Achitophel." *Dryden's England*. Donald Thomas, ed. *John Dryden: Selected Poems*. London: J. M. Dent Ltd, Everyman's Library, 1993. — 291

Eliot, George. *Silas Marner*. Walter Loban and Rosalind Olmsted, eds. *Adventures in Appreciation*. New York: Harcourt, Brace & World, Inc., 1963. — 47, 148, 245

------. *The Mill on the Floss*. New York: Dodd, Mead and Co., 1960. — 189

Elliot, Elizabeth. *Shadow of the Almighty: The Life and Testament of Jim Elliot*. New York: Harper & Brothers, 1958.
Quoting: Jim Elliot — 33

Elliott, Lawrence. *George Washington Carver: The Man Who Overcame*. Englewood Cliffs, NJ: Prentice Hall, Inc., 1966.
Quoting: George Washington Carver — 83

Ellis, William T. *Billy Sunday: The Man and His Message*. Chicago: Moody Press, 1959.
Quoting: Billy Sunday — 331

Elson, William. *Elson Readers*. New York: Scott, Foresman and Co., 1912. Book Four. — 283.

Emerson, Ralph Waldo. "Heroism." Richard Aldington, ed., *The Viking Book of Poetry*. New York: The Viking Press, 1958. Vol. II. — 347

Fitt, Arthur Percy. *The Shorter Life of D. L. Moody*. Chicago: Moody Press, 1900.
Quoting: Dwight L. Moody — 353

Frost, Robert. In Louis Untermeyer, ed., *Modern American Poetry*. New York: Harcourt, Brace and Co., 1950.
"The Death of the Hired Man" — 58, 134
"The Road Not Taken" — 189

Gibbs, Nancy, and Michael Duffy. *The Preacher and the Presidents*. New York: Center Street, Hatchet Book Group USA, 2007.
Quoting: Lyndon Baines Johnson — 140
Ronald Reagan — 23
Referring to: Billy Gtaham — 254

Gibran, Kahlil. *Sand and Foam*. New York: Alfred A. Knopf, Inc., 1926. — 284

------. *The Prophet*. New York: Alfred A. Knopf, 1926. — 226, 238, 248, 336, 340

------. *Thoughts and Meditations*. New York: The Citadel Press, 1960. — 339

Goethe, Johann Wolfgang von. *Faust*. Bayard Taylor, tr. New York: The Macmillan Company, 1937. — 114, 119, 120, 139, 141, 157, 160, 161, 165, 168, 171, 182, 185, 186, 188, 197, 200, 206, 208, 218, 232, 248, 251, 253, 255, 266, 267, 276, 291, 303, 337, 347, 361, 366

Graham, Billy. A letter sent to the supporters of the Billy Graham Evangelistic Association, April 2009. — 61

Gray, Thomas. "Elegy Written in a Country Churchyard." Richard Aldington, ed. *The Viking Book of Poetry*. New York: The Viking Press, 1958. Vol. I. — 256

------. "Elegy Written in a Country Churchyard: The Epitaph." Ernest Bernbaum, ed. *Anthology of Romanticism*. New York: Thomas Nelson & Sons, 1929. Vol. Two. — 251

Harris, Jon R. *Wings of the Morning*. No city: Xulon Press, 2006.
— 176

Hawthorne, Nathaniel. *The Scarlet Letter*. New York: Books, Inc., n.d.
— 48, 66, 103, 109, 296, 305, 344

Holmes, Oliver Wendell. "The Voiceless." Richard Aldington, ed. *The
Viking Book of Poetry*. New York: The Viking Press, 1958.
Vol. II. — 162

Homer. *The Odyssey of Homer*. S. H. Butcher and A. Lang, trs.
New York: The Macmillan Company, 1911. — 26, 37, 86, 189,
215, 347

Horace (Quintus Horatius Flaccus). *Horace: Satires, Epistles, Ars
Poetica*. H. Rushton Fairclough, tr. Cambridge, MA: Harvard
University Press, 1991. — 6, 225, 233, 246, 275, 279, 281, 284,
291, 300, 311, 313, 316, 333, 361, 367

Hume, David. *An Inquiry Concering the Principles of Morals*. Charles
W. Hendel, ed. New York: The Bobbs-Merrill Company, Inc.,
1957. — 212

Jamieson, Robert, A. R. Fausset, and David Brown. *Commentary*.
Grand Rapids: Wm. B. Eerdmans Publishing Co., 1945. Vol. III.
Quoting: Alfonso — 310
          Sophocles — 79

Johnson, Ben Campbell. *To Will God's Will*. Philadelphia: The
Westminster Press, 1987. — 74, 78

Kesler, Jay. *Too Big to Spank*. Glendale, CA: RegalBooks, GIL
Publications, 1978. — 123

Kidner, Derek. *Proverbs*. D. J. Wiseman, ed. *The Tyndale Old
Testament Commentaries*. Downers Grove, IL: InterVarsity
Press, 1964. — 157, 302

Kierkegaard, Soren. *Attack Upon Christendom*. Walter Lowrie, tr.
Boston: The Beacon Press, 1956. — 207, 280, 299, 309

Kinlaw, Dennis F. "Behind Scholars' Closed Doors." *Christianity Today*. Carol Stream, IL, April 29, 1991. — 314

------. *Preaching in the Spirit*. Grand Rapids: Francis Asbury Press of Zondervan, 1985. — 227

Kipling, Rudyard. "Mother O' Mine." Richard C. Mackenzie, ed. *The New Home Book of Best Loved Poems*. Garden City, NY: Garden City Books, Doubleday, 1946. — 167

------. "Recessional." Louis Untermeyer, ed. *Modern British Literature*. New York: Harcourt, Brace and Co., 1950. — 146

------. *The Light That Failed*. New York: Books, Inc., n.d. — 11, 56, 62, 128, 149, 182, 206, 264, 356

------. "When Earth's Last Picture Is Painted." Miles and Pooley, eds. *Literature and Life in England*. New York: Scott, Foresman and Co., 1943. — 135

Kiser, S. E. "My Creed." A. L. Alexander, ed. *Poems That Touch the Heart*. Garden City, NY: Hanover House, 1958. — 282

Leibniz, Gottfried Wilhelm von. Quote from Google site. — 133

Lewis, C. S. *God in the Dock*. Grand Rapids: William B. Eerdmans Publishing Co., 1970. — 30, 63, 201, 262

------. *Mere Christianity*. New York: The Macmillan Company, 1960. — 116, 141, 160, 168, 185, 227, 294, 302, 333, 345, 362, 364

------. *Perelandra*. New York: Macmillan Publishng Co., 1944. — 2, 121, 150, 171, 184, 195, 352

------. *The Abolition of Man*. New York: Macmillan Publishing Co., 1947. — 119

------. *The Great Divorce*. New York: Macmillan Publishing Co., 1978. — 109, 213, 298

------. *The Horse and the Body*, Book 5 in *The Chronicles of Narnia*. New York: Collier Books, Macmillan, 1978. — 198

------. *The Last Battle*, Book 7 in *The Chronicles of Narnia*. New York: Collier Books, Macmillan, 1978 — 115, 144, 171, 195, 308

------. *The Lion, the Witch and the Wardrobe*, Book 1 in *The Chronicles of Narnia*. New York: Collier Books, Macmillan, 1978. — 265

------. *The Magician's Nephew*, Book 6 in *The Chronicles of Narnia*. New York: Collier Books, Macmillan, 1978. — 127, 241

------. *The Pilgrim's Regress*. Grand Rapids: Wm. B. Eerdmans Publishing Co., 1979. — 124, 209, 353, 357

------. *The Problem of Pain*. New York: Macmillan Publishing Co., 1978. — 62

------. *The Silver Chair*, Book 4 in *The Chronicles of Narnia*. New York: Collier Books, Macmillan, 1953. — 49

------. *The Weight of Glory*. Grand Rapids: William B. Eerdmans Publishing Co., 1977. — 329

------. *Till We Have Faces*. Grand Rapids: William B. Eerdmans Publishing Co., 1966. — 278, 289, 317, 361

Locke, John. *An Essay Concerning Human Understanding*. London: Dent & Sons, LTD, 1961. — 20

Longfellow, Henry Wadsworth. *Best Loved Poems of Longfellow*. Chicago: The Spencer Press, 1949.
"A Psalm of Life" — 144, 166
"Evangeline" — 161
"The Village Blacksmith" — 135
"Tomorrow" — 336

------. "I Heard the Bells on Christmas Day." *The Broadman Hymnal*. Nashville: Broadman, 1940. — 151

------. "Some Day, Some Day." Richard Aldington, ed. *The Viking Book of Poetry*. New York: The Viking Press, 1958. Vol. II. — 151

Markham, Edwin. "The Man With the Hoe." Louis Untermeyer, ed. *Modern American Poetry*. New York: Harcourt, Brace and Co., 1950. — 143

McCollister, John. *God and the Oval Office*. Nashville: W Publishing Group, Thomas Nelson, 2005.
Quoting: Calvin Coolidge — 104
Abrahan Lincoln — 146
George Washington — 127

McEntyre, Marilyn Chandler. "Why the Care of Language Is More Important than Ever." *Christianity Today*. Carol Stream, IL, September 2009. — 205

Meacham, Jon. *Franklin and Winston*. New York: Random House, 2003.
Quoting: Sir Winston Churchill — 76, 207
Franklin Delano Roosevelt — 197

Merchant, Jane. *Because It's Here*. Nashville: Abingdon Press, 1970.
"Builder" — 258
"Prescription for Pride" — 324
"Though It Be Little" — 293

------. *Every Good Gift*. Nashville: Abingdon Press, 1968.
"Unless I Ask" — 350

Milton, John. *Paradise Lost*. Indianapolis: ITT Bobbs-Merrill Educational Publishing Co., 1962. — 21, 261, 265, 270, 288, 289, 327, 330, 338, 340, 348, 350, 354, 356

------. *Paradise Regained*. Douglas Bush, ed. *The Portable Milton*. New York: Penguin Books, The Viking Press, 1949. — 288, 326, 340, 353, 363

Mitchell, Helen Buss. *Roots of Wisdom*. Belmont, CA: Wadsworth Publishing Co., 1996, 2002.
Quoting: Dante Alighieri (2002 edition) — 172
Abraham Lincoln (in 1996 edition) — 105

Morgan, Robert J. *Then Sings My Soul: 300 of the World's Greatest Hymn Stories*. Nashville: Thomas Nelson, 2006.
Quoting: Fanny J. Crosby — 160
Referring to: Civilla Martin — 170
Isaac Watts — 130

Morrison, H. C. *From Sanai to Calvary*. Louisville, KY: Pentecostal Publishing Co., 1942. — 213.

Muck, Terry. "Interview With President Ellsworth Kalas." *The Asbury Herald*. Wilmore, KY, Summer 2009 issue.
Quoting: Ellsworth Kalas — 203

Murphree, Jon Tal. *Autographed by God*. University Park, IA: Vennard College, 2006. — 227

------. *Giant of a Century Trail*. Apollo, PA: West Publishing Co., 1969.
Quoting: John L. Brasher — 199

------. *The Road to SIFAT*. Columbus, GA: Quill Publications, 1990.
Referring to: Sarah Corson — 256

Murphree, Marisa. Personal letter, 2005. — 200

Neff, David. "Drunk on Money." *Christianity Today*. Carol Stream, IL, April 8, 1988. — 44

Neibuhr, Reinhold. *Moral Man and Immoral Society*. New York: Charles Scribner's Sons, 1960. — 29

Ovid (Publius Ovidius Naso). *Metamorphoses*. David Damrosch and David L. Pike, eds. *The Longman Anthology of World Literature*. New York: Pearson Longman, 2008. — 13

Pascal, Blaise. *Pensées*. A. J. Krailsheimer, tr. London: Penguin Books, 1995. — 124, 204, 309, 348

Paton, Alan. *Cry, the Beloved Country*. New York: Macmillan Pub. Co., 1948. — 21, 39, 85, 125, 190, 231, 266, 305

Plato. *Epistle VII*. Albert B. Hakim, ed. *Historical Intro to Philosophy*. Upper Saddle River, NJ: Prentice Hall, 2001. — 300

------. *The Republic*, Book V. Dagobert Runes, ed. *Treasury of Philosophy*. New York: Philosophical Library, 1955. — 190, 192

Poe, Edgar Allan. "A Dream Within a Dream." Gordon N. Ray, ed. *Masters of American Literature*. Boston: Houghton Mifflin Company, 1959. — 336

------. "The Raven." Richard Aldington, ed. *The Viking Book of Poetry*. New York: The Viking Press, 1958. Vol. II. — 272

Procter, Adelaide Anne. "My God, I Thank Thee." *The Methodist Hymnal*. Nashville: The Methodist Publishing House, 1966. — 163, 219, 238

------. "Per Pacem Ad Lucem." *English Sacred Lyrics*. University of California Library, YA01604. Selection 133. — 324

Reed, Isaiah. *Boyhood Memories and Lessons*. Jim Kerwin, ed. Chesapeake, VA: Parbar Westward Publications, 2007. — 108, 124

Ringenberg, William C. *Letters to Young Scholars*. Upland, IN: Taylor University Press, 2003.
Quoting: Albert Einstein — 244
Joaquin Miller — 133

Rusthoi, Esther Kerr. "When We See Christ." *Great Gospel Songs and Hymns*. Dallas: Stamps-Baxter of Zondervan, 1976. — 195

Samri, Cal and Rose. *More Holy Humor*. Nashville: Thomas Nelson, 1997.
Quoting: G. K. Chesterton — 170
John Kelly — 170

Schulz, Charles M. *Peanuts* comic strip. September 14, 1955. — 75

------. *The Complete Peanuts*. Seattle: Fantagraphics Books, 2007.
Vol. 1957-58 — 83
Vol. 1963-64 — 57

Schumacher, E. F. *Small Is Beautiful*. New York: Harper & Row, 1973. — 163

Scott, Sir Walter. *Marmion*. New York: Macmillan Co., 1901 — 259

------, *The Lady of the Lake*. New York: The New American Library, 1962. — 192, 193, 207, 214, 238, 251, 258, 278, 309, 328, 336

Shaftsbury, Lord. "An Inquiry Concerning Virtue and Merit." Ernest Bernbaum, ed. *Selections From the Pre-Romantic Movement*. New York: Thomas Nelson and Sons, 1929. — 203

Shakespeare, Willliam. *The Complete Works of Shakespeare*. W. G. Clark and W. Aldis Wright, eds. Garden City, NY: Nelson Doubleday, Inc., n.d. Volumes I and II.
A Midsummer Night's Dream — 125, 136, 297, 323, 339
As You Like It — 4, 40, 81, 96, 107, 110, 125, 141, 148,162, 199, 213, 229, 256, 365
Julius Ceasar — 50, 61, 62, 76, 86, 90, 110, 164, 250, 347, 365
King Richard II — 28, 91
Macbeth — 16, 93, 104, 120, 125, 134, 141, 142, 147, 158, 160, 165, 193, 211, 240, 276, 279, 295, 296, 343, 351
Othello — 3, 10, 25, 38, 44, 65, 69, 85, 224, 277, 280, 307, 321, 328, 334, 338, 350, 359
"Sonnets" — 90, 98, 228
The Merchant of Venice — 45, 204, 221, 232, 242, 255, 280, 282, 283, 323, 334, 335, 349, 361, 366
The Taming of the Shrew — 82

------. *Hamlet, Prince of Denmark*. New York: The Macmillan Co., 1922. — 17, 25, 30, 37, 41, 51, 70, 74, 85, 100, 116, 127, 155, 162, 169, 234, 236, 243, 257, 274, 281, 282, 291, 347, 365

Shaw, George Bernard. *Arms and the Man: Act III*. M. H. Abrams, ed. *The Norton Anthology of English Literature*. New York: W. W. Norton & Company, 1962. Vol. 2. — 257

------. *Saint Joan*. London: Penguin Group, 1946. — 176

Sheen, (Archbishop) Fulton J. "Bottom-Line Theology." *Christianity Today*. Carol Stream, IL, June 3, 1977. — 154

Sider, Ronald J. *Rich Christians in an Age of Hunger.* Downers Grove, IL: InterVarsity Press, 1977. — 111

Smith, Hannah Whitall. *The Christian's Secret of a Happy Life.* Westwood, NJ: Fleming H. Revell Company, 1952. — 200

Soccio, Douglas J. *Archetypes of Wisdom.* Belmont, CA: Wadsworth Publishng Co., 1998.
Quoting: Heraclitus — 63

------. *Archetypes of Wisdom.* Belmont, CA: Wadsworth, Thomas Learning, 2001.
Quoting: Guatama the Buddha — 298
Martin Luther King, Jr. — 306
Lao-tzu — 149
Sophocles — 188

Sophocles. *Oedipus the King.* New York: Washington Square Press, Inc., 1959. — 11, 77, 132, 183, 189, 191

Springer, Rebecca R. *My Dream of Heaven.* Tulsa, OK: Harrison House, n.d. Originally published in 1898 as *Intra Muros.* — 364

Spurgeon, Charles H. "The Minister's Fainting Fits," Lecture XI. *Lectures to My Students.* Lynchburg, VA: The Old Time Gospel Hour, n.d. Reprinted from edition in England, 1865. — 139

Stevenson, Robert Louis. "The Sire de Malétroit's Door." *The Great Short Stories of Robert Louis Stevenson.* New York: Pocket Books, Inc. 1951. — 1

Stowe, Harriet Beecher. *Uncle Tom's Cabin.* New York: Everyman's Library, Alfred A. Knopf, Inc., 1994. — 15, 25, 88, 114, 133, 144, 153, 162, 197, 282, 336, 346

Strachey, Lytton. *Eminent Victorians.* London: Bloomsbury Publishing Ltd., 1988.
Referring to: Florence Nightingale — 59

Swinburne, Algernon Charles. "Hymn to Proserpine." M. H. Abrams, ed. *The Norton Anthology of English Literature.* New York: W. W. Norton & Co., 1962. Vol. 2. — 336

Tan, Paul Lee, ed. *Encyclopedia of 7,700 Illustrations.* Rockville, MD:
　　Assurance Publishers, 1979.
　　Quoting:　Aristotle — 118
　　　　　　　Anonymous — 344
　　　　　　　Native Indian Tribe — 233
　　　　　　　Charles H. Spurgeon — 137
　　　　　　　Daniel Webster — 38, 295

Tennyson, Alfred, Lord. "In Memoriam," poem 96. M. H. Abrams, ed.
　　The Norton Anthology of English Literature. New York: W. W.
　　Norton & Co., 1962. Vol. 2. — 127, 246

------. "The Higher Pantheism." *The Poetical Works of Tennyson.* New
　　York: Crowell, n.d. — 177

The Book of Psalms in Metre: The Scottish Hymnal. Edinburgh: Thomas
　　Nelson and Sons, 1882. 35, 84, 97, 232, 246

The New Book of Knowledge. New York: Grolier, Inc., 1967. Vol. 12.
　　— 316

Tolkien, J. R. R. "On Faerie Stories." *The Tolkien Reader.* New York:
　　Ballantine, 1966. — 97

Velasquez, Manuel. *Philosophy: A Text with Readings.* Belmont, CA:
　　Wadsworth Publishing Co., 1999.
　　Quoting:　Lady Burton — 154
　　　　　　　Frederick the Great — 175
　　　　　　　George Bernard Shaw — 357
　　　　　　　Socrates — 244
　　　　　　　Mark Twain — 173
　　　　　　　Oscar Wilde — 152

Virgil (Publius Vergilius Maro). *The Aeneid.* W. F. Jackson Knight, tr.
　　London: Penguin Books, 1958. — 210, 216, 222, 228, 237, 239,
　　248, 249, 264, 268, 273, 286, 288, 298, 306, 309, 324, 328, 347,
　　358, 362

Waterman, Nixon. "To Know All Is to Forgive All." Richard C.
　　MacKenzie, ed. *The New Home Book of Best Loved Poems.*
　　Garden City, NY: Garden City Books, 1946. — 324

Watts, Isaac. "When I Can Read My Title Clear." *Baptist Hymnal.* Nashville: Convention Press, 1956. — 360

Weatherhead, Leslie D. *Why Do Men Suffer?* Nashville: Abingdon Press, 1936. — 200, 216

Wells, James. "Treasures." *Gospel Harmony.* Dalton, GA: The A. J. Showalter Co, 1936. — 95

Wesley, Charles. "Come Father, Son, and Holy Ghost." *The Methodist Hymnal.* Nashville: Methodist Publishing House, 1964. — 244

Whedon, Daniel D., ed. *Whedon's Commentary.* New York: Phillips and Hunt, 1885. Vol. VI.
    Quoting: Old German Proverb — 320
        Saadi — 108

Whittier, John Greenleaf. "O Brother Man." *The Broadman Hymnal.* Nashville: Broadman Press, 1940. — 187

------. "The Eternal Goodness." Edmund Fuller and B. Jo Kinnick, eds. *Adventures in American Literature.* New York: Harcourt, Brace & World, Inc., 1963. — 200, 319

------. In Donald McQuade, ed. *The Harper American Literature.* No city: Addison-Wesley Educational Publishers, Inc., 1994. Vol. I.
    "First-Day Thoughts" — 52
    "Ichabod" — 245
    In a note explaining his writing of "Ichabod" — 309

Wiersbe, Warren. *God Isn't in a Hurry.* Grand Rapids: Baker Books, 1994. — 213

Wilde, Oscar. *The Works of Oscar Wilde.* Leicester, UK: Bookmart Limited, 1990.
    "An Ideal Husband," Act II — 180
    "The Ballad of Reading Gaol" — 177

------. *The Works of Oscar Wilde.* Cambridge, Eng: Blitz Editions, 1990.
    "Lady Windermere's Fan" — 340

Williamson, G. I. *The Shorter Catechism.* No city given: Presbyterian and Reformed Publishing Co., 1976. Vol. I. — 337

Winchester, C. T. *The Life of John Wesley.* New York: The Macmillan Company, 1906. — 130

Wise, George C. *Rev. Bud Robinson.* Louisville, KY: The Pentecostal Publishing Co., 1946 — 68

Woodrum, Lon. *Eternity in Their Heart.* Grand Rapids: Zondervan, 1955. — 11, 36, 164, 227, 291

------. "Judgin'." *Take My Heart.* Kansas City, MO: Beacon Hill Press, n.d. — 225

------. *Stumble Upon the Dark Mountains.* Waco, TX: Word Books, 1956. — 34, 87, 109, 216, 229, 289

------. *The Rebellious Planet.* Grand Rapids: Zondervan, 1965.— 101, 179, 236, 362

Wordsworth, William. Richard Aldington, ed. *The Viking Book of Poetry.* New York: The Viking Press, 1958. Vol. II.
"My Heart Leaps Up" — 269
"Strange Fits of Passion" — 327

Young, William P. *The Shack.* Newbury Park, CA: Windblown Media, 2007. — 16, 85, 165, 215, 216, 257, 273

33654691R00232

Made in the USA
Lexington, KY
03 July 2014